Advance Praise for *The Three Ages of International Commercial Arbitration*

One of the great strengths of this remarkable book is that it makes use of countless new documents and archival research – such as unpublished ICC arbitral awards, rare periodicals, and all successive versions of the ICC Rules of Arbitration – to retrace the modern history and evolution of international commercial arbitration. Through this in-depth research, Dr. Schinazi is able to explore the field's inner dynamics. An elegantly written book, *The Three Ages* is a must-read for anyone interested in the history of international arbitration and international law in the making.

**– Yas Banifatemi,**
**Founding Partner,**
**Gaillard Banifatemi Shelbaya Disputes;**
**Lecturer, Panthéon-Sorbonne University;**
**Visiting Lecturer, Yale Law School and Harvard Law School**

Dr. Schinazi's *The Three Ages of International Commercial Arbitration* is brilliant and momentous – nothing short of a tour de force. It is a meticulously researched but also deeply rich and imaginative work, eclipsing anything that has been produced up to now on the genesis and evolution of international commercial arbitration. I confess to finding it a real page-turner.

**– George Bermann,**
**Gellhorn Professor of Law**
**and Monnet Professor in European Union Law,**
**Columbia Law School**

This is one of the most detailed works exploring the International Chamber of Commerce's past since Ridgeway's 1938 *Merchants of Peace.* Dr. Schinazi's book offers a detailed panorama of the arbitration landscape to coincide with the ICC's centennial. Readers will discover a wealth of hitherto unpublished information about the ICC and the beginnings of its International Court of Arbitration. This is a major book about the history and evolution of the ICC arbitration system, informed by keen insights drawing on legal theory and intellectual history. It is a delight to see the book in print, the fitting culmination of Dr. Schinazi's doctoral research.

**– Emmanuel Jolivet,**
**General Counsel,**
**International Chamber of Commerce**
**and International Court of Arbitration**

As a practicing lawyer and later a Supreme Court Justice, I have always been fascinated by international commercial arbitration institutions, including the ICC. Now, after reading Dr. Schinazi's brilliant work, I can better understand the development and essence of those modern institutions over the ages. The book is therefore immensely important for researchers as well as practitioners in the field of international arbitration. It seems to me that we are now facing a New Age in this field due to the huge influence of social networks and the opportunities they present. I hope that Dr. Schinazi will provide similar illumination on these aspects, too, in the future.

**– Justice Hanan Melcer,**
**Deputy President, Supreme Court of Israel**

At last an in-depth historical presentation! Arbitration has firmly established itself as the choice method of dispute resolution in the international legal order, progressively and almost imperceptibly overshadowing state courts. It is important to understand how this development came about, and the key can be found in Dr. Schinazi's remarkably intelligent and synthetic account. The insights he offers are essential to understanding not only the current situation but also its risks and prospects.

**– Pierre Tercier,**
**Emeritus Professor, University of Fribourg;**
**Honorary President, ICC International Court of Arbitration**

Dr. Schinazi's meticulously researched monograph extends the turn to history in international legal scholarship to international arbitration. Relying on impressive archival research at the International Chamber of Commerce and beyond, *The Three Ages* uncovers the ideas and actors over two centuries that led to the emergence of the modern system of international commercial arbitration. A thoughtful, original book, and beautifully written to boot. Highly recommended!

**– Michael Waibel,**
**Professor of International Law,**
**University of Vienna**

# CAMBRIDGE STUDIES IN INTERNATIONAL AND COMPARATIVE LAW: 163

Established in 1946, this series produces high quality, reflective and innovative scholarship in the field of public international law. It publishes works on international law that are of a theoretical, historical, cross-disciplinary or doctrinal nature. The series also welcomes books providing insights from private international law, comparative law and transnational studies which inform international legal thought and practice more generally.

The series seeks to publish views from diverse legal traditions and perspectives, and of any geographical origin. In this respect it invites studies offering regional perspectives on core *problématiques* of international law, and in the same vein, it appreciates contrasts and debates between diverging approaches. Accordingly, books offering new or less orthodox perspectives are very much welcome. Works of a generalist character are greatly valued and the series is also open to studies on specific areas, institutions or problems. Translations of the most outstanding works published in other languages are also considered.

After seventy years, Cambridge Studies in International and Comparative Law sets the standard for international legal scholarship and will continue to define the discipline as it evolves in the years to come.



*A list of books in the series can be found at the end of this volume.*

# THE THREE AGES OF INTERNATIONAL COMMERCIAL ARBITRATION

Drawing on a wide range of previously unpublished sources, this unique history of international commercial arbitration in the modern era identifies three periods in its development: the Age of Aspirations (c. 1780–1920), the Age of Institutionalization (1920s–1950s), and the Age of Autonomy (1950s–present). Mikaël Schinazi analyzes the key features of each period, arguing that the history of international commercial arbitration has oscillated between moments of renewal and anxiety. During periods of renewal, new approaches, instruments, and institutions were developed to carry international commercial arbitration forward. These developments were then reined in during periods of anxiety, for fear that international arbitration might be overstepping its bounds. The resulting tension between renewal and anxiety is a key thread running through the evolution of international commercial arbitration. This book fills a key gap in the scholarship for anyone interested in the fields of international arbitration, legal history, and international law.

Mikaël Schinazi is an international dispute resolution lawyer and a visiting lecturer at Sciences Po Law School, Paris. A member of the New York Bar, he holds a BA *magna cum laude* with highest honours from Harvard University, an LLB from the University of Cambridge (John Eliot Scholar), an LLM from Columbia Law School (Harlan Fiske Stone Scholar), and a PhD in law from the Institut d'Études Politiques de Paris (Sciences Po).

# THE THREE AGES OF INTERNATIONAL COMMERCIAL ARBITRATION

MIKAËL SCHINAZI

CAMBRIDGE
UNIVERSITY PRESS

CAMBRIDGE
UNIVERSITY PRESS

Shaftesbury Road, Cambridge CB2 8EA, United Kingdom

One Liberty Plaza, 20th Floor, New York, NY 10006, USA

477 Williamstown Road, Port Melbourne, VIC 3207, Australia

314–321, 3rd Floor, Plot 3, Splendor Forum, Jasola District Centre, New Delhi – 110025, India

103 Penang Road, #05–06/07, Visioncrest Commercial, Singapore 238467

Cambridge University Press is part of Cambridge University Press & Assessment,
a department of the University of Cambridge.

We share the University's mission to contribute to society through the pursuit of education, learning and research at the highest international levels of excellence.

www.cambridge.org
Information on this title: www.cambridge.org/9781108799775

DOI: 10.1017/9781108891837



First published 2022
First paperback edition 2024

*A catalogue record for this publication is available from the British Library*

ISBN 978-1-108-83517-6 Hardback
ISBN 978-1-108-79977-5 Paperback

*In memoriam Emmanuel Gaillard (1952–2021)*

# CONTENTS

# FIGURES

# TABLES

# FOREWORD

When, in the winter of 2013, Mikaël Schinazi approached me to discuss his project of undertaking doctoral studies on the modern history of international commercial arbitration, I immediately found the project to be both innovative and fascinating. While it is obvious that the field has grown exponentially over the past few decades, and now occupies a key position in the broader legal landscape, the reasons as to *why* and *how* this happened have not been fully elucidated. A major work in this area remains Yves Dezalay and Bryant Garth's 1996 *Dealing in Virtue*, but this sociological study, as Schinazi aptly notes in his introduction, no longer reflects the complex reality of the field. A few other scholars (mostly in France and England) were also conducting research in this area, but they were writing mostly from the vantage point of their respective disciplines and, for the most part, outside the legal field.

This was therefore an excellent topic for a doctoral dissertation, although an extremely difficult one. As any scholar of international arbitration is well aware, many primary and secondary sources are confidential or difficult to access. The topic was also vast. While I share Schinazi's reluctance to trace the origins of international commercial arbitration to the ancient world, starting the narrative in the late eighteenth century, as he does, was a daunting task. Schinazi, however, was ideally positioned to tackle this challenge, possessing stellar credentials, the required background (in both law and history), and a rigor and intellectual maturity beyond his years.

Schinazi first started exploring the various sources and archives available to him. He went to the National Archives in France and England. He visited courts and tribunals. He went to many research libraries in Paris, as well as various libraries and archives outside Paris, exploring, for instance, the Clémentel papers in the city of Clermont-Ferrand. (Étienne Clémentel, a now largely forgotten figure of the French Third Republic, played a key role as the founding president of the International Chamber of Commerce, as Schinazi explains in the book.)

At times, his research felt like a detective story, tracking down and interviewing the families of various individuals who played a key role in the modern history of arbitration. (Did their fathers or grandfathers leave unpublished papers, letters, or documents behind them? Why did they become interested in international arbitration in the first place?) As with any good historical work, some of Schinazi's efforts were unsuccessful. But many led to important breakthroughs, as when Schinazi gained access to all the archives of the International Chamber of Commerce and its Court of Arbitration in Paris, the world's preeminent arbitral institution, which only a handful of scholars had been able to explore in depth. (The ICC, and in particular its General Counsel Dr. Emmanuel Jolivet, should be thanked for granting Schinazi full access to its archives.) This is the first book to make use of so many new documents – including more than 130 mostly unpublished arbitral awards, rare periodicals, and all successive version of the ICC Rules of Arbitration – to retrace the modern history of international commercial arbitration.

Through this research, Schinazi was able to divide the history of the field into three broad waves or periods, which he calls the Age of Aspirations (*ca.*1780–1920), the Age of Institutionalization (1920s–1950s), and the Age of Autonomy (1950s–present). Schinazi clearly explains that this division of time is deliberately approximative. He further argues (borrowing from the terminology used by David Kennedy in a different context) that this history oscillates between moments of renewal and moments of anxiety, an idea which I find highly convincing but with which others may, of course, disagree.

Schinazi's comprehensive presentation of the primary and secondary sources and excellent knowledge of both the theory and the practice of international commercial arbitration are used to contradict some well-worn myths about the history of the field. They are also used to trace the genealogy of key concepts and ideas. I was especially impressed by Schinazi's thorough analysis of the origins and evolution of the so-called "French school of international arbitration" (in Part III of the book), which blends legal and intellectual history, brings to life the main protagonists (Goldman, Fouchard, and others), and cogently discusses their ideas.

One may expect that the questions raised in this book – and the answers provided by Schinazi – will be of interest to at least three audiences. Academics working in the fields of international arbitration (both commercial and investor-state), public international law, legal history, and intellectual history will find answers to some of their questions about the origins of the modern regime of international arbitration and the International Chamber of Commerce, which has been in operation for a century. Arbitrators, lawyers, and practitioners will be interested in finding out more about the evolution of international commercial arbitration – how it originated and where it might be heading. This is especially true in a field where theory and practice are so closely connected. Finally, members of the broader public interested in current debates and controversies over the state of international arbitration (especially in the investment treaty context) may find that an awareness of the historical background can provide new perspectives on these debates.

Schinazi's dissertation was a delight to supervise, along with my colleague Professor Mikhaïl Xifaras. It was unanimously described as an outstanding work of scholarship by all five members of his PhD defense committee, all of whom are warmly thanked for agreeing to serve on the PhD defense committee: Professors Horatia Muir Watt, Carine Jallamion, Joshua Karton, and Jérôme Sgard, and Mr. V. V. Veeder QC, a dear friend and brilliant colleague, who left us in 2020. The book is now an absolute pleasure to read, and a treasure trove of new information. It is to be expected that it will continue to garner praise and become a reference work for those seeking more information about the modern history and evolution of international commercial arbitration.

*Emmanuel Gaillard*
*Professeur agrégé des Facultés de droit*
*Visiting Professor, Yale Law School and Harvard Law School*
*Founding Partner, Gaillard Banifatemi Shelbaya Disputes*
*January 15, 2021*

# ACKNOWLEDGMENTS

This book is dedicated to my doctoral supervisor, Professor Emmanuel Gaillard, who passed away unexpectedly on April 1, 2021, as the book was about to go to print. Professor Gaillard was a source of inspiration for academics and lawyers around the world. As will become clear in the book's final chapters, his vision framed international arbitration's development into its current state. Over the past eight years or so, he provided constant advice, support, and mentorship. I am grateful for his faith in me and my ideas. Professor Gaillard made seminal intellectual contributions to the field, but above all else I will remember him for his wit, youthful energy, and kindness. Like so many others, I feel privileged to have known him.

This book is based on a doctoral thesis completed at Sciences Po Law School in Paris, France. I would like to express my sincere gratitude to Professor Mikhaïl Xifaras, who jointly supervised the project along with Professor Gaillard. Both supervisors provided incisive comments on successive versions of my draft. I thank them for being demanding but never impatient, honest but always optimistic, and for making sure that I brought my work to fruition.

In addition to my supervisors, I would like to thank all the jury members for agreeing to serve on the PhD defense committee: Professors Carine Jallamion, Joshua Karton, Horatia Muir Watt, Jérôme Sgard, and Mr. V. V. Veeder QC (whose kindness, both at the PhD defense and after, is fondly remembered). They agreed to spend precious time and effort reading a long – and surely imperfect – document, and this work greatly benefited from their thorough feedback.

I also wish to express my deepest thanks to Dr. Yas Banifatemi of Gaillard Banifatemi Shelbaya Disputes (formerly of Shearman & Sterling LLP), who first hired me as a legal assistant ten years ago, in 2011, and has advised me ever since. I have had the great privilege of being able to seek Dr. Banifatemi's advice on a wide range of academic, professional, and personal matters over the years, and I am grateful for her guidance and mentorship.

I feel lucky to have had the opportunity to carry out this project at Sciences Po, which provided funding and excellent working conditions during my time there. In addition to my supervisors, I would like to thank the faculty members of Sciences Po Law School for creating such a vibrant and supportive academic community. Many thanks are also due to my fellow graduate students in the PhD program in law for their constant support and general cheerfulness and the law school's administrative staff, without whose dedication the PhD program would not run so smoothly.

While writing a dissertation can be a solitary endeavor, I was fortunate enough to be surrounded by a group of more experienced scholars, who were interested in some of the same issues and research questions. I would like to thank, at Sciences Po, Professor Jérôme Sgard and, in the early stages of my research, Professor Claire Lemercier; at King's College London (and now Oxford University), Professor Florian Grisel; and, at the International Chamber of Commerce (ICC), Dr. Emmanuel Jolivet and Mr. Alexander Fessas. At the ICC, I also benefited from the guidance and expertise of the jurists and research librarians Ms. Sylvie Picard Renaut, Mr. Damien Schoenstein, and Ms. Stéphanie Torkomyan, all of whom answered many questions and received me several times during my research. Many scholars and experts offered their time and advice. In addition to the individuals listed earlier, I greatly benefited from informal conversations with Professors Frédéric Audren, Thomas Clay, Julie Saada, Emmanuelle Tourme-Jouannet, and Dina Waked.

When revising my thesis and locating photographs for this book, I had the pleasure of meeting Dr. Marie-Christine Kessler, a political scientist and Étienne Clémentel's granddaughter, and Dr. Guy Rousseau, a history professor, both of whom provided illuminating insights into Clémentel's early life and work. Dr. Louise Arizzoli provided the photograph of Clémentel posing near his bust by Auguste Rodin; and Dr. Sigvard Jarvin kindly sent me photographs of two eminent Swedish scholars, Algot Bagge and Emil Sandström, which unfortunately could not be included in this book.

At Cambridge University Press, I would also like to thank Mr. Tom Randall for believing in this project and the production team for giving me the pleasure of seeing it turn into print. I am also grateful to the three anonymous reviewers chosen by Cambridge University Press.

In addition, several individuals agreed to read portions or all of my draft and help with various aspects of my research. Ms. Virginia Hamilton, copy-editor, provided outstanding editorial advice and assistance and helped prepare the manuscript for submission to the publishers. Mr. Arthur Schott Lopes read large portions of an early draft. At Shearman & Sterling, Ms. Nanou Leleu-Knobil, Mr. Michel Szczepanski, Mr. Jean-Marc Elsholz, Ms. Bénédicte Baudot-Soubrane, and members of the word processing center, among others, were always available to assist or discuss specific aspects of the research or publication process.

Many close friends provided support and much-needed respite from academic life over the course of this project. They are too numerous to list in full here, but I would particularly like to thank Marie-Joe Abi-Nassif, Daniel Barbosa, Jérôme Baudry, Aaron Bauhs, Margot Dazey, Delphine Dogot, Mona El Khoury, Alexis Foucard, Florian Grisel, Sylvaine Guyot, Anouk Kemp, Anne-Marie Lacoste, Ashish Mitter, Lauriane Mouysset, Zeina Obeid, Elsa Paparemborde, the Rachmanises, Céline Ramstein, Arianna Rosato, Abdallah Salam, Yann Schinazi, Jessica Schönberg, Alexandre Senegačnik, Romain Zamour, Roman Zinigrad, and, for everything they taught me, the roommates of Quincy 627.

Lastly, and most fundamentally, this book would not have been possible without Maxime and my close family – my parents Isabelle and Ilan, my sisters Jessica and Barbara, and my little niece Hannah. Their unconditional love and constant encouragement form the bedrock upon which so many aspects of my life rest. For this, my gratitude is beyond words.

# 1

# General Introduction

This book is an exploration of the history of international commercial arbitration – the mechanism by which parties' mutual rights and liabilities are determined with binding effect by a third person, the arbitrator, instead of by a court of law.[1] It divides the history of international commercial arbitration into three broad waves or periods, which I call the Age of Aspirations, the Age of Institutionalization, and the Age of Autonomy. I argue that this history oscillates between moments of renewal and moments of anxiety. During periods of renewal, new instruments, devices, and institutions were created to carry international commercial arbitration forward. These initiatives were then reined in during periods of anxiety, seemingly out of fear that international commercial arbitration might go too far (e.g., by encroaching on state sovereignty). The resulting tension or pendulum-like movement – from renewal to anxiety and from anxiety to renewal – is a key feature of the history of international commercial arbitration and helps explain the course of its development.

In this chapter, I explain the general background and justification of the study (Section 1.1) and its objectives and arguments (Section 1.2). I also describe the sources used and make a few caveats (Section 1.3).

## 1.1 Background and Justification

This study is based on a startling paradox: despite the ever-growing importance of international commercial arbitration in today's world (Section 1.1.1), relatively little scholarly attention has been devoted to its modern history and evolution (Section 1.1.2).

[1] See, generally, Emmanuel Gaillard and John Savage (eds.), *Fouchard, Gaillard, Goldman on International Commercial Arbitration* (The Hague: Kluwer Law International, 1999), chapter 1. For an approach to delineating the notion of arbitration, see Charles Jarrosson, *La notion d'arbitrage* (Paris: LGDJ, 1987); Jarrosson, "Les frontières de l'arbitrage," *Revue de l'arbitrage*, 2001, 5–41.

### 1.1.1 Setting the Stage: The Current Landscape of International Commercial Arbitration

It has become customary to describe international commercial arbitration as the preferred method for resolving business disputes between parties from different countries.[2] The data made available by the International Chamber of Commerce (ICC) show that since its creation in 1923, the International Court of Arbitration (hereinafter the "ICC Court") has administered 25,000 cases.[3] While the first 3,000 cases were filed over a period of 53 years, the next 3,000 cases took only 11 years to arrive.[4] During the first eighteen months of its existence, the ICC Court received sixty-eight cases from seventeen countries.[5] In 2019, it recorded 851 new cases, involving 2,498 parties from 147 countries and independent territories.[6] These figures testify to the "explosive" growth[7] and "meteoric rise"[8] of international commercial arbitration.

Although no exhaustive study has yet been made of this sector's weight in the global economy,[9] it is clear that the economic implications of international arbitration are enormous. The surveys conducted by the Queen Mary School of International Arbitration in London have repeatedly shown that international arbitration plays a key role in today's business world.[10] It has been found that membership of the 1958 New York Convention, the leading treaty in the field, leads to an increase

[2] See, for example, Gaillard and Savage, *Fouchard, Gaillard, Goldman*, 1; Gary Born, *International Commercial Arbitration* (The Hague: Kluwer Law International, 2014), 1.

[3] International Chamber of Commerce, "ICC Celebrates Case Milestone, Announces Record Figures for 2019" (January 9, 2020), https://iccwbo.org/media-wall/news-speeches/icc-celebrates-25000th-case-milestone-and-announces-record-figures-for-2019/.

[4] Laurence Craig, William Park, and Jan Paulsson, *International Chamber of Commerce Arbitration* (New York: Oceana Publications, 1990), 4.

[5] International Chamber of Commerce, *Arbitration Report No. 3* (July 1924), 1.

[6] International Chamber of Commerce, "2019 ICC Dispute Resolution Statistics," *ICC Dispute Resolution Bulletin*, 2020, no. 2, 20.

[7] Charles Brower, "The Global Court: The Internationalization of Commercial Adjudication and Arbitration," *University of Baltimore Law Review*, 26, no. 3 (1996), 10.

[8] Stavros Brekoulakis, "International Arbitration Scholarship and the Concept of Arbitration Law," *Fordham International Law Journal*, 36 (2013), 745.

[9] Emmanuel Gaillard, "L'apport de la pensée juridique française à l'arbitrage international," *Journal du droit international*, 2017, 531.

[10] In the 2015 survey, 90 percent of participants named international arbitration as their preferred dispute resolution mechanism. *2015 International Arbitration Survey: Improvements and Innovations in International Arbitration*, 5. That figure reached 97 percent in the 2018 survey. *2018 International Arbitration Survey: The Evolution of International Arbitration*, 5.

in bilateral trade.[11] Furthermore, the amounts in dispute keep reaching new heights. The most striking and highly publicized example is the *Yukos* saga. In July 2014, an arbitral tribunal sitting in The Hague under the auspices of the Permanent Court of Arbitration ordered the Russian Federation to pay more than USD 50 billion in damages to the former majority shareholders of Yukos Oil Company.[12] While most international commercial arbitration cases do not compare with "mammoth arbitrations"[13] of this kind, they typically involve large amounts. As the ICC has reported, the aggregate value of all pending disputes before the ICC Court at the end of 2019 was USD 230 billion, with an average value of USD 140 million and a median value of USD 10 million.[14]

Not only has the market *for* arbitration grown exponentially, so too has the market *in* arbitration. Law firms, counsel, arbitrators, arbitral institutions and centers, and even international arbitration journals[15] compete for power, influence, and prestige.[16] As Oppetit wrote in 1998, not without some dismay at the path arbitration was taking, "highly valued both by governments and in economic circles, much in favor with the judiciary, arbitration has become a key part of merchant society institutions: there now exists a true arbitration *market* in every sense of the word."[17] In fact, arbitration has become the daily business of several hundreds, if not thousands, of practitioners around the world.

International commercial arbitration has also been embraced with enthusiasm in academic circles and is now a vibrant area of study and research. As recalled by a leading US arbitration lawyer, "[i]n 1960,

[11] Thomas Hale, *Between Interests and Law: The Politics of Transnational Commercial Disputes* (Cambridge: Cambridge University Press, 2015), 46. See also Thomas Hale, "What Is the Effect of Commercial Arbitration on Trade?," in Walter Mattli and Thomas Dietz (eds.), *International Arbitration and Global Governance: Contending Theories and Evidence* (Oxford: Oxford University Press, 2014).

[12] *Yukos Universal Limited (Isle of Man)* v. *Russian Federation*, PCA Case No. AA 227, Final Award (July 18, 2014).

[13] Ibid., ¶ 4.

[14] International Chamber of Commerce, "2019 ICC Dispute Resolution Statistics," 26.

[15] Jacques Werner, "Editorial: Competition within the Arbitration Industry," *Journal of International Arbitration*, 2, no. 2 (1985), 5. See also Philippe Fouchard, "Où va l'arbitrage international?," *McGill Law Journal*, 34 (1989), 439; Michael Mustill, "Is It a Bird . . . ?," in *Liber amicorum Claude Reymond: Autour de l'arbitrage* (Paris: LexisNexis, 2004).

[16] See Joshua Karton, *The Culture of International Arbitration and the Evolution of Contract Law* (Oxford: Oxford University Press, 2013), 56–75; Karton, "International Arbitration as Comparative Law in Action," *Journal of Dispute Resolution*, no. 2 (2020), 317.

[17] Bruno Oppetit, *Théorie de l'arbitrage* (Paris: Presses Universitaires de France, 1998), 10. See also Pierre Lalive, "Sur une 'commercialisation' de l'arbitrage international," in *Liber amicorum Claude Reymond*.

international arbitration was not a familiar subject among US lawyers. There were no law schools in the US teaching the subject" and "no textbook or coursebook to be used."[18] The contrast with today could not be starker. Over the past few decades, we have seen an inexorable rise in the number of schools offering courses and promoting research in international arbitration.[19] There are now countless outlets for research in this area, including peer-reviewed journals, websites, and forums reporting the latest news and trends in the field.

In addition to being a market and a thriving area of study and research, international commercial arbitration can be considered an "international legal field," as defined by Bourdieu.[20] The notion of "an arena where struggle takes place"[21] and a "symbolic terrain with its own networks, hierarchical relationships, and expertise, and more generally its own 'rules of the game'"[22] prompts an analysis of international commercial arbitration in sociological terms. Gaillard, for instance, has identified three categories of actors in the field of international commercial arbitration – "essential actors," "service providers," and "value providers" – and has described the various rituals they perform as part of their activity in the field.[23] Closely

[18] Gerald Aksen, "A Dozen Differences in International Arbitration in the Last Half-Century," in *Liber amicorum en l'honneur de William Laurence Craig* (Paris: LexisNexis, 2016), 3.

[19] Gaillard, "L'apport," 530. See also Mirèze Philippe, "Autant en emporte le vent… de l'arbitrage," in Nassib Ziadé (ed.), *Liber Amicorum Samir Saleh: Reflections on Dispute Resolution with Particular Emphasis on the Arab World* (Alphen aan den Rijn: Wolters Kluwer, 2020), 253.

[20] According to the sociologist, a field is an area of structured activity, characterized by the unequal position of social agents in their competitive struggle to accumulate different sorts of resources or capital (whether economic, cultural, social, or symbolic). See Pierre Bourdieu, "Foreword," in Yves Dezalay and David Sugarman (eds.), *Professional Competition and Professional Power: Lawyers, Accountants and the Social Construction of Markets* (London: Routledge, 1995), xi–xii. See also Bourdieu, "Foreword," in Yves Dezalay and Bryant Garth, *Dealing in Virtue*, vii; Bourdieu, "The Force of Law: Toward a Sociology of the Juridical Field," trans. Richard Terdiman, *Hastings Law Journal*, 38 (1987), 816; and, generally, Pierre Bourdieu and Loïc Wacquant, *An Invitation to Reflexive Sociology* (Chicago: University of Chicago Press, 1992), 97.

[21] Mikael Madsen and Yves Dezalay, "The Power of the Legal Field: Pierre Bourdieu and the Law," in Reza Banakar and Max Travers (eds.), *An Introduction to Law and Social Theory* (Oxford: Hart, 2002), 192.

[22] Yves Dezalay and Bryant Garth, "Merchants of Law as Moral Entrepreneurs: Constructing International Justice from the Competition for Transnational Business Disputes," *Law and Society Review*, 29 (1995), 32.

[23] Emmanuel Gaillard, "Sociology of International Arbitration," *Arbitration International*, 31 (2015), 1. See also Gaillard, "Nouvelles réflexions sur la sociologie de l'arbitrage," *Procédures*, 2 (2020), 35–37.

related to the notion of field is the idea of an "epistemic community" – that is, "a network of professionals with recognized expertise and competence in a particular domain and an authoritative claim to policy-relevant knowledge within that domain or issue-area."[24] People involved in the field of international commercial arbitration have clearly formed an "epistemic community" of professionals who share a set of normative beliefs and values – a distinct legal "culture" specific to international commercial arbitration.[25]

### 1.1.2 *Literature Gap and Reassessments*

Despite all the "wealth and legal, economic and sociological complexity"[26] of international commercial arbitration, its history – or, even better, its genealogy[27] – has attracted relatively little scholarly attention. This is not to say that there have been no attempts to retrace or understand its evolution. Roebuck compiled a remarkable bibliography of "sources for the history of arbitration," which filled an entire issue of *Arbitration International*.[28] As will be explained in Chapter 2, numerous studies have appeared on the ancient history of international arbitration, stretching as far back as Mesopotamia and Ancient

[24] Peter Haas, "Epistemic Communities and International Policy Coordination," *International Organization*, 46 (1992), 3. See also Andrea Bianchi, "Epistemic Communities in International Arbitration," in Thomas Schultz and Frederico Ortino (eds.), *The Oxford Handbook of International Arbitration* (Oxford: Oxford University Press, 2020), 569–90; Jean d'Aspremont, *Epistemic Forces in International Law: Foundational Doctrines and Techniques of International Legal Argumentation* (Cheltenham: Edward Elgar, 2015).

[25] Karton, *Culture*, 5. For an early essay on the topic, see Tom Ginsburg, "The Culture of Arbitration," *Vanderbilt Journal of Transnational Law*, 36 (2003), 1335. Won Kidane has authored a book entitled *The Culture of International Arbitration* (New York: Oxford University Press, 2017), but his argument is that the leading theories of international arbitration do not adequately account for the impact of local cultures; as such, he is more interested in the role of cultures *in* arbitration than a single culture *of* arbitration.

[26] Gaillard, "L'apport," 542.

[27] The genealogical method consists in analyzing a modern idea as the confluence of previous, successively transformed ideas. For a prime example, see Duncan Kennedy, "Savigny's Family/Patrimony Distinction and Its Place in the Global Genealogy of Classical Legal Thought," *American Journal of Comparative Law*, 58 (2010), 811, 831–32. The two classic texts are Friedrich Nietzsche, *On the Genealogy of Morality* (1887), ed. Keith Ansell-Pearson, trans. Carol Diethe (Cambridge: Cambridge University Press, 2007); Michel Foucault, "Nietszche, la généalogie, l'histoire" (1971), in Daniel Defert, François Ewald, and Jacques Lagrange (eds.), *Dits et écrits I: 1954–1988* (Paris: Gallimard, 2001).

[28] Derek Roebuck, "Sources for the History of Arbitration: A Bibliographical Introduction," *Arbitration International*, 14 (1998), 237.

Greece.[29] It has indeed become standard practice for textbooks and treatises to begin with references to this distant past. In addition, an increasing number of scholars have analyzed the construction of the contemporary regime of international commercial arbitration.

In France, David, the eminent comparative law scholar, devoted multiple studies, as well as a chapter in his autobiography,[30] to international arbitration, including a historical study of arbitration in the nineteenth and twentieth centuries.[31] Hilaire's work also paved the way for much historical work in the field.[32] Closer to us, Jallamion has studied the practice of arbitration in civil matters from 1650 to 1789, initially focusing on Montpellier[33] and later expanding the scope of her research.[34]

Also in France, Grisel has worked on the application and creation of law in international arbitration;[35] along with Stone Sweet, he has been engaged in a large-scale project on the judicialization of international commercial arbitration, which also draws on archival material to chart the history and evolution of the field.[36] Lemercier and Sgard have been investigating the

[29] For a recent essay dividing the history of interstate arbitration into five "moments" (starting with the "Greek moment"), see Alexis Keller, "Inter-State Arbitration in Historical Perspective," in Thomas Schultz and Frederico Ortino (eds.), *The Oxford Handbook of International Arbitration* (Oxford: Oxford University Press, 2020), 843–73.

[30] René David, *Les avatars d'un comparatiste* (Paris: Economica, 1982), 244–57.

[31] René David, "Arbitrage du XIXe et arbitrage du XXe siècle," in *Mélanges offerts à René Savatier* (Paris: Dalloz, 1965).

[32] Jean Hilaire, "L'arbitrage dans la période moderne (XVIe–XVIIIe siècles)," *Revue de l'arbitrage*, 2000, 187.

[33] Carine Jallamion, "L'arbitrage en matière civile du XVIIe au XIXe siècle: L'exemple de Montpellier" (PhD diss., University of Montpellier 1, 2004).

[34] See, for example, Carine Jallamion, "La jurisprudence française et l'arbitrage de 1843 à 1958: De la défaveur à la faveur jusqu'à l'avènement de l'arbitrage international," *Revue de l'arbitrage*, 2015, 739 (pt. 1), 1037 (pt. 2); Jallamion, "Le juge français au service de l'investissement: Le développement en France de l'arbitrage commercial international (XIXe–XXe siècle)," in Luisa Brunori, Serge Dauchy, Olivier Descamps, and Xavier Prévost (eds.), *Le droit face à l'économie sans travail*, vol. 1, *Sources intellectuelles, acteurs, résolution des conflits* (Paris: Classiques Garnier, 2019); Jallamion and Thomas Clay, "Justice publique et arbitrage: hier et aujourd'hui," in Loïc Cadiet, Serge Dauchy, and Jean-Louis Halpérin (eds.), *Itinéraires d'histoire de la procédure civile* (Paris: IRJS Éditions, 2014).

[35] Florian Grisel, *L'arbitrage international ou le droit contre l'ordre juridique* (Paris: LGDJ, 2011). See also Eduardo Silva Romero, Emmanuel Jolivet, and Florian Grisel, "Aux origines de l'arbitrage commercial contemporain: L'émergence de l'arbitrage CCI (1920–1958)," *Revue de l'arbitrage*, 2016, 403.

[36] Alec Stone Sweet and Florian Grisel, *The Evolution of International Arbitration: Judicialization, Governance, Legitimacy* (Oxford: Oxford University Press, 2017). See also Florian Grisel and Alec Stone Sweet, "L'arbitrage international: Du contrat dyadique au système normatif," *Archives de philosophie du droit*, 52 (2009), 75.

modern history of international commercial arbitration, drawing on a wide range of primary and secondary sources and completing a final report in 2015.[37] Finally, Gaillard's Hague Academy course, though primarily concerned with the "legal theory" of international arbitration, imparts a vision of its overall development – or that of its "mental representations."[38]

In England, Mustill helpfully tried to sketch the history of international commercial arbitration,[39] while Veeder authored numerous studies on famous arbitrations or key episodes in the history of international arbitration.[40] Hale drew on various historical sources when exploring the transnational commercial dispute resolution regime,[41] and Schultz's study of "transnational legality," though a work of legal theory, also contains useful insights into the formation of the current international arbitration regime.[42] A recent collection of essays also

[37] Claire Lemercier and Jérôme Sgard, *Arbitrage privé international et globalisation(s): Rapport final* (March 2015), which followed an initial research report by the same authors in 2013. See also Jérôme Sgard, "A Tale of Three Cities: The Construction of International Commercial Arbitration," in Grégoire Mallard and Jérôme Sgard (eds.), *Contractual Knowledge: One Hundred Years of Legal Experimentation in Global Markets* (Cambridge: Cambridge University Press, 2016).

[38] Emmanuel Gaillard, *Legal Theory of International Arbitration* (Leiden: Martinus Nijhoff, 2010).

[39] Michael Mustill, "Arbitration: History and Background," *Journal of International Arbitration*, 6, no. 2 (1989), 43; Mustill, "The History of International Commercial Arbitration: A Sketch," in Lawrence Newman and Richard Hill (eds.), *The Leading Arbitrators' Guide to International Arbitration*, 3rd ed. (Huntington, NY: Juris, 2014). On English arbitral history, see also Michael Mustill and Stewart Boyd, *Commercial Arbitration*, 2nd ed. (London: Butterworths, 1989), 431–58.

[40] See, for example, V. V. Veeder, "The Tetiube Mining Concession: 1924–1932: A Swiss-Russian Story (Where the Arbitral Dog Did Not Bark)," in *Liber amicorum Claude Reymond*; Veeder, "Lloyd George, Lenin and Cannibals: The Harriman Arbitration; The 1999 Freshfields Lecture," *Arbitration International*, 16 (2000), 115; Veeder, "The Lena Goldfields Arbitration: The Historical Roots of Three Ideas," *International and Comparative Law Quarterly*, 47 (1998), 747; Veeder, "Two Arbitral Butterflies: Bramwell and David," in Martin Hunter, Arthur Marriott, and V. V. Veeder (eds.), *The Internationalisation of International Arbitration: The LCIA Centenary Conference* (London: Graham & Trotman/Martinus Nijhoff, 1995); Veeder and Brian Dye, "Lord Bramwell's Arbitration Code 1884–1889," *Arbitration International*, 8 (1992), 329.

[41] Hale, *Between Interests and Law*. My project and Hale's are distinct in that Hale uses the history of the ICC to address the question of variations in institutional attitudes towards global governance, whereas I explore the modern origins of the international arbitration regime. In other words, Hale uses international arbitration as a laboratory for shifts in global governance, whereas my goal is to retrace the very history of international commercial arbitration.

[42] Thomas Schultz, *Transnational Legality: Stateless Law and International Arbitration* (Oxford: Oxford University Press, 2014).

contains fascinating studies on specific episodes in the history of international adjudication, including international arbitration.[43]

Even though some of these works seem to be part of a broader effort "to write a critical history of international arbitration in commercial and investment matters,"[44] historical scholarship relating to international commercial arbitration is much less developed or comprehensive than that relating to investment treaty arbitration. In fact, recent scholarship has explored the history of investor-state arbitration. For instance, building on earlier work by Anghie and Lipson,[45] Miles has traced the origins of international investment law in the commercial and political expansionism of Western states from the seventeenth to the early twentieth century and cogently argued that "these origins still resonate within its modern principles, structures, agreements, and dispute resolution systems."[46] Yackee has provided a detailed account of "the first investor-state arbitration" – the 1864 dispute between the Suez Canal Company and Egypt, which was arbitrated by a commission headed by Napoleon III.[47] Several recent works have been devoted to the history of the investment treaty regime[48] or have tried to put the investment treaty regime in its historical context.[49] The attempt to understand the roots and causes of the current investment treaty regime is unmatched in the world of international commercial arbitration.

[43] Ignacio de la Rasilla and Jorge Viñuales (eds.), *Experiments in International Adjudication: Historical Accounts* (Cambridge: Cambridge University Press, 2019).

[44] Anne-Charlotte Martineau, "A Forgotten Chapter in the History of International Commercial Arbitration: The Slave Trade's Dispute Settlement System," *Leiden Journal of International Law*, 31 (2018), 219.

[45] Antony Anghie, *Imperialism, Sovereignty and the Making of International Law* (Cambridge: Cambridge University Press, 2004); Charles Lipson, *Standing Guard: Protecting Foreign Investment in the Nineteenth and Twentieth Centuries* (Berkeley: University of California Press, 1985).

[46] Kate Miles, *The Origins of International Investment Law: Empire, Environment, and the Safeguarding of Capital* (Cambridge: Cambridge University Press, 2013), 3.

[47] See Jason Yackee, "The First Investor-State Arbitration? The Suez Canal Dispute of 1864 and Some Reflections on the Historiography of International Investment Law," in Stephan Schill, Christian Tams, and Rainer Hofmann (eds.), *International Investment Law and History* (Cheltenham: Edward Elgar, 2018).

[48] Taylor St. John, *The Rise of Investor-State Arbitration: Politics, Law, and Unintended Consequences* (Oxford: Oxford University Press, 2018); St. John, "The Creation of Investor-State Arbitration," in Thomas Schultz and Frederico Ortino (eds.), *The Oxford Handbook of International Arbitration* (Oxford: Oxford University Press, 2020), 792–814; Schill, Tams, and Hofmann, *International Investment Law*.

[49] See, for example, Jonathan Bonnitcha, Lauge Poulsen, and Michael Waibel, *The Political Economy of the Investment Treaty Regime* (Oxford: Oxford University Press, 2017), chapter 1; Chester Brown and Kate Miles (eds.), *Evolution in Investment Treaty Law and Arbitration* (Cambridge: Cambridge University Press, 2011).

Parra's comprehensive history of the International Centre for Settlement of Investment Disputes (ICSID), now in its second edition,[50] may have filled a "glaringly empty space on the serious bookshelf,"[51] but no similar attempt has been made with regard to the ICC or other leading arbitral institutions. Mustill's statement that "[a]rbitration has a long [p]ast, but scarcely any [h]istory"[52] – though no longer fully accurate – seems to apply to international commercial arbitration more than it does to investment treaty arbitration. One of the aims of this book is to help fill that gap.

### *1.1.3 Reassessing Some Aspects of* Dealing in Virtue

Another of the book's goals is to challenge key aspects of one of the most successful and enduring works about the modern evolution of international commercial arbitration, Dezalay and Garth's *Dealing in Virtue.*[53] Published in 1996, this work sought to "trace in the mechanism of this increasingly global private justice the emergence of a transnational legal profession, institutionalized in new kinds of 'courts' – international commercial arbitration – and a special body of 'law' – the so-called *lex mercatoria.*"[54] Viewing international commercial arbitration as a "process of social construction,"[55] Dezalay and Garth explained how international arbitrators had succeeded in "gaining enough identification with virtue . . . to be entrusted with and to profit from major business disputes."[56] Relying on Bourdieu's structural analysis, they mapped the field of international commercial arbitration, showing how it "reveals and contributes to the reorganization and reshuffling of hierarchies of positions, modes of legitimate authority, and structures of power."[57]

50 Antonio Parra, *The History of ICSID*, 2nd ed. (Oxford: Oxford University Press, 2017); Parra, "'Black's Bank' and the Settlement of Investment Disputes," in David Caron, Stephan Schill, Abby Smutny, and Epaminontas Triantafilou (eds.), *Practising Virtue: Inside International Arbitration* (Oxford: Oxford University Press, 2015).

51 Frank Berman, "Book Report: *The History of ICSID* by Antonio R Parra," *ICSID Review – Foreign Investment Law Journal*, 28 (2013), 144.

52 Michael Mustill, "Sources for the History of Arbitration," *Arbitration International*, 14 (1998), 235.

53 Yves Dezalay and Bryant Garth, *Dealing in Virtue: International Commercial Arbitration and the Construction of a Transnational Legal Order* (Chicago: Chicago University Press, 1996).

54 Ibid., 3.

55 Ibid., 5.

56 Bryant Garth, "One Window into the State of Insiders' Arbitration Scholarship," *Journal of World Investment and Trade*, 19 (2018), 155 n1.

57 Dezalay and Garth, *Dealing in Virtue*, 17, 61.

According to Dezalay and Garth, the contrast between "grand old men" and "young technocrats" was one of the most important divides in the field of international arbitration – a "key source of conflict, and also of transformation."[58] The "grand old men" were part of the pioneering generation of arbitration; they already had legitimacy and "national aura" before starting as arbitrators and saw arbitration as a "duty, not a career."[59] Dezalay and Garth argued that, beginning in the late 1970s and accelerating in the 1980s, a new generation of "young technocrats" used their technical expertise to criticize the "'amateurism' or 'idealism' of their predecessors."[60] This "'generational warfare' between the grand old men and the younger 'arbitration technocrats' – aided by U.S. multinational law firms – transformed an informal justice centered on the European grand professors into a U.S.-style 'offshore litigation.'"[61]

Dezalay and Garth's book was very much a pioneering work, the first full-scale inquiry into the construction of international commercial arbitration from a sociological perspective.[62] It was largely a success, quickly stimulating discussion and earning praise.[63] The book is still often cited and remains one of the most popular works in the field.[64] *Dealing in Virtue* has inspired further studies on the sociology of international arbitration,[65]

[58] Ibid., 34.

[59] Ibid., 34–35.

[60] Ibid., 36–37.

[61] Ibid., 10.

[62] Note, however, an earlier text by Bruno Oppetit, "Eléments pour une sociologie de l'arbitrage," *L'Année sociologique*, 27 (1976), 179, reproduced in *Théorie de l'arbitrage* (Paris: Presses Universitaires de France, 1998).

[63] Yves Dezalay, Didier Bigo, and Antonin Cohen, "Enquêter sur l'internationalisation des noblesses d'État: Retour réflexif sur des stratégies de double jeu; Entretien avec Yves Dezalay," *Cultures et Conflits*, no. 98 (2015), 24.

[64] According to Schultz and Ridi, it is the most cited work in arbitration literature (in English) in absolute terms, with a total of 1,394 cites. See Thomas Schultz and Niccolò Ridi, "Arbitration Literature," in Thomas Schultz and Frederico Ortino (eds.), *The Oxford Handbook of International Arbitration* (Oxford: Oxford University Press, 2020), 5. See also Thomas Schultz, "Celebrating 20 Years of 'Dealing in Virtue.'" *Journal of International Dispute Settlement*, 7 (2016), 531. The book's title is echoed in that of a collection of writings about international commercial arbitration: David Caron, Stephan Schill, Abby Smutny, and Epaminontas Triantafilou (eds.), *Practising Virtue: Inside International Arbitration* (Oxford: Oxford University Press, 2015).

[65] See, for example, Thomas Clay, "Qui sont les arbitres internationaux? Approche sociologique," in Centre français de droit comparé, *Les arbitres internationaux*, vol. 8 (Paris: Editions de la Société de législation comparée, 2005); Jean-Baptiste Racine, "Eléments pour une sociologie de l'arbitrage: Actes de la Journée d'étude du Groupe Sociologie de l'arbitrage du Comité français de l'arbitrage," *Revue de l'arbitrage*, 2012, 709; Sergio Puig, "Social Capital in the Arbitration Market," *European Journal of International Law*, 25

including some that postulate the emergence of a third generation of arbitrators, the "Managers."[66] At a more subconscious level, the book may have shaped some of our perceptions about what it means to be an international arbitrator. As Schultz points out, "[t]hanks in no small part to Dezalay and Garth, we tend to associate being an arbitrator with virtue."[67]

Nevertheless, voices are increasingly calling for a reassessment of key aspects of Dezalay and Garth's thesis. Lemercier and Sgard contest the argument that the opposition between "grand old men" and "young technocrats" was a key force in structuring the modern field of international commercial arbitration: "At the beginning of our history, grand old men were not that grand. ... The group that built international commercial arbitration was to a great extent made up of outsiders by comparison to both the legal professionals and the most famous public institutions."[68] Likewise, Grisel convincingly argued that the crucial period of institutional transformation did not take place in the 1980s and 1990s, as Dezalay and Garth had argued, but between the 1950s and 1970s.[69] That was the time when international commercial arbitration became dominated by "secant marginals," that is, "individuals who, while being members of multiple social groups (national, ethnic, professional), do not develop a sense of primary identity, or exclusive loyalty, with regard to any one of these groups."[70] According to Grisel, these "secant marginals" largely determined the evolution of international commercial arbitration, by "building a hybrid system, made up of bridges that connected different legal systems and professions" and "combining elements from different systems in order to create a system at once new and familiar."[71]

My objection to Dezalay and Garth follows broadly similar lines. As a preliminary point, the group that "built" the contemporary regime of international commercial arbitration was not exclusively composed of

(2014), 387; Magdalene D'Silva, "Dealing in Power: Gatekeepers in Arbitrator Appointment in International Commercial Arbitration," *Journal of International Dispute Settlement*, 5 (2014), 605.

66 Thomas Schultz and Robert Kovacs, "The Rise of a Third Generation of Arbitrators? Fifteen Years after Dezalay and Garth," *Arbitration International*, 28 (2012), 161.

67 Schultz, "Celebrating 20 Years," 531–33.

68 Lemercier and Sgard, *Arbitrage privé international*, 143.

69 Florian Grisel, "Competition and Cooperation in International Commercial Arbitration: The Birth of a Transnational Legal Profession," *Law and Society Review*, 51 (2017), 790; see also Grisel, "Marginals and Elites in International Arbitration," in Thomas Schultz and Frederico Ortino (eds.), *The Oxford Handbook of International Arbitration* (Oxford: Oxford University Press, 2020), 260–82.

70 Grisel, "Competition and Cooperation," 793.

71 Ibid.

men, let alone "grand old men." To give but one example, Frances Kellor (1873–1952), a brilliant arbitration scholar and social reformer who was active in progressive circles, played an important (and often-overlooked) role in promoting arbitration in the United States in the 1930s and 1940s (see Figure 1.1).[72] More importantly, Dezalay and Garth have consistently overlooked the *historical* dimension of international commercial arbitration. In their work, they have constructed narratives around a series of oppositions: grand old men vs. young technocrats, academics vs. practitioners, North vs. South. While some of these make sense, others are less plausible and harder to demonstrate. In fact, by relegating history to the background, Dezalay and Garth have built a largely two-dimensional field, made up of these binary oppositions, which do not provide a full, or even adequate, picture of the history and evolution of international commercial arbitration. In other words, their account lacks a third dimension – namely, temporal or historical depth.

This book seeks to explore the historical dimension of international commercial arbitration, to which Dezalay and Garth paid relatively little attention. It will do so by adopting a sociologically inspired approach, looking at the actors (jurists, attorneys, academics, members of arbitral institutions, etc.), organs (diplomatic conferences, arbitral institutions, law firms, etc.), and modes of action (negotiation, codification, etc.). However,

[72] Kellor is one of the least-known figures in international arbitration, despite her key role as the first vice-president of the American Arbitration Association (AAA) and a member of its board of directors from its foundation in 1926 through the 1940s. She was its only female founder. According to Kessler, this neglect for Kellor's life and career stems in large part from "a gendered narrative of Progressive legal reform – one that has tended to lionize certain heroic, male icons (usually law professors or judges) as the courageous exponents of legal change." Amalia Kessler, "Arbitration and Americanization: The Paternalism of Progressive Procedural Reform," *Yale Law Journal*, 124 (2015), 2974. Tellingly, Kellor's obituary in the *New York Times* on January 5, 1952, was headlined "Frances Kellor, 78, Arbitration Aide." In addition to *American Arbitration: Its History, Functions, and Achievements* (Washington, DC: Beard Books, 1999 [1948]), Kellor wrote *The United States and the International Court* (New York: Thomas Seltzer, 1925) (with Antonia Hatvany); *Arbitration in Action: A Code for Civil, Commercial and Industrial Arbitrations* (New York: Harper, 1941); *Arbitration in International Controversy* (New York: Commission to Study the Organization of Peace and American Arbitration Association, 1944) (with Martin Domke); "Western Hemisphere Systems of Commercial Arbitration," *University of Toronto Law Journal*, 6 (1946), 307 (also with Martin Domke); and *Arbitration and the Legal Profession: A Report Prepared for the Survey of the Legal Profession* (New York: American Arbitration Association, 1952). Kellor was active in the women's suffrage movement; her partner, Mary Dreier, was the head of the legislative league of a New York women's reform movement. On Kellor generally, see John Press, "Frances Kellor, Americanization, and the Quest for Participatory Democracy" (PhD diss., New York University, 2009) (on file with author).

in order not to find myself trapped in the same pitfalls as Dezalay and Garth, I expand the boundaries of my research, both temporally (by covering a much longer period in the history of international commercial arbitration) and qualitatively (by exploring a much wider range of sources than just interviews, on which their work was principally based). This approach enables me to divide the history of international commercial arbitration into three broad periods, or ages, and to illuminate long-term patterns and discontinuities – the alternating surges of confidence and hesitation in arbitration, for instance – which Dezalay and Garth were unable to grasp.

## 1.2 Objectives and Arguments

In addition to the aforementioned general objective of dividing the history of international commercial arbitration into three broad periods (Section 1.2.1), a more specific objective will be to demonstrate that the history of international commercial arbitration has witnessed a kind of pendulum movement between broad periods of renewal and anxiety (Section 1.2.2). I will also argue that common to all three periods is an abiding tension between the State and the efforts of the merchant community to expand the reach of international commercial arbitration (Section 1.2.3).

### *1.2.1 The Three Ages of International Commercial Arbitration*

The first period, from approximately the 1780s to the 1920s – described by some historians as the "long nineteenth century"[73] – was the Age of Aspirations. It can be traced to the beginning of the French Revolution, which initially saw arbitration as fundamental to the settlement of disputes between citizens (before later displaying extreme hostility toward it). The Age of Aspirations was marked by an intense exploration of arbitration in all its forms. In private relations, arbitration was commonly used to settle commercial disputes, for example through the many trade associations in Europe. In the public arena, when used among states, arbitration was seen as a way of fostering peace and stability. The Age of Aspirations lasted until the 1920s, when arbitral institutions were founded; the importance of merchants and statesmen yielded to that of

[73] The expression "long nineteenth century" was most famously used by British historian Eric Hobsbawm to describe the 125-year period from 1789 (beginning of the French Revolution) to 1914 (outbreak of World War I). The "Age of Aspirations" described here is slightly longer, lasting until the 1920s (when arbitral institutions such as the ICC were founded).

**Figure 1.1** Anonymous photograph of Frances Kellor in 1942. Mary Elisabeth Dreier Papers, Schlesinger Library, Radcliffe Institute, Harvard University.

members of these arbitral institutions, and various efforts were made to recognize the validity of arbitration clauses.

The Age of Institutionalization followed from approximately the 1920s to the 1950s. It witnessed the creation of arbitral institutions, such as the Court of Arbitration of the ICC in 1923 and the American Arbitration Association (AAA) in 1926. These institutions not only administered cases but also established rules and principles, such as the ICC Rules of Arbitration. Through such codification efforts, they also developed international commercial arbitration from within. The Age of Institutionalization was marked by a much more internationalist spirit or legal consciousness. It lasted until the 1950s, when the 1958 Convention on the Recognition and Enforcement of Foreign Arbitral Awards ushered international commercial arbitration into a new era.

We are currently in the Age of Autonomy, which started in the 1950s. It has been marked by the autonomy of the mercatocracy, that is, increased specialization in the field and the rise of experts, specialized arbitration practitioners and academics. Another hallmark of the third age is the autonomous character of the law expounded by these experts and academics through such concepts as *lex mercatoria* and the arbitral legal order, which can be seen as attempts to give arbitration a theoretical foundation and explain its development as a system of law in its own right.

Table 1.1 summarizes the three ages of international commercial arbitration explored in successive parts of this book.

### *1.2.2 The Pendulum Movement between Anxiety and Renewal*

I argue that the history of international commercial arbitration is characterized by a *pendulum movement* between periods of *renewal* and *anxiety*. A "renewal," in common parlance, is the resumption of an activity after an interruption. Far from being rectilinear, the history of international commercial arbitration has been marked by periods of intense activity or renewal, followed by interruptions or caesurae as doubts arose over the meaning of international commercial arbitration and its position in the broader legal landscape, giving rise to anxiety, apprehension, and even fear.

The novelty of this idea does not lie in the choice of terms. In a profound article, David Kennedy used similar language when he described the evolution of international law in the United States as a "story of disciplinary renewal and consolidation punctuated by periods of anxiety and disputation."[74] Rather, what is new about renewal and anxiety as used here is their application to the field of international commercial arbitration. To the best of my knowledge, no other attempt has been made to frame the history of that field using these notions and categories.

This methodology draws inspiration from the work of several earlier scholars. Various historians and international lawyers have described the

[74] David Kennedy, "When Renewal Repeats: Thinking against the Box," *NYU Journal of International Law and Politics*, 32 (2000), 342. Kennedy was interested in international law's intellectual style and mainstream voice – "a voice of stability, associated vaguely with the past, and an updated, or reforming, vision which is more complex, relevant, and up-to-date" (ibid., 343). Kennedy also used the image of a pendulum movement to refer to the "back and forth between the formal law/community sides in periods of consensus, and … the anti-formal/sovereign autonomy sides in periods of anxiety" (ibid., 376). Terré, too, used the image of the pendulum to describe the meaningful oscillation between the opposing poles of contract and judiciality in arbitration. See François Terré, "L'arbitrage, essence du juridique," in *Liber amicorum Claude Reymond*, 309.

Table 1.1 *The three ages of international commercial arbitration*

| | The Age of Aspirations | The Age of Institutionalization | The Age of Autonomy |
|---|---|---|---|
| Period | 1780s–1920s | 1920s–1950s | 1950s–present |
| Defining features | Diffuse sense of an arbitral consciousness and an awareness of arbitration's potential as a source of stability between parties | Creation of key institutions, such as the ICC and the ICC Court of Arbitration; codification efforts (e.g., drafting of the ICC Arbitration Rules) | Increased specialization within the field, with experts discussing complex legal and theoretical issues such as *lex mercatoria* and the arbitral legal order |
| Preoccupation | Use of arbitration to settle disputes between traders and individuals and, in some instances, states | Creation of arbitral institutions to administer arbitration cases | Construction of a body of law and the theoretical foundations of arbitration as an autonomous system |
| Main bodies | Trade associations, diplomatic conferences | Arbitral institutions | Arbitral institutions, law firms, and educational establishments offering specialized courses of study in arbitration |
| Main figures | Merchants in trade associations, diplomats/statesmen | Members of arbitral institutions | Professional lawyers, arbitration practitioners |
| Modes of action | Commodity markets arbitration; diplomatic negotiation | Codification; drafting of arbitration rules | Specialized and technical writings about arbitration as an autonomous system |

structure of their field in terms of a binary opposition between two conflicting notions. In his classic work on the structure of international legal argument, Koskenniemi identified "ascending and descending patterns of argument" in international legal discourse and argued that "[a]ny doctrine, argument or position can be criticized because either utopian or apologist."[75] Koskenniemi argued that international law must constantly oscillate between these two extremes, leaving any middle ground as "a terrain of irreducible adversity."[76] Similarly, Tourme-Jouannet has studied international law from the perspective of its "double ultimate end of a liberal law-providence."[77] For her, this dualism provides a "key" to understanding the practice of international law past and present: "the original coexistence of the two purposes of international law . . . still remains today."[78] These exemplary studies offer valuable pointers for analyzing the field of international commercial arbitration.

### 1.2.3 The Ongoing Tension between the State and the Mercatocracy

Another aim of this book is to examine the ongoing tension between the State and the mercatocracy, defined by Cutler as the "global corporate elite" made up of transnational merchants, private international lawyers, representatives of international organizations, and so on, which "operates globally and locally to develop new merchant laws governing international commerce and the settlement of international commercial disputes and to universalize the laws through the unification and harmonization of national commercial legal orders."[79] The mercatocracy has played a key role throughout the modern history of international commercial arbitration, not as some kind of secret society but as a merchant group deeply committed to expanding the reach of, and developing rules and institutions peculiar to, international arbitration.

As such, the mercatocracy may be viewed as the latest stage in the development of Hegel's "civil society" (*bürgerliche Gesellschaft*), the realm in which individual human beings exist as "*private persons* who have their

[75] Martti Koskenniemi, *From Apology to Utopia: The Structure of International Legal Argument* (Cambridge: Cambridge University Press, 2005), 65.

[76] Ibid., 597.

[77] Emmanuelle Tourme-Jouannet, *Le droit international libéral-providence: Une histoire du droit international* (Brussels: Bruylant, 2011), 1.

[78] Ibid., 8.

[79] Claire Cutler, *Private Power and Global Authority: Transnational Merchant Law in the Global Political Economy* (Cambridge: Cambridge University Press, 2003), 4–5.

own interest as their end."[80] "In civil society," Hegel explained, "each individual is his own end, and all else means nothing to him."[81] In other words, individuals must depend on themselves to achieve their own welfare and "contingent needs" and interests.[82] Through its emphasis on individuals as disposers of their own private property, the concept of civil society therefore captured the essence of the then-nascent modern market economy.[83] Even though Hegel's thought needs to be understood in the context of the Prussian state as it existed in the 1820s, the notion of civil society reveals something more profound about modernity: the loss of sovereignty considered as the "attribute of a powerful individual whose legitimacy over territory . . . rested on a purportedly direct or delegated or divine or historic authority."[84] To a large extent, then, the mercatocracy is not very far removed from the *Bürgher* or bourgeois asserting his own ends at a time of destabilization and radical transformation of state sovereignty.

The tension between the State and the mercatocracy – a key aspect of the political history of arbitration – will be seen on numerous occasions in this book. What should be the proper function of arbitration in society? And should this be decided the State or "civil society"? At times, it has seemed as if both entities were working toward the same goal, as when the right of citizens to choose arbitrators to rule on their disputes was enshrined in France's constitutions of 1793 and 1795, or more recently when a former

80 Georg Wilhelm Friedrich Hegel, *Elements of the Philosophy of Right* (1821), ed. Allen Wood, trans. Hugh Barr Nisbet (Cambridge: Cambridge University Press, 2003), 224 (emphasis in original).

81 Ibid., 220.

82 Ibid., 222. For Hegel, civil society was one of three "moments" in the "ethical life" (*Sittlichkeit*) of modernity, coming after the "family" and before the individual as a member of the "public life" of the state (ibid., 198). Marx likewise divided history into three stages but, unlike Hegel, he maintained that "[f]ree individuality, based on the universal development of individuals and on their subordination of their communal, social productivity as their social wealth, is the third stage." Karl Marx, *Grundrisse: Foundations of the Critique of Political Economy* (1939), trans. Martin Nicolaus (London: Penguin, 1993), 158. The third stage, the result of the "social wealth" that the society creates, involved a complete transformation of "civil society."

83 See, generally, Steven Smith, "At the Crossroads: Hegel and the Ethics of *bürgerliche Gesellschaft*," *Laval théologique et politique*, 51 (1995), 346; Allen Wood, "Editor's Introduction," in Georg Wilhelm Friedrich Hegel, *Elements of the Philosophy of Right* (1821), ed. Allen Wood, trans. Hugh Barr Nisbet (Cambridge: Cambridge University Press, 2003).

84 Michael Reisman, "Sovereignty and Human Rights in Contemporary International Law," *American Journal of International Law*, 84 (1990), 867. The classic work remains Ernst Kantorowicz's 1957 study *The King's Two Bodies: A Study in Medieval Political Theology* (1957; Princeton: Princeton University Press, 2016).

French minister of justice, Robert Badinter, proclaimed: "International arbitration is one of the spontaneous but harmonious expressions of Justice. In order that it may prosper, it is better that it should remain outside the government's hold."[85] But the relationship between the State and the mercatocracy has not always been easy. The tension between the two stems from the constant opposition between two opposing tendencies: the centralization of the State and the diffusing forces of the mercatocracy.

This tension will serve as a sort of metanarrative, a story *about* the story of international commercial arbitration. Of course, there may be objections from those who, like Lyotard, detect an "incredulity toward metanarratives" in an age of fragmentation, where "[t]he narrative function is losing its functors, its great hero, its great dangers, its great voyages, its great goal."[86] Rejecting the grand narratives of modernity (the Enlightenment, the emancipation of humanity, Marxism, etc.), Lyotard calls for "little narratives" or *petits récits* centered on "singularities and 'incommensurabilities.'"[87] While these profound objections may apply to the present metanarrative as well, the value of an overarching account should not be dismissed out of hand. Lyotard's own ideas often took on narrative forms; as he once wrote, "[o]ne *must*, certainly, inscribe in words, in images. One cannot escape the necessity of representing."[88] This book's metanarrative is precisely a *representation* of the history of international commercial arbitration that weaves together its various parts.

## 1.3 Sources and Caveats

In exploring the history of international commercial arbitration, this book draws on a wide range of primary and secondary sources (Section 1.3.1), with regard to which a few caveats need to be mentioned (Section 1.3.2).

[85] Robert Badinter, "Formal Opening," in *60 Years of ICC Arbitration: A Look at the Future* (Paris: ICC Publishing, 1984), 23.

[86] Jean-François Lyotard, *The Postmodern Condition: A Report on Knowledge* (1979), trans. Geoff Bennington and Brian Massumi (Manchester: Manchester University Press, 1984), xxix.

[87] Ibid., 60.

[88] Jean-François Lyotard, *Heidegger and 'the jews'* (1988), trans. Andreas Michel and Mark Roberts (Minneapolis: University of Minnesota Press, 1990), 26.

### *1.3.1 Sources*

One of my principal sources was the documentation relating to my dissertation topic currently available at the ICC's headquarters in Paris. It included 131 arbitral awards from the years 1922–1969, for the most part unpublished.[89] I have also read the confidential minutes of the ICC Court of Arbitration's Executive Committee meetings between 1923 and 1932, at which the Court's ongoing cases were discussed. In addition, I obtained all fourteen of the successive versions of the ICC Rules of Arbitration, with the accompanying explanatory commentaries where available.

Various periodicals and other printed publications available at the ICC or, in some cases, the *Bibliothèque nationale de France* and other libraries provided a fascinating window on the history of international arbitration. They include all nineteen issues of the *Journal of the International Chamber of Commerce*, from July 1924 to October 1928; issues three to eight of the *Arbitration Reports*, printed as supplements to the *Journal of the International Chamber of Commerce* (I could not locate the first two issues in Paris); the *Bulletin* and *Record* of the ICC; and all available issues of *World Trade/L'Économie internationale*, a bilingual ICC periodical, from 1929 to 1959. I have also consulted various brochures (from 1921 (no. 13) to 1959 (no. 207)), digests, and internal documents relating to the ICC's structure and organization, the biennial ICC congresses, and other ICC activities over the years related to international commercial arbitration.

In Clermont-Ferrand, I explored the Clémentel papers, which are housed at the Puy-de-Dôme Departmental Archives. Étienne Clémentel (1864–1936) was a French politician who served as *député* and senator and was the first president of the ICC. He also sponsored a bill affirming the validity of arbitration clauses in France, which was a thorny issue at the time. It prompted me to visit the archives of the French National Assembly, where I read the relevant parts of the parliamentary debates on this issue that took place in the Chamber of Deputies in 1907 and 1908 and in the Senate between 1921 and 1925.

Other attempts to locate new sources on the modern history of international commercial arbitration have been less successful. I went to the Paris Court of Appeal in the hope of finding old judicial decisions relating to international arbitration that would have shown, for

89 Assisted by a team of Sciences Po students, I transcribed these awards in 2017. I venture to hope that the ICC will one day publish them for the benefit of other researchers.

instance, whether any of the arbitration cases I had read about had been the subject of annulment proceedings. The *greffière* at the court registry kindly let me read various documents but none of them were directly relevant to my research. My searches at the Paris Departmental Archives (where the old archives of the Paris Court of Appeal are kept) were equally unfruitful.[90]

I also tried to locate the archives of the American Arbitration Association (AAA), which was founded in 1926 and continues to play an important role in the field of alternative dispute resolution. I was told that the AAA archives containing the type of historical information in which I was interested were no longer housed at the AAA's headquarters in New York but had been acquired by Pepperdine University Law School in Malibu, California,[91] which boasts a large conflict resolution library. Upon further inquiry, however, I found out that the materials acquired by Pepperdine "did not include the institutional archives or any founding materials."[92]

My research project also led me to speak to various individuals over the years. Although, unlike Dezalay and Garth, my intention was never to undertake extensive interviewing, I reached out to the families of various individuals who had played a key role in the modern history of arbitration, asking them whether their parents or grandparents had left behind unpublished papers, letters, or documents. Professor Hans Smit's son, a distinguished arbitration attorney in his own right, and Me Jean Robert's son, a lawyer in Paris, were kind enough to respond to my queries. However, I learned little that was not already publicly available – apart from a few fascinating anecdotes that said a lot about the spirit of the time.[93] Perhaps other scholars with the necessary language skills will find other documents; for example, the archives of the Swedish national committee are kept at the Royal Library of Sweden, those of the Swiss national committee are kept in Zurich, and there is also a Sanders Law

[90] Judicial decisions kept in the Archives de Paris are released 100 years after their date of issue. Readers may order no more than ten documents on any one day, which makes such research difficult, if not impossible.

[91] Email of Mr. Ted Pons, Vice-President, Publications and ADR Resources (May 12, 2015).

[92] Email of Ms. Katie Kerr Dodds, Assistant Dean, Law Library, Pepperdine University School of Law (May 12, 2015).

[93] See, for example, Robert Smit, "Remembrance and Reminiscence: Thoughts on Arbitrator Selection: Why My Father Was (Usually) a Good Choice," *American Review of International Arbitration*, 23 (2012), 583 (explaining that Hans Smit often "'suggested' that the parties convene their arbitral hearings in Southern France rather than Paris" because it "provided an opportunity to bring the parties together in an atmosphere conducive to settlement").

Library at the Erasmus School of Law in Rotterdam.[94] I have also spoken to various experts over the years. They are listed in the acknowledgment.

With regard to secondary sources, I have used a wide range of books (or their relevant sections), dissertations, journal articles, reports, and so on. These are also listed in the bibliography at the end of this book.

### *1.3.2 Caveats*

#### 1.3.2.1 Geographical Focus

This book concentrates particularly on the European origins of international commercial arbitration. There are two main reasons for this choice. The first is purely practical: France is where I chose to undertake my research. This is notably where the archives of the Paris-based ICC are located. These archives contain a wealth of documents that have remained largely unexplored by scholars. Someone else might have picked another institution or a different vantage point from which to consider the history of international commercial arbitration. I suspect, however, that my argument about the oscillation between periods of anxiety and renewal holds true in other geographical contexts, too. As sociologists have pointed out, studying the "local" can provide a useful way to study the "global."[95]

The second reason is that Europe, and France in particular, has played a key role in the modern history and evolution of international commercial arbitration. Discussing the "pervasive and crucial role"[96] that French courts, jurists, and institutions have played throughout the history of international commercial arbitration, von Mehren – a true internationalist, who studied law in three countries and taught in nine – explained that "[t]hese French developments may well constitute the most creative and probing contemporary experimentation and reflection respecting the

[94] Calls and emails to the Sanders Law Library – to inquire whether Prof. Sanders (1912–2012) had left unpublished personal papers – remained unanswered. A compilation of personal letters addressed to Prof. Sanders was produced to mark his 100th birthday; see ICCA Pieter Sanders Collection, www.arbitration-icca.org/historic-treasures/profsanders.html.

[95] See, for example, Saskia Sassen, "The Global inside the National: A Research Agenda for Sociology," *Sociopedia.isa* (2010), 3; Saskia Sassen, *Territory, Authority, Rights: From Medieval to Global Assemblages* (Princeton: Princeton University Press, 2006). The concept of "glocalization" – a portmanteau of "globalization" and "localization" – is particularly useful here, conveying the idea that law can be studied at both the global and local levels.

[96] Arthur Taylor von Mehren, "International Commercial Arbitration: The Contribution of the French Jurisprudence," *Louisiana Law Review*, 46 (1986), 1046.

nature of – and the characteristics required by – an effective dispute resolution process for international commercial activities."[97]

I am not of course suggesting that the history of international commercial arbitration was shaped exclusively in Europe. That is simply not the case. International arbitration has a rich and varied history in many parts of the world. It is beyond the scope of this book to inquire why European influences came to play such a prominent role in the history of international commercial arbitration, be it through cross-fertilization between legal systems or more profound phenomena, including Western expansionism and colonialism.[98] When reading about the history of international law and related fields, it is important to bear in mind that not so long ago Europe still served as "the origin, engine and *telos* of historical knowledge."[99] Under the influence of the

[97] Ibid., 1059. In an article whose title hearkened to von Mehren's earlier paper, Gaillard referred to a clear "*pensée juridique française*" (French legal thinking) in international arbitration (Gaillard, "L'apport," 529). Elsewhere, he has described French Court of Cassation case law on international arbitration as "strong and coherent," a powerfully resonating voice in modern arbitration law (Emmanuel Gaillard, "La jurisprudence de la Cour de cassation en matière d'arbitrage international," *Revue de l'arbitrage*, 2007, 697). See also Jan Paulsson, *The Idea of Arbitration* (Oxford: Oxford University Press, 2013), 44. This pro-arbitration approach was enshrined in France's bold 2011 arbitration reform.

[98] This will be explored briefly in Chapter 3, Section 3.2.1. As van Hulle notes, "[t]he role that international arbitration has played as part of the imperial legal infrastructure of states has not yet been fully appreciated" (Inge van Hulle, "Imperial consolidation through arbitration: Territorial and boundary disputes in Africa (1870–1914)," in Ignacio de la Rasilla and Jorge Viñuales (eds.), *Experiments in International Adjudication: Historical Accounts* (Cambridge: Cambridge University Press, 2019), 56). Anghie has probed the relationship between colonialism and the emergence of transnational law (Anghie, *Imperialism*, 223–44), and Shalakany has argued that international arbitration of investment disputes became necessary "only after gunboat diplomacy was no longer the acceptable way to settle trade disputes with the (newly independent) former colonies of the Third Word" (Amr Shalakany, "Arbitration and the Third World: A Plea for Reassessing Bias Under the Specter of Neoliberalism," *Harvard International Law Journal*, 41 (2000), 430–31; see also Muthucumaraswamy Sornarajah, "The Climate of International Arbitration," *Journal of International Arbitration*, 8 (1991), 47). For a contrasting view (arguing that "the dice are loaded no longer. A new generation of Third World officials, executives, and lawyers has learned to use the mechanism of international arbitration"), see Jan Paulsson, "Third World Participation in International Investment Arbitration," *ICSID Review – Foreign Investment Law Journal*, 2 (1987), 21.

[99] Martti Koskenniemi, "Histories of International Law: Dealing with Eurocentrism," *Rechtsgeschichte*, 19 (2011), 158. See also Arnulf Becker Lorca, "Eurocentrism in the History of International Law," in Bardo Fassbender and Anne Peters (eds.), *The Oxford Handbook of the History of International Law* (Oxford: Oxford University Press, 2012).

"turn to history" in the study of international law[100] and international adjudication[101] – in no small part due to Koskenniemi's seminal research[102] – and recent trends in intellectual[103] and global history,[104] a new generation of international law scholars are rewriting the history of international law as "seen from the peripheries."[105] In considering the historical narrative from a new perspective, they have shown that "the international law we deem universal and Western is in fact heterogeneous and global."[106] Over the past decade, critical voices have also been raised, arguing that "private international law has contributed very little to the global governance debate, remaining remarkably silent

[100] See Thomas Skouteris, "The Turn to History in International Law," *Oxford Bibliographies*, www.oxfordbibliographies.com/view/document/obo-9780199796953/obo-9780199796953-0154.xml (last modified June 27, 2017). On the various ways in which the relationship between international law and history may be envisaged (as history of international law, history in international law, or international law in history), see Matthew Craven, "Introduction: International Law and Its Histories," in Matthew Craven, Malgosia Fitzmaurice, and Maria Vogiatzi (eds.), *Time, History and International Law* (Leiden: Martinus Nijhoff, 2007). See also Matthew Craven, "Theorizing the Turn to History in International Law," in Anne Orford, Florian Hoffmann, and Martin Clark, *The Oxford Handbook of the Theory of International Law* (Oxford: Oxford University Press, 2016).

[101] See, for example, Ignacio de la Rasilla, "The Turn to the History of International Adjudication," in Ignacio de la Rasilla and Jorge Viñuales (eds.), *Experiments in International Adjudication: Historical Accounts* (Cambridge: Cambridge University Press, 2019), 32–52; Mary O'Connell and Lenore VanderZee, "The History of International Adjudication," in Cesare Romano, Karen Alter, and Yuval Shany (eds.), *The Oxford Handbook of International Adjudication* (Oxford: Oxford University Press, 2013), 40–62.

[102] See, for example, Martti Koskenniemi, *The Gentle Civilizer of Nations: The Rise and Fall of International Law 1870–1960* (Cambridge: Cambridge University Press, 2001).

[103] See, for example, David Armitage, "The International Turn in Intellectual History," in Darrin McMahon and Samuel Moyn (eds.), *Rethinking Modern European Intellectual History* (New York: Oxford University Press, 2014); David Armitage, *Foundations of Modern International Thought* (Cambridge: Cambridge University Press, 2013).

[104] See, for example, Martti Koskenniemi, "Expanding Histories of International Law," *American Journal of Legal History*, 56 (2016), 104; Lynn Hunt, *Writing History in the Global Era* (New York: Norton, 2014); Bardo Fassbender and Anne Peters, "Introduction: Towards a Global History of International Law," in Bardo Fassbender and Anne Peters (eds.), *The Oxford Handbook of the History of International Law* (Oxford: Oxford University Press, 2014), 1–24.

[105] Recent examples are Miles, *Origins*; Juan Pablo Scarfi, *The Hidden History of International Law in the Americas: Empire and Legal Networks* (Oxford: Oxford University Press, 2017); Mamadou Hebié, *Souveraineté territoriale par traité: Une étude des accords entre puissances coloniales et entités politiques locales* (Paris: Presses Universitaires de France, 2015).

[106] Arnulf Becker Lorca, *Mestizo International Law: A Global Intellectual History 1842–1933* (Cambridge: Cambridge University Press, 2015), 14.

before the increasingly unequal distribution of wealth and authority in the world," and calling for a "radical reappraisal of its traditional methodologies."[107] One can only hope that a similar trend will develop in international arbitration scholarship, perhaps building on (mostly European) accounts like the present one to write a more hybrid – or "*mestizo*"[108] – history of the discipline.

#### 1.3.2.2 Anxiety and Renewal

My intention in writing this book is not only to retrace the modern history of international commercial arbitration but also to explore the field's inner dynamics. My reference to the pendulum-like oscillation between anxiety and renewal is not simply a heuristic device, an interpretive tool to make sense of the rich and varied history of international commercial arbitration; it is also a graphic way of exposing the broader forces that have been and arguably still are at play, shaping the contemporary landscape of international commercial arbitration.

That said, I am not positing that history is endlessly cyclical, or that the dialectical opposition (thesis/antithesis) between anxiety and renewal should be resolved in favor of a middle ground (synthesis). Nor am I arguing that the periods of renewal and anxiety were necessarily good or bad. Anxiety often has negative connotations, but it can also be beneficial in some situations (as when it alerts us to dangers). Likewise, we tend to associate renewal with a sense of optimism – a rebirth or positive transformation. But renewal is not necessarily positive, and sometimes the status quo is the better option.[109]

[107] Horatia Muir Watt, "Private International Law's Shadow Contribution to the Question of Informal Transnational Authority," *Indiana Journal of Global Legal Studies*, 25 (2018), 40. See also Muir Watt, "International Arbitration: A Critical Private International Law Perspective," in Thomas Schultz and Frederico Ortino (eds.), *The Oxford Handbook of International Arbitration* (Oxford: Oxford University Press, 2020), 513–36; Muir Watt, "Private International Law Beyond the Schism," *Transnational Legal Theory*, 2 (2011), 347.

[108] See Lorca, *Mestizo International Law.*

[109] For example, various authors have expressed opposition to proposals to amend the New York Convention, preferring the status quo to renewal. See Emmanuel Gaillard, "The Urgency of Not Revising the New York Convention," in Albert Jan van den Berg (ed.), *50 Years of the New York Convention*, ICCA Congress Series No. 14 (The Hague: Kluwer Law International, 2009) (arguing that "the New York Convention should be left alone," even if "its language is at times dated," ibid., 690); V. V. Veeder, "Is There a Need to Revise the New York Convention?," *Journal of International Dispute Settlement*, 1 (2010), 499.

Of course, any attempt to rationalize a complex reality is inherently problematic. I use the terms renewal and anxiety because they convey my overall impression of the history of international commercial arbitration. But, like Tourme-Jouannet's argument about the liberal-welfarist law of nations, my classificatory scheme may be imperfect at times – "a particular hypothesis" that seeks to "expand the range of our current historical interpretations through a historical reading that more often complements the other suggested histories than is opposed to them."[110]

#### 1.3.2.3 Dividing History into Periods

This leads me to my third caveat. The tripartite division advanced in this book reflects the impression I have acquired, in the course of studying the many documents on which it relies, that certain landmark events – the creation of the ICC in the aftermath of World War I, the enactment of the New York Convention, and so on – propelled the discipline into a new era. At the same time, however, the chronological references used to define the three periods – from the 1780s to the 1920s for the first age, the 1920s to the 1950s for the second, and the 1950s to the present for the third – are deliberately approximative. Duncan Kennedy, who divided the history of American legal thought from the early nineteenth century to World War II into three key periods, warned of the "spurious precision of dates,"[111] and this is especially true for a topic as complex as the history of international commercial arbitration.

Of course, as French historian Jacques Le Goff explained in his last book, programmatically titled *Faut-il vraiment découper l'histoire en tranches?* [Must We Really Divide History into Periods?],[112] "dividing history into periods is never a neutral or innocent act."[113] Any periodization is "a complex act,"[114] a practice that is both "artificial and

[110] Tourme-Jouannet, *Le droit international*, 9.

[111] Duncan Kennedy, *The Rise and Fall of Classical Legal Thought* (Washington, DC: Beard Books, 2006), 1. In this study, originally published in 1975, Kennedy proposed a new understanding of three key periods in American legal history: from the Revolution to the Civil War (labeled "pre-Classical legal thought"), the late nineteenth and early twentieth centuries (labeled "Classical Legal Thought"), and the early modern period from before World War I onward. According to Kennedy, Classical Legal Thought differed "radically, discontinuously, from the model that dominated up to the Civil War, but was conceptually similar to the one we employed in 1975," ibid., x–xi.

[112] Jacques Le Goff, *Faut-il vraiment découper l'histoire en tranches?* (Paris: Seuil, 2014). I owe this reference to Jérôme Sgard.

[113] Ibid., 37.

[114] Ibid., 15.

temporary."[115] Le Goff explains how the division of time into distinct periods originated in religious practice.[116] While acknowledging the need to divide history into periods,[117] he alerts us to some of the pitfalls that such an approach can have: "this breaking down is not merely chronological, it also expresses the idea of moving on, a turning point, or even a disavowal of the society and values of the previous period."[118]

It is not my intention to suggest that any one period was better than or superior to any other.[119] I do not believe that we live in a golden age of international arbitration or that there was ever such an age in the past. Each period has its strengths and weaknesses, its cast of great characters and more controversial figures. As with the three representations of international arbitration identified by Gaillard, there is no right or wrong period, or periodization, of international commercial arbitration; "there is room for divergence on the systematization of the discipline, the appreciation of solutions, or propositions as to the trend of the evolution in the field."[120]

* * *

Why international commercial arbitration?, one might ask. Because its history, as this introduction has tried to show, has not yet been fully explored or written. But also because through international commercial arbitration jurists can contemplate a number of fundamental questions, such as the nature and function of law and its place in a globalized world. "There is something mesmerizing in arbitration," Oppetit once wrote.[121] Three decades later, Racine also described international commercial arbitration as "a pragmatic law that confuses and fascinates."[122] This book has been inspired by a similar sense of

[115] Ibid., 37.
[116] Ibid., 17.
[117] Ibid., 190.
[118] Ibid., 13.
[119] On the periodization of the history of international law and the "remarkable inclination towards 'narrations of progress,'" see Oliver Diggelmann, "The Periodization of the History of International Law," in Bardo Fassbender and Anne Peters (eds.), *The Oxford Handbook of the History of International Law* (Oxford: Oxford University Press, 2012), 1008.
[120] Gaillard, *Legal Theory*, 11.
[121] Oppetit, *Théorie de l'arbitrage*, 9.
[122] Jean-Baptiste Racine, "L'arbitrage: propos liminaire sur un droit pragmatique," in Yves Strickler and Jean-Baptiste Racine (eds.), *L'arbitrage: Questions contemporaines* (Paris: L'Harmattan, 2012), 11.

fascination. It might, like international commercial arbitration itself, be viewed as "an act and place of freedom," even tempting some readers to "play truant" by loitering outside their disciplines.[123] But perhaps it will also reveal something deeper – namely, where international commercial arbitration comes from and where it is heading.

[123] Jean-Baptiste Racine, *Droit de l'arbitrage* (Paris: Presses Universitaires de France, 2016), 633.

# PART I

## The Age of Aspirations

# 2

# Introduction to the Age of Aspirations

During the Age of Aspirations (1780s–1920s), arbitration was practiced in a wide range of contexts, from trade associations in London or Liverpool to diplomatic conferences in Geneva. Early adepts believed that arbitration "represented an essential means to achieving the lofty goal of peace through law in a complex and divided world."[1]

The main figures of this period were (1) merchants in trade associations and (2) diplomats and statesmen desirous of settling disputes peacefully at diplomatic conferences rather than resorting to war. Through the efforts of these players, modern international arbitration developed some of its distinctive characteristics, such as the binding force of arbitral awards and the requirement that they state the reasons on which they are based.

In the Age of Aspirations, the mercatocracy had not yet become fully organized, so there was little tension between it and the State. It is true that there were what Lagarde called "pockets of organization"[2] – that is, individuals who started envisioning the arbitral process as removed from the preserve of states – but arbitration remained largely local, confined to a specific trade or geographical area (e.g., British trade associations applying English law). Widespread *international* arbitration, however, remained an ideal, a set of aspirations. States took center stage; by and large, they alone decided whether arbitration should be used and in what contexts.

The situation slowly changed at the end of the Age of Aspirations, when the mercatocracy became more organized and increasingly began to assert its authority. In the 1920s, the Age of Aspirations gave way to the Age of Institutionalization (1920s–1950s). International arbitration did not suddenly cease being seen as an instrument for peace – on the

[1] Bruno Oppetit, *Théorie de l'arbitrage* (Paris: Presses Universitaires de France, 1998), 10.

[2] Paul Lagarde, "Approche critique de la *lex mercatoria*," in Philippe Fouchard, Philippe Kahn, and Antoine Lyon-Caen (eds.), *Le droit des relations économiques internationale: Études offertes à Berthold Goldman* (Paris: Litec, 1982), 139.

contrary, the discourse on "peace through arbitration" continued into the 1920s and 1930s – but arbitral institutions started to emerge, causing merchants and statesmen to become less important than technicians and the members of those institutions. It was they, the true members of the mercatocracy, who sought to consolidate the arbitration system by creating legal rules and methods.

Chapters 3 and 4 adopt contrasting perspectives. Exploring international arbitration in a global context, Chapter 3 looks at two strains of arbitration in the eighteenth and nineteenth centuries: commodity market arbitrations and state-to-state arbitrations. It argues that this was a period of intense renewal, with the beginnings of an "arbitral consciousness," even though "international arbitration" had various meanings and did not yet exist as we know it today. Chapter 4 has a narrower geographical focus, concentrating on France. Through the debates on arbitration clauses that marked the period leading up to the twentieth century, it explores, more broadly, the differing attitudes toward arbitration at the time. By identifying waves of enthusiasm and hostility toward arbitration, the chapters in this part show the movement between renewal and anxiety at play over an extended period of time in the modern history of international arbitration.

Before delving into the Age of Aspirations, however, this chapter looks at how a history of international commercial arbitration may be written. There are many possible answers to this deceptively simple question. After considering some of them (Section 2.1), the chapter will draw attention to various methodological pitfalls that may be encountered when studying the history of international arbitration, especially its distant origins (Section 2.2).

## 2.1 Different Ways of Writing a History of International Commercial Arbitration

There is no one way of writing the modern history of international commercial arbitration, but rather a "radical pluralism" of historical methods and approaches,[3] several of which will be used in this book.

[3] Mikhaïl Xifaras, "Comment rendre le passé contemporain?," in Nicolas Laurent-Bonne and Xavier Prévost (eds.), *Penser l'ancien droit privé: Regards croisés sur les méthodes des juristes (II)* (Paris: LGDJ, 2018), 19–20. For a recent study exploring the variety of approaches and methods in contemporary legal history, see Frédéric Audren, Anne-Sophie Chambost, and Jean-Louis Halpérin, *Histoires contemporaines du droit* (Paris: Dalloz, 2020).

Schematically, one could focus on the history of events, the history of concepts, or the history of individual people (there are indeed many well-known, as well as less known but no less fascinating,[4] figures in the modern history of international arbitration).[5] When it comes to concepts, one could trace the history of the notion of *lex mercatoria*[6] or that of the arbitral legal order,[7] for example.

With regard to events, one could explore narrow timescales, focusing, for example, on a few key events and explaining how they led to the present state of international commercial arbitration. This approach – which some might call *histoire événementielle* or event-based history,[8] with its "brief, rapid, nervous fluctuations"[9] – views history as closely tied to specific events. Applied to the study of international arbitration, it would focus on a few key moments that led to the current state of affairs. For example, the genesis of the New York Convention was a seminal moment and turning point in the modern history of international commercial arbitration. Participants from a wide range of national, cultural, and legal backgrounds gave detailed thought to the role that individual states should play in the modern international arbitration compact. This event had broader implications for the modern history of international commercial arbitration.

Alternatively, one could adopt a longer-term narrative, focusing on the deep and slowly evolving historical structure of international commercial arbitration. Such an approach – which Braudel famously called the

[4] For examples, see Chapter 6, Section 6.2.2 (and n. 67) with details about Étienne Clémentel, a key founder of the International Chamber of Commerce and its Court of Arbitration, whose life is frequently overlooked by arbitration scholars; and Chapter 4, Section 4.3.2 (and n. 59) with details about Louis Louis-Dreyfus, a member of the French parliament who promoted arbitration in legislative and business circles in the first decades of the twentieth century.

[5] See Bardo Fassbender and Anne Peters, "Introduction: Towards a Global History of International Law," in Bardo Fassbender and Anne Peters (eds.), *The Oxford Handbook of the History of International Law* (Oxford: Oxford University Press, 2014), 11–14.

[6] See Section 9.2.

[7] See Section 10.4.1.

[8] See, for example, Pierre Nora, "Le retour de l'événement," in Le Goff and Nora, *Faire l'Histoire*. See also Paul Ricœur, "Le retour de l'événement," *Mélanges de l'École française de Rome*, 104 (1992), 29.

[9] Fernand Braudel, "Preface to the First Edition" (1946), in *The Mediterranean and the Mediterranean World in the Age of Phillip II*, trans. Siân Reynolds (Berkeley: University of California Press, 1995), 2. Braudel famously posited a trinity of time: (1) structural and geographic time (*structure*), (2) social time of intermediate duration (*conjoncture*), and (3) events and individual time (*événement*). *The Mediterranean* consists of three sections, following this division of time.

"longue durée"[10] and which still has powerful advocates in the anglophone world today[11] – encourages us to examine the long sweep of history. While this approach was primarily used to analyze long periods of structural and geographic time, and even the history of mentalities,[12] there is no reason why it should not be applied to the study of legal history,[13] such as that of international commercial arbitration over an extended period of time.

Moreover, one could study the history of international commercial arbitration across time and space, or focus on a single geographical setting.[14] The narrative in England, for instance, would focus on the courts of piepowders, which had jurisdiction over disputes between merchants at local fairs and were described by Blackstone as "[t]he lowest, and at the same time the most expeditious, court of justice known to the law of England."[15] It would also explore the quality or control arbitrations of such bodies as the London or Liverpool Corn Trade Associations and the London Flour Trade Association. It would then discuss the Arbitration Act 1889, which consolidated previous practices, and, in the more recent past, the Arbitration Acts 1950, 1975, 1979, and 1996. A US narrative would explore judicial and legislative hostility to commercial arbitration in the nineteenth century,

10 For a programmatic essay, see Fernand Braudel, "Histoire et Sciences sociales: La longue durée," *Annales: Economies, Sociétés, Civilisations*, 13 (1958), 725; trans. as Braudel, "History and the Social Sciences: The *Longue Durée*," in Braudel, *On History*, trans. Sarah Matthews (Chicago: Chicago University Press, 1982), 25.

11 See, in particular, David Armitage and Jo Guldi, *The History Manifesto* (Cambridge: Cambridge University Press, 2014); Armitage and Guldi, "The Return of the *Longue Durée*: An Anglo-American Perspective," *Annales: Histoire, Sciences Sociales*, 70 (2015), 289.

12 See, for example, Jacques Le Goff, "Les mentalités: Une histoire ambiguë," in Jacques Le Goff and Pierre Nora (eds.), *Faire l'Histoire: Nouveaux problèmes, nouvelles approches, nouveaux objets* (1974; Paris: Gallimard, 2011).

13 See, for example, Dominique Gaurier, *Histoire du droit international: de l'Antiquité à la création de l'ONU* (Rennes: Presses Universitaires de Rennes, 2014).

14 For an important work of scholarship, covering the arbitral process in three contexts (interstate relations, international commercial relations, and municipal relations), see J. Gillis Wetter, *The International Arbitral Process: Public and Private* (New York: Oceana, 1979). For a recent exploration of the modern history of international commercial arbitration in three geographical settings (England, the United States, and France), see Jérôme Sgard, "A Tale of Three Cities: The Construction of International Commercial Arbitration," in Grégoire Mallard and Jérôme Sgard (eds.), *Contractual Knowledge: One Hundred Years of Legal Experimentation in Global Markets* (Cambridge: Cambridge University Press, 2016).

15 William Blackstone, *Commentaries on the Laws of England; Book III: Of Private Wrongs*, ed. Thomas Gallanis (Oxford: Oxford University Press, 2016), 21.

encapsulated in Story's statement that "courts of justice are presumed to be better capable of administering and enforcing the real rights of the parties, than any mere private arbitrators."[16] It would then consider the 1925 Federal Arbitration Act, which marked a complete reversal of attitudes, establishing an extremely pro-arbitration regime,[17] and the birth of the American Arbitration Association in 1926.[18]

Finally, the history and evolution of international commercial arbitration can also be studied from a more abstract angle, though this is less common in legal scholarship, at least in Europe, and thus more novel. One such approach is to rely on aesthetic notions, building on Schlag's key insight that "[l]aw is an aesthetic enterprise."[19] Schlag identified four "aesthetics within which American law is cast"[20] and which "shape the ways in which we think law, do law, and imagine law's future identities":[21] (1) the *grid aesthetic*, according to which "law is framed as a field, a territory, a two-dimensional space that can be mapped or charted";[22] (2) the *energy aesthetic*, in which "law is cast in the image of energy," meaning that "[l]egal rules, principles, policies, and values have magnitude that must be quantified, measured, and compared";[23] (3) the *perspectivist aesthetic*, which "enables a variety of different political perspectives and social phenomena to be translated faithfully into the language of the law";[24] and (4) the *dissociative aesthetic*, which represents "a specter of dissolution that haunts all these aesthetics" and "does not and cannot last."[25] According to Schlag, these four aesthetics combine in various ways and operate through us, "choosing us, enacting us, directing us."[26]

[16] Joseph Story, *Commentaries on Equity Jurisprudence* (London: Stevens and Haynes, 1884), 440.

[17] See, for example, section 2 of the Federal Arbitration Act (1925), which provides that arbitration agreements "shall be valid, irrevocable, and enforceable, save upon such grounds as exist at law or in equity for the revocation of any contract."

[18] See, for example, Frances Kellor, *American Arbitration: Its History, Functions, and Achievements* (1948; Washington, DC: Beard Books, 1999).

[19] Pierre Schlag, "The Aesthetics of American Law," *Harvard Law Review*, 115 (2002), 1049. I owe this reference to Horatia Muir Watt.

[20] Ibid., 1051.

[21] Ibid., 1102.

[22] Ibid., 1055. For example, the distinction between contract and tort, which itself is divisible into negligence and intentional tort, etc.

[23] Ibid., 1051.

[24] Ibid., 1087.

[25] Ibid., 1054.

[26] Ibid., 1053.

Schlag's framework could be usefully applied to international arbitration, and legal history more broadly, as a means of alerting us to the overall "color" or "texture" of that history. For example, one may argue that law in the Age of Aspirations, with its emphasis on the proper boundaries of arbitration (i.e., what falls outside the scope of an arbitration clause, the distinction between national and international arbitration, etc.), was cast in the grid aesthetic. The Age of Institutionalization, with its emphasis on the creation of new institutions and the sense that arbitration law was in motion, would correspond much more to the energy aesthetic. The dominant aesthetic in our current Age of Autonomy (1950s–present), in which multiple actors – arbitration experts as well as individuals from outside the arbitration world – seek to express their own legal, social, and political views on arbitration, might correspond to the perspectivist aesthetic. It remains an open question whether we are entering a new age in the history of international arbitration, characterized by so much backlash and anxiety that the three aforementioned aesthetics may collapse and give way to an Age of Disruption, in which law would be cast in the dissociative aesthetic.

## 2.2 Methodological Pitfalls in Studying the Ancient Origins of International Arbitration

"Must we go back in time to the Biblical episode of the Tower of Babel, with which the diversity of human societies, and thus of legal orders, is said to have begun?" Ancel asks at the beginning of his history of private international law.[27] It appears indeed that each historical narrative has an "initial and unassignable reference, the absolute condition for any possibility of its historicization," as Michel de Certeau once wrote.[28] But focusing excessively on the origins of a given historical phenomenon has its risks, notably the danger of succumbing to what Marc Bloch called "obsession with origins."[29]

Many arbitration scholars have indeed tried to locate the precise origins of international commercial arbitration. Bibliographies of international commercial arbitration show that there have been studies on

[27] Bertrand Ancel, *Eléments d'histoire du droit international privé* (Paris: Panthéon-Assas, 2017), 20.

[28] Michel de Certeau, *The Writing of History* (1975), trans. Tom Conley (New York: Columbia University Press, 1988), 90–91.

[29] Marc Bloch, *Apologie pour l'histoire ou métier d'historien* (1949; Paris: Armand Colin, 2018), 53.

ancient tribes and distant peoples, from Mesopotamia[30] to Ancient Egypt,[31] Greece,[32] and Rome.[33] In the space of thirty years, from 1981 to 2011, the *Revue de l'arbitrage* published no fewer than eighteen articles on the ancient history of arbitration.[34] Even more telling, the late Professor Roebuck founded a publishing house (Holo Books) and imprint (The Arbitration Press) to disseminate his own writings about arbitration in Ancient Greece, Rome, the Middle Ages, the Elizabethan era, and seventeenth-century England, which together cover several thousands of pages.[35] Although the literature on the origins of international arbitration may offer illuminating insights into the early history

[30] Sophie Lafont, "L'arbitrage en Mésopotamie," *Revue de l'arbitrage*, 2000, 557. See also Thomas Clay, "Arbitre," in Loïc Cadiet (ed.), *Dictionnaire de la justice* (Paris: Presses Universitaires de France, 2004).

[31] Margit Mantica, "Arbitration in Ancient Egypt," *Arbitration Journal*, 12 (1957), 155.

[32] Nicholas Hammond, "Arbitration in Ancient Greece," *Arbitration International*, 1 (1985), 188; Jackson Ralston, *International Arbitration from Athens to Locarno* (Stanford: Stanford University Press, 1929), chapter 15 ("Ancient Arbitrations").

[33] Bruno de Loynes de Fumichon and Michel Humbert, "L'arbitrage à Rome," *Revue de l'arbitrage*, 2003, 285.

[34] In chronological order: Jean-Jacques Clère, "L'arbitrage révolutionnaire: Apogée et déclin d'une institution (1790–1806)," *Revue de l'arbitrage*, 1981, 3; Jean-François Poudret, "Deux aspects de l'arbitrage dans les pays romands du Moyen Age: L'arbitrabilité et le juge-arbitre," *Revue de l'arbitrage*, 1999, 3; Yves Jeanclos, "La pratique de l'arbitrage du XIIe au XVe siècle: Éléments d'analyse," *Revue de l'arbitrage*, 1999, 417; Serge Dauchy, "Le recours contre les décisions arbitrales en perspective historique: Aux origines des articles 1481–1491 NCPC," *Revue de l'arbitrage*, 1999, 763; Julie Velissaropoulos-Karakostas, "L'arbitrage dans la Grèce antique: Époques archaïque et classique," *Revue de l'arbitrage*, 2000, 9; Jean Hilaire, "L'arbitrage dans la période moderne (XVIe–XVIIIe siècles)," *Revue de l'arbitrage*, 2000, 187; Daphné Papadatou, "L'arbitrage byzantin," *Revue de l'arbitrage*, 2000, 349; Lafont, "L'arbitrage en Mésopotamie,"; Fabrizio Marrella, "L'arbitrage à Venise (XIIe–XVIe siècles)," *Revue de l'arbitrage*, 2002, 263; Derek Roebuck, "L'arbitrage en droit anglais avant 1558," *Revue de l'arbitrage*, 2002, 535; de Loynes de Fumichon and Humbert, "L'arbitrage à Rome"; Dominique Gaurier, "Le règlement privé des conflits dans la Chine impériale: arbitrage ou médiation?," *Revue de l'arbitrage*, 2004, 189; Carine Jallamion, "Arbitrage et pouvoir politique en France du XVIIe au XIXe siècle," *Revue de l'arbitrage*, 2005, 3; Anne Lefebvre-Teillard, "L'arbitrage en droit canonique," *Revue de l'arbitrage*, 2006, 5; Ali Mezghani, "Le droit musulman et l'arbitrage," *Revue de l'arbitrage*, 2008, 211; Lefebvre-Teillard, "Arbiter, Arbitrator Seu Amicabilis Compositor," *Revue de l'arbitrage*, 2008, 369; Fatou Camara and Abdoullah Cissé, "Arbitrage et médiation dans les cultures juridiques négro-africaines: Entre la prédisposition à dénouer et la mission de trancher," *Revue de l'arbitrage*, 2009, 285; Charles Leben, "L'arbitrage par un tribunal rabbinique appliquant le droit hébraïque," *Revue de l'arbitrage*, 2011, 87.

[35] See, for example, Derek Roebuck, *Ancient Greek Arbitration* (Oxford: Holo Books, 2001); Roebuck and Bruno de Loynes de Fumichon, *Roman Arbitration* (Oxford: Holo Books, 2004); Roebuck, *Arbitration and Mediation in Seventeenth-Century England* (Oxford: Holo Books, 2017).

of key concepts and ideas, it is sometimes prey to methodological pitfalls. These include drawing far-fetched historical parallels (Section 2.2.1) and presenting international commercial arbitration as a story of linear progress (Section 2.2.2).

### 2.2.1 *Far-Fetched Historical Parallels*

The historical parallels drawn in some works on the origins of international arbitration are at times dubious and not backed up by solid evidence. For instance, in an otherwise interesting article, an author appeals to common sense for want of clear arguments: "Common sense inclines us to think that over the 3,000 years of history of Mesopotamian history . . . there must have been places and times where arbitration existed."[36] Not surprisingly, the same author then has to acknowledge, in a remarkable series of caveats, that (1) "the word [arbitration] does not seem to exist in the Sumerian and Akkadian vocabulary,"[37] (2) her research is based on mere "intuition,"[38] and (3) "clear and indisputable occurrences of real arbitration are still rare and technical criteria difficult to check."[39] Another author, after asserting that "arbitration is omnipresent in the medieval sources of the countries that make up what is now French-speaking Switzerland,"[40] then goes on to draw a direct and unsubstantiated comparison with the present: "arbitration was not just very widespread but *more widely accepted* in the Middle Ages than today."[41]

Another related pitfall consists in treating international arbitration, or some of its features, as already apparent in the past. The problem here arises when the historian looks for earlier "anticipations" of later doctrines, "as if the fully developed form of the doctrine was always in some sense immanent in history."[42] One writer goes so far as to praise the "striking modernism" of arbitration in the fourth century BCE,

[36] Lafont, "L'arbitrage en Mésopotamie," 558.
[37] Ibid.
[38] Ibid.
[39] Ibid., 589.
[40] Poudret, "Deux aspects."
[41] Ibid., 11 (emphasis added).
[42] Quentin Skinner, "Meaning and Understanding in the History of Ideas," *History and Theory*, 8, no. 1 (1969), 10. For a critical reading of Skinner, see Anne Orford, "On International Legal Method," *London Review of International Law*, 1 (2013), 166; see also Anne Orford, "What Is the Place of Anachronism in International Legal Thinking" (lecture, Panthéon-Sorbonne University, Paris, January 23, 2013).

evidenced "in the binding nature of the arbitration award which is enforceable without any need for official approval."[43]

Some writers went even further, maintaining that already in earlier times arbitration not only displayed features that were later to distinguish it but also served a broadly similar function in society, apparently disregarding differences in the historical contexts. Two authors explain that "arbitration is as old as humanity and . . . had already been used since the dawn of civilization. Whether Athens, Rome, pre-Islamic Arabia, Ancient Law, or France in the 19th century, it is always the same arbitration which is practiced, often in a very precise way."[44] Similarly, we are told that "from the twelfth to the fifteenth centuries, as at the turn of the twenty-first century, the peaceful, quick, effective, economical and non-judicial way to resolve disputes is arbitration."[45] More generally, it has been said that "arbitration seems to be a universal practice among human communities"[46] and that, "[o]f all mankind's adventure in search of peace and justice, arbitration is among the earliest."[47] Statements as broad and general as these are of course impossible to verify, let alone refute.

### *2.2.2 A Linear History?*

Some authors, moreover, seem to believe that the march of international arbitration has always been clear and unambiguous, advancing in a linear fashion. As Viñuales notes, most accounts of the history of international adjudication take the form of a "progression narrative," which tends to obscure the "'trials' and 'errors' in the long process of experimentation relating to international adjudication."[48] For example, Gary Born's *Commentary and Materials* originally contained little historical

[43] Velissaropoulos-Karakostas, "L'arbitrage dans la Grèce antique," 24–25.
[44] Thomas Clay and Philippe Pinsolle, "General Introduction: The Major Cases of the French Case Law on International Arbitration," in Thomas Clay and Philippe Pinsolle (eds.), *French International Arbitration Law Reports* (Huntington, NY: JurisNet, 2014), vi.
[45] Jeanclos, "La pratique de l'arbitrage," 472.
[46] Velissaropoulos-Karakostas, "L'arbitrage dans la Grèce antique," 9.
[47] Kellor, *American Arbitration*, 3.
[48] Jorge Viñuales, "Experiments in International Adjudication: Past and Present," in Ignacio de la Rasilla and Jorge Viñuales (eds.), *Experiments in International Adjudication: Historical Accounts* (Cambridge: Cambridge University Press, 2019), 11. See also Cesare Romano, "Trial and Error in International Judicialization," in Cesare Romano, Karen Alter, and Yuval Shany (eds.), *The Oxford Handbook of International Adjudication* (Oxford: Oxford University Press, 2013), 111–34.

background on arbitration[49] but by 2015 had thirty pages on the history of international arbitration,[50] while the second edition of his three-volume authoritative treatise devotes no less than sixty-nine pages to the history of international commercial arbitration,[51] concluding with the following panoramic statement:

> Arbitration has been an enduring feature of dispute resolution – both state-to-state and commercial – since the beginning of recorded history. In societies of profoundly different characters, ranging from Sumerian and Egyptian, to ancient Greek and Roman, to medieval English, French, Swiss, German and Italian, to Colonial American, Asian and Latin American, to Islamic and Arab, to Jewish, to more modern common law and civil law jurisdictions, arbitration has been used equally by both states and state-like entities, and by businessmen and women, to resolve their disputes, and particularly, their international disputes.[52]

Mixing highly diverse geographical contexts and epochs, this statement views the trajectory of international arbitration as a linear narrative, stretching back from the "beginning of recorded history" to the present day.

Such description of the development of international arbitration is hardly surprising. At a time of increasing hostility toward international arbitration, particularly in the investment treaty context, invoking its historical lineage is a way of legitimizing an activity on which the careers of countless scholars and practitioners depend. Dezalay and Garth observed that "history is a key legitimator in the legal field. ... The passage of time also tends to obscure the politics that created an institution, thereby giving it an aura of naturalness. And this kind of legitimacy is probably especially important in a field where it is important to be able to claim a distance from business and politics."[53] Gordon likewise noted that "lawyers' uses of history have generally been apologetic, designed to endow currently dominant claims to entitlements and distributions of legal advantage and modes of legitimating property and power with the

[49] Gary Born, *International Commercial Arbitration: Commentary and Materials*, 2nd ed. (The Hague: Kluwer Law International, 2001).

[50] Gary Born, *International Commercial Arbitration: Cases and Materials*, 2nd ed. (The Hague: Kluwer Law International, 2015).

[51] Gary Born, *International Commercial Arbitration*, 2nd ed. (The Hague: Kluwer Law International, 2014).

[52] Ibid., 68.

[53] Yves Dezalay and Bryant Garth, *Dealing in Virtue: International Commercial Arbitration and the Construction of a Transnational Legal Order* (Chicago: Chicago University Press, 1996), 45.

authority of the past."[54] These words are useful to remember when reading some linear and triumphalist narratives about the history of international arbitration, which may "have more than a whiff of propaganda about them."[55]

## 2.3 Conclusion

This chapter has inquired into the different ways of approaching the history of international commercial arbitration – through long- or short-term narratives, deep structures or key events, or wide or narrow geographical settings. It has also looked at various studies on the distant origins of international arbitration, identifying some of the methodological pitfalls that may await writers who go back too far in time and draw far-fetched parallels. The narrative in Chapter 3 starts in the late eighteenth century, which – heeding the salutary advice of Foucault, and Nietzsche before him, to "laugh at the solemnities of the origin"[56] – should be regarded not as *the* beginning of international arbitration but as one of its many beginnings.

[54] Robert Gordon, "The Past as Authority and as Social Critic: Stabilizing and Destabilizing Functions of History in Legal Argument," in *Taming the Past: Essays on Law in History and History in Law* (Cambridge: Cambridge University Press, 2017), 288.

[55] Jan Paulsson, *The Idea of Arbitration* (Oxford: Oxford University Press, 2013), 10.

[56] Michel Foucault, "Nietszche, la généalogie, l'histoire" (1971), in Daniel Defert, François Ewald, and Jacques Lagrange (eds.), *Dits et écrits I: 1954–1988*, (Paris: Gallimard, 2001), 1007.

# 3

# Genealogy of International Commercial Arbitration

## 3.1 Introduction

This chapter asks whether, and to what extent, modern international arbitration practice is related to pre-twentieth-century dispute settlement methods. It argues that international arbitration can be analyzed within (1) the narrow context of (private) arbitrations practiced in local trade associations, and (2) the broader context of (public) international adjudication, which has evolved considerably over time. While it does not claim that these forms of arbitration, which were important mechanisms in the late eighteenth and the nineteenth centuries, are the sole "ancestors" of the modern international arbitration system, it shows how some of their characteristics were developed and became defining features of modern international arbitration practice. This chapter thus attempts to explore the complex genealogy (or genealogies) of international arbitration by exploring two influential strands discernable at a time when "arbitration" had various meanings and the field was less structured than it is today.[1]

The chapter points to the emergence of an "arbitral consciousness" in the late eighteenth and the nineteenth centuries. I use "consciousness" with the meaning Duncan Kennedy gives it when he defines "legal

[1] "Arbitration" had different meanings in the different contexts in which it was used (interstate relations, international commercial relations, and municipal relations); in the interstate context, for instance, it had a largely diplomatic and political meaning throughout the nineteenth century. Moreover, there was no clear divide between international commercial arbitration and investment treaty arbitration before the second half of the twentieth century, when states began to enter into bilateral investment treaties (BITs), beginning with a 1959 treaty between the Federal Republic of Germany and Pakistan. Thus, "international arbitration" and "adjudication" should be interpreted broadly in this chapter.

consciousness" as "the particular form of consciousness that characterizes the legal profession as a social group, at a particular moment."[2] I apply this notion to the field of arbitration, using the expression "arbitral consciousness" to refer to the ideals that manifested themselves in the Age of Aspirations, when it seemed that arbitration could be used for the higher purpose of ensuring peace and stability between parties. As will be seen, this form of legal consciousness was powerful at the time and extended into the twentieth century.

This chapter is divided into two parts. It first singles out two threads in the genealogy of international arbitration: dispute resolution through arbitration in the commodity markets, notably in England, on the one hand; and international adjudication through the so-called mixed commissions and arbitration by sovereign, on the other hand (Section 3.2). Second, it argues that these adjudicative mechanisms had a lasting impact on modern international arbitration. In allocating the dispute resolution process to an arbitral tribunal, they provided a blueprint for successful arbitration and helped to develop key notions that are still in use today (Section 3.3).

To begin with, however, an introductory comment needs to be made about sources, several of which – mainly collections of international arbitration awards – are specific to this chapter. Collections of arbitral awards began to appear in the nineteenth century (e.g., under the authorship of Francis Wharton[3] and John Bassett Moore[4]) and continued into the twentieth century. In 1902, Henri La Fontaine, a Belgian senator and lawyer who was deeply committed to the international peace movement,[5] published the *Pasicrisie Internationale*, which contained several hundred

[2] Duncan Kennedy, *The Rise and Fall of Classical Legal Thought* (Washington, DC: Beard Books, 2006), 27. According to Kennedy, people who practice legal reasoning do so with a preexisting structure of categories, concepts, and arguments, and this legal consciousness can be studied over time.

[3] Francis Wharton (ed.), *A Digest of the International Law of the United States, Taken from Documents Issued by Presidents and Secretaries of State, and from Decisions of Federal Courts and Opinions of Attorneys-General*, 3 vols. (Washington, DC: W. H. Lowdermilk, 1886).

[4] John Bassett Moore, *History and Digest of the International Arbitrations to Which the United States Has Been a Party, Together with Appendices Containing the Treaties Relating to such Arbitrations, and Historical and Legal Notes on Other International Arbitrations Ancient and Modern, and on the Domestic Commissions of the United States for the Adjustment of International Claims*, 6 vols. (Washington: Government Printing Office, 1898).

[5] See Nadine Bernard, "Henri La Fontaine (1854–1943) ou la paix par le droit," *Revue belge de droit international*, 28 (1995), 342–56.

documents (mostly arbitration clauses) relating to 177 international arbitrations that took place between 1794 and 1900.[6] In 1905 and 1923, Lapradelle and Politis produced the two volumes of their *Recueil des arbitrages internationaux*, published by Pedone;[7] and, from 1928 to 1934, Arthur Nussbaum edited a four-volume work on international arbitration.[8] In 1948, the Secretariat of the United Nations and the Registry of the International Court of Justice created a systematic collection of international arbitral and judicial awards, the *Reports of International Arbitral Awards*; thirty-two volumes have appeared to date.[9] The *Reports* did not include "the awards which appear in the relevant collections of La Fontaine, Lapradelle-Politis and Moore."[10] Nor did they contain detailed analysis or discussion of the arbitral awards they reproduced. More recent works have tried to fill that gap.[11]

## 3.2 Two Threads: Commodity Market Arbitration and State-to-State Arbitration

Two distinct threads may be singled out in the genealogy of international arbitration. The first is arbitration in the commodity markets, as practiced in the British trade associations, for example (Section 3.2.1). The second consists of the adjudicative mechanisms that were used in the international sphere throughout the late eighteenth and the nineteenth centuries.[12] This period was marked by various "experiments in

[6] Henri La Fontaine, *Pasicrisie Internationale 1794–1900: Histoire documentaire des arbitrages internationaux* (The Hague: Martinus Nijhoff, 1997 [1902]), xi–xii.

[7] Albert de Lapradelle and Nicolas Politis, *Recueil des arbitrages internationaux* (Paris: Pedone, 1905 and 1923). Volumes 1 (1798–1855) and 2 (1855–72) were reproduced in a second edition published by Éditions Internationales in 1957 following its publication of the third volume in 1954.

[8] Arthur Nussbaum, *Internationales Jahrbuch für Schiedsgerichtswesen in Zivil- und Handelssachen* 4 vols. (Berlin: Carl Heymanns, 1926 (vol. 1), 1928 (vol. 2), 1931 (vol. 3), 1934 (vol. 4)).

[9] United Nations, Codification Division, *Reports of International Arbitral Awards*, http://legal.un.org/riaa/.

[10] United Nations, "Foreword," *Reports of International Arbitration Awards*, 15 (2006), ix, http://legal.un.org/docs/?path=../riaa/cases/vol_XV/foreword.pdf&lang=O (accessed August 15, 2020).

[11] See, for example, Vincent Coussirat-Coustère and Pierre Michel Eisemann, *Répertoire de la jurisprudence arbitrale internationale*, vol. 1 *1794–1918*, vol. 2 *1919–1945*, vol. 3 *1946–1988* (Dordrecht: Martinus Nijhoff, 1989 [vols. 1, 2], 1991 [vol. 3]); Jean-Louis Iten et al., *Les grandes décisions de la jurisprudence internationale* (Paris: Dalloz, 2018).

[12] Louis Cavaré, *Le Droit international public positif*, vol. 2, *Les Modalités des relations juridiques internationales, les compétences respectives des États* (Paris: Pedone, 1962), 218.

international adjudication,"[13] as well as famous cases like the 1872 *Alabama* Arbitration between the United States and Great Britain, which raised the standing of international arbitration on the global stage (Section 3.2.2).

### *3.2.1 Arbitration within Local Trade Associations*

Commercial arbitration was widely practiced in local trade associations in Europe throughout the nineteenth century and thereafter, offering a key window through which to study its genealogy. As Vulliemin explained in 1931, "[t]he form of the first arbitration courts and the great arbitration movement that we are witnessing was clearly more corporative."[14] Vulliemin's portrayal of that trend is worth quoting in detail:

> In Hamburg, the creation of the first permanent arbitration body coincided with the setting up of an association of cereal traders close to Hamburg Stock Exchange. In 1872, alcohol trade followed suit, then potato derivatives in 1879, and in 1888 under the auspices of the Commerce Chamber an arbitration court was created the competences of which extended to all the branches of trade. . . . In 1901, an arbitration court for fodder trade, in 1907, metal trade established an arbitration body, rubber trade followed it in 1911, butter trade in 1913. . . . In 1872 in Bremen, a committee was created for cotton trade, which, like the Liverpool Cotton Association which was created before, included an arbitration court. That committee later on officially became Bremen Cotton Exchange.[15]

In England, the continued success of commercial arbitration was largely due to that country's key position among industrial nations at the time. As is well known, during the Industrial Revolution, which began in the 1760s and continued well into the 1830s and 1840s,[16]

[13] The expression is from de la Rasilla and Viñuales, who define "experiments" as "attempts, sometimes fully developed – whether subsequently successful in their operation or not – but sometimes also aborted at an early stage, to resort to international adjudication for a variety of purposes." See Ignacio de la Rasilla and Jorge Viñuales, "Introduction," in Ignacio de la Rasilla and Jorge Viñuales (eds.), *Experiments in International Adjudication: Historical Accounts* (Cambridge: Cambridge University Press, 2019), 2.

[14] Robert Vulliemin, *Du recours à l'arbitrage dans les matières commerciales à la fin du XIXe et au début du XXe siècle et de l'organisation de l'arbitrage commercial international* (Paris: Arthur Rousseau, 1931), 135.

[15] Ibid., 137.

[16] See Eric Hobsbawm, *The Age of Revolution: Europe 1789–1848* (New York: Vintage, 1996 [1962]), 29. Some scholars place the origins of the Industrial Revolution earlier; see, for example, the discussion in Fernand Braudel, *Civilization and Capitalism: 15th–18th*

Great Britain became the dominant world economic power.[17] During the French Revolutionary and Napoleonic wars (1792–1815), London became the world's financial capital "almost by default," being safe "from invasion and at the cross-roads of the international trade routes."[18] During the so-called imperial century (1815–1914), Britain kept expanding its overseas empire and establishing new colonial possessions,[19] and this, too, contributed to more widespread use of arbitration.[20]

Policy developments also played a key role in accelerating trade; the Corn Laws, a prime example of British mercantilism, and the Navigation Acts were repealed in 1846 and 1849, respectively, opening markets to outside competition. In 1860, a free trade agreement was signed between

*Century*, vol. 2, *The Wheels of Commerce*, trans. Siân Reynolds (Berkeley: University of California Press, 1992 [1979]), 239.

17 Growth was extremely fast in many sectors such as metallurgy and cotton textiles; between 1770 and 1815, the cotton industry grew at 7 percent per year. See Ronald Findlay and Kevin O'Rourke, *Power and Plenty: Trade, War, and the World Economy in the Second Millennium* (Princeton: Princeton University Press, 2007), 313 (presenting data collected by N. F. R. Crafts and C. K. Harley).

18 Richard Tames, *Economy and Society in Nineteenth Century Britain* (London: Routledge, 1972), 90.

19 See Ronald Hyam, *Britain's Imperial Century, 1815–1914: A Study of Empire and Expansion* (New York: Palgrave Macmillan, 2002). Meanwhile, in France, under the Second Empire (1852–1870), Napoleon III and Chasseloup-Laubat, his Minister of the Navy and the Colonies and an advocate of French colonialism, tripled the area of the French overseas empire – an expansionism that continued under the Third Republic (1870–1940).

20 The imperial project and colonial confrontation between European and non-European states led to a radical reconceptualization of international law, with jurists developing new tools and techniques aimed at "civilizing the uncivilized" (Antony Anghie, *Imperialism, Sovereignty and the Making of International Law* (Cambridge: Cambridge University Press, 2004), 37). For example, in 1875, a few years after the completion of the Suez Canal (1869), Mixed Courts were established in Egypt (see, e.g., Jasper Brinton, *The Mixed Courts of Egypt* (New Haven: Yale University Press, 1930); Mark Hoyle, *Mixed Courts of Egypt* (London: Graham & Trotman, 1991)). The Mixed Courts had exclusive jurisdiction over trade disputes involving Western countries governed by a commercial code drafted by European jurists (see Amr Shalakany, "Arbitration and the Third World: A Plea for Reassessing Bias under the Specter of Neoliberalism," *Harvard International Law Journal*, 41 (2000), 432; according to Shalakany, Mixed Courts were "strikingly similar, both in terms of technical and political attributes, to the modern institutional arrangements of international arbitration"). Colonialism undoubtedly created "a sphere of a seemingly dispassionate and juridified dispute settlement process," furthering the use of arbitration to resolve territorial and other disputes (Inge van Hulle, "Imperial Consolidation through Arbitration: Territorial and Boundary Disputes in Africa (1870–1914)," in Ignacio de la Rasilla and Jorge Viñuales (eds.), *Experiments in International Adjudication: Historical Accounts* (Cambridge: Cambridge University Press, 2019), 58).

Great Britain and France, starting a "golden age of free trade."[21] This was also the beginning of the so-called Second Industrial Revolution, which was marked by an increase in economic growth, rapid industrialization, and the expansion of rail and telegraph lines, leading to greater movement of people and ideas.[22] Technological advances – such as the laying of a submarine telegraph cable under the English Channel in 1851 and under the Atlantic Ocean in 1866 – also meant that financial markets were more integrated. These factors contributed to making Great Britain "the focal point for both buyers and sellers in the 19th century grain market"[23] as well as in other commodity markets.

The development of arbitration in England and other countries should therefore be seen as part of the "globalization boom"[24] that took place in the century prior to 1914. As the volume of trade increased, so too did disputes between buyers and sellers. Rosenbaum, a Philadelphia lawyer who in 1915 spent seven months in London writing a report on commercial arbitration, noted that arbitration was used in a very wide range of disputes.[25] He further observed that many disputes had arisen between cotton traders in Southern states and merchants in Liverpool during and after the American Civil War, and that this gave "greatest impetus to the spread of arbitration in England."[26]

[21] Stephen Krasner, "State Power and the Structure of International Trade," *World Politics*, 28, no. 3 (1976), 325. On the treaty, also known as the Cobden-Chevalier Treaty, see Arthur Dunham, *The Anglo-French Treaty of Commerce of 1860 and the Progress of the Industrial Revolution in France* (Ann Arbor: University of Michigan Press, 1930). The 1860 treaty was followed by many bilateral trade agreements between European states.

[22] The Second Industrial Revolution is generally dated between 1870 and 1914, even though some scholars place the end of the Second Industrial Revolution in the 1930s (see, for example, James Hull, "From Rostow to Chandler to You: How Revolutionary Was the Second Industrial Revolution?," *Journal of European Economic History*, 25, no. 1 (1996), 194–96).

[23] Morton Rothstein, "Centralizing Firms and Spreading Markets: The World of International Grain Traders, 1846–1914," *Business and Economic History*, 17 (1988), 103. On the impact of cheap grain on the European economy in the late nineteenth century, see Kevin O'Rourke, "The European Grain Invasion, 1870–1913," *Journal of Economic History*, 57, no. 4 (1997), 775–801. On the broader evolution of trade and global chains of commodities during the Second Industrial Revolution, see Steven Topik and Allen Wells, *Global Markets Transformed: 1870–1945* (Cambridge, MA: Harvard University Press, 2014).

[24] See Kevin O'Rourke and Jeffrey Williamson, *Globalization and History: The Evolution of a Nineteenth-Century Atlantic Economy* (Cambridge, MA: MIT Press, 1999).

[25] Samuel Rosenbaum, *A Report on Commercial Arbitration in England*, Bulletin 12 (Chicago: American Judicature Society, 1916), 7.

[26] Rosenbaum mentioned disputes over the "quality and condition of consignments of grain, cotton, sugar, coffee, fruit, rubber, timber, meats, hides, seeds, fibres, fats, and

The Liverpool cotton market was especially important, as it was "the first commodity market in Europe to develop futures trading, considerably ahead of the London markets which still trade futures today."[27] To settle disputes arising in the cotton industry, the Liverpool Cotton Association (founded in 1841) set up an arbitration committee.[28] Before long, virtually all disputes between buyers and sellers in the Liverpool cotton market were being settled through arbitration. Other trade associations, both in Liverpool and London, followed suit, and arbitration committees were soon set up within the corn, oil seed, and coffee trade associations, to name but three.[29]

The London Corn Trade Association (LCTA) came to play a particularly important role, arguably acting as "the benchmark model that was emulated by other professions in the following years and decades."[30] Founded by international traders in 1878, the LCTA sought to facilitate the grain trade by, among other activities, setting quality standards, standardizing shipping documents for major exporting

countless other articles of commerce, as well as every conceivable variety of dispute that can arise out of a contract for sale and delivery, such as questions of delays, quantities, freights, interpretation, etc." (ibid., 14).

27 Nigel Hall, "The Liverpool Cotton Market: Britain's First Futures Market," *Transactions of the Historical Society of Lancashire and Cheshire*, 149 (2000), 99–100; see also Nigel Hall, "The Governance of the Liverpool Raw Cotton Market, c.1840–1914," *Northern History*, 53, no. 1 (2016), 98–115.

28 See Anthony Connerty, "International Cotton Arbitration," *Arbitration International*, 29 (2013), 295–318.

29 For a study of the organization and operation of the London and Liverpool commodity markets, see Ross Cranston, "Law through Practice: London and Liverpool Commodity Markets c.1820–1975," *Society and Economy Working Papers* (London: LSE Law, 2007). Cranston pays close attention to the functions of clearing and settling transactions in commodity markets, leaving the "crucial feature of dispute resolution through arbitration . . . for another day" (ibid., 2).

30 Jérôme Sgard, "A Tale of Three Cities: The Construction of International Commercial Arbitration," in Grégoire Mallard and Jérôme Sgard (eds.), *Contractual Knowledge: One Hundred Years of Legal Experimentation in Global Markets* (Cambridge: Cambridge University Press, 2016), 157. On other trades, see, for example, Masaichiro Ishikazi, *Le droit corporatif international de la vente des soies: Les contrats-types américains et la codification lyonnaise dans leurs rapports avec les usages des autres places* (Paris, Marcel Giard, 1928); J. C. A. Faure, "Commodity Market Arbitrations with Special Reference to the Incorporated Oil Seed Association Rules," *International and Comparative Law Quarterly*, 15 (1966), 736–42; Lisa Bernstein, "Private Commercial Law in the Cotton Industry: Creating Cooperation through Rules, Norms, and Institutions," *Michigan Law Review*, 99 (2001), 1724–90.

nations, and clarifying arbitration procedures.[31] Its arbitration mechanism proved highly successful.[32]

In addition to Great Britain's leading role as a global trading nation, various other reasons can be advanced to explain the growth and success of commercial arbitration in the British commodity markets. A key factor was the widespread use of standard contracts containing arbitration clauses.[33] These contracts were regularly revised, becoming increasingly precise and sophisticated over time.[34] As Sgard has explained, in 1896 the LCTA had a total of fifty-one standard contracts covering such specialized areas as the grain trade with Argentina, the Black Sea, and Manchuria.[35] Schwob, who in 1928 authored a detailed study of the LCTA contracts, explained that these contracts "represent a codification of customs that the parties have to comply with upon entering into a contract based on a formulation of the LCTA."[36]

The LCTA standard contracts were authoritative, sometimes even being used by parties who had no commercial relations with England.[37] All these standard contracts contained arbitration clauses providing that any dispute arising out of the contract would be finally settled under LCTA rules.[38] This helps explain why parties engaged in global trade had little choice but to submit their disputes to the arbitration mechanisms of

[31] See, generally, Hugh Barty-King, *Food for Man and Beast: The Story of the London Corn Trade Association, the London Cattle Food Trade Association, and the Grain and Feed Trade Association, 1878–1978* (London: Hutchinson Benham, 1978). The LCTA no longer exists; in 1906, a group of traders broke away and formed the London Cattle Food Trade Association; in 1969, merger talks began between the two organizations and the Grain and Feed Trade Association – which continues to provide arbitration services to this day – was born in 1971. See Grain and Feed Trade Association, "About," www.gafta.com/about.

[32] Rosenbaum, *Report*, 31; see also Gershon Ellenbogen, "English Arbitration Practice," *Law and Contemporary Problems*, 17 (1952), 668.

[33] On standard contracts and their role in the unification and harmonization of international trade law, see Clive Schmitthoff, "The Unification or Harmonization of Law by Means of Standard Contracts and General Conditions," *International and Comparative Law Quarterly*, 17 (1968), 551–70.

[34] Vulliemin, *Du recours à l'arbitrage*, 159–60.

[35] Sgard, "Tale of Three Cities," 158.

[36] Georges Schwob, *Les contrats de la London Corn Trade Association (Vente CAF)* (Paris: Arthur Rousseau, 1928), 25.

[37] Vulliemin, *Du recours à l'arbitrage*, 167. According to a decision delivered by a court in Rennes, France, on June 4, 1926, "London standard contracts, especially those of the London Corn Trade Association (LCTA), have earned considerable fame in the grain trade and are commonly used in France." Quoted in Schwob, *Les contrats*, 7.

[38] Ibid., 72–80.

the LCTA and other trade associations, as a result of which Great Britain secured its place as a major provider of legal services through arbitration.

Finally, another reason for the success of the English arbitration model was the fact that, as the number of commercial arbitrations increased, England regularly made improvements to the legal framework within which they were handled. This resulted in a complex arbitration regime made up of a "disparate patchwork of statute and common law."[39] It is beyond the scope of this book to describe this regime; suffice it to say that in 1889 an Act consolidating previous practice was passed,[40] which, along with its "historical siblings"[41] – the London Court of International Arbitration,[42] the Commercial Court, and Lord Bramwell's Arbitration Code[43] – provided a more robust framework for dealing with arbitration. The 1889 Act – at one and the same time "a consolidation of existing law" and "innovatory legislation"[44] – contained a set of rules intended to govern the arbitral procedure. It provided a stable regime for arbitration, remaining in force for several decades.

### *3.2.2 Arbitration between States*

Switching the focus of inquiry from the private to the public sphere, a second thread in the genealogy of international arbitration is international adjudication in the late eighteenth and the nineteenth centuries. It covers the so-called mixed commissions and arbitration by sovereign, as well as famous events like the *Alabama* Arbitration of 1872.

[39] V. V. Veeder and Brian Dye, "Lord Bramwell's Arbitration Code 1884–1889," *Arbitration International*, 8 (1992), 333.

[40] Arbitration Act 1889. The Act was amended by the Arbitration Clauses (Protocol) Act 1924 (enacting the 1923 Geneva Protocol on Arbitration Clauses), the Arbitration (Foreign Awards) Act 1930) (enacting the 1927 Geneva Convention on the Execution of Foreign Arbitral Awards), and the Arbitration Act 1934 (enacting many of the recommendations of the 1927 MacKinnon Committee); the arbitration legislation was then consolidated in the Arbitration Act 1950.

[41] Veeder and Dye, "Lord Bramwell's Arbitration Code."

[42] The name "London Court of International Arbitration" dates from 1981. The institution was inaugurated as "The City of London Chamber of Arbitration" in 1892; it was renamed the "London Court of Arbitration" in 1903, and acquired its present name in 1981. See London Court of International Arbitration, "History," www.lcia.org/lcia/history.aspx.

[43] The Bramwell Code was a "draft annotated code of English arbitration law and practice which its promoters introduced unsuccessfully to Parliament on several occasions between 1884 and 1889." Veeder and Dye, "Lord Bramwell's Arbitration Code," 331.

[44] Michael Mustill and Stewart Boyd, *Commercial Arbitration*, 2nd ed. (London: Butterworths, 1989), 444.

#### 3.2.2.1 Mixed Commissions

Mixed commissions, which have been defined as "collegiate organs created by treaty by two or more subjects of international law in order to achieve a given goal,"[45] were frequently used throughout the nineteenth century. At least three different types of mixed commissions have been identified: (1) mixed dispute settlement commissions, which can be further divided into (a) mixed diplomatic commissions (normally composed of an even number of commissioners, whose function was akin to direct negotiation between the parties) and (b) mixed arbitral commissions (normally composed of an even number of commissioners, plus a neutral umpire); (2) mixed cooperation commissions (whose purpose was to further cooperation between two or more states in various areas); and (3) mixed boundary commissions (established for delimitation and/or demarcation purposes).[46] Of these, the mixed arbitral commissions can plausibly be considered as "the ancestors of modern arbitral tribunals"[47] in that they sometimes led to final and binding decisions made by adjudicators who had been selected by the parties themselves.

The most important mixed commissions were undoubtedly those created under the 1794 Jay Treaty between the United States and Great Britain.[48] This treaty, named after one of its negotiators, John Jay, Chief Justice of the United States from 1789 to 1795, was made for the purpose of settling matters left unresolved after the War of Independence. They included the British occupation of military forts, which the British Government had previously agreed to vacate in the Treaty of Paris (1783); British seizure of American ships and impressment of American sailors into the Royal Navy to fight against revolutionary France; British interference in American trade and exports, especially to the British West Indies; the northwestern boundary between the United States and Canada; and compensation for prerevolutionary debts.[49]

[45] Laurence Boisson de Chazournes and Danio Campanelli, "Mixed Commissions," *Max Planck Encyclopedia of Public International Law* (December 2006), ¶ 4.

[46] Ibid., ¶¶ 8–14.

[47] Ibid., ¶ 10.

[48] Treaty of Amity Commerce and Navigation, between His Britannic Majesty and The United States of America, by Their President, with the advice and consent of Their Senate ("Jay Treaty"), November 19, 1794.

[49] See Katja Ziegler, "Jay Treaty (1794)," *Max Planck Encyclopedia of Public International Law* (April 2013), 3.

Proclaiming a "firm inviolable and universal Peace" between the United States and Great Britain,[50] the treaty partially resolved some of these issues.[51] It further provided that other outstanding issues would be resolved by arbitration. Three mixed commissions were set up under the treaty[52] to resolve some of the issues raised.[53] Between 1794 and 1804, a total of 536 awards were rendered under the Jay Treaty.[54]

Given the large number of awards and their significance, legal scholars generally concur that the Jay Treaty was highly successful and constituted a turning point in the history of international arbitration. It has been described as "a crucial act which clearly separates former habits and modern practice"[55] and "the first modern arbitration Convention,"[56] which inaugurated "a new era for international arbitration."[57] Contemporary scholars have even described 1794 as the "precise year when international dispute resolution began to develop"[58] and "a kind of golden age of arbitration."[59]

#### 3.2.2.2 Arbitration by Sovereign

Another form of arbitration that was used in the course of the nineteenth century may be described as arbitration by sovereign (known in French as *arbitrage par souverain*). It was thought that this form of arbitration, which "correspond[s] to the idea that justice emanates from a higher power,"[60]

50 Jay Treaty, Article 1.

51 For example, it established a special commercial relationship between the two countries, while continuing to restrict US commercial access to the British West Indies. It also included the withdrawal of British army units from some military forts.

52 The St. Croix River Commission, to determine the location and source of the St. Croix River located on the Canada–Maine boundary; the British Debts Commission, to settle issues related to debts owed by US citizens to British creditors; and the Maritime Claims Commission, to deal with US claims resulting from seizures of ships and cargoes by Britain.

53 The first commission reached a settlement in 1798, though it took two further treaties, in 1814 and 1842, to finally resolve the St. Croix River delimitation process. The second commission rendered a few decisions but was dissolved in 1799. The third commission was more successful and completed its work in 1804, after awarding USD 11.65 million to US claimants and USD 143,428 to British claimants.

54 Mary O'Connell and Lenore VanderZee, "The History of International Adjudication," in Cesare Romano, Karen Alter, and Yuval Shany (eds.), *The Oxford Handbook of International Adjudication* (Oxford: Oxford University Press, 2013), 44.

55 Albert de Lapradelle and Nicolas Politis, *Recueil des arbitrages internationaux* (Paris: Pedone, 1905), 1:xxix.

56 La Fontaine, *Pasicrisie*, 1.

57 Nicolas Politis, *La Justice internationale* (Paris: Panthéon-Assas, 2017 [1924]), 30.

58 Iten et al., *Les grandes décisions*, xi.

59 O'Connell and VanderZee, "History of International Adjudication," 44.

60 Cavaré, *Le Droit international public positif*, 219.

had several major advantages: a simple procedure based on documentary evidence alone (without hearing the parties); the presumed impartiality of the arbitrator as a neutral figure from a third country; and the authority vested in the arbitrator's person by virtue of their position as monarch or emperor.[61]

The *arbitrage par souverain* model was used throughout the nineteenth century, often with a successful outcome.[62] A key example – one that played an especially important role in the broader history of international arbitration – was the decision rendered by Napoleon III in the dispute between the Suez Canal Company and Egypt in 1864.[63] This case, which has been described as "the first investor-state arbitration,"[64] concerned the Suez Canal Company's claim of "expropriation" by Egypt. A five-member commission was constituted, with Louis-Napoleon as the titular arbitrator. His award was rendered on April 21, 1864,[65] and the Suez Canal was completed within a few years.

Despite such successes, *arbitrage par souverain* was not without its critics. As Politis remarked, "[t]he advantage of the system is that it simplifies the procedure and ensures that the judge is perfectly independent; its drawback is that there is a lack of competence and, in short, a distortion of justice."[66] There was concern that "the arbitrator, whose political position is dominant, is a bad judge, caring as much, if not more, about the country's interests rather than the rights of the plaintiffs."[67] These assessments show how, in the Age of Aspirations, the development of the international arbitration system was still in its embryonic stages.

[61] Ibid., 220.

[62] For examples, see "Success of Arbitration," *American Advocate of Peace*, 55 (1893), 151–53 and 162–63. See also Charles Richet, *Les Guerres et la Paix: Étude sur l'arbitrage international* (Paris: Schleicher Frères, 1899), 109–13.

[63] Napoléon III, *Sentence arbitrale rendue par Sa Majesté l'Empereur des Français sur les réclamations réciproques de Son Altesse le Bey de Tunis et du général Benaïad* (Paris: Eugène Penaud, 1857).

[64] Yackee, "First Investor-State Arbitration?"

[65] "Sentence arbitrale rendue par l'Empereur Napoléon III, le 6 juillet 1864, entre le Vice-Roi d'Egypte et la Compagnie universelle du canal de Suez," Final Award, April 21, 1864, *in* La Fontaine, *Pasicrisie*, 122–29.

[66] Politis, *La Justice internationale*, 77.

[67] Albert de Lapradelle and Nicolas Politis, "Introduction," in Lapradelle and Politis, *Recueil des arbitrages internationaux* (Paris: Pedone, 1905), 2:xix. According to the two authors, in the Suez arbitration "Napoleon III was legitimately influenced by the very precarious financial situation of the Company" (ibid., 2:381). See also Cavaré, *Le Droit international public positif*, 221.

#### 3.2.2.3 A "High-Water Mark": The *Alabama* Arbitration of 1872

The *Alabama* Arbitration was a pivotal moment in the history of international arbitration in the nineteenth century.[68] It has been described as the "high-water mark"[69] and "an unprecedented international tribunal in history,"[70] which led to the "revival" of international arbitration in the nineteenth century.[71] As will be seen, it also marked the emergence of an arbitral consciousness, leading "the movement of arbitration [to] accelerate and spread" and symbolizing "a new spirit" of "confidence in arbitration,"[72] and may be seen to some extent as a template for the modern system of international arbitration.

The background to the *Alabama* Arbitration, which has captured the imagination of historians and artists alike, can be succinctly summarized. The arbitration concerned a diplomatic dispute between the United States and Great Britain that arose out of the American Civil War. In the course of that war, Great Britain had allowed several ships, including CSS *Alabama* and some of her raiders, to be built in British shipyards for the use of the Confederate States. The *Alabama* captured about thirty-eight Northern merchant ships before being sunk in June 1864 off the coast of France, as shown in Figure 3.1.

In 1869, in what was called the *Alabama* Claims, the United States claimed "direct" and "collateral" damage against Great Britain on the ground that the British Government had violated its legal duty to

[68] On the *Alabama* Arbitration, see, for example, Adrian Cook, *The Alabama Claims: American Politics and Anglo-American Relations, 1865–1872* (Ithaca: Cornell University Press, 1975); Tom Bingham, *Lives of the Law: Selected Essays and Speeches: 2000–2010* (Oxford: Oxford University Press, 2011), chapter 2; Tom Bingham, "Alabama Arbitration," in *The Max Planck Encyclopedia of Public International Law* (Oxford: Oxford University Press, 2006); Tom Bingham, "The *Alabama* Claims Arbitration," *International and Comparative Law Quarterly*, 54 (2005), 1–25; V. V. Veeder, "The Historical Keystone to International Arbitration: The Party-Appointed Arbitrator; From Miami to Geneva," in David Caron et al. (eds.), *Practising Virtue: Inside International Arbitration* (Oxford: Oxford University Press, 2015); Bruno de Loynes de Fumichon and William Park, "Retour sur l'affaire de l'*Alabama*: De l'utilité de l'histoire pour l'arbitrage international," *Revue de l'arbitrage*, 2019, 743–834.

[69] Moore, *History and Digest*, 4:ix.

[70] Lapradelle and Politis, *Recueil*, 1:906. See also Politis, *La Justice internationale*, 34; Veeder, "Historical Keystone," 142.

[71] James Brierly, *Brierly's Law of Nations: An Introduction to the Role of International Law in International Relations* (Oxford: Oxford University Press, 2012 [1928]), 410.

[72] Lapradelle and Politis, *Recueil*, 1:xvii.

**Figure 3.1** Édouard Manet, "The Battle of the USS 'Kearsarge' and the CSS 'Alabama,'" oil on canvas (1864). Philadelphia Museum of Art, John G. Johnson Collection, 1917, Cat. 1027. The painting depicts the sinking of the CSS *Alabama*.

respect neutrality. After several years of unsuccessful diplomatic efforts, an agreement was reached in 1871. Known as the Treaty of Washington, it established a five-member tribunal made up of Brazilian, Swiss, and Italian arbitrators appointed, respectively, by the Emperor of Brazil, the President of the Swiss Federation, and the King of Italy; and American and British arbitrators appointed by each of the parties.[73] The arbitral

[73] Treaty between the United States and Great Britain ("Treaty of Washington"), May 8, 1871, Article I. The five arbitrators were Marcos Antônio de Araújo, Baron d'Itayubá (a former professor and the Brazilian ambassador in Paris); Jakob Stämpfli (the former

**Figure 3.2** Charles Édouard Armand-Dumaresq, "The Geneva Conference, The Alabama Arbitration," oil on canvas (*ca.*1873). Gift of Mr. and Mrs. Kenneth R. Giddens © Courtesy of the Mobile Museum of Art, Mobile, Alabama. The painting shows members of the arbitral tribunal and others sitting in the Salle de l'Alabama in Geneva.

commission met in 1871 in Geneva's Town Hall, in what is still known as the Salle de l'Alabama (as shown in Figure 3.2), and rendered its decision on September 14, 1872.[74] The arbitrators found that Great Britain had an obligation to remain neutral during the American Civil War and had failed to do so.[75] The tribunal ordered Great Britain to pay

president of the Swiss Confederation); Count Frederico Sclopis (an Italian lawyer and statesman); Charles Francis Adams (the grandson and son of the second and sixth presidents of the United States and a former US minister in London); and Sir Alexander Cockburn (then chief justice of the Queen's Bench Division). Count Sclopis was selected as president. See Veeder, "Historical Keystone," 134 and Bingham, *Lives of the Law*, ¶ 8.

[74] "Award Rendered on September 14, 1872 by the Tribunal of Arbitration Established by Article I of the Treaty of Washington of May 8, 1871," in Moore, *History and Digest*, 1:653, also available at http://legal.un.org/riaa/cases/vol_XXIX/125-134.pdf.

[75] Ibid., 1:657.

the United States as compensation within a year the considerable sum of USD 15.5 million in gold.[76]

## 3.3 The Impact of These Mechanisms on Modern Arbitration Practice

In the Age of Aspirations, the two threads described earlier, though they unfolded in very different contexts, helped develop or strengthen key ideas and principles that proved important for the modern international arbitration regime. Arbitration both in trade associations and between states was marked by a strong sense of renewal, with innovations and improvements leading to features that still play a role in modern international arbitration practice (Section 3.3.1). In addition, this period witnessed the emergence of a distinct form of arbitral consciousness, with arbitration being seen as an efficient way of settling disputes and ensuring stability between parties (Section 3.3.2).

### *3.3.1 Developing Key Features of Modern International Arbitration Practice*

#### 3.3.1.1 Dispute Resolution by One or More Arbitrators

First, adjudication methods used in the eighteenth and nineteenth centuries reaffirmed the belief that it was possible, and even desirable, to entrust the dispute resolution process to an "arbitral tribunal" – even though this notion, of course, was not defined as clearly as it is today. In British trade associations, even before the LCTA was founded, contracts in the corn trade stipulated that disputes would be settled by arbitrators; parties would appoint a "London Corn Factor" and the decision of these arbitrators would be final.[77] In 1870, a committee of arbitrators composed of twenty members of the London Corn Trade was established, with half of its members being elected from buyers and the other half from sellers.[78] The LCTA continued that practice, using arbitrators who were "engaged in the corn trade as merchants, millers, factors, or

[76] "Sentence du 14 septembre 1872," in Lapradelle and Politis, *Recueil*, 2:889–94. This was equivalent to the staggering amount of approximately USD 225 billion today. See Veeder, "Historical Keystone," 133. On the amount of the award, see also Roy Jenkins, *Gladstone* (London: Macmillan, 1995), 359; Loynes de Fumichon and Park, "Retour," 747.

[77] Chris Chattaway, "Arbitration in the Foreign Corn Trade in London," *Economic Journal*, 17 (1907), 428.

[78] Ibid., 429.

brokers," as well as "members of the London Corn Exchange, Baltic or London Corn Trade Association."[79]

When the arbitration concerned the quality of materials, the arbitrators would often "meet and compare a sample portion with a standard lot of the same material, and render their award, giving or refusing an allowance on the price and fixing the amount if any; in this they are guided solely by their knowledge of the material under discussion."[80] This practice of testing and inspecting samples had an important impact on international commercial arbitration.[81]

Turning to the international sphere, we find that "the same reasoning that was invoked historically in state-to-state arbitrations has been adopted, in almost identical terms, in the context of contemporary international commercial arbitration, where party-nominated co-arbitrators have been a central feature of the arbitral process since the historical record begins."[82] An interesting example is provided by Article 5 of the Jay Treaty (concerning the St. Croix River Commission), which stated that each party was to name one member (called "commissioner") and the two commissioners were to choose or draw by lot a third commissioner.[83] The three commissioners were to decide the dispute on the basis of the evidence produced by the parties,[84] and were granted the power to appoint a secretary if necessary.[85] The determinations of the three commissioners were to be "final and conclusive"[86] – a feature that would find its way into subsequent arbitration mechanisms.

Likewise, the *Alabama* Arbitration was the result of two major powers entrusting the dispute resolution process to an arbitral tribunal, which then issued a binding decision. The deliberations certainly did not meet modern standards of neutrality and confidentiality, with the arbitrators commenting on the case with the parties and deliberating in their presence. But this may be explained by the fact that the arbitral tribunal drew on the two

[79] Ibid., 430.
[80] Rosenbaum, *Report*, 27.
[81] As discussed in Chapter 7, it was followed by the ICC Court of Arbitration, where disputes in the 1920s and 1930s often concerned the quality of goods and arbitrators physically inspected them.
[82] Born, *International Commercial Arbitration*, 1:24.
[83] Jay Treaty, Article 5.
[84] Ibid.
[85] Ibid.
[86] Ibid., Articles 5, 6, and 7.

forms of arbitration discussed earlier.[87] Despite its hybrid nature, the arbitral tribunal succeeded in rendering an award that was binding on the parties.[88] This was a powerful sign that entrusting the dispute resolution process to an arbitral tribunal could yield positive results.

#### 3.3.1.2 A "Template" for International Arbitration

Second, these pre-twentieth-century adjudicative mechanisms provided a solid model for international arbitration. The very first issue of the *Revue de l'arbitrage*, in 1955, contained an article by Carabiber that specifically mentioned the London Corn Trade Association (LCTA) as well as some other British trade associations.[89] Taking stock of the ICC's experience after forty years of existence, Eisemann likewise referred with great admiration to "the elaborate arbitral systems created within the framework of such highly organized trade associations as, for instance, the London Corn Trade Association or the Incorporated Oilseed Association."[90] While these references may have been part of an effort by Carabiber, Eisemann, and others to build a respectable past for ICC arbitration, they suggest that the examples of the LCTA and other British trade associations were very present in the minds of those who contributed to the creation of the ICC arbitration system.

When it comes to disputes between states, commentators are divided over whether state-to-state disputes such as the *Alabama* Arbitration can be said to provide the template par excellence for modern international arbitration practice.[91] On the one hand, Bingham argued that the *Alabama* Arbitration could be "recognized as a model for resolving international and

[87] The arbitration may be described as both a "mixed commission," with parties negotiating directly with each other, and an *arbitrage par souverain*, with three arbitrators nominated by their respective sovereigns. See Cavaré, *Le Droit international public positif*, 224.

[88] Sir Alexander Cockburn, the British arbitrator, did not sign the award and published a long and angry dissent in London ten days later. But even he felt that Great Britain should comply with the award. The Chancellor of the Exchequer scolded Cockburn publicly for not signing the award with the other arbitrators, and Queen Victoria, in her speech at the state opening of Parliament in 1873, expressed her belief that Great Britain should comply with the award. See Lapradelle and Politis, *Recueil*, 2:895–96.

[89] Charles Carabiber, "Les centres d'arbitrage: Leur rôle dans le développement de l'arbitrage," *Revue de l'arbitrage*, 1955, 5.

[90] Frédéric Eisemann, "Arbitrations under the International Chamber of Commerce," *International and Comparative Law Quarterly*, 15 (1966), 726.

[91] As a clear indication of continued interest in this topic, the 2018 Berthold Goldman Lecture of the International Academy for Arbitration Law, delivered by William Park, was entitled "Revisiting the Alabama Arbitration: The Use and Abuse of History." It was published in expanded form as Loynes de Fumichon and Park, "Retour."

commercial disputes according to law."[92] Likewise, Veeder called it "the first international tribunal of its kind in modern times and the basic model for international arbitration today"[93] and "the basic model for investment arbitration today."[94] On the other hand, Paulsson has argued that the *Alabama* Arbitration was "not so much an achievement of the arbitral process as a splendid feat of diplomacy."[95] Paulsson pointed to ten features distinguishing the *Alabama* Arbitration from modern international arbitrations,[96] making it a "splendid example of the intelligent use of the arbitral process in the interest of peace,"[97] but not much more.

Paulsson may be correct insofar as many features of the *Alabama* Arbitration would be inconceivable today. However, there is no denying that it was a successful international arbitration, even if its qualification as a "model" for today's arbitral process is something of an exaggeration. As already seen, the tribunal was not "neutral" by modern standards, but it did succeed in rendering a binding award with which the parties complied. Moreover, it possessed attributes typical of a jurisdictional body,[98] and the tribunal even provided reasons for its decision (even though this was not required by the arbitration agreement). Three years after the *Alabama* Award was rendered, the practice of providing reasons for decisions was enshrined in the Institute of International Law's 1875 code of procedure for arbitration[99] as well as other instruments.[100] Thus,

[92] Tom Bingham, "Alabama Arbitration," in *The Max Planck Encyclopedia of Public International Law* (Oxford: Oxford University Press, updated 2006), ¶ 11.

[93] Veeder, "Historical Keystone."

[94] V. V. Veeder, "Investor-State Disputes and the Development of International Law Arbitral Lessons from the Private Correspondence of Queen Victoria and Lenin," *Proceedings of the ASIL Annual Meeting*, 98 (2004), 34. These statements seem to echo Louis Renault's assertion in 1905 that the *Alabama* Arbitration was "the classic arbitration as far as the forms used and the importance of involved interests were concerned." See Louis Renault, "Préface," in Lapradelle and Politis (eds.), *Recueil*, 1:xi.

[95] Jan Paulsson, "The *Alabama Claims Arbitration*: Statecraft and Stagecraft," in Ulf Franke, Annette Magnusson, and Joel Dahlquist (eds.), *Arbitrating for Peace: How Arbitration Made a Difference* (The Hague: Kluwer Law International, 2016), 7.

[96] For example, the arbitrators "did not have the authority of *compétence-compétence*"; the two party-appointed arbitrators "were remunerated by the respective appointing governments" and "discussed the progress of the case and the acceptability of its outcome with their appointing governments"; the three neutral arbitrators were not conversant with English, the language of the proceedings, and deliberated in French instead; and the deliberations were "mostly in the presence of the parties" (ibid., 18).

[97] Ibid., 20.

[98] See Iten et al. (eds.), *Les grandes décisions*, xii.

[99] See Projet de règlement pour la procédure arbitrale internationale (1875), Article 23.

[100] The requirement also made its way into Article 79 of the 1907 Hague Convention and Article 56 of the Statute of the International Court of Justice.

although perhaps not strictly the "model" for contemporary international arbitration that it is sometimes claimed to be, the *Alabama* Arbitration did provide an example of an adjudicative procedure resulting in a reasoned and binding award, and at the same time infused international arbitration with a "new vigour even for claims relating to matters of national honour."[101]

### 3.3.1.3 Awards Based on Legal Grounds

A third feature that deserves emphasis is the fact that, at least in public international law arbitrations, arbitrators increasingly relied on legal reasoning in their awards.[102] Even though state-to-state arbitrations were mostly practiced by statesmen and diplomats, arbitration slowly left the diplomatic arena and entered the legal world. This continued into the twentieth century, when international arbitration became truly the preserve of jurists and members of arbitral institutions, marking the shift from the Age of Aspirations to the Age of Institutionalization.

An interesting example is the Jay Treaty's mixed commissions, which issued awards based on law. The "commissioners" were not only diplomats; they also acted as judges and nominated a third-party umpire to help them adjudicate the dispute. And while they often decided the case on equitable grounds, they were also required to have regard to "Justice" and, at times, "the Laws of Nations."[103] As such, they were "the first prominent example of arbitration by a collegial tribunal issuing reasoned awards based on law."[104] In the words of Politis, "[a]rbitration was hitherto above all diplomatic. Henceforth, by virtue of the technicality and freedom of the discussions within the mixed commission, it was gradually to become judicial."[105]

[101] Charles Brower, "Arbitration," in Rüdiger Wolfrum (ed.),*The Max Planck Encyclopedia of Public International Law* (Oxford: Oxford University Press (updated 2007), 22.

[102] See Georges Abi-Saab, "De l'arbitrage dans ses rapports avec la justice internationale," in Christian Dominicé, Robert Patry, and Claude Reymond (eds.), *Études de droit international en l'honneur de Pierre Lalive* (Basel: Helbing & Lichtenhahn, 1993), 379.

[103] Jay Treaty, Articles 6 and 7.

[104] Brower, "Arbitration," ¶ 17.

[105] Politis, *La Justice internationale*, 32. See also A. M. Stuyt, "Preface to the 1939 Edition," *Survey of International Arbitrations 1794–1970* (Leiden: A. W. Sijthoff, 1972), ix; Alexis Keller, "Inter-State Arbitration in Historical Perspective," in Thomas Schultz and Frederico Ortino (eds.), *The Oxford Handbook of International Arbitration* (Oxford: Oxford University Press, 2020), 855–56.

Likewise, the *Alabama* Arbitration raised some questions that were "clearly legal."[106] In fact, as Bingham noted, the *Alabama* Arbitration continues to be a reference for several principles of international law.[107] The first, as expressed by the International Court of Justice in the *Nottebohm Case*, is that "in the absence of any agreements to the contrary, an international tribunal has the right to decide as to its own jurisdiction and has the power to interpret for this purpose the instruments which govern that jurisdiction."[108] The second, as expressed in the *Fisheries Case*, is that "a State can never plead a provision of, or lack of provision in, its internal law or an act or omission of its executive power as a defence to a charge that it has violated international law."[109] Both principles can be traced back to the *Alabama* Arbitration, which shows that the arbitrators relied to a certain extent on legal reasoning.

### *3.3.2 An Arbitral Consciousness*

Less tangibly but just as importantly, these threads were crucial in raising a general arbitral consciousness. The discourse on international arbitration was often imbued with a vision of arbitration as a force for good and progress, a means of ensuring peace and stability among nations. This arbitral consciousness progressively permeated the arbitration world and was still palpable in the early decades of the twentieth century, when various arbitral institutions were created with the stated goal of maintaining peaceful relationships between men. As Sgard has observed, "[t]he powerful utopian or messianic dimension that often imbued the public discourse on arbitration found its way as well into the International Congress of Chambers of Commerce and later into the language of the American Arbitration Association."[110]

As is often the case when trying to grasp something as amorphous as arbitral consciousness, it may be helpful to turn to literature and the arts. A short story by Strindberg in 1915 refers to the *Alabama* Arbitration,

106 Lapradelle and Politis, *Recueil*, 1:904–5. For example, Article VI of the Treaty of Washington clearly laid down the "principles of international law" according to which the US claims were to be assessed.

107 Bingham, "Alabama Arbitration," ¶ 10 (making reference to the following two cases).

108 *Nottebohm Case (Liechtenstein* v. *Guatemala)*, Judgment of November 18, 1953 (Preliminary Objection), *I.C.J. Reports 1953*, 119.

109 *Fisheries Case (United Kingdom* v. *Norway)*, December 18, 1951, Dissenting Opinion of Sir Arnold McNair, *I.C.J. Reports 1951*, 181.

110 Jérôme Sgard, "A Tale of Three Cities," 163.

highlighting the value of arbitration as means of achieving peace. In it, an Englishman receives a telegram stating that

> the first International Tribunal at Geneva has finished its work; this means that a war between two nations, or what would have been worse – a war against the future, has been prevented; that a hundred thousand Americans and as many Englishmen have to thank this day that they are alive. The Alabama Question has been settled not to the advantage of America, but of justice, not to the injury of England, but for the good of future generations.[111]

A major global crisis had been averted.[112] At a time when "America felt betrayed, insulted, and injured,"[113] international arbitration was seen as a safeguard against war and became widely used,[114] which explains why, after the *Alabama* Arbitration, the US House of Representatives unanimously passed a motion to include arbitration clauses in all future treaties.[115]

Two paintings also convey the spirit of the time and illustrate the Age of Aspirations more broadly. The first, by Manet, shows the 1864 battle near Cherbourg, during which, after the infliction of heavy losses on Union ships, the *Alabama* was sunk. The second portrays the arbitral tribunal finalizing its award in the Salle de l'Alabama in 1872.

Manet's painting, realized shortly after the naval battle, uses dark, somber tones to convey a looming sense of defeat after a chaotic, violent confrontation.[116] In sharp contrast, Armand-Dumaresq uses bright, vivid colors to express the hopefulness brought by a new dawn in international affairs – a sense that "arbitration is an instrument of peace," as

[111] August Strindberg, *The German Lieutenant and Other Stories*, trans. Claud Field (London: Werner Laurie, 1915), 65; quoted in David Caron, "War and International Adjudication: Reflections on the 1899 Peace Conference," *American Journal of International Law*, 94 (2000), 9.

[112] In fact, as Veeder has shown, the *Alabama* Arbitration was important not only from a legal perspective but also in terms of diplomatic history, averting an imminent war between Great Britain and the United States. See Veeder, "Historical Keystone."

[113] Cook, *The Alabama Claims*, 19.

[114] For examples, see William Darby, *International Arbitration. International Tribunals: A Collection of the Various Schemes which Have Been Propounded; and of Instances in the Nineteenth Century* (London: J. M. Dent, 1899).

[115] O'Connell and VanderZee, "History of International Adjudication," 45. See also Mary O'Connell, "Arbitration and Avoidance of War: The Nineteenth-Century American Vision," in Cesare Romano (ed.), *The United States and International Courts and Tribunals* (New York: Cambridge University Press, 2009), 37.

[116] Manet did not witness the battle but read about it in the newspapers. See Juliet Wilson-Bareau and David Degener, *Manet and the American Civil War: The Battle of U.S.S.* Kearsarge *and the C.S.S.* Alabama (New Haven: Yale University Press, 2003).

a nineteenth-century author wrote.[117] The tribunal members, diplomats from around the world, are negotiating peace composedly around a large wooden table. That painting illustrates not just the *Alabama* Arbitration but the Age of Aspirations more broadly: the notion that international arbitration can be used to avert war – the dark naval battles of the past – and maintain harmonious relations between parties.

The utopian discourse surrounding the *Alabama* Arbitration had a profound impact on international arbitration more broadly. In January 1872, the *Alabama* Arbitration directly inspired Swiss jurist Gustave Moynier to make the first proposal to establish a permanent international criminal court for violations of humanitarian law.[118] It also marked an important step in the process of judicialization of international courts and tribunals, which became even more important with the Hague Conferences of 1899 and 1907.[119] Even though the primary goal of these two conferences was to consider common problems such as the laws of war and the limitation of armaments, they also sought to make international arbitration more effective.[120]

This arbitral consciousness was so powerful that it continued well into the twentieth century. Speaking at the 1925 ICC Congress, Clémentel

117 Ferdinand Dreyfus, *L'arbitrage international* (Paris: Calmann Lévy, 1892), 248.

118 Gustave Moynier, "Note sur la création d'une institution judiciaire internationale propre à prévenir et à réprimer les infractions à la Convention de Genève," *Bulletin international des Sociétés de secours aux militaires blessés*, 11 (1872), 3–4.

119 The Hague Conferences of 1899 and 1907 gave a prominent role to international arbitration. The First Hague Conference (1899) led to the establishment of the Permanent Court of Arbitration (PCA) as a third-party dispute settlement forum (the PCA continues to provide case administration services to parties to this day and also has its own set of procedural rules, which were updated in 2012). The Second Hague Conference (1907) contemplated the creation of a permanent arbitral institution, the Judicial Arbitration Court, which was to exist alongside the PCA in The Hague. The plan ultimately failed, as delegates could not agree on the future court's exact composition or on the process for selecting judges. With the two Hague Conferences, international arbitration slowly left the diplomatic arena and became more judicialized, governed by new rules, standards, and principles.

120 In particular, the 1907 Convention for the Pacific Settlement of International Disputes contained new standards that had been lacking at the time of the *Alabama* Arbitration. The convention provided that arbitrators would be selected because of their "known competency in questions of international law" and "highest moral reputation," as opposed to their standing in the diplomatic arena (Article 44). It also contained an obligation for the tribunal to "consider its decisions in private" and ensure that "the proceedings remain secret" (Article 78), and a duty for the tribunal to give reasons for its awards (Article 79). Finally, another, surprisingly modern provision contained in the convention was the idea that the PCA was "competent to settle the 'Compromis'" (Article 53) – an early formulation of the principle of *compétence-compétence*.

described the "innate longing for speedy justice, based on equity, that has led many nations to institute a legal procedure for arbitration."[121] Kellor described the American Arbitration Association as "an institution unique in the history of keeping peace and goodwill among men," bringing "tranquility and happiness out of the chaos which disputes make in the lives of men and of nations."[122] Likewise, in 1932, René David explained that "not only is arbitration conquering new domains, and becoming more widely used in modern international law as a means of peacefully calming conflicts among nations, but also, even in the field of private law pure, recourse to arbitration is more frequent than ever in all countries."[123]

David was making the connection between public international law arbitration and private arbitration explicit, noting that the pacifying virtues of the former – "peacefully calming conflicts among nations" – could be used in the latter context as well. This view can still be found today. For example, in 2013, the Jerusalem Arbitration Center was launched for the resolution of commercial disputes between businesses in Palestine and Israel; those involved in its creation insisted that arbitration, and the development of trade more broadly, could foster peace.[124] Likewise, the title of the book released during the centenary celebrations of the Arbitration Institute of the Stockholm Chamber of Commerce in 2017 was *Arbitrating for Peace: How Arbitration Made a Difference.*[125] This appears to echo the arbitral consciousness that existed during the eighteenth and nineteenth centuries.

121 "Address by M. Étienne Clémentel (June 25, 1925)," in *Proceedings of the Third Congress of the ICC (Brussels, 21–27 June 1925)*, 209.

122 Kellor, *American Arbitration*, xi. Kellor later spoke of the need to coordinate the "existing systems of arbitration and agencies interested in international commercial arbitration . . . not only for the settlement of disputes among parties, but as creating an economic foundation for international peace and security." See Frances Kellor, "La coordination des systèmes d'arbitrage commercial," in International Chamber of Commerce, *Conférence sur l'arbitrage commercial international: Compte rendu des séances destiné aux Membres de la Conférence (June 13–15, 1946)*, 24.

123 René David, *Rapport sur l'arbitrage conventionnel en droit privé: Étude de droit comparé* (Rome: L'Universale Tipografia Poliglotta, 1932), 5.

124 See, for example, Nadia Darwazeh, "The Jerusalem Arbitration Centre: From Tradition to Innovation," *Journal of International Arbitration*, 31 (2014), 122. Darwazeh referred to Montesquieu's famous idea known as "gentle commerce" (*doux commerce*), namely that "[t]he natural effect of commerce is to bring peace. Two nations that negotiate between themselves become reciprocally dependent; for if one has an interest in buying, the other has an interest in selling; and all unions are based upon mutual needs." Montesquieu, *De l'esprit des lois* (1748), book 20, in Roger Callois (ed.), *Œuvres complètes*, vol. 2 (Paris: Gallimard, 1951), chapter 2.

125 Franke, Magnusson, and Dahlquist (eds.), *Arbitrating for Peace.*

## 3.4 Conclusion

This chapter has analyzed two "threads" in the genealogy of international arbitration: commodity market arbitration and public international adjudication. These forms of dispute resolution contributed to the development (or strengthening) of several features of modern international arbitration practice at a time when arbitration was not such a clearly defined field or concept as it is today. The chapter has also explored the emergence of an arbitral consciousness in the late eighteenth and the nineteenth centuries. In Chapter 4, the perspective will be narrowed down to France.

# 4

# The Arbitration Clause Saga in French Law and the Emergence of a Special Regime for International Commercial Arbitration

## 4.1 Introduction

While Chapter 3 sought to situate international commercial arbitration in the wider context of international adjudication, this chapter focuses on a specific context – that of France. It uses a key concept, the arbitration clause, to explore a wider set of attitudes toward international commercial arbitration that prevailed in the nineteenth and early twentieth centuries. Before exploring this idea further, it is worth briefly recalling the definition of an arbitration clause. As is well known, an arbitration clause (or *clause compromissoire*) should be distinguished from a submission agreement (or *compromis*). Both are "species" of the wider category – the "genus"[1] – of arbitration agreements, which is the key basis for arbitration. But while an arbitration clause is concluded *before* a dispute arises, a submission agreement is made *after* a dispute has arisen and relates exclusively to the dispute to which the agreement refers.[2] The difference between the two is, therefore, essentially of a chronological nature.

Even though there is no longer any formal division between the provisions of the French Code of Civil Procedure that relate to the arbitration clause and those that relate to the submission agreement – which renders the distinction between the two largely meaningless

[1] Thomas Clay, "Liberté, égalité, efficacité: la devise du nouveau droit français de l'arbitrage. Commentaire article par article," *Journal du droit international*, 2012, 469. See also French Code of Civil Procedure, Article 1442 ("An arbitration agreement may be in the form of an arbitration clause or a submission agreement").

[2] See, for example, Christophe Seraglini and Jérôme Ortscheidt, *Droit de l'arbitrage interne et international*, 2nd ed. (Paris: LGDJ, 2019), ¶ 581, at 533–34.

today[3] – this was not always the case. In French legal history, the question of the validity of arbitration clauses long preoccupied judges, lawmakers, and scholars. For more than eighty years, from 1843 to 1925, French law did not recognize the validity of an arbitration clause. This revealed deeper anxieties about arbitration – the fear that it might encroach on the jurisdiction of the competent courts or have deleterious effects on the justice system more broadly. It was not until 1925 that French legislators expressly recognized the validity of an arbitration clause in *commercial* matters. This acted as a strong impetus for renewal, which strengthened the legal regime for international commercial arbitration in French law.

This chapter is divided into two parts. First, it explores the movement from *renewal to anxiety* in eighteenth- and nineteenth-century France – the largely pro-arbitration regime of the French Revolution and the current of hostility toward arbitration that emerged during the Consulate and the First Empire (Section 4.2). It then describes the reverse movement from *anxiety to renewal* in the late nineteenth and early twentieth centuries. This seminal period for arbitration saw French legislators recognize the validity of arbitration clauses in commercial contracts and create a special regime for international commercial arbitration (Section 4.3).

In short, this chapter is about the "saga" of the arbitration clause – the "crucial position"[4] it occupied in French legal history for a considerable length of time. As one author explains, "[w]hen one aims to harm arbitration, one takes on the arbitration clause, not the arbitration agreement; when one aims at furthering arbitration, one validates the clause and tries to ensure its efficiency."[5] In other words, the arbitration clause offers a unique means of exploring the dynamic of renewal and anxiety in the Age of Aspirations. Like a seismograph, it has registered the impact of successive waves of enthusiasm and hostility toward arbitration.

[3] See Emmanuel Gaillard and John Savage (eds.), *Fouchard, Gaillard, Goldman on International Commercial Arbitration* (The Hague: Kluwer Law International, 1999), ¶ 386, at 194. This does not mean that the distinction between an arbitration clause and a submission agreement is wholly irrelevant; for example, the drafting of each raises different issues: see Nigel Blackaby et al., *Redfern and Hunter on International Arbitration* (Oxford: Oxford University Press, 2015), 139 and 161–62.

[4] Matthieu de Boisséson, *Le droit français de l'arbitrage interne et international* (Paris: Joly, 1990), ¶ 5, at 19.

[5] Ibid.

## 4.2 From Renewal to Anxiety: Changing Attitudes toward Arbitration in Eighteenth- and Nineteenth-Century France

None of the debates surrounding the validity of an arbitration clause during the first half of the twentieth century can be understood without examining the historical antecedents of these debates. At the time of the French Revolution, arbitration, as it was then understood,[6] was a fundamental way of settling disputes between private citizens (Section 4.2.1). Within a few years, however, this revolutionary fervor provoked a deep sense of anxiety, culminating in the *Prunier* decision of 1843, which invalidated arbitration clauses and must be analyzed on both legal and ideological grounds (Section 4.2.2).

### *4.2.1 The French Revolution's Fervor toward Arbitration*

As is well documented, the justice system under the *Ancien Régime* was harshly criticized, for example in the writings of Montesquieu, Voltaire, and Beccaria.[7] The Constituent National Assembly rapidly decided to give France a new judicial organization. On August 17, 1789, Nicolas Bergasse presented a report on behalf of the Committee on the Constitution, proposing a reorganization of the justice system.[8] The following month, on September 10, 1789, a commission led by Jacques-Guillaume Thouret[9] was mandated to carry out an immediate

[6] The term "arbitration" often denoted "compulsory arbitration" (*arbitrage forcé*), meaning that parties were obligated to submit to arbitration in matters determined by law. "Arbitrage forcé" was thus very different from "arbitration" as we know it today.

[7] In *De l'esprit des lois* (1748), Montesquieu sharply criticized the organization of the judiciary; Voltaire also leveled devastating blows against the judicial system, particularly during the Calas, Sirven, and La Barre affairs, which unfolded from roughly 1762 to 1771. Meanwhile, Beccaria's *Dei delitti e delle pene* (published in Italian in 1764 and translated into French in 1766) significantly influenced Voltaire, who wrote a *Commentaire sur le Traité des délits et des peines* in 1766. See Jean-Pierre Royer et al., *Histoire de la justice en France du XVIIIe siècle à nos jours*, 5th ed. (Paris: Presses Universitaires de France, 2016), 155–78.

[8] Nicolas Bergasse, "Rapport par M. Bergasse sur l'organisation du pouvoir judiciaire, lors de la séance du 17 août 1789," in Jérôme Mavidal and Emile Laurent (eds.), *Archives parlementaires de 1787 à 1860: Première série (1787–1799)* (Paris: Librairie Administrative P. Dupont, 1875), vol. 8.

[9] Jacques-Guillaume Thouret (1746–1794), a Girondin revolutionary, was four times president of the Constituent Assembly and president of the Court of Cassation; he was executed in Paris during the Reign of Terror. See Assemblée Nationale, "Jacques-Guillaume Thouret," www.assemblee-nationale.fr/gouv_parl/fiches_personnalites/Thouret.asp.

reform of French criminal law. Meanwhile, the Constituent Assembly drafted various projects for a complete reform of the courts, and its work on the reorganization[10] of the judicial system was embodied in the law of August 16–24, 1790.

That law gave arbitration a prominent role in settling disputes between private citizens.[11] Title I of the law, entitled "Des arbitres," contained six articles explaining arbitration's use in the reformed judicial system. Article 1 affirmed that "as arbitration is the most reasonable means of ending disputes among citizens, legislators cannot enact any provision aimed at making arbitration agreements less favored or effective."[12] Article 2 stated further that "all persons able to freely exercise their rights and actions can appoint one or more arbitrators to rule on their private interests, in all situations and subject matters without exception."[13] During the parliamentary debates, Thouret stressed how important it was to "discreetly quell disputes between spouses or close relatives, which otherwise, after scandalizing society, sometimes end up ruining an entire family."[14] As these words suggest, the Revolution placed an emphasis on the conciliatory nature of arbitration in settling disputes between private citizens.[15]

Soon enough, the provisions relating to arbitration were incorporated in the constitutions of 1793 (Year I) and 1795 (Year III). The constitution of June 24, 1793 stated that "[t]he rights of citizens to choose arbitrators to rule on their disputes shall not be infringed."[16] The constitution of August 22, 1795 similarly affirmed that, "[t]he rights of the parties to choose arbitrators to rule on their dispute shall

[10] The report was adopted more or less in its entirety and became law on October 10, 1789.

[11] Carine Jallamion, "Arbitrage et pouvoir politique en France du XVIIe au XIXe siècle," *Revue de l'arbitrage*, 2005, 21–28; Jean-Jacques Clère, "L'arbitrage révolutionnaire: Apogée et déclin d'une institution (1790–1806)," *Revue de l'arbitrage*, 1981, 3; Bruno de Loynes de Fumichon, "La passion de la Révolution française pour l'arbitrage," *Revue de l'arbitrage*, 2014, 3; Jean-Louis Halpérin, "Le juge et le jugement en France à l'époque révolutionnaire," in Robert Jacob (ed.), *Le juge et le jugement dans les traditions juridiques européennes: Études d'histoire comparée* (Paris: LGDJ, 1996), 233.

[12] Law of August 16–24, 1790, Article 1.

[13] Ibid., Article 2.

[14] *Réimpression de l'Ancien Moniteur depuis la réunion des États-Généraux jusqu'au Consulat (Mai 1789–Novembre 1799)* (Paris: Plon Frères, 1847), 5:312.

[15] Eric Loquin, "Arbitrage – Aperçu historique – Aperçu de droit comparé," *Juris-Classeur Procédure Civile*, fascicle 1010 (Paris: LexisNexis, 2013), ¶ 23.

[16] Constitution of June 24, 1793, Article 86. The constitution's (radical and highly egalitarian) provisions were never implemented because of the French Revolutionary War.

not be infringed."[17] These constitutional provisions were followed by numerous laws making arbitration compulsory in various kinds of legal relations.[18] As Jallamion observed, the Revolutionary period, at least in its early stages, was marked by a "deep-seated distrust towards state justice and clear preference for arbitration."[19]

### *4.2.2 The Backlash against Arbitration*

#### 4.2.2.1 Legislative Hostility toward Arbitration

The enthusiasm for arbitration displayed by lawmakers during the early days of the Revolution was short-lived; in the space of a few years, judicial attitudes swung from one extreme to the other.[20] In the words of Loquin, a "radical change" took place during the Consulate (1799–1804) and the start of the First Empire (1804–1814 and from March–July 1815).[21]

The sense of anxiety appears most prominently in contemporary transcripts and reports. Speaking in the Council of State in 1805, Édouard Mounier[22] suggested that the entire section of the Code of Civil Procedure that dealt with arbitration should be removed.[23] "The Law," he said, "should not deal with submission agreements."[24] Mounier argued that "the custom of submission agreements is but a parody of judicial administration" and that "citizens should be required to recognize judges as the only ministers of the law."[25] Mounier's words were met with the disapproval of Jean-Baptiste Treilhard, who explained that "courts were created to force defendants to face trial; but . . . when the parties agree on how to end their dispute, respect

[17] Constitution of August 22, 1795, Article 210.

[18] See Loquin, "Arbitrage," ¶ 23.

[19] Carine Jallamion, "La jurisprudence française et l'arbitrage de 1843 à 1958: De la défaveur à la faveur jusqu'à l'avènement de l'arbitrage international," *Revue de l'arbitrage*, 2015, 744 (pt. 1, ¶ 10).

[20] See, for example, Henri Motulsky, *Écrits*, vol. 2, *Études et notes sur l'arbitrage* (Paris: Dalloz, 2010), 29.

[21] Loquin, "Arbitrage," ¶ 3.

[22] Claude-Philibert-Édouard Mounier (1784–1843), the son of Jean-Joseph Mounier (1758–1806) – himself a politician and jurist who played an important role in the early days of the French Revolution – became an auditor at the Conseil d'État in 1806. See Jean Tulard, "Mounier (Claude-Philibert-Édouard)," in Jean Tulard (ed.), *Dictionnaire Napoléon* (Paris: Fayard, 1987), 1203.

[23] "Procès-verbaux du Conseil d'État: Séance du 25 prairial an XIII (14 juin 1805), tenue sous la présidence de M. L'Archichancelier," in Jean-Guillaume Locré, *La législation civile, commerciale et criminelle de la France, ou commentaire et complément des codes français* (Paris: Treuttel et Würtz, 1830), 23:391.

[24] Ibid., 391.

[25] Ibid., 392.

owed to freedom requires that they be not disappointed."[26] In the end, Mounier's proposal was not adopted. But the expression "a parody of judicial administration," a convenient catchphrase, would be used again in subsequent decades, becoming something of a rallying cry for lawmakers and commentators on both sides of the debate.

Equally symptomatic of a strong current of hostility toward arbitration was Claude-Joseph Mallarmé's speech before the Tribunat – the assembly set up in 1800 to discuss draft laws before their adoption by the legislature. Mallarmé[27] explained that

> the former laws and case law may have accorded arbitration too little favor, but the law of August 24, 1790, and other more recent ones, gave it too much. The liberal ideas that informed the drafting thereof no doubt inspired great confidence in this respectable institution for what it is, but they should not go as far as deforming it.[28]

According to Mallarmé, measures had to be taken to safeguard against arbitration's "exorbitant" role in society: the subject matter of the dispute and the identity of the arbitrators would have to be identified,[29] and parties would need to specify, "in writing and expressly," that they wished to forgo "a generally established right."[30]

The 1806 Code of Civil Procedure indeed made the validity of arbitration agreements subject to numerous technical and procedural conditions. In particular, Article 1006 provided that arbitration agreements would need to specify the subject matter of the dispute and the identity of the arbitrators, "failing which they would be void."[31] The various provisions relating to arbitration were grouped under the single heading "*Des arbitrages.*" They were placed in the third book of part two, at the very end of the code – a clear indication of the "decline of the institution in the

[26] Locré, *La législation civile*, 392.

[27] Claude-Joseph Mallarmé (1758–1835) was elected to the Council of Five Hundred in 1795 as *député* for Meurthe and re-elected in 1799. See Jean Tulard, "Mallarmé (Claude-Joseph)," in Tulard, *Dictionnaire Napoléon*, 1122.

[28] Claude-Joseph Mallarmé, "Discours prononcé par M. Mallarmé, orateur du Tribunat, dans la séance du Corps législatif du 29 avril 1806, pour motiver le vœu d'adoption émis par la section de législation du Tribunat" (April 26, 1806), in Jean-Guillaume Locré, *La législation civile*, 23:435.

[29] Ibid., 437.

[30] Ibid., 439.

[31] In addition, Article 1007 imposed strict time limitations on an arbitrator's mandate, and Article 1018 explained that, in some instances, the third arbitrator "will have to conform to the opinion of one of the other arbitrators."

legislator's mind."[32] This reflected the overall spirit of the time, which was characterized by a strong sense of anxiety with regard to arbitration.[33]

#### 4.2.2.2 The *Prunier* Decision

This was the setting in which, in 1843, the Civil Chamber of the Court of Cassation in *Compagnie L'Alliance* v. *Prunier* rendered a decision invalidating arbitration clauses in the insurance field.[34] The facts of the case can be summarized as follows: In 1837, the insured, Sieur Prunier, entered into a fire insurance contract with the insurance company L'Alliance. Article 15 of the insurance contract stated that all disputes between the insurance company and the policyholder concerning damages resulting from fire would be resolved by a panel of three arbitrators sitting at the company's headquarters in Paris. In 1839, a fire destroyed Prunier's buildings, but L'Alliance refused to pay the sum owed under the insurance contract. Prunier brought a case before the *tribunal civil* in Lyon; from there, the case went first to the *Cour royale* in Lyon and then to the Court of Cassation, where L'Alliance argued, inter alia, that Article 1003 of the 1806 code – allowing private parties to "submit to arbitration [*compromettre*] rights that they may dispose of freely" – had been violated.

On July 10, 1843, the Court of Cassation's Civil Chamber, presided by Joseph-Marie Portalis,[35] ruled in favor of Prunier and invalidated the arbitration clause contained in the fire insurance contract. The court held that Article 1003 could not be considered "on its own and as representing a general principle free of any condition"; on the contrary, Article 1003 must be combined with Article 1006 of the code, which stated that to be valid, an arbitration agreement had to specify the subject matter of the

[32] Glasson, Tissier, and Morel, *Traité de procédure civile* (1936), quoted in Loquin, "Arbitrage," ¶ 25.

[33] It is true that arbitration was still compulsory in some contexts, such as maritime insurance disputes and certain corporate partnership agreements, but these exceptions were limited.

[34] *Compagnie L'Alliance* v. *Prunier*, Court of Cassation (France), Civil Chamber, July 10, 1843, *Sirey* 1843, I, 561, note Devilleneuve, conclusions Advocate General Hello. The case was reprinted in the *Revue de l'arbitrage*, 1992, 399. For a recent analysis of the case, see Ibrahim Fadlallah and Dominique Hascher, *Les grandes décisions du droit de l'arbitrage commercial* (Paris: Dalloz, 2019), 3–10.

[35] Joseph-Marie Portalis (1778–1858), the son of Jean-Étienne-Marie Portalis, joined the judiciary in 1813; he was appointed to the Court of Cassation in 1815, where he became the presiding judge of the Criminal Division in 1824 and *premier président* in 1829. Jean-Louis Halpérin, "Portalis Joseph-Marie," in Patrick Arabeyre, Jean-Louis Halpérin, and Jacques Krynen (eds.), *Dictionnaire historique des juristes français, XII–XXe siècle* (Paris: Presses Universitaires de France, 2015), 831–32.

dispute and the identity of the arbitrators.[36] *Prunier* rendered most arbitration clauses unenforceable because the subject matter of a future dispute and the names of potential arbitrators could hardly be specified in advance.

The court's decision revealed deep-seated concerns and anxieties about arbitration. Even though *Prunier* concerned a specific situation – the validity of an arbitration agreement in a fire insurance contract – the court chose to speak in general terms, using broad language that could be applied to a wide range of contexts.[37] As the court stated, if arbitration clauses were enforced, they would be adopted generally and individuals "would be deprived of the guarantees that the courts afford."[38] In terms that were clearly reminiscent of the Revolutionary era, the court also warned against the enormous power wielded by arbitrators.[39]

Expressions of anxiety were quick to follow. In his commentary of the decision, Devilleneuve predicted that it was likely to cause "a great furor, from both a doctrinal and a practical standpoint."[40] He noted that arbitration clauses were already being used in "many contracts such as insurance policies, partnerships, undertakings, and fixed-price contracts, etc."[41] and that it would be necessary "to wait for case law to say its last word."[42] *Prunier* thus had an immediate and visible impact on French

[36] *Compagnie L'Alliance* v. *Prunier, Sirey* 1843, I, 567. In addition to this technical argument about the proper interpretation of Articles 1003 and 1006 of the 1806 code, the court reasoned on what could be described as policy grounds, arguing that the effect of L'Alliance's behavior was to "force the insured party, whatever their residence and however serious or slight the damage they have sustained, to establish an arbitral tribunal in Paris, where perhaps most of them have no business relation and know nobody, far away from the place where the damage was inflicted, which place is the only one where the damage can be checked and assessed" (ibid., 567). As Jarrosson has explained, *Prunier* may therefore be seen as a "prefiguration of consumer rights laws" (see Charles Jarrosson, "La clause compromissoire (art. 2061 C. civ)," *Revue de l'arbitrage*, 1992, 262).

[37] Jallamion, "La jurisprudence française," 748 (pt. 1, ¶ 17). See also Carine Jallamion, "L'arbitrage en matière civile du XVIIe au XIXe siècle: L'exemple de Montpellier" (PhD diss., University of Montpellier 1, 2004), 454–56. *Prunier*'s opening words – "Whereas jurisdiction *ordinarily* lies with the courts" – are particularly significant. *Compagnie L'Alliance* v. *Prunier, Sirey* 1843, I, 567 (emphasis added).

[38] *Compagnie L'Alliance* v. *Prunier, Sirey* 1843, I, 568.

[39] In his conclusions, Advocate General Hello perceptively noted the parallel with the backlash against arbitration that had occurred decades earlier. Hello used Mounier's words "a parody of judicial administration," though without referring to their author, and argued that arbitration clauses should be viewed as ordinary contracts to which ordinary principles of contract law should apply. *Compagnie L'Alliance* v. *Prunier, Sirey* 1843, I, 564–67.

[40] *Compagnie L'Alliance* v. *Prunier, Sirey* 1843, I, 561.

[41] Ibid., 561.

[42] Ibid., 562.

jurisprudence, although it should not be overstated.[43] The decision was confirmed by the Civil Chamber of the Court of Cassation in two decisions rendered on February 21 and December 2, 1844, under the presidency of Portalis.[44] It was not long before arbitration clauses were held to be invalid in commercial contracts too.[45]

The *Prunier* decision meant that the arbitration regime was much less favorable in France, compared to its European neighbors. To back up their objections and highlight France's isolated position in Europe, scholars undertook comparative analyses,[46] exploring the issue of the validity of arbitration clauses under English,[47] Belgian,[48] and German law,[49] all of which were more liberal than the French regime. *Prunier*

[43] As Jallamion has shown, courts rapidly made inroads on the *Prunier* rule, with some judges displaying less severity by upholding agreements to arbitrate made after the dispute arose. So, even in the 1840s, a "tradition favoring arbitration" existed in France. See Jallamion, "La jurisprudence française," 741.

[44] Court of Cassation (France), Civil Chamber, February 21, 1844, *Compagnie du Soleil* v. *Lorents*, *Journal du palais*, 1844, I, 596; Court of Cassation (France), Civil Chamber, December 2, 1844, *Compagnie d'assurances du Phénix* v. *Perret*, *Journal du palais*, 1844, II, 567. See Jallamion, "L'arbitrage en matière civile," 456–57.

[45] Jallamion, "L'arbitrage en matière civile," 457–58. Jallamion cites, for example, a case by the Rouen Court of Appeal on January 18, 1845, reported in *Journal du palais*, 1845, I, 271.

[46] See, for example, Jacques Godron, *La clause compromissoire: Étude de droit comparé (jurisprudences française et belge, droit anglais) et de droit international privé* (Paris: Arthur Rousseau, 1916).

[47] Scholars often referred to Article 27 of the 1889 English Arbitration Act, which defined "submission" as a "written agreement to submit present or future differences to arbitration, *whether an arbitrator is named therein or not*" (emphasis added). In order to highlight its relevance for French law, the 1889 Arbitration Act was translated into French by none other than Raymond Saleilles and published in the *Annuaire de législation étrangère* the same year. Saleilles expressed the wish that France might "greatly benefit" from the "precedents of the practice of English courts." See Raymond Saleilles, "Loi du 26 août 1889 pour amender et codifier les dispositions légales relatives à l'arbitrage," in Société de législation comparée, *Annuaire de législation étrangère* (1889), 42.

[48] The principle of the validity of the arbitration clause was firmly established in Belgian law; in a judgment dated February 17, 1888, the Belgian Court of Cassation stated that, "there is no law forbidding arbitration clauses . . . they are not contrary to public order either and belong under private agreements to which the principles on personal capacity and contractual matters apply." See Court of Cassation (Belgium), First Chamber, February 17, 1888, *Dugniolle* v. *Ceulemans*, *Recueil Dalloz* 1889, II, 168.

[49] In Germany, arbitration clauses had been valid – provided certain requirements were met – since 1877 (see Article 1026 of the German Code of Civil Procedure (ZPO) of January 30, 1877). This provision was still being applied in Alsace-Lorraine (where important pieces of new German imperial legislation had been introduced following Germany's annexation of the region in 1871), which raised a conundrum: an arbitration

was seen as a somber moment in French jurisprudence, an "eclipse"[50] that would "plunge arbitration in France into complete darkness for long decades."[51]

## 4.3 From Anxiety to Renewal: Overcoming *Prunier* to Create a Pro-Arbitration Regime

Between 1904 and 1925 – when the law setting aside the *Prunier* rule for commercial contracts was finally promulgated – no fewer than six bills on the issue of the validity of arbitration clauses were introduced in the Chamber of Deputies and the Senate (Section 4.3.1). These bills provide insight into the changing landscape of arbitration (Section 4.3.2). They were discussed not just behind the closed doors of the parliament but also within the business community and academic circles.[52] Discussions about the validity of the arbitration clause also strengthened the distinct regime created in France for international commercial arbitration (Section 4.3.3).

clause contained in a contract between two parties from Alsace-Lorraine was valid (provided it complied with the requirements of Article 1026 of the Alsace-Lorraine Code of Civil Procedure), whereas the same arbitration clause in a contract between two French citizens from outside Alsace-Lorraine could be held invalid by a court. For many lawmakers at the time, this inconsistency was yet another reason why the French law on arbitration clauses had to be reformed.

[50] Motulsky, *Écrits*, 29.

[51] Jean-Baptiste Racine, *Droit de l'arbitrage* (Paris: Presses Universitaires de France, 2016), 130–31.

[52] To give but a few examples of works published on the topic in the 1920s and 1930s: Maurice Picard, "La clause compromissoire et l'arbitrage dans les rapports internationaux," *Journal du droit international*, 1923, 508–19; Louis Louis-Dreyfus, "La clause compromissoire," *Revue politique et parlementaire*, 1925, 370–87; Joseph Hamel, "La clause compromissoire dans les rapports de commerce internationaux: À propos de quelques récents projets et propositions de loi," *Revue de droit international privé*, 18 (1923), 721–40 (pt. 1) and 19 (1924), 15–30 (pt. 2); René Leray, "L'arbitrage et la loi nouvelle sur la clause compromissoire," *Revue des ventes et transports*, 1926, no. 1, 301–37; René Morel, "La clause compromissoire en matière commerciale," *Revue critique de législation et jurisprudence*, 46 (1926), 486–540; Albert Viatte, "Clause compromissoire: Validité en matière commerciale; Commentaire de la loi du 31 décembre 1925," *Recueil général des lois, décrets et arrêtés – Première partie – Commentaires et revues de jurisprudence*, 56 (1926), 19–24; Jean Rudler, *La clause compromissoire et l'arbitrage civil* (Nancy: A. Suzaine, 1927); Jean Robert, *La clause compromissoire et l'organisation de l'arbitrage* (Paris: Sirey, 1929); Otto Rothé, *La clause compromissoire et l'arbitrage depuis la loi de 1925* (Paris: Domat/Montchrestien, 1934); Charles Refort, *Les difficultés soulevées par l'application de la loi du 31 décembre 1925 sur la clause compromissoire* (Paris: M. Lavergne, 1939).

### 4.3.1 *Legislative Efforts to Set Aside the* Prunier *Rule*

Proposals to reform the law on arbitration clauses took place with increasing frequency in the early decades of the twentieth century. This was a period of intense activity for arbitration, both domestically and internationally, with the adoption of the Geneva Protocol on Arbitration Clauses on September 24, 1923. Bills were sponsored by the then *député* Flandin in 1904 – the year in which the French Court of Cassation sanctioned the inclusion of an arbitration clause in a contract,[53] suggesting that certain judges were already adopting a more pro-arbitration stance – and Louis-Dreyfus in 1907. They were among the many "bills which – the Clémentel bill apart – fell into a seemingly everlasting sleep in Parliament boxes."[54]

The archives of the French National Assembly provide a window on the various legislative efforts to set aside the *Prunier* rule invalidating arbitration clauses. Table 4.1 lists, in chronological order, the major bills that were submitted to the French parliament on this topic between 1908 and 1925.

Even though it was Louis-Dreyfus's bill that ultimately passed in the Senate in 1925, it took several attempts – including a second by Flandin, who had become a senator in 1909[55] – for both chambers to finally agree on a legislative reform.

The approaches taken in the various reform proposals can be divided into three main categories.[56] First, some bills tried to overturn the *Prunier* line of cases entirely by recognizing the validity of *all* arbitration clauses, whether concluded in France or abroad.[57] A second approach was to treat an arbitration clause as valid only if it was part of

[53] Court of Cassation (*Chambre des requêtes*) (France), June 21, 1904, *Georges Bernard* v. *General Mercantile Company*, *Dalloz* 1906, I, 395 (the contract had been concluded in Belgium, where arbitration clauses were valid, between French and Belgian parties). The year 1904 was also marked by (i) the creation of the International Congress of Chambers of Commerce by Belgian industrialist Louis Canon-Legrand (see Chapter 6, Section 6.2.1) and (ii) the Entente Cordiale between Britain and France, which settled a number of outstanding colonial disputes between the two countries. Both events likely contributed to spreading the idea that disputes could be settled peacefully outside the courts.

[54] Leray, "L'arbitrage et la loi nouvelle," 311.

[55] Senate (France), "Flandin Etienne," www.senat.fr/senateur-3eme-republique/flandin_etienne1832r3.html.

[56] See Hamel, "La clause compromissoire," 727. For an analysis of the different bills, see also André Prudhomme, "The Present Position of the Arbitration Clause under the Law of France," in Arthur Nussbaum, *International Yearbook on Civil and Commercial Arbitration* (Oxford: Oxford University Press, 1928), vol. 1.

[57] This approach was followed by Flandin in 1904 and 1921 and Achille Fould in 1923. Even though the Flandin bill was endorsed by the Paris Chamber of Commerce in 1904 and by

Table 4.1 *Bills on the validity of arbitration clauses introduced in the French parliament between 1908 and 1925*

| | |
|---|---|
| July 2, 1908 | The Louis-Dreyfus bill passes in the Chamber of Deputies;[1] it is referred to the Senate on July 3,[2] but nothing happens for the next eighteen years. |
| January 18, 1921 | A bill by Étienne Flandin is introduced in the Senate.[3] |
| July 7, 1921 | A bill by Aristide Briand, President of the Council and Minister of Foreign Affairs, is introduced in the Chamber of Deputies.[4] |
| February 13, 1923 | A bill by Achille Fould is introduced in the Chamber of Deputies.[5] |
| March 13, 1923 | A bill by Étienne Clémentel is introduced in the Senate.[6] |
| December 8, 1925 | The Louis-Dreyfus bill passes in the Senate.[7] |
| December 31, 1925 | The Louis-Dreyfus bill becomes law. |

1 *Annales de la Chambre des députés*, July 2, 1908, second session, 620.
2 *Annales du Sénat* (July 3, 1908), 1066.
3 *Documents parlementaires: Sénat*, 1921, app. 4, at 2.
4 *Documents parlementaires: Sénat*, 1921, app. 566, at 1019.
5 *Documents parlementaires: Chambre*, 1923, app. 5566, at 340.
6 *Documents parlementaires: Sénat*, 1923, app. 168, at 134.
7 *Annales du Sénat*, December 8, 1925, at 144.

a commercial contract involving at least one foreign party.[58] The third approach, followed by Louis-Dreyfus, was to consider arbitration clauses as valid only in *commercial* cases, regardless of whether they involved a foreign party. The third approach appealed to many chambers of commerce and local business organizations. The Louis-Dreyfus bill,

Jeanneney, a *député*, in a report dated February 26, 1906, it did not pass the Chamber of Deputies, and Flandin subsequently reintroduced the bill in the Senate in 1921.

58 This idea was contained in the Clémentel bill, which was far from perfect, however, because it treated contracts between two French nationals differently from those between a French national and a foreign national (see Hamel, "La clause compromissoire," 739). The Clémentel bill therefore provided an inadequate solution.

which had initially passed in the Chamber of Deputies in 1908, was eventually adopted by the Senate in 1925.

### *4.3.2 Louis-Dreyfus's "Propaganda" Efforts and the Rise of the Mercatocracy*

A closer look at the Louis-Dreyfus bill and its author gives a sense of how the business community became the driving force behind many developments in international commercial arbitration toward the end of the Age of Aspirations and the beginning of the Age of Institutionalization. In other words, the mercatocracy – at least in France – became more organized and started increasingly to assert itself vis-à-vis the state.

The fact that it was the Louis-Dreyfus bill that ultimately succeeded – despite efforts by others to make the arbitration clause valid under French law – is hardly surprising. Given his family background and training, Louis-Dreyfus was the ideal figure to defend such a law. The son of a wealthy industrialist from Alsace who, by the early twentieth century, had become a global grain distributor, he sought to promote arbitration in the wider business community.[59] Louis-Dreyfus was also a member of the French parliament (first as a *député* and later a senator) and could therefore use his power and influence to convince French business of its value.

As Louis-Dreyfus explained, reforming the law on arbitration clauses would have far-reaching legal and economic consequences:

[59] As Chatriot points out, relatively little is known about the figure of Louis-Dreyfus (see Alain Chatriot, *La politique du blé: Crises et régulation d'un marché dans la France de l'entre-deux-guerres* (Paris: Institut de la gestion publique et du développement économique, Comité pour l'histoire économique et financière de la France, 2016), chapter 2, n. 207). Louis-Dreyfus studied law before joining the family business. From 1905 to 1910, the period during which he introduced his bill in the Chamber of Deputies, he served in the French parliament as a *député* representing the Lozère department (see "Louis-Dreyfus (Louis)," in Jean Jolly (ed.), *Dictionnaire des Parlementaires français: Notices biographiques sur les ministres, députés, et sénateurs français de 1889 à 1940* (Paris: Presses Universitaires de France, 1970), 6:2306). Then, in 1915, following the death of his father, he led the family business, along with his brother Charles, further expanding it to Russia and the Americas. In the 1920s and 1930s, their company dominated the grain trade, and Louis-Dreyfus became known as the "King of Wheat" or "King Two Louis" (*le roi deux Louis*) – a reference to the highest-valued gold coin of the *Ancien Régime* (see Robert Paxton, *French Peasant Fascism: Henry Dorgères' Greenshirts and the Crises of French Agriculture, 1929–1939* (Oxford: Oxford University Press, 1997), 19). Louis-Dreyfus soon returned to politics, serving as a *député* representing the Alpes-Maritimes department from 1930 to 1936 and as a senator from 1937 to 1940 (*Dictionnaire des Parlementaires français*, 6:2306). On July 10, 1940, he voted for the constitutional change that effectively established the regime of Philippe Pétain.

> Arbitration clauses, once their effects are recognized as valid, will contribute to the country's commercial and industrial development in that it will facilitate business by allowing difficulties to be settled quickly and at little expense; it will no doubt lead to the establishment of arbitral chambers, like those that already exist in all the great nations of Europe, especially in England; it will increase the number and importance of the trade associations and will therefore benefit both domestic and international trade, for there is no doubt that foreign merchants will be more willing to become our clients if they find the same advantages here as in other countries.[60]

Louis-Dreyfus deployed similar arguments in an article published in 1925 while the Senate was considering the bill.[61] Legislative reform could contribute to the economic growth of the country by ensuring that "arbitration becomes increasingly frequent."[62] He further explained that, through the development of trade associations, arbitration would make it possible, "with the involvement of all concerned, to draw up general regulations constituting a kind of Charter of Commerce and Industry."[63] This was an ambitious agenda, going far beyond the simple legislative reform that Louis-Dreyfus had been advocating.

Shortly thereafter, Louis-Dreyfus spoke at various conferences and events – described by one author as "propaganda conferences."[64] In 1926 and 1927, he delivered speeches in Marseille,[65] Lyon,[66] and Troyes.[67] These speeches constituted "the sole preparatory work, as it were, for the law, an observation that clearly underlines the private nature of the new law, made *by* and *for* a few big corporations."[68]

60 Louis-Dreyfus bill, "Exposé des motifs."

61 Louis-Dreyfus, "La clause compromissoire," 380–81. The article was still at press when the Senate passed the bill in 1925.

62 Ibid., 372.

63 Ibid., 380.

64 Leray, "L'arbitrage et la loi nouvelle," 325.

65 The local newspaper in which the Marseille conference (on February 22, 1926) was reported – the March 8, 1926 issue of the *Journal commercial et maritime de Marseille* – is unavailable due to decay. I have located two copies of this issue – one in Paris and the other in Marseille – but was unable to have access to them.

66 The Lyon conference (on June 25, 1926) was reported in three consecutive issues of the *Courrier du commerce* on July 7, 1926 (5.204), July 10, 1926 (5.205), and July 14, 1926 (5.206).

67 The proceedings of the Troyes conference (on June 27, 1927) were published as a brochure, *La clause compromissoire et l'arbitrage commercial: Conférence faite par M. Louis Louis-Dreyfus à Troyes, le 27 juin 1927* (Paris: Imprimerie de publications périodiques, 1927).

68 Leray, "L'arbitrage et la loi nouvelle," 325 (emphasis in original).

In those conferences, Louis-Dreyfus introduced himself by highlighting his position as both lawmaker and a member of the business elite. "I am a convinced parliamentarian," Louis-Dreyfus explained in Lyon.[69] But he also viewed himself as a business leader, speaking to his peers about some of the challenges they faced. Taking a jab at magistrates, he sided with the business leaders:

> Through our very occupation, we have experience of practical issues, which judges might not have. With all the respect we owe them, we are nonetheless entitled to say that their lives are spent reading codes and in the dust of files. As the businessmen that we are, we act more expeditiously, we are not afraid of responsibilities, we are better at remaining forthright, we will not hesitate to recognize the fault of a merchant who is at fault, even if they be our best client. We will condemn them if our conscience tells us to.[70]

Louis-Dreyfus contrasts the figure of the judge – reading dust-covered documents – with that of the efficient businessman, making no secret of where his allegiances lay.[71]

In addition to promoting the use of arbitration – for all commercial actors, including "*small* traders, *small* manufacturers"[72] – Louis-Dreyfus sought to allay some of the doubts expressed by business leaders and others at the time. What would happen if a party refused to appoint an arbitrator? Louis-Dreyfus suggested that there should be moral sanctions – "publication of your name or exclusion" from local trade associations and commercial groups.[73] How would appeals work? Louis-Dreyfus adopted a pragmatic stance: "I think it would be wise, at least to begin with, not to prevent appeals against arbitration."[74] In order to avoid frequent appeals, which would cause undue delays and defeat a key purpose of arbitration, Louis-Dreyfus contemplated various possibilities. One option was to increase administrative costs: "I unhesitatingly recommend that the costs of the second proceedings be much higher, though not prohibitive, than those of the first."[75] This would avoid the "chicanery" of losers systematically appealing.[76]

[69] *Courrier du commerce*, July 7, 1926.
[70] Ibid.
[71] It is telling that Louis-Dreyfus uses the first-person plural pronoun ("we," "us," "our") thirteen times in just four sentences, as if to insist that he, too, is more a businessman than a politician.
[72] *La clause compromissoire et l'arbitrage commercial*, 15 (emphasis in original).
[73] *Courrier du commerce*, July 7, 1926.
[74] *Courrier du commerce*, July 10, 1926.
[75] Ibid.
[76] Ibid.

Louis-Dreyfus's "propaganda" efforts therefore show how, in the 1920s, arbitration was being actively promoted to the business community as a key method for maintaining peaceful commercial relations. He was of course not alone in undertaking such promotion. The French press covered arbitration extensively at the time, making it more widely known to readers. An article in *Les Débats* referred to the arbitration treaties that France had recently concluded with foreign nations and stressed that the situation in France was "paradoxical and slightly ridiculous": "two French individuals could not validly conclude what France has just concluded with England and Italy."[77] The article went on to call for legislative reform that would "abolish an unfair regime not expressly established by law but through mere interpretation, with greater or lesser subtlety, of the Code [of Civil Procedure]."[78] Another article in *Le Matin* stated that arbitration was an "extremely simple" procedure that could "end within a few weeks without costing anything apart the arbitrators' and lawyers' fees!" Through arbitration, the article explained, one could "avoid the specific horrors of judicial ordeals."[79]

To a large extent, these statements illustrate the changing world of international arbitration at the end of the Age of Aspirations, when the private interests of the mercatocracy created a fertile ground on which contemporary international commercial arbitration could flourish. At the same time, a separate *legal* regime was being strengthened specifically for international arbitration in France.

### *4.3.3 Strengthening the Legal Regime for International Commercial Arbitration*

The debates surrounding the validity of the arbitration clause in France were linked to broader reflection on the distinction between domestic and international arbitration. As Godron pointed out, the conditions under which French courts would recognize arbitration clauses as valid were hardly workable in practice and needed further clarification.[80] In particular, the discussions and cases that followed in the wake of the

77 "A propos des traités d'arbitrage," *Journal des débats politiques et littéraires*, January 27, 1904, 1.
78 Ibid.
79 "De l'arbitrage," *Le Matin*, August 15, 1905, 2.
80 See Jacques Godron, "La clause compromissoire dans les rapports internationaux devant les Tribunaux français" (pt. 2), *Journal du droit international*, 1919, 658–59 (see ibid., 47–62 for pt. 1).

*Prunier* rule led courts, scholars, and lawmakers to address the fate of contracts involving at least one foreign party.[81] As von Mehren pointed out, this was how "a separate and distinct legal regime for international arbitration began to emerge in French law,"[82] culminating in such cases as *Pélissier du Besset* (1927) and *Mardelé* (1930). This body of cases played a key role in shaping the contemporary French international commercial arbitration regime. As more recent scholars have noted, "without the distinction between domestic and international arbitration, arbitration would not have flourished as it did, as international arbitration benefitted from exceptions tailored to the needs of international trade."[83]

*Pélissier du Besset* was arguably "the leading French [arbitration] case prior to the 1981 reform,"[84] establishing that "a transaction will be international where it produces a movement across borders with reciprocal consequences in more than one country."[85] The case concerned a sixty-one-year lease agreement for shops in Algeria – then under French rule – concluded in 1883 between a French national, Pélissier du Besset, and an English company, The Algiers Land and Warehouse Co. Ltd. The rent was to be paid in pounds sterling, but in 1923 Pélissier du Besset's heirs, faced with the depreciation of the French franc against the British pound, refused to pay, arguing that the gold clause was invalid under French law. The English company, meanwhile, alleged that the clause was valid because the parties were of different nationalities and the lease agreement was, therefore, an international contract. The court had to decide whether "the respondent company, when renting the vaults in the port of Algiers . . ., conducted an operation that, for the purposes of the trial, could be characterized as an overseas or international operation."[86]

81 As many commentators noted, a special regime had already been carved out for disputes relating to a contract involving at least one foreign party. See, for example, Court of Cassation (*Chambre des requêtes*) (France), July 17, 1899, *Ospina* v. *Ribon*, *Revue des sociétés*, September–October 1899, 497 (confirming the validity of an arbitration clause between two foreign (Colombian) parties).

82 Arthur Taylor von Mehren, "International Commercial Arbitration: The Contribution of the French Jurisprudence," *Louisiana Law Review*, 46 (1986), 1049.

83 Benoit Le Bars and Joseph Dalmasso, *Arbitrage commercial international: Les grands arrêts du droit français* (Paris: LexisNexis, 2016), 2.

84 Gaillard and Savage, *Fouchard, Gaillard, Goldman*, ¶ 108, at 56.

85 Ibid.

86 Court of Cassation (France), May 17, 1927, *Pélissier du Besset* v. *The Algiers Land and Warehouse Co. Ltd.*, *Dalloz* 1928), 2, at 25, conclusions by Matter, and note Capitant.

Advocate General Matter addressed the issue by adopting an economic rather than a legal definition of international transactions. He famously expressed the view that "[t]o be thus characterized [as international], the contract must have reciprocal effects, as a sort of ebb-and-flow movement across borders, in the two countries."[87] According to Matter, "the renting of a real property right in Algiers by an Englishman to a Frenchman has not resulted in France in the entry of goods or money, the operation was entirely local, so payment therefor must necessarily be subject to French public policy laws."[88] This approach was endorsed by the Court of Cassation.

A few years later, the Court of Cassation revisited the issue in two cases, *Mardelé* (1930) and *Dambricourt* (1931), both of which concerned contracts that had been concluded prior to the legislative reform of December 31, 1925. *Mardelé*[89] concerned the arbitration of a dispute under a contract concluded in France between two French merchants for the sale of 100 tons of Chilean wheat, CIF Le Havre. The contract was held to be international. The Court of Cassation noted that the goods were of foreign origin; the seller was the subsidiary of a Dutch company; and the contract was subject to the conditions of the London Corn Trade Association, which provided for arbitration in London. The Court of Cassation reasoned that the situation involves the interests of international commerce. Where such is the case, and given that the nullity of the arbitration clause provided for in Article 1006 of the Code of Civil Procedure is not part of public policy in France, the parties, even if they are both French, may, in a contract concluded abroad or in France, validly derogate from the provisions of the aforementioned text and choose a foreign law to govern their agreements, such as English law, which considers such clauses as valid.[90]

The Court of Cassation adopted exactly the same reasoning in *Dambricourt* a year later.[91]

In *Mardelé*, the Court of Cassation therefore laid down a different criterion from that in *Pélissier du Besset*. Whereas it had previously referred to the economic concept of "ebb-and-flow movement across borders," it now relied on the notion of "interests of international commerce." This was a broader notion and "such flexibility will allow

[87] Ibid., 31.

[88] Ibid.

[89] Court of Cassation (France), February 19, 1930, *Mardelé* v. *Muller*, *Sirey* 1933, I, 41.

[90] Ibid.

[91] Court of Cassation (France), January 27, 1931, *Dambricourt* v. *Rossard*, *Sirey* 1933, I, 41, note Jean-Paulin Niboyet.

the development of an autonomous arbitration regime specific to international matters."[92] Von Mehren's illuminating assessment of *Mardelé* is worth quoting in detail:

> the *jurisprudence* that culminated in *Mardelé* also implied ideas and techniques that were to continue to shape the French law's handling and understanding of international commercial arbitration. In particular, this case strongly suggests that various aspects of the legal regime applicable to domestic arbitrations do not apply to arbitrations which involve the interests of international commerce. The *jurisprudence* further intimates that certain of the rules and principles governing the regime applicable to international commercial arbitration need not flow from rules and principles found in a national law. Particular rules and principles of a non-national character can be developed to take into account the special qualities and requirements of international commercial arbitration as a dispute-resolution process.[93]

One can clearly see how these cases and the debates surrounding the validity of the arbitration clause contributed to the establishment of a special regime for international commercial arbitration in France. This distinction between domestic and international arbitration was enshrined in the Decree of May 12, 1981[94] and maintained in the Decree of January 13, 2011.[95] Such reforms made it possible to apply more liberal principles to international arbitration, which was thus freed from unnecessary restrictions.

## 4.4 Conclusion

Part I analyzed key features of the Age of Aspirations, when the discourse on "peace through arbitration" was prevalent and a coherent international arbitration framework began to emerge. Chapter 3 explored two "threads" in the genealogy of international arbitration in the late eighteenth and the nineteenth centuries: arbitration in the commodity

92 Le Bars and Dalmasso, *Arbitrage commercial international*, 3, at 4.

93 Von Mehren, "International Commercial Arbitration," 1050.

94 Decree No. 81–500 of May 12, 1981.

95 Decree No. 2011–48 of January 13, 2011. See Ministère de la Justice et des Libertés, "Rapport au Premier ministre relatif au décret n° 2011–48 du 13 janvier 2011 portant réforme de l'arbitrage," *Journal officiel de la République française*, January 14, 2011, www.legifrance.gouv.fr/affichJO.do?idJO=JORFCONT000023417459. The decree has been the subject of several analyses; see, for example, Emmanuel Gaillard and Pierre de Lapasse, "Le nouveau droit français de l'arbitrage interne et international," *Dalloz*, 2011, 3, 175. A complete bibliography can be found in Thomas Clay, *Code de l'arbitrage commenté* (Paris: LexisNexis, 2021), 453–55.

markets (particularly in the British trade associations), and arbitration between states. It also identified the arbitral consciousness that existed at the time. Chapter 4 retraced the part played by the arbitration clause in the broader evolution of international commercial arbitration.[96] It explored the dual movement from renewal to anxiety in the eighteenth and nineteenth centuries, culminating in the 1843 *Prunier* case invalidating arbitration clauses; and from anxiety to renewal in the twentieth century, culminating in the law of December 31, 1925. It also explained how these debates contributed to the establishment of a distinct regime for international (as opposed to domestic) arbitration in France.

International arbitration witnessed many concrete results and achievements in the Age of Aspirations. However, its widespread use and acceptance remained, to a large extent, an ideal and an aspiration. It was necessary to wait until the 1920s and 1930s for the modern regime of international commercial arbitration to fully develop. As remarked by Loquin, "there is no doubt that the promotion of arbitration, and the growth resulting from its institutionalization, date from that moment."[97] For its internationalization, one must therefore look to the early decades of the twentieth century.

[96] Even though this chapter ends in the 1920s and 1930s, at the beginning of the Age of Institutionalization, the "saga" of the arbitration clause continues into the present era. In 1972, the French legislature decided that an arbitration clause was invalid unless otherwise provided by law. The situation was reversed in 2001, when arbitration clauses became valid in contracts between professionals, unless otherwise provided by specific legislative provisions (Law No. 2001–420 of May 15, 2001 relating to new economic regulations; see also Charles Jarrosson, "Le nouvel essor de la clause compromissoire après la loi du 15 mai 2001," JCP, 2001, no. 27). The law entitled Justice for the Twenty-First Century introduced yet further changes, modifying Article 2061 of the Civil Code for the third time since 1804; it provided that arbitration clauses are valid in all contracts, but cannot be enforced against nonprofessionals (Law No. 2016–1547 of November 18, 2016 Modernizing Twenty-First Century Justice, Article 2061). In a recent decision, the Court of Cassation further held that the negative effect of competence-competence does not apply to international consumer contracts even if the contract contains an arbitration clause, so consumers can bring their disputes before domestic courts without waiting for arbitrators to decide first on their own jurisdiction (Court of Cassation (France), First Civil Chamber, September 30, 2020, *PWC Landwell-PricewaterhouseCoopers Tax & Legal Services* v. *Mme L . . . Y . . . et autres*, *Journal du droit international*, 2020, 1327, note Gaillard; *Hebdo édition privée*, October 15, 2020, note Vidal; *Dalloz actualité*, October 21, 2020, note Jourdan-Marques).

[97] Loquin, "Arbitrage," 19.

# PART II

# The Age of Institutionalization

# 5

# Introduction to the Age of Institutionalization

By the beginning of the twentieth century, the pro-arbitration movement had gained such traction that the creation of institutions specializing in international commercial arbitration no longer seemed far off. Efforts to build new institutions were interrupted by World War I, however, which had a devastating effect on many national economies. After the war, the need to build permanent institutions to maintain peaceful relations between commercial parties from different countries became more urgent than ever. It was in this context that the International Chamber of Commerce (ICC) was founded in 1920, following the 1919 Atlantic City Conference. Its Court of Arbitration was created in 1923 and started administering cases soon thereafter. A few years later, in 1926, the American Arbitration Association (AAA) was established through the merger of the Arbitration Society of America and the Arbitration Foundation. In the words of a contemporary scholar, "international arbitration ha[d] entered the organizational and expansive phase."[1]

The Age of Institutionalization (*ca.*1920–1950) was a seminal period for the subsequent development of the international commercial arbitration regime. It was marked by the emergence of a new class of arbitration scholars and practitioners. This reflected a broader phenomenon, described as the "technocratisation of the economy," manifested in "a new class of actors in international relations: the experts."[2] These individuals – early members of the mercatocracy – displayed a much more internationalist spirit than was previously the case. They sought, often successfully, to enlist

[1] Maurice Picard, "La clause compromissoire et l'arbitrage dans les rapports internationaux," *Journal du droit international*, 1923, 508, 519.

[2] Yann Decorzant, "Internationalism in the Economic and Financial Organisation of the League of Nations," in Daniel Laqua (ed.), *Internationalism Reconfigured: Transnational Ideas and Movements Between the World Wars* (London: I. B. Tauris, 2011), 115–16. As Decorzant explains, studies on the role of experts in the interwar years built on Richard Kuisel, *Le capitalisme et l'État en France: Modernisation et dirigisme au XXe siècle* (Paris: Gallimard, 1984).

the support of states to carry out their projects. But states still played a powerful role in the Age of Institutionalization, for example by deciding under what conditions an award could be enforced abroad.

The key figures in the Age of Institutionalization were lawyers and scholars who, working mainly in arbitral institutions, sought to establish international commercial arbitration as a specialist discipline. Even though some of them had strong diplomatic or government experience – the prime example is Étienne Clémentel, the first president of the ICC – others worked in relative obscurity, devoting their time and efforts to mastering the art of arbitration. Like the diplomats of the previous age, their vision was still imbued with idealism and colored by a belief in arbitration as a force for good.[3] But they were also eager to develop the specific rules and techniques that would enable the modern system of international commercial arbitration to grow and become more effective. It is arguably they who were responsible for constructing international commercial arbitration as it is known today, more so than the "grand old men" described by Dezalay and Garth.

This part is divided into two chapters. Chapter 6 explores the origins of the ICC and its Court of Arbitration, and the movement between renewal and anxiety that is palpable in the major instruments adopted in the Age of Institutionalization. The Geneva Protocol on Arbitration Clauses (1923) and the Geneva Convention on the Execution of Foreign Awards (1927) reflected a highly territorial mindset situated at the anxiety end of the spectrum, while the Convention on the Recognition and Enforcement of Foreign Arbitral Awards (1958) marked a shift from territorialism to internationalism, pushing the pendulum toward renewal and anticipating the Age of Autonomy. This swing can be analyzed as part of the broader changes in the overall legal consciousness at the time, with scholars and practitioners displaying a much more internationalist outlook than was previously the case.

Chapter 7 adopts a narrower focus, exploring the establishment and evolution of the ICC's arbitration system, paying close attention to how the institution codified existing rules and practices through its Rules of Arbitration. These codification efforts are a prime example of the institutionalization of international commercial arbitration that took place in the 1920s and thereafter.

But first, let us ponder the apparent neglect of the ICC's history by jurists and historians alike (Section 5.1) and venture to offer some explanations (Section 5.2).

[3] On this point, see also Claire Lemercier and Jérôme Sgard, *Arbitrage privé international et globalisation(s): Rapport final* (March 2015), 96–97.

## 5.1 A Gap in the Literature

Only a handful of works about the ICC's origins and history appeared in the early decades of its existence. The first seems to have been Léon Magnier's doctoral study *La Chambre de commerce internationale*, which was published in Paris in 1928.[4] Dedicated to Étienne Clémentel, the book provided an overview of the constitution of the International Chamber of Commerce, its organization, and its biennial congresses, as well as a brief description of its arbitration system at the time. A decade later, in 1938, George Ridgeway, a history professor who also served in the US Department of State,[5] produced *Merchants of Peace*.[6] The book was sponsored by the Carnegie Endowment for International Peace and constituted a full-length study of the first twenty years of the ICC from an American viewpoint.[7] A revised and updated edition was published, with a different subtitle, in 1959.[8] Besides these two works, there was little about the ICC's history available to people unfamiliar with the institution.[9]

It was not until the end of the century that the ICC's history and work once again received serious academic attention in dissertations by Jolivet in French[10] and Rosengarten in German.[11] They were quickly followed by Druelle-Korn's 2004 thesis exploring the origins of the ICC, which

[4] Léon Magnier, *La Chambre de commerce internationale* (Paris: Arthur Rousseau, 1928).

[5] See obituary, "Memorials: George Loveland Ridgeway," *Princeton Alumni Weekly*, November 26, 1968, 21.

[6] George Ridgeway, *Merchants of Peace: Twenty Years of Business Diplomacy through the International Chamber of Commerce; 1919–1938* (New York: Columbia University Press, 1938).

[7] Nigel Blackburn, *World Peace through World Trade*, ICC Publication No. 342 (Paris: International Chamber of Commerce, 1979), 10.

[8] George Ridgeway, *Merchants of Peace: The History of the International Chamber of Commerce* (Boston: Little, Brown, 1959).

[9] Note, however, a 1972 thesis by Chen-Wen Tsai, "La Chambre de commerce internationale, un groupe de pression international: Son action et son rôle dans l'élaboration, la conclusion et l'application des conventions internationales établies au sein des organisations intergouvernementales à vocation mondiale (1945–1969)" (Katholieke Universiteit te Leuven, 1972), referenced in Monika Rosengarten, "Die Internationale Handelskammer: Wirtschaftspolitische Empfehlungen in der Zeit der Weltwirtschaftskrise 1929–1939" (PhD diss., Freie Universität Berlin, 1999), 54n103; and Claude Paillat, *Dossiers secrets de la France contemporaine*, vol. 1, *1919: Les illusions de la gloire* (Laffont, 1979), 224–28.

[10] Emmanuel Jolivet, "Les Incoterms, étude d'une norme du commerce international" (PhD diss., University of Montpellier 1, 1999) (on file with author). Published by Litec in 2003, this authoritative study on the uniform rules for interpreting trade terms introduced by the ICC in 1936 includes a brief account of the origins of the ICC.

[11] Rosengarten, *Die Internationale Handelskammer*.

drew on a wide range of historical sources.[12] Closer to the present time, Lemercier and Sgard have probed the modern roots of international commercial arbitration in France, though they mention the Atlantic City Conference only once in their research report.[13]

Outside the historical field, a mere handful of scholars have studied the beginnings of the ICC from the perspective of their own disciplines. Drawing on theories of transnational governance and international cooperation, Hale referred to the history of the ICC in his study of institutional attitudes toward global governance.[14] Kelly, an international relations scholar, also used the ICC as a case study to show that during the second, third, and fourth decades of the twentieth century non-governmental organizations (NGOs) were "performing diplomatic roles on a regular basis,"[15] which, he argues, disproves the assumption that structural power in the global political economy has been in the hands of non-state actors only since the late 1960s. Other political scientists who have used the ICC's history in their research include Ronit and Schneider, who explain that the birth of the ICC can be seen as part of a larger movement toward increased international and global cooperation between private actors after World War I.[16] Beside these scholars, however, few political scientists and international relations

[12] Clotilde Druelle-Korn, "Un laboratoire réformateur, le département du commerce en France et aux États-Unis de la Grande Guerre aux années vingt" (PhD diss., Institut d'études politiques de Paris, 2004) (on file with author), esp. 277–329. Druelle-Korn, however, was interested not so much in international commercial arbitration as in the trade ministries in France and the United States from World War I until the 1920s. Badel also mentions the origins of the ICC (and its contribution in areas other than arbitration) in her thesis; see Laurence Badel, *Un milieu libéral et européen: Le grand commerce français 1925–1948* (Vincennes: Institut de la gestion publique et du développement économique, Comité pour l'histoire économique et financière de la France, 1999), chapter 1.

[13] Lemercier and Sgard, *Arbitrage privé international*, 12. Jérôme Sgard delivered a paper on the birth of the ICC, "Naissance d'une institution: La Chambre de commerce internationale de Paris" at a conference entitled "Perspectives historiques sur l'arbitrage international en matière de commerce et d'investissements" at the Ecole Normale Supérieure in Paris on June 13, 2017.

[14] Thomas Hale, *Between Interests and Law: The Politics of Transnational Commercial Disputes* (Cambridge: Cambridge University Press, 2015).

[15] Dominic Kelly, "The International Chamber of Commerce as a Diplomatic Actor" (discussion paper, Centre for the Study of Diplomacy, University of Leicester, 2000), 19–20.

[16] Karsten Ronit and Volker Schneider, "Private Organizations and their Contribution to Problem-Solving in the Global Arena," in Karsten Ronit and Volker Schneider (eds.), *Private Organizations in Global Politics* (London: Routledge, 2000), 1. See also Ronit and Schneider, "Global Governance through Private Organizations," *Governance*, 12 (July 1999), 243.

scholars have studied the origins of the ICC and its Court of Arbitration. Indeed, the *Routledge Handbook of International Organization* mentions the ICC only once, in a chapter on the consultative status of NGOs.[17]

## 5.2 Why the Lack of Research?

There may be several reasons for this apparent neglect of ICC history. From a purely practical standpoint, the ICC archives are not freely accessible, meaning that not all scholars interested in the history and evolution of the ICC have had access to the full range of primary sources available. In addition, the ICC Court of Arbitration, whose primary mission is the administration of cases and not the advancement of scholarly research, has done little to make its rich institutional history more widely known. Although the ICC recognizes important moments in its history,[18] it has conducted little research itself into the history of its origins.

But there seems to be another, more profound explanation for the lack of research in this area. Many scholars in the field of international relations have paid more attention to states than to private organizations. As Kelly observed, "In most analyses of global politics, private organizations are ignored or attributed a minor role. . . . For a long time, and with considerable consequences, private organizations were ignored in international affairs research because state-centric approaches were stubbornly defended within this field."[19] In other words, many approaches have been "quite clearly theoretically incapable of capturing the significance of nonstate authority and law" because of the "tendency to theorize authority as a construct of both states and the public sphere, ruling *private authority* out theoretically as an analytically significant consideration."[20] Because of this strong state-centric focus, many researchers have failed to view private institutions such as the ICC as topics worthy of serious academic inquiry.

[17] Felicity Vabulas, "Consultative and Observer Status of NGOs in Intergovernmental Organizations," in Bob Reinalda (ed.), *Routledge Handbook of International Organization* (New York: Routledge, 2013). Druelle-Korn also notes several books on international governance and cooperation in the post–World War I period that make no mention of the ICC; see Druelle-Korn, "Un laboratoire réformateur," 119n42.

[18] See, for example, "ICC Merchants of Peace Recognised," International Chamber of Commerce, https://iccwbo.org/media-wall/news-speeches/icc-merchants-peace-recognised/.

[19] Kelly, *International Chamber of Commerce*, 25.

[20] Claire Cutler, *Private Power and Global Authority: Transnational Merchant Law in the Global Political Economy* (Cambridge: Cambridge University Press, 2003), 79.

Despite these reasons, the scarcity of detailed studies remains puzzling. For instance, the ICC could be considered through the prism of the internationalization of economic activities and institution building at the transnational level, which are topics that have attracted considerable interest from sociologists, political scientists, and international relations scholars.[21] And it is surprising that the ICC, an organization that outlasted the League of Nations and predated the United Nations and the institutions established at the Bretton Woods Conference, has been given short shrift by those interested in these institutions and their associated organs,[22] especially when one considers that the ICC played a major role in brokering the Dawes Plan, which in 1924 attempted to solve the issue of reparations between the Allies and Germany, and took part in no fewer than twenty-nine official conferences convened by the League of Nations between 1927 and 1932.[23]

To this day, the ICC continues to maintain close relations with major international organizations, including the United Nations. In 1946, the ICC was granted general consultative status with the UN Economic and Social Council, a status reserved for organizations that have "substantive and sustained contributions to make to the achievement of the objectives of the United Nations," a "considerable" membership, and are "broadly representative of major segments of society in a large number of countries in different regions of the world."[24] In 2012, France's permanent representative to the United Nations requested that the matter of granting the ICC observer status at the UN General Assembly be added to the provisional agenda for the sixty-seventh session.[25] Several delegations initially opposed this request on the ground that the ICC did not constitute an intergovernmental

[21] See, for example, Marie-Laure Djelic and Sigrid Quack, "Conclusion: Globalization as a Double Process of Institutional Change and Institution Building," in Marie-Laure Djelic and Sigrid Quack (eds.), *Globalization and Institutions: Redefining the Rules of the Economic Game* (Cheltenham: Edward Elgar, 2003).

[22] On the ICC's relationship with the League of Nations, see Lemercier and Sgard, *Arbitrage privé international*, esp. 103–5.

[23] Lyman White, *International Non-Governmental Organizations: Their Purposes, Methods, and Accomplishments* (New Brunswick: Rutgers University Press, 1951), 31 (mentioning that the ICC attended these conferences "at times with full voting rights, at other times in a consultative capacity").

[24] These criteria were set out in ECOSOC Resolution 1996/31 of July 25, 1996, which is the most recent version of the rules on NGO accreditation for consultative status.

[25] "Request for the Inclusion of a Supplementary Item in the Agenda of the Sixty-Seventh Session," UN Doc. A/67/191 (August 15, 2012), www.un.org/en/ga/search/view_doc.asp?symbol=A/67/191.

organization under applicable UN criteria.[26] But on December 13, 2016, in what has been described as "an unprecedented move," the ICC became the first business organization to acquire observer status at the UN General Assembly.[27] The ICC's long-standing relations with the United Nations and its unique position as "the regulator of business globalization"[28] further justify treating its roots and history as subjects of academic inquiry.

[26] See session information, UN General Assembly, Sixth Committee, 69th Session, "Observer Status for the International Chamber of Commerce in the General Assembly (Agenda Item 170)," www.un.org/en/ga/sixth/69/chamber_of_commerce.shtml.

[27] See "ICC Granted UN Observer Status," International Chamber of Commerce, https://iccwbo.org/media-wall/news-speeches/un-general-assembly-grants-observer-status-international-chamber-commerce-historic-decision/.

[28] Michel Aurillac, "La Cour internationale d'arbitrage de la CCI régulatrice de la mondialisation," in Gerald Aksen et al. (eds.), *Global Reflections on International Law, Commerce and Dispute Resolution: Liber Amicorum in Honour of Robert Briner* (Paris: ICC Publishing, 2005).

# 6

# The Construction of a Coherent Framework for International Commercial Arbitration

## 6.1 Introduction

Between October 20 and 24, 1919, a year after the end of World War I, business leaders from Great Britain, France, Belgium, Italy, and the United States met at an international trade conference in Atlantic City, New Jersey. The stated aim of this private business conference was to ascertain "the material and economic needs of the four principal allied nations" and "to what extent the United States could and should supply those needs, and how."[1] Attended by 4,000 people, the conference was described by one of its members as nothing less than "the most important trade meeting in history" and "a corollary to the Peace Conference."[2] The event saw the creation of a so-called Committee on Permanent Organization to discuss plans for establishing an international chamber of commerce. Paris was selected as the city where representatives from the Allied countries would meet again to finalize these plans. In 1920, the constitution and rules of the newly formed organization were adopted, marking the official founding of the International Chamber of Commerce (ICC). Three years later, in 1923, the ICC inaugurated a Court of Arbitration, which soon started administering cases.

The birth of the ICC and its Court of Arbitration brought with it the promise of a new beginning in international arbitration, and international affairs more broadly. Nonetheless, the pendulum movement between

[1] *International Trade Conference* (Atlantic City: Chamber of Commerce of the United States of America, 1919), 11.

[2] *International Trade Conference*, 10. These were the words of Alfred Bedford, who chaired the executive committee for the conference and was the vice-president of the US Chamber of Commerce.

renewal and anxiety could still be seen in the Age of Institutionalization. For example, the Geneva Convention on the Execution of Foreign Awards (1927), which the ICC helped to broker, was strongly colored by a highly territorial mindset, reflecting fears that international arbitration continued to arouse at the time. And yet the ICC also played a major role in the genesis of the New York Convention on the Recognition and Enforcement of Foreign Arbitral Awards (1958), which was an embodiment of renewal, marking the shift from territorialism to internationalism, from the Age of Institutionalization to the Age of Autonomy, and ushering international commercial arbitration into a new era.

This chapter is divided into two sections. The first retraces the origins of the ICC and its Court of Arbitration in the 1920s. The creation of the Court, a body set up to administer cases, was a clear sign that international commercial arbitration was becoming more institutionalized (Section 6.2). The second section explores the tension between renewal and anxiety in the Age of Institutionalization. It presents the Geneva Protocol and the Geneva Convention as expressions of that anxiety and the New York Convention as signaling the swing toward renewal. It also explores the history of each of these instruments and situates some of the *travaux préparatoires* for the New York Convention – in particular, the draft conventions produced by the ICC and the United Nations Economic and Social Council (ECOSOC) – on the renewal/anxiety spectrum (Section 6.3).

Along the way, this chapter hopes to demonstrate that the principal figures who fashioned today's international commercial arbitration regime were private business leaders (that is, potential *users* of the arbitration system) and members of arbitral institutions, rather than Dezalay and Garth's "grand notable arbitrators" and "grand old men" of the 1980s and 1990s.[3] Defying claims that the current system of international commercial arbitration dates from 1963,[4] when the seminal *Gosset* decision was rendered,[5] this chapter looks back to a more distant but no less important past, some forty years earlier.

[3] Yves Dezalay and Bryant Garth, *Dealing in Virtue: International Commercial Arbitration and the Construction of a Transnational Legal Order* (Chicago: Chicago University Press, 1996), 35.

[4] Thomas Clay and Philippe Pinsolle, "General Introduction: The Major Cases of the French Case Law on International Arbitration," in Thomas Clay and Philippe Pinsolle (eds.), *French International Arbitration Law Reports* (Huntington, NY: JurisNet, 2014), v.

[5] Court of Cassation (France), First Civil Chamber, May 7, 1963, *Etablissements Raymond Gosset* v. *Frère Carapelli S.p.A.*, *Revue critique de droit international privé*, 1963, note Motulsky.

## 6.2 The Origins of the International Chamber of Commerce and Its Court of Arbitration

Chronologically, three important milestones should be noted. In 1919, business leaders from Allied countries gathered at the Atlantic City Conference (Section 6.2.1). Then, in 1920, they decided to create a permanent institution, the ICC (Section 6.2.2). And finally, in 1923, realizing that it could play a key role in administering commercial disputes between private parties, the ICC launched its Court of Arbitration (Section 6.2.3).

These dates – 1919, 1920, and 1923 – are frequently overlooked in the literature. Yet they emblematize key aspects of international commercial arbitration: its supranational character, the overlap between public and private interests, and the interrelationship between business and legal circles.

### *6.2.1 The Atlantic City Conference*

#### 6.2.1.1 Historical Background

The 1919 meeting in Atlantic City was not the first international conference to envision a system of business cooperation between business leaders from different countries. It can be seen as part of a broader movement – the "unexpected blossoming"[6] or "proliferation" of international gatherings, "some formed by governments, but most of them resulting from private enterprise"[7] – that predated World War I and was to resume shortly afterward. One such gathering was the International Congress of Chambers of Commerce, which was instituted in 1904 and first convened in 1905 in Liège, Belgium, under the presidency of Louis Canon-Legrand, a Belgian industrialist who later served as a vice-president of the ICC.[8] The congress's purpose was to "secure harmony of action on all international questions affecting commerce and trade by enlisting the cooperation of the various nations to obtain uniform laws with reference to commercial matters."[9] Its wider goal was "to facilitate the commercial intercourse of

[6] Henri la Fontaine and Paul Otlet, "La Vie Internationale et l'effort pour son organisation," *La Vie Internationale*, 1 (1912), 14.

[7] F. S. Northedge, *The League of Nations, Its Life and Times, 1920–1946* (Leicester: Leicester University Press, 1986), 16.

[8] *Fifth International Congress of Chambers of Commerce and Commercial and Industrial Associations* (Boston: Boston Chamber of Commerce, 1912), 5–6. See also John Fahey, "The International Chamber of Commerce," *Annals of the American Academy of Political and Social Science*, 94 (1921), 126.

[9] *Fifth International Congress*, 5.

nations and to promote cordial relationships between them"[10] (similar words would be used in the ICC's 1920 constitution).[11]

In the years leading up to World War I, the International Congress of Chambers of Commerce met biennially – in Milan (1906), Prague (1908), London (1910), Boston (1912), and Paris (1914). On each occasion, the congress grew in both scope and attendance, with the number of delegates reaching 1,000 in Boston and 2,000 in Paris.[12] Some of them would subsequently attend the Atlantic City Conference after the war. Canon-Legrand, the permanent president of the International Congress of Chambers of Commerce, was a member of the Belgian mission in Atlantic City,[13] where he actively participated in the Committee on Permanent Organization.[14] Edward A. Filene, the Massachusetts businessman and philanthropist, and John H. Fahey, who held positions in the newspaper industry,[15] both attended the 1914 congress in Paris.[16] In 1919, Filene returned to Paris as a member of the American delegation that met with Clémentel and others to discuss Allied business interests in the reconstruction of Europe,[17] while, at the Atlantic City Conference, Fahey chaired the Committee on Permanent Organization tasked with creating "some form of permanent international organization."[18]

The subjects covered at these biennial congresses were wide-ranging and numerous, covering such disparate topics as postal reform, maritime routes, and customs formalities, and they soon extended to international commercial arbitration as well.[19] At the 1912 congress in Boston, the following resolution was introduced:

[10] Ibid.

[11] International Chamber of Commerce, *Constitution and Rules of Procedure*, Brochure No. 17 (Paris: ICC International Headquarters, 1920), Article I(2).

[12] *International Trade Conference*, 478–79.

[13] Ibid., 14.

[14] Ibid., 459.

[15] "John H. Fahey Papers," Franklin D. Roosevelt Presidential Library and Museum, www.fdrlibrary.marist.edu/archives/collections/franklin/index.php?p=collections/findingaid&id=147&q=&rootcontentid=116439.

[16] Clotilde Druelle-Korn, "Un laboratoire réformateur, le département du commerce en France et aux États-Unis de la Grande Guerre aux années vingt" (PhD diss., Institut d'études politiques de Paris, dir. Serge Bernstein, 2004) (on file with author), 297.

[17] George Ridgeway, *Merchants of Peace: The History of the International Chamber of Commerce* (Boston: Little, Brown and Company, 1959), 22. See also Druelle-Korn, "Un laboratoire réformateur," 297.

[18] *International Trade Conference*, 461.

[19] *Fifth International Congress*, 10–12.

> The Congress affirms its desire to see convene, as soon as possible, official international conferences which will assure between nations the existence of arbitral jurisdiction conceived in the widest sense of the term, and of a nature to assure an equitable solution of all international disputes either between individuals of different States or between the States themselves.[20]

International commercial arbitration was again discussed at the Paris Congress of Chambers of Commerce two years later. A report on arbitration prepared by the Committee on Arbitration of the Chamber of Commerce of the State of New York, chaired by Charles L. Bernheimer, was submitted to the congress, along with a draft plan for international commercial arbitration.[21] "The spread of the idea of Commercial Arbitration is most encouraging," the report noted.[22] The plan further stated that "organizations such as a Chamber of Commerce, Board of Trade, Merchants' Association or Exchange of high standing or moral influence" should exist in "each important commercial community" to maintain "a system of commercial arbitration" between merchants.[23] Even though this plan was described as "a mere outline or draft presented for the consideration and criticism of commercial bodies throughout the world,"[24] it already contained the idea of a permanent arbitral organization.

At the 1914 Paris congress, further resolutions envisioning an international convention that would unify arbitration laws were passed.[25] They included the following decision:

> It is furthermore VOTED
>
> That the Permanent Committee of the Congress call an international conference composed of representatives of Chambers of Commerce and of Commercial and Industrial Federations and Associations, assisted by lawyers from the different countries represented at the Congress, for the purpose of collecting and considering all the data relative to the practical application of the principle of arbitration between citizens of different

[20] Ibid., 16 (Resolution IX).

[21] Chamber of Commerce of the State of New York, *International Arbitration of Individual Commercial Disputes: Tentative Plan Suggested by the Chamber of Commerce of the State of New York* (New York: Chamber of Commerce of the State of New York, 1914).

[22] "Report of the Chamber of Commerce of the State of New York: International Commercial Arbitration," in Chamber of Commerce of the State of New York, *International Arbitration of Individual Commercial Disputes*, 5.

[23] "Outline of a Plan for International Commercial Arbitration," in Chamber of Commerce of the State of New York, *International Arbitration of Individual Commercial Disputes*, 7.

[24] Ibid., 10.

[25] International Chamber of Commerce, *Commercial Arbitration*, Brochure No. 13 (Paris: ICC International Headquarters, 1921), 6–7.

> countries, and of drawing up a plan for an International Convention on the unification of laws on arbitration;
>
> And that thereupon the Permanent Committee shall transmit this plan to the Government of the French Republic with the request that it invite other nations to an International Diplomatic Conference that shall have for its object the establishment, on the basis of the plan drawn up by the said Conference, of an international agreement with respect to arbitration for the settlement of disputes between citizens of different countries.[26]

As this resolution makes clear, when the Paris congress closed on June 10, 1914, just before the outbreak of war, the idea of a "business men's League of Nations," to use Ridgeway's words, was already germinating.[27]

A key problem, however, was the absence of a permanent secretariat to translate the policies decided at each biennial congress into practice.[28] This problem was highlighted by numerous commentators, who lamented the absence of "a permanent institution responsible for executing the wishes expressed"[29] or "a fundamental organization on which [the congress] might rest."[30] A plan to set up such a body in Brussels had to be abandoned when war broke out.[31] The establishment of the ICC can therefore be seen as the resumption of work begun episodically at the international congresses before the war and its continuation through the creation of a permanent instrument for action.[32]

#### 6.2.1.2 Postwar Efforts to Build a Permanent Organization

The idea of organizing an international business conference in Atlantic City came not from state officials, who were busy attending the Paris Peace Conference, but from private individuals consisting largely of business leaders and members of the nascent mercatocracy. The Chamber of Commerce of the United States played a key and underestimated role in this process, showing how, through the exchange of ideas, business circles on both sides of the Atlantic contributed to building the new institution.

26 Ibid., 7.

27 Ridgeway, *Merchants of Peace*, 15.

28 Fahey, "International Chamber of Commerce," 126.

29 Léon Magnier, *La Chambre de commerce internationale* (Paris: Arthur Rousseau, 1928), 7.

30 Roberto Pozzi, "Conciliation and Arbitration between Merchants of Different Countries. Memorandum Submitted by M. Roberto Pozzi," in International Chamber of Commerce, *Commercial Arbitration*, Brochure No. 13, 8.

31 Nigel Blackburn, *World Peace through World Trade*, ICC Publication No. 342 (Paris: International Chamber of Commerce, 1979), 4.

32 See Eugène Schneider, *Le voyage des missions économiques des pays alliés aux États-Unis et le Congrès d'Atlantic-City, octobre-novembre 1919* (Paris: Imprimerie Chaix, 1919), 27.

Schneider's account of the origins of the ICC relates that, before the armistice, representatives from the British Chambers of Commerce invited their American counterparts to visit them in England. The Chamber of Commerce of the United States, which had been founded in 1912 with the support of the Taft administration,[33] declined the invitation on account of the war effort. When the war was over, however, it was they who invited the British Chambers of Commerce to visit the United States, and their invitation was extended to other members of Allied countries as well.[34]

The American business leaders' proposal to meet reached the French in April 1919. Druelle-Korn tells us that on April 28, 1919, Jean Monnet, head of the London mission of the ministry of commerce, wrote a note to Clémentel, the French minister of commerce, recounting his meeting with Edward A. Filene and Edward G. Miner. (Monnet had been introduced to Filene and Miner by Thomas W. Lamont, a banker at J. P. Morgan & Co., who served as the US Treasury Department's representative at the Paris Peace Conference.)[35] The Monnet memorandum described the Americans' goals as being: "a) to realize a project to organize an international chamber of commerce, b) study Europe's economic needs locally and explore the form that American aid might take."[36] The memorandum went on: "Acknowledging that the European economic problem could be solved only if America were to grant Europe large loans, and realizing that American public opinion was insufficiently alert to the question, Messrs. Filene and Miner suggested that a sort of economic propaganda mission be sent to the U.S."[37] The memorandum further stated that the US Chamber of Commerce would be in charge of logistics and cover a portion of the expenses.[38]

Shortly after that memorandum was written, a meeting was organized in Paris between members of the American delegation, Clémentel, and Georges Pascalis, who was the president of the Paris Chamber of Commerce.[39] The

33 "U.S. Chamber of Commerce. The Early Years," US Chamber of Commerce, www.uschamber.com/sites/default/files/uscc_HistoryBook.pdf, 5–7.

34 Schneider, *Le voyage*, 4.

35 Edward M. Lamont, *The Ambassador from Wall Street: The Story of Thomas W. Lamont, J. P. Morgan's Chief Executive* (Lanham: Madison Books, 1994). This reference is in Druelle-Korn, "Un laboratoire réformateur," 280n407.

36 "Note de Jean Monnet à Clémentel en date du 28 avril 1919," in Druelle-Korn, "Un laboratoire réformateur," app. VIII(a), 586.

37 Ibid.

38 Ibid., 587.

39 *Proceedings: Organization Meeting of the International Chamber of Commerce; Paris, France, June 23 to 30, 1920* (Paris: ICC International Headquarters, 1920), 162.

American delegation's objective was "crystal clear. It was a matter of impressing US businessmen and, through them, American public opinion as a whole, of fully illuminating the problem of American aid for their European allies, and determining how this aid could be provided."[40] Practical solutions to the problems of the day would be found if business leaders from Allied countries all met at the same time. "Just come to America," the American delegation told Clémentel and Pascalis. "You will make our compatriots over there understand what you have convinced us of in France."[41]

It took no time for Clémentel to grasp the potential significance of this "economic propaganda mission." As Schneider recalled, Clémentel "had the merit of immediately grasping the value that the suggestions put to him by the American delegates would have for France."[42] ("The only merit I have, if indeed I have any, is to have understood the importance of economic cooperation," Clémentel would later proclaim.[43]) At a time when negotiations at the Paris Peace Conference were becoming tense, Clémentel saw the American proposal as a way to push forward the French economic postwar agenda.[44] Furthermore, Clémentel may also have been trying to promote the newly founded Confédération générale de la production française (CGPF) by giving it a key role in selecting the French delegation.[45]

An important question was who should lead the French delegation. As *Le Matin* reported, it needed to be headed by "one of the foremost men, best informed about the country's affairs."[46] The person chosen was Eugène Schneider, a wealthy industrialist, who had become the chairman of the French iron and steel mill Schneider-Creusot in 1898 and also served as a *député*.[47] Schneider had already made a name for himself in the United States, and Clémentel thought this would help ensure the success of the French delegation.[48] Moreover, the selection of Schneider made commercial sense: as the *New York Times* reported, the meeting

40 Schneider, *Le voyage*, 6.

41 *Le Matin*, May 19, 1919, 1.

42 Schneider, *Le voyage*, 7.

43 *Proceedings: Organization Meeting*, 22.

44 Druelle-Korn, "Un laboratoire réformateur," 278.

45 Ibid.

46 "Vers une politique économique interalliée," *Le Matin*, July 25, 1919, 1.

47 "Eugène Schneider 1868–1942," Assemblée nationale, www2.assemblee-nationale.fr/sycomore/fiche/(num_dept)/6351. As his obituary would recall at the time of his death, "[t]hat very young man had immediately understood how important the collaboration of private industry would be to his country in the event of an international conflict." Léon Guillet, "Notice biographique. Eugène Schneider (1868–1942)," *Revue de métallurgie*, 5 (1943), 156.

48 Druelle-Korn, "Un laboratoire réformateur," 286–87.

would be "of particular interest to steel manufacturers," since the delegations present would include "representatives of steel interests, as well as men concerned with financial and shipping affairs."[49]

Looking more widely at the composition of the entire French delegation, one is struck by the number of business leaders, as opposed to government officials, politicians, or jurists.[50] One of the few jurists in the group was Édouard Dolléans, an *agrégé* in law who wrote a multivolume history of the French labor movement.[51] Under Clémentel's tenure as president of the ICC, Dolléans became general secretary of the ICC, much to the surprise of contemporary biographers.[52] Other delegations, too, were likewise predominantly composed of business and industrial leaders,[53] which shows the influence private business interests had on the genesis of the Atlantic City Conference, and by consequence the ICC. Indeed, both resulted from a private business initiative to which the public authorities tacitly assented. In this respect, the birth of the ICC lay at the intersection between public and private interests, marking a new dynamic in the relationship between the State and the mercatocracy.

The French delegation was ready at the end of the summer of 1919 and in early October, along with the delegations from Belgium, Italy, and the United Kingdom, set sail for the United States aboard the troopship *Northern Pacific*, which was repatriating American soldiers who had fought in the war.

[49] "Steel Men Coming to Trade Meeting," *New York Times*, October 12, 1919.

[50] In addition to Schneider, the French delegation included Baron du Marais, director of Credit Lyonnais; Homberg, vice-president of the Société Générale; Roche, director of Poulene Brothers; and François-Poncet, delegate of the Steel Committee in France. See *International Trade Conference*, 14–15.

[51] Édouard Dolléans, *Histoire du mouvement ouvrier* (Paris: Armand Colin, 1948 [vols. 1, 2], 1953 [vol. 3]).

[52] See, for example, Jean-François Eck, "La Chambre de commerce internationale: les positions des représentants français," in Sylvain Schirmann (ed.), *Organisations internationales et architectures européennes 1929–1939: Actes du colloque de Metz (31 mai–1er juin 2001); En hommage à Raymond Poidevin* (Metz: Centre de recherche histoire et civilisation, 2003), 304. Druelle-Korn shares the same sense of surprise (Druelle-Korn, "Un laboratoire réformateur," 312n461).

[53] For example, in addition to Canon-Legrand, the Belgian delegation included representatives of the National Bank of Belgium, the Savings Bank of Belgium, and the Antwerp Chamber of Commerce. Likewise, the British delegation included officers of the Bank of Liverpool, the London Chamber of Commerce, and the Federation of British Industries. The full list of foreign delegates at Atlantic City can be found in Appendix 6.1 to this chapter.

### 6.2.2 The Founding of the International Chamber of Commerce

#### 6.2.2.1 Paris as the Location of the ICC's Headquarters

Even though the Atlantic City Conference was an exercise in economic propaganda, delegates hoped that a more permanent organization would come out of it. The idea of a permanent organization was evoked by delegates as soon as they set foot in the United States to attend the conference. In the *New York Times*, Schneider was quoted as saying: "The organization of some kind of permanent business establishment, not unlike a world chamber of commerce, will be one of the things accomplished at the International Conference at Atlantic City next week."[54]

At the conference, a so-called Committee on Permanent Organization was constituted to discuss, as its name implied, plans for establishing a permanent organization. The committee was chaired by John H. Fahey and included individuals who had been involved in prewar efforts to set up a permanent organization,[55] such as Canon-Legrand, the permanent president of the International Congress of Chambers of Commerce. During the committee's discussions over several days, two matters appeared to be of particular importance.

The first concerned which countries should be allowed to join the new organization. It was unanimously decided that the five Allied nations of Belgium, France, Italy, the United Kingdom, and the United States should be founding members, and that other "approved Allied and neutral nations" would be allowed to join, "leaving the approval to the discretion of the proper governing body of the organization."[56] So, "only the five nations that attended the Atlantic City Congress were to form the permanent organization."[57] It was clear that "Germany and her allies are barred from the international body and no provision was made for their entrance at a later date."[58] (Millerand later predicted that, eventually, "other members, other Allies, neutral parties will join you. A time will come when even those who have fought against us will be admitted."[59] Germany did indeed join the newly formed organization in 1925.[60]) On the question of

[54] "Wants a Business League for World: Eugène Schneider of Creusot Works Urges a Great Chamber of Commerce," *New York Times*, October 15, 1919.

[55] The full list of committee members can be found in Appendix 6.2 to this chapter.

[56] *International Trade Conference*, 461.

[57] Schneider, "Le voyage," 27.

[58] "To Start World's Business League: Committee of Trade Leaders Adopts Plan for International Chamber of Commerce," *New York Times*, October 22, 1919.

[59] "Inauguration de la Chambre de commerce internationale," *Le Temps*, June 30, 1920, 4.

[60] Druelle-Korn, "Un laboratoire réformateur," 305.

membership, it was also decided that "membership should be confined to business and financial men, inviting government co-operation."[61] Thus, the ICC's relative independence vis-à-vis states was a key feature from the outset.

A second question of importance was where the future organization should be located. A draft document discussed on October 21, 1919, stated: "It is desired that the seats of the permanent organization be located in (*to be determined*)."[62] At another meeting of the committee on the same day, delegates expressed the view that "probably it would be wise to have the permanent headquarters of this organization in close proximity to the headquarters of the organization of the League of Nations, perhaps in the same city," but that the matter "should be given further consideration" at a later date.[63]

There was widespread speculation as to where the new headquarters would be located. As the press initially reported, "[i]t was predicted, following the meeting, that the headquarters would be in Geneva," whereas France would be "the Big Buyer."[64] For a while, Atlantic City was also considered "as the official headquarters of the proposed World League of Business." All delegates attending the conference were "delighted with the arrangements and hospitality for the week at the shore, and are in a favorable frame of mind to act in choosing the resort as a permanent meeting place."[65] Ultimately, Paris was selected as the city where the representatives of the five Allied countries would meet to put together a complete plan for the organization.

Many reasons can be advanced for the choice of Paris as the location of the ICC's headquarters. It could arguably be seen as a gesture to Étienne Clémentel,[66] a national figure in France[67] and instrumental in the

[61] *International Trade Conference*, 461.

[62] Ibid., 466 (emphasis added).

[63] Ibid., 475.

[64] *New York Times*, October 22, 1919.

[65] "May be a World Centre: Atlantic City Hopes to be Permanent Home of Business League," *New York Times*, October 27, 1919.

[66] See *World Peace through World Trade*.

[67] A native of the Auvergne region, Étienne Clémentel (1864–1936) came from a modest background. Recent research by Guy Rousseau (as yet unpublished) reveals that Clémentel did not receive a university education in the humanities and the law (as was previously thought); he took his *baccalauréat* exam in 1883, worked in the French administration (as *surnuméraire de l'Enregistrement*) from 1883 to 1888, and then managed to take a law exam (*capacité de droit*) and become a notary public. Clémentel taught himself economics and in 1900 (not 1930, as was previously thought) wrote a textbook on international commerce, which remained unpublished (see Archives départementales du Puy-de-Dôme, Fonds

creation of the ICC.[68] As minister of commerce, he was responsible for sending the French delegation to the Atlantic City Conference (1919).[69] He became the ICC's first president (from 1920 to 1923) and was also particularly committed to the establishment of its Court of Arbitration.[70] His role at the ICC, prior to his illness in 1930, has been described as "pivotal."[71] He made a number of important speeches and also established close contacts with the League of Nations. (Clémentel was close to Léon Bourgeois, the first president of the League of Nations, and both men belonged to the same party, the Gauche radicale.)[72]

Clémentel, Doc. 5J97; Clotilde Druelle-Korn, "De la pensée à l'action économique: Étienne Clémentel (1864–1936), un ministre visionnaire," *Histoire@Politique*, 16 (2012), 40–54). He then moved into local and national politics, serving as a deputy between 1900 and 1919 and as a senator between 1920 and 1936. He held various government portfolios as, successively, minister for France's colonies (1905–1906), agriculture (1913), finance (1914), and commerce, industry, and postal/telegraphy services (1915–19). He played a key role during World War I, helping to shape French economic policy and insisting on inter-Allied cooperation over a reparations system (see Marc Trachtenberg, "'A New Economic Order': Étienne Clémentel and French Economic Diplomacy during the First World War," *French Historical Studies*, 10 (1977), 315–41). In addition, Clémentel was an art patron and collector and an artist himself, notably exploring color photography at a time when it was still in its infancy (see Louise Arizzoli, "Clémentel photographe: les autochromes," in Marie-Christine Kessler and Guy Rousseau (eds.), *Étienne Clémentel. Politique et action publique sous la Troisième République* (Brussels: Peter Lang, 2018); Arizzoli, "Autochromes by Étienne Clémentel (-1864–1936): An Enlightened Approach to Early Color Photography," *Études photographiques*, 35 (2017); Edmond Haraucourt, *L'œuvre artistique d'Étienne Clémentel* (Paris: Lapina, 1927)). His friends included Monet and Rodin, who sculpted the bust of Clémentel (see Figure 6.1) that continues to adorn the ICC's headquarters in Paris to this day. See also, for example, Marie-Christine Kessler and Guy Rousseau (eds.), *Étienne Clémentel: Politique et action publique sous la Troisième République* (Brussels: Peter Lang, 2018); Guy Rousseau, *Étienne Clémentel (1864–1936): Entre idéalisme et réalisme, une vie politique* (Clermont-Ferrand: Archives départementales du Puy-de-Dôme, 1998); Claude Paillat, *Dossiers secrets de la France contemporaine*, vol. 1, *1919: Les illusions de la gloire* (Paris: Laffont, 1979), 200–28; Richard Kuisel, *Le capitalisme et l'État en France: Modernisation et dirigisme au XXe siècle* (Paris: Gallimard, 1984), whose twenty-five plus pages on Clémentel (and preface to the book by Jean-Noël Jeanneney) have done much to raise awareness of him among modern readers.

[68] See Clotilde Druelle-Korn, "Étienne Clémentel président-fondateur de la Chambre de commerce internationale," in Marie-Christine Kessler and Guy Rousseau (eds.), *Étienne Clémentel: Politique et action publique sous la Troisième République* (Brussels: Peter Lang, 2018).

[69] See Section 6.2.1.2.

[70] Blackburn, *World Peace*; Magnier, *La Chambre de commerce internationale*, 21.

[71] Clotilde Druelle-Korn, "The Great War: Matrix of the International Chamber of Commerce, a Fortunate Business League of Nations," in Andrew Smith, Kevin Tennent, and Simon Mollan (eds.), *The Impact of the First World War on International Business* (London: Routledge, 2016), 109.

[72] Ibid., 110. See also Claire Lemercier and Jérôme Sgard, *Arbitrage privé international et globalisation(s): Rapport final* (March 2015), 103.

**Figure 6.1** Anonymous photograph of Étienne Clémentel posing near his bust by Auguste Rodin, taken at the Galerie Bernheim Jeune in Paris in 1926. Private collection. Started in 1915, the bust was to be Rodin's last sculpture before his death in 1917. On the sculpture, see Arizzoli, "Clémentel photographe"; Albert Elsen, *All the Masks Fall Off: Rodin's Last Sculpture, The Portrait of Clémentel* (Memphis: Memphis Brooks Museum of Art, 1988).

A more strategic reason, suggested by Druelle-Korn, was that Paris seemed like a good compromise between the Americans, who wanted the new organization to be located "close to Geneva and potential market opportunities"; the French, who had suggested Washington; and the English, who had suggested Brussels or Paris.[73] In addition, France had been heavily affected by the war: "In choosing Paris as the seat for its future Permanent Organization Congress," Schneider wrote, "the Atlantic City Conference demonstrated its

[73] Druelle-Korn, "Great War," 106–7.

**Figure 6.2** Anonymous photograph of a founding meeting of the International Chamber of Commerce in Paris in 1920. Private collection of Dr. Guy Rousseau. All rights reserved.

faith and trust in our country."[74] Clémentel also explained that choosing Paris was a way to "express gratitude to France – France, who during four tragic years fought for the common cause without flinching even for a moment, because she had confidence in her ideal."[75]

With hindsight, the decision to locate the permanent organization in Paris can be seen as highly significant. By bringing together scholars and practitioners in the same city, it contributed to shaping modern (French) international commercial arbitration law and practice. It also brought important direct and indirect economic benefits to the city. And it doubtless goes some way to explaining why Paris is today portrayed as "the home of international arbitration."[76]

[74] Schneider, "Le voyage," 28.
[75] *Proceedings: Organization Meeting*, 15.
[76] "Paris Arbitration, the Home of International Arbitration," Paris Arbitration, www.parisarbitration.com/en/.

#### 6.2.2.2 The ICC's Organization Meeting

The so-called Organization Meeting of the ICC commenced on June 23, 1920, in the Salle du Comité des Forges.[77] More than 140 representatives from American chambers of commerce and industrial organizations attended the meeting.[78] Lengthy discussions took place on the new organization's constitution, which was adopted unanimously.[79] It opened with the statement, "This association shall be known as the International Chamber of Commerce." Reiterating the lofty goals that had been mentioned at the prewar International Congress of Chambers of Commerce, it went on to describe the organization's purpose as being: "to facilitate the commercial intercourse of nations, to secure harmony of action on all international questions affecting commerce and industry, and to promote peace, progress, and cordial relations among countries and their citizens by the cooperation of business men and their organizations devoted to the development of commerce and industry."[80]

On June 28, 1920, the ICC was officially constituted at a public meeting in the Sorbonne's *Grand Amphithéâtre* in Paris, in the presence of Millerand, the prime minister and future president of France, and other senior politicians.[81] "It is under the auspices of this comforting and symbolic event encapsulating an entire program that I place the destinies of the International Chamber of Commerce and officially declare it established," Clémentel announced.[82] Schneider, who spoke on behalf of the French delegation, referred to two recurrent themes: the ICC's independence vis-à-vis states and its membership consisting of private business and industrial leaders. "What will become of the League of Nations?" Schneider asked, at a time when no one could have guessed that the ICC would outlive the League of Nations. "I cannot say. Time will tell. But I can

77 *Proceedings: Organization Meeting*, 177, app. A. This place could be seen as symbolizing the "bridge" that was being "thrown over the Atlantic" (ibid., 23).

78 Ibid., 16. This is Clémentel's figure; the *New York Times* mentioned 170 delegates. See "Commerce Chamber to Discuss Prices: Delegates to Go to Paris," *New York Times*, April 26, 1920; "Delegates Sail for Commerce Meeting," *New York Times*, May 24, 1920; "Ready for New Trade Body: Plans Drawn for First Meeting of International Chamber of Commerce," *New York Times*, May 22, 1920.

79 *Proceedings: Organization Meeting*, 35.

80 Ibid., 195, app. C.

81 "Inauguration de la Chambre de commerce internationale," 3–4. The speeches delivered that day – by Clémentel and the heads of the five delegations from the Allied countries – do not appear in the Organization Meeting's official brochure, but they can be found in a detailed two-page article published in the French newspaper *Le Matin* on June 30.

82 "Inauguration de la Chambre de commerce internationale," 3.

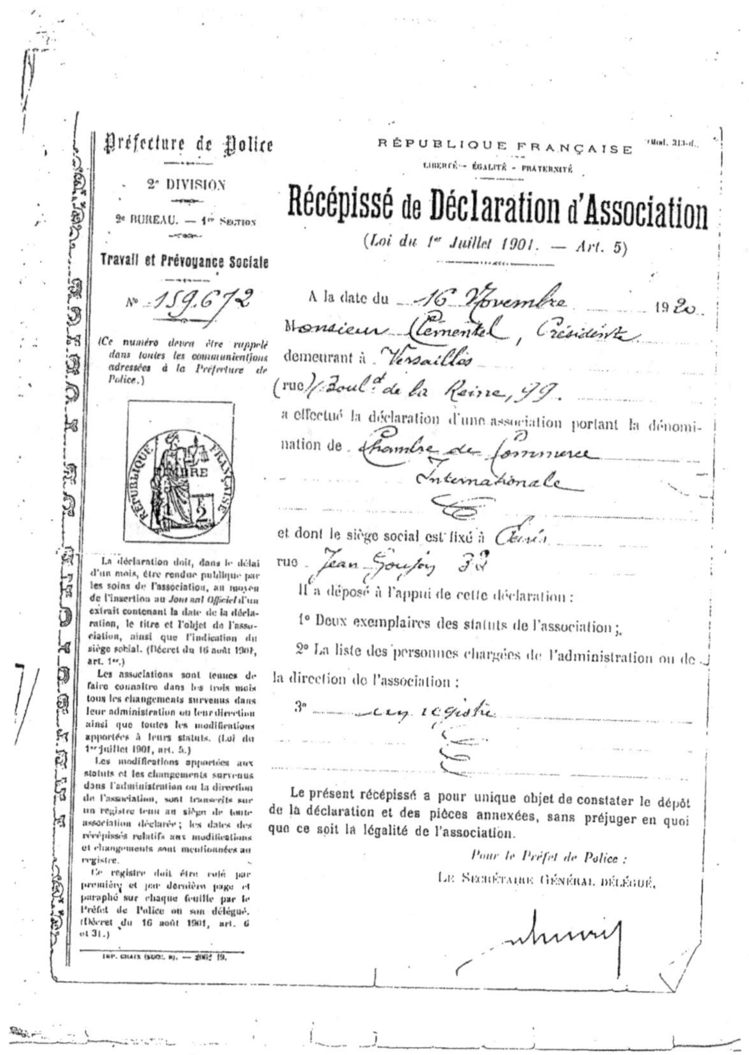

Préfecture de Police

2e DIVISION

2e BUREAU. — 1re SECTION

Travail et Prévoyance Sociale

N° 159672

(Ce numéro devra être rappelé dans toutes les communications adressées à la Préfecture de Police.)

RÉPUBLIQUE FRANÇAISE

LIBERTÉ - ÉGALITÉ - FRATERNITÉ

Récépissé de Déclaration d'Association

(*Loi du 1er Juillet 1901. — Art. 5*)

A la date du 16 Novembre 1920

Monsieur Clementel, Président

demeurant à Versailles

(rue) Boul^d de la Reine, 99.

a effectué la déclaration d'une association portant la dénomination de Chambre de Commerce Internationale

et dont le siège social est fixé à Paris

rue Jean Goujon 33

Il a déposé à l'appui de cette déclaration :

1° Deux exemplaires des statuts de l'association ;

2° La liste des personnes chargées de l'administration ou de la direction de l'association :

3° un registre

Le présent récépissé a pour unique objet de constater le dépôt de la déclaration et des pièces annexées, sans préjuger en quoi que ce soit la légalité de l'association.

*Pour le Préfet de Police :*

LE SECRÉTAIRE GÉNÉRAL DÉLÉGUÉ,

La déclaration doit, dans le délai d'un mois, être rendue publique par les soins de l'association, au moyen de l'insertion au *Journal Officiel* d'un extrait contenant la date de la déclaration, le titre et l'objet de l'association, ainsi que l'indication du siège social. (Décret du 16 août 1901, art. 1er.)

Les associations sont tenues de faire connaître dans les trois mois tous les changements survenus dans leur administration ou leur direction ainsi que toutes les modifications apportées à leurs statuts. (Loi du 1er juillet 1901, art. 5.)

Les modifications apportées aux statuts et les changements survenus dans l'administration ou la direction de l'association, sont transcrits sur un registre tenu au siège de toute association déclarée ; les dates des récépissés relatifs aux modifications et changements sont mentionnées au registre.

Ce registre doit être coté par première et par dernière page et paraphé sur chaque feuille par le Préfet de Police ou son délégué. (Décret du 16 août 1901, art. 6 et 31.)

IMP. CHAIX (SUCC. B). — 2062 19.

**Figure 6.3** Declaration by the ICC of an *association* in its name under the Law of July 1, 1901. Reproduced with kind permission of Dr. Emmanuel Jolivet. The ICC's legal status under French law is that of a non-profit-making organization, known in French as an *Association Loi 1901*. The ICC has changed its location in Paris three times in the course of its existence. It was originally housed at 33 rue Jean Goujon in Paris, as shown on the declaration of association; on October 9, 1926, the headquarters were officially transferred to 38 Cours Albert 1er; and, on October 30, 2013, they were officially transferred to 33–43 avenue du Président Wilson, in a wing of the Palais d'Iéna, within walking distance of Cours Albert 1er.

affirm that the private men that we are carry within us the spirit of the League of Nations and as such, whatever happens, it is certain not to die. For straightaway we are putting its ideal into practice."[83]

### 6.2.3 *The Birth of the ICC Court of Arbitration*

#### 6.2.3.1 Plans to Create a Court of Arbitration

Although the administration of disputes was not the primary purpose of the ICC, the organization quickly became "vitally interested" in the subject of international commercial arbitration.[84] As Eisemann explained, "the setting up of a centre of international commercial arbitration within the framework of the institution" became a top priority for its members.[85] The subject found its way onto the drafting agenda for the original constitution, which was drawn up by the Committee on Permanent Organization under the presidency of John H. Fahey and adopted at the 1920 congress in Paris. This constitution included the following provision:

> When the parties to a contract bearing on international commerce agree to submit to arbitration a difference of opinion due to the execution of such contract, they may choose as an arbitration board one or several of the members of the Administration Commission, who shall act as an arbitration board. The decision of the arbitration board shall be submitted to the General Secretary who shall forthwith transmit it to the parties concerned.[86]

From the outset, therefore, the Administrative Commission was to play a key role. Chaired by the general secretary of the International Headquarters[87] – Édouard Dolléans at the time – it was composed of individuals selected by ICC member organizations at national level.[88]

[83] Ibid.

[84] "Arbitration and the ICC," *ICC News*, 29, no. 3 (1958), 2.

[85] Frédéric Eisemann, "The Court of Arbitration: Outline of Its Changes from Inception to the Present Day," in *60 Years of ICC Arbitration: A Look at the Future* (Paris: ICC Publishing, 1984), 391.

[86] Article VII, section 3, of the 1920 constitution. See *Proceedings: Organization Meeting*, 204.

[87] Article VII, section 2, of the 1920 constitution. See ibid.

[88] Article VII, section 2, of the 1920 constitution. See ibid., 203. Members of the Administrative Commission were required to reside at the place where the International Headquarters were situated, namely Paris, in order to keep the general secretary informed of "the special interests and problems of their respective countries" and of "the progress in their respective countries of the policies of the International Chamber."

After the 1920 Paris congress, a special so-called Committee on International Commercial Arbitration was set up under the chairmanship of Lyon-Caen, permanent secretary of the Académie des sciences morales et politiques and formerly dean of the Paris law faculty.[89] The committee appointed two subcommissions[90] and tasked Roberto Pozzi, the legal adviser to the Italian Cotton Association, with the drafting of a general report on conciliation and arbitration, which was to be presented at the 1921 congress in London.[91] Noting in his report that "the use of conciliation and arbitration has become more and more widely diffused,"[92] Pozzi described the ICC as "a sort of Supreme Court of International Commerce."[93] Pozzi explained that the Committee on International Commercial Arbitration had "recognized the wisdom and timeliness of the creation of an organism for conciliation and arbitration to form part of the International Chamber of Commerce, and to be based upon its Constitution."[94] The report concluded by expressing the hope that the committee had made "a first step towards the organization and actuation of international arbitration."[95]

A few weeks after the Pozzi report was completed, the first congress of the ICC opened in London. It was attended by 500 delegates and chaired by Albert Hobson, vice-president of the ICC and chairman of the British national committee. The congress considered twenty-seven resolutions, two of which concerned arbitration.[96] They were adopted unanimously. All that remained was to launch a permanent organization to implement them.

89 Ridgeway, *Merchants of Peace*, 319. The committee included Edouard Huysmans (Belgium), Oliver Bodington (Great Britain), Roberto Pozzi and Ugo Capitani (Italy), Philip von Hemert (Netherlands), S. G. Archibald (United States), and Édouard Dolléans (general secretary of the Chamber). International Chamber of Commerce, *Commercial Arbitration*, Brochure No. 13, 3.

90 The legal subcommission was to consider legislative reforms necessary to unify arbitration procedure, while the regulations' subcommission was to draw up regulations to govern international arbitration conducted by the International Chamber of Commerce. Ibid., 3.

91 Pozzi, "Conciliation and Arbitration," 5.

92 Ibid., 5–6.

93 Ibid., 8.

94 Ibid., 9.

95 Ibid., 21.

96 International Chamber of Commerce, *London Congress 1921: Resolutions Adopted*, Brochure No. 18, 20–22. Resolution XIV sought to make the arbitration clause valid in all countries and stated that the procedure in legal arbitration should be uniform in all countries. Resolution XV approved the proposals for rules relating to conciliation and arbitration presented by the legal subcommission of the Committee on International Commercial Arbitration.

#### 6.2.3.2 The Inauguration of the Court of Arbitration

Plans to create "an international court for hearing commercial disputes between nationals of the various countries" were approved by the Executive Committee of the ICC in late May 1922.[97] On January 19, 1923, the Court of Commercial Arbitration of the ICC was finally inaugurated. The meeting took place in the large hearings chamber of the Tribunal de Commerce de la Seine and was attended by more than 500 people, including members of the French government[98] and various other personalities.[99] The choice of venue is significant: the implication is that, despite being a private initiative, the ICC and the broader arbitration community would endeavor to work hand in hand with the domestic courts.

The speeches delivered on that day included some that praised the justice system – as if to forestall criticism about arbitration – and others that subtly pointed to its weaknesses – as if to promote the work of the Court of Arbitration. For instance, Clémentel, whose speech, filled with handwritten notes, can be found in his personal papers, profusely thanked the officials in the room and described the ICC's agenda as "work of general interest."[100] As he explained, "I feel sure that all the traders, manufacturers, and financiers of the world pay, as I do, a sincere tribute to the Law Courts of the various countries. Their equity, their impartiality, their devotion to the public cause are above all criticism."[101] He added that "the root principle of the Rules [of Arbitration] is that the Court of Arbitration of the ICC is not a Court which judges: it is the organization which appoints the arbitrators and directs the procedure of the disputes under consideration."[102] In a passage that seemed targeted at van Hamel, representing the general secretary of the League of

[97] "Adopts World Court for Trade Disputes: International Chamber of Commerce Plan to Be Put in Effect at Once," *New York Times*, May 27, 1922; "Form World Court for Arbitration of Trade Disputes: United States and 27 Other Nations to Be Represented on International Tribunal," *New York Times*, November 6, 1922.

[98] Maurice Colrat, minister of justice, and Lucien Dior, minister of commerce.

[99] The president of the British National Committee and vice-president of the ICC Sir Albert J. Hobson, the director of the legal section of the League of Nations Dr. van Hamel, the president of the Dutch Chamber of Commerce in Paris and president of the executive committee of the Court of Arbitration Philip von Hemert, and the ambassadors and ministers from the thirty-two countries in which the International Chamber of Commerce had national member organizations. The full list of initial members of the Court of Arbitration of the International Chamber of Commerce can be found in Appendix 6.3 to this chapter.

[100] *Inauguration of the Court of Commercial Arbitration: January 19th 1923*, Brochure No. 22 (Paris: ICC International Headquarters, 1923), 14.

[101] Ibid., 16.

[102] Ibid., 17.

Nations Sir Eric Drummond, Clémentel recalled that "[t]here are already in existence a certain number of international institutions, which hold authority in arbitration matters," and made it clear that the ICC "does not wish to compete with these existing organizations, it merely wishes to complete their work by extending it as much as possible."[103]

Alongside these qualifications, Clémentel deftly included criticism of the domestic justice system. He noted that

> [s]trict justice ... has the very defects of its qualities: this equity, this impartiality demand on the part of the judges a much closer examination of the matters in hand, all the more so as those being judged are a long way from their judges. The procedure will therefore of necessity be longer when it is a question of settling an international dispute. The two parties will be put to a certain amount of expense and, owing to delays, may suffer from a locking up of capital which may cause them considerable inconvenience. Moreover, international disputes usually bear on questions of a technical nature, which can only be settled by a technical expert. The judge will therefore have to consult an expert and in many cases his opinion will determine the award.[104]

Many arguments used to promote arbitration in subsequent decades can already be found in Clémentel's inaugural address. While domestic courts, as Clémentel claimed, would lead to delays, extra expense, and "considerable inconvenience" in international disputes, the Court of Arbitration would be cheaper and faster in comparison. And while judges often had to consult an expert and frequently ended up following the expert's advice, the Court of Arbitration made it possible to have direct recourse to such an individual. Implied in Clémentel's address was the notion that, for "business men and practical men of action,"[105] international arbitration might be a superior form of justice.

Clémentel's speech was well received by those in attendance. Colrat, the minister of justice, assured the audience that "[t]he French Government is glad that Paris has been chosen as the seat of the International Chamber of Commerce."[106] A reception took place in the gallery of the Tribunal de Commerce de la Seine. Clémentel then read an "acceptance of warrant," which was unanimously approved by the Court of Arbitration.[107] The warrant stated that the 1922 Rules of Conciliation and Arbitration would be put into force and that the procedure of

103 Ibid., 18.
104 Ibid., 16.
105 Ibid.
106 Ibid., 32.
107 Ibid., 33.

conciliation and arbitration was "at the disposail [*sic*] of manufacturers, business men and financiers of any country for the settlement of their international commercial disputes, whether they are, or not, Members of the ICC and whether, or not, their country is affiliated to the Chamber, or to the League of Nations."[108]

Members of the Court of Arbitration later met with President Millerand, who, as prime minister, had been present at the 1920 meeting at the Sorbonne. He "recalled the fact that he had always been a warm advocate of arbitration and stated that he viewed the creation of such an institution, as the Arbitration Court of the ICC, with the keenest interest."[109] The Court of Arbitration of the ICC was thus launched.

## 6.3 The ICC's Efforts to Build a Coherent Framework for International Commercial Arbitration

The birth of the ICC and its Court of Arbitration can be seen as emblematic of the Age of Institutionalization, marking a new phase in the modern history of international commercial arbitration. This period was nonetheless marked by an oscillation between anxiety and renewal. The movement toward anxiety can be seen most clearly in two international instruments that were developed in the 1920s for international arbitration: the Geneva Protocol on Arbitration Clauses (1923) and the Geneva Convention on the Execution of Foreign Awards (1927). They reflected a highly *territorial* mindset, underscoring some of the fears that were still associated with international commercial arbitration at the time (Section 6.3.1). By contrast, the end of the Age of Institutionalization and the beginning of the Age of Autonomy gravitated in the opposite direction, from anxiety to renewal. This change of mindset – from territorialism to internationalism – is reflected in the Convention on the Recognition and Enforcement of Foreign Arbitral Awards (1958), which heralded a new age in international commercial arbitration (Section 6.3.2). It can also be seen in the writings of scholars and practitioners, who investigated new questions and laid the groundwork for future developments in the field (Section 6.3.3).

[108] Ibid.
[109] Ibid., 43.

### *6.3.1 Territorialism in the Age of Institutionalization: The Geneva Framework*

No sooner had the ICC been founded than it started to become intensely active in the field of international arbitration. Despite some early difficulties in making its voice heard, it succeeded in building a coherent international framework for international commercial arbitration. The Geneva Protocol on Arbitration Clauses, which was adopted on September 24, 1923, and entered into force on July 28, 1924, dealt with the international validity of arbitration *clauses*, while the Geneva Convention on the Execution of Foreign Awards, which was adopted on September 26, 1927, and entered into force on July 25, 1929, concerned the international recognition and enforcement of arbitration *awards*.

#### 6.3.1.1 The 1923 Geneva Protocol on Arbitration Clauses

In the 1920s, it was becoming increasingly clear in legal and economic circles that an international instrument was needed to ensure the international validity of arbitration clauses. As Brachet explained, international arbitration was enjoying "ever increasing favor. . . . But the full development of this arbitration depends on solving two big problems: the international validity of arbitration clauses and the international enforcement of arbitral awards."[110] The International Chamber of Commerce felt that this was a question worth exploring. At the 1921 congress in London, it adopted a resolution recommending that arbitration clauses "be declared valid by all countries" and that "in all countries an effort be made to secure legislation that will render executory the awards of foreign arbitrators without reference to the nationality of the parties."[111] At its following congress, held in Rome in March 1923, it returned to the issue of the validity of arbitration clauses:

> The International Chamber of Commerce considers that it is of the highest importance to the commerce of the world that the practice of international commercial arbitration should be facilitated and extended, and is of [the] opinion that it is an indispensable condition for the

[110] Paul Brachet, *De l'exécution internationale des sentences (étude de droit comparé et de droit international privé)* (Paris: Rousseau, 1928), 2.

[111] Resolution XIV of the International Chamber of Commerce, *London Congress 1921: Resolutions Adopted*, Brochure No. 18, 20.

> extension of this practice that the validity of arbitration clauses in international commercial contracts shall be fully and generally respected.[112]

This was a matter of concern for ICC members, who believed that the absence of an adequate international regime for dealing with arbitration clauses would prevent international arbitration – and, therefore, the ICC's Court of Arbitration – from expanding further. At an ICC meeting, von Hemert, the president of the Executive Committee of the ICC's Court of Arbitration, explained that "Members of the Council might been [*sic*] disappointed seeing the few cases which have been dealt with by the Chamber till now."[113] Von Hemert "laid stress upon two hindrances which prevented immediate progress: 1. The fact that the Arbitration Clause was not valid in any country. . . . 2. Another obstacle was the lack of knowledge about laws concerning arbitration."[114] The ICC could, and in fact did, address the second point by publishing various brochures on arbitration laws in different countries,[115] but only a large-scale international effort was capable of solving the first issue.

While the ICC hoped to lead this effort, it was the League of Nations, and more specifically its English representatives, that initially made a key contribution to the subject.[116] Lemercier and Sgard have shown that the

112 Resolution V of the International Chamber of Commerce, *Resolutions Adopted at the Second Congress (Rome, March 1923)*, Brochure No. 31 (Paris: ICC International Headquarters, 1923), 37.

113 International Chamber of Commerce, "Proceedings of the Thirteenth Meeting of the Council," November 9, 1923, 37.

114 Ibid.

115 For example, Swiss National Committee of the International Chamber of Commerce, *Commercial Arbitration under Swiss Law*, Brochure No. 61 (Paris: ICC International Headquarters, 1927); Roberto Pozzi, *Commercial Arbitration under Italian Law*, Brochure No. 62 (Paris: ICC International Headquarters, 1927); W. L. P. A. Molengraaff, *Commercial Arbitration under Dutch Law*, Brochure No. 63 (Paris: ICC International Headquarters, 1927); Jean Duchenois, *Commercial Arbitration under French Law*, Brochure No. 65 (Paris: ICC International Headquarters, 1927); German National Committee of the International Chamber of Commerce, *Commercial Arbitration under German Law*, Brochure No. 72 (Paris: ICC International Headquarters, 1930); E. Huysmans, *Commercial Arbitration under Belgian Law*, Brochure No. 88 (Paris: ICC International Headquarters, 1934); J. E. James, *Commercial Arbitration under British Law (England and Wales, Scotland and Northern Ireland)*, Brochure No. 91 (Paris: ICC International Headquarters, 1936); Swedish National Committee of the International Chamber of Commerce, *Commercial Arbitration under Swedish Law*, Brochure No. 122 (Paris: ICC International Headquarters, 1947). All these brochures were prepared in collaboration with the Secretariat of the International Chamber of Commerce.

116 Veeder has also shown the connection between the Entente's Genoa Economic and Financial Conference in 1922 and the League of Nations' 1923 Geneva Protocol, as well

ICC left "*no imprint*" in the text of the 1923 Protocol,[117] which was, initially at least, "a British initiative."[118] As they explain, Sir Hubert Llewellyn Smith, the British member of the Economic Committee of the League of Nations from 1920 to 1927,[119] stated in March 1922 that arbitration clauses were not recognized in all countries, which caused some parties to renege on their contractual undertakings.[120] A working group was constituted under the presidency of F. D. MacKinnon;[121] it issued a report in 1922, which was followed by a League of Nations' recommendation for the recognition of arbitration clauses.[122] A second group was then formed in 1923 for the purpose of drawing up a draft protocol on arbitration clauses; notwithstanding some difficulties, it managed to draft the text that was approved by the League of Nations at its meeting on September 24, 1923.[123] Thus, it is not exactly true to say that both the Geneva Protocol and the Geneva Convention were "adopted at the behest of the ICC, under the auspices of the League of Nations that was recently created."[124] In fact, "[i]n this very first episode, the ICC was not only absent from the Geneva debates but ignored, and even spurned."[125]

The protocol was brief – eight articles, only four of which covered the validity and effect of arbitration clauses. Yet it addressed some of the issues that were hindering the development of international commercial arbitration at the time. The protocol required each contracting state to recognize "the validity of an agreement whether relating to existing or future differences between parties, subject respectively to the jurisdiction

as the influence of Soviet-German arbitral practice on modern arbitration treaties; see V. V. Veeder, "Chancellor Wirth and the Mologales Concession 1923-1927: The German-Speaking Origins of the 1965 ICSID Convention," in Christina Binder, Ursula Kriebaum, August Reinisch, and Stephan Wittich (eds.), *International Investment Law for the 21st Century: Essays in Honour of Christoph Schreuer* (Oxford: Oxford University Press, 2009), 383–84. It is, however, a relatively faint legal connection.

117 Lemercier and Sgard, *Arbitrage privé international*, 104.

118 Ibid., 98.

119 See Decorzant, "Internationalism," 115. The Economic and Financial Organisation (EFO) of the League of Nations was created in 1920 and "staffed by international and national civil servants, together with financial and economic experts."

120 Llewellyn Smith, quoted in Lemercier and Sgard, *Arbitrage privé international*, 98–99.

121 MacKinnon became a King's Counsel in 1914 and was elevated to the Court of Appeal in 1937.

122 Lemercier and Sgard, *Arbitrage privé international*, 99–100.

123 Ibid., 102–3.

124 Pierre Tercier, "The 1927 Geneva Convention and the ICC Reform Proposals," *Dispute Resolution International*, 2, no. 1 (2008), 21.

125 Lemercier and Sgard, *Arbitrage privé international*, 105.

of different Contracting States."[126] It allowed the parties to determine "[t]he arbitral procedure, including the constitution of the arbitral tribunal,"[127] and required contracting states to ensure that arbitration agreements[128] and arbitral awards[129] would be enforced. Article 1 limited the application of the convention to disputes concerning a "contract relating to commercial matters or to any other matter capable of settlement by arbitration"[130] and allowed each contracting state to limit its obligations under the protocol to "contracts which are considered as commercial under its national law."[131] (France made this reservation when ratifying the protocol on June 7, 1928.)[132] As Born points out, such language "presaged the 'commercial relationship' and the arbitrability requirements of the New York Convention."[133]

The protocol was ratified or acceded to by thirty states, many of which were members of the international trading community at the time. These included Belgium, Brazil, the British Empire, France, Germany, India, Italy, Japan, and Spain.[134] It had an immediate and palpable impact on international commercial arbitration. In Born's words, it "planted the seeds for a number of principles of profound future importance to the international arbitration process."[135] In France, it had the effect of accelerating legislative reform, prompting legislators to adopt the 1925 bill affirming the validity of arbitration clauses in order to comply with the international obligations it would impose.[136] Also in 1925, the Federal Arbitration Act (FAA) was passed in the United States, providing that arbitration agreements "shall be valid, irrevocable, and enforceable, save upon such grounds as exist at law or

126 Geneva Protocol on Arbitration Clauses, Article 1.
127 Ibid., Article 2.
128 Ibid., Article 4.
129 Ibid., Article 3.
130 Ibid., Article 1, ¶ 1.
131 Ibid., Article 1, ¶ 2.
132 United Nations Treaty Collection, League of Nations Treaties, "6. Protocol on Arbitration Clauses: Ratifications," https://treaties.un.org/Pages/LONViewDetails.aspx?src=LON&id=547&chapter=30&clang=_en.
133 Born, *International Commercial Arbitration* (The Hague: Kluwer Law International, 2014), 1:20.
134 United Nations Treaty Collection, "Protocol on Arbitration Clauses (Geneva, September 24, 1923): Ratifications," https://treaties.un.org/Pages/LONViewDetails.aspx?src=LON&id=548&chapter=30&clang=_en.
135 Born, *International Commercial Arbitration*, 1:66.
136 Matthieu de Boisséson, *Le droit français de l'arbitrage interne et international* (Paris: Joly, 1990), 23.

in equity for the revocation of any contract."[137] Like France's 1925 law, the FAA established a resolutely pro-arbitration regime that bolstered the development of international commercial arbitration. Overall, it seems that the protocol had "a decisive impact on the future of arbitration throughout the world"[138] and "a major – if often underappreciated – role in the development of the legal framework for international commercial arbitration."[139]

However, the protocol reflected a highly territorial mindset, reflecting the somewhat narrow vision of international commercial arbitration prevalent in the 1920s. In particular, Article 3 stated that "[e]ach Contracting State undertakes to ensure the execution by its authorities and in accordance with the provisions of its national laws of arbitral awards made in its own territory."[140] Foreign awards were not included in this definition, which could lead to serious difficulties.[141] Another international instrument capable of resolving some of these difficulties was therefore necessary.

#### 6.3.1.2 The 1927 Geneva Convention on the Execution of Foreign Awards

Unlike the 1923 protocol, the 1927 convention was chiefly the work of the ICC, which had grown steadily since its creation in 1920. A resolution adopted by the ICC at its 1925 congress in Brussels called upon "the various Governments to adopt agreements wherever possible on the basis of reciprocity between States whereby provision is made for the mutual enforcement of arbitration awards."[142] The resolution listed

137 9 U.S.C. § 2A law providing for the validity of arbitration agreements was already in force in the state of New York; New York Laws 1920, Chapter 275.

138 Emmanuel Gaillard and John Savage (eds.), *Fouchard, Gaillard, Goldman on International Commercial Arbitration* (The Hague: Kluwer Law International, 1999), ¶ 242, at 121.

139 Born, *International Commercial Arbitration*, 1:65.

140 Geneva Protocol on Arbitration Clauses, Article 3.

141 A concrete example was given in a report by the ICC: "[T]he German administration of justice will recognize the validity of a clause of this kind [an arbitration clause] agreed upon between a German and an Englishman. At the Englishman's request it will bring the German before the arbitrators in case he should, in spite of the clause he had signed, claim to submit his case to the ordinary Courts. And the German State will facilitate the arbitration proceedings which may take place in its territory and will insure the execution of the award if it is made within its frontiers. But the limits of the scope of this Protocol will be seen at once: the German state binds itself only with regard to awards made in Germany: it retains its freedom of action with regard to awards made, for example, in England. This is a serious gap." International Chamber of Commerce, *Arbitration Report No. 8* (July 1927), 2.

142 Resolution VIII.2; see International Chamber of Commerce, *Resolutions Passed at the Third Congress*, Brochure No. 40 (Paris: ICC International Headquarters, 1925), 33.

the requirements that foreign awards had to fulfill in order to be recognized in the country where enforcement was sought.[143] The resolution ended with a clear exhortation: "The International Chamber of Commerce recommends that the League of Nations be invited to consider the possibility of promoting an International Convention on these lines."[144]

The ICC's call for action did not fall on deaf ears. Even though the precise nature of the consultations that took place between the ICC and the League of Nations regarding the Geneva Convention is difficult to determine, it is clear that the two institutions exchanged ideas and technical knowledge.[145] Three main stages can be identified in the genesis of the Geneva Convention: First, individual members of the League of Nations spent a year exchanging preliminary ideas.[146] Then, in 1927, the League of Nations set up a special committee to discuss the draft convention and address some differences between the common law and civil law approaches.[147] Lastly, a report was submitted to the World Economic Conference, and the Geneva Convention was adopted on September 26, 1927.

The convention had clear limitations. It was open only to the parties to the Geneva Protocol, and it would apply only if nine conditions were satisfied:[148] (1) the arbitration submission pursuant to which the award was made had to be valid under the law applicable to it;[149] (2) the subject matter of the award had to be "capable of settlement by arbitration" under the law of the country in which the award was to be relied upon;[150] (3) the arbitral tribunal must have been constituted "in the manner agreed upon by the parties and in conformity with the law governing the arbitration

[143] Ibid., 35. The requirements were as follows: "(a) That the award contains nothing contrary to the public order or the public policy of the State in which its enforcement is sought; (b) That it is final according to the laws of the country where it was rendered; (c) That, according to the same law, the copy of the award has been duly authenticated; (d) That the parties have been legally summoned, represented, or declared to be in default."

[144] Ibid., 35.

[145] Lemercier and Sgard, *Arbitrage privé international*, 107–8.

[146] Ibid., 109–110.

[147] Ibid.

[148] Briner and Hamilton should be credited for grouping the nine conditions into a single list: see Robert Briner and Virginia Hamilton, "The History and General Purpose of the Convention: The Creation of an International Standard to Ensure the Effectiveness of Arbitration Agreements and Foreign Arbitral Awards," in Emmanuel Gaillard and Domenico di Pietro (eds.), *Enforcement of Arbitration Agreements and International Arbitral Awards: The New York Convention in Practice* (London: Cameron May, 2008).

[149] Convention on the Execution of Foreign Arbitral Awards, Article 1(a).

[150] Ibid., Article 1(b).

procedure";[151] (4) the award should have become "final in the country in which it [had] been made";[152] (5) the recognition or enforcement of the award should not infringe public policy or "the principles of the law of the country in which it is sought to be relied upon";[153] (6) the award must not have been annulled in the country where it was made;[154] (7) the party against whom the award was to be invoked must have been given "notice of the arbitration proceedings in sufficient time to enable him to present his case," and must have been "properly represented" if lacking legal competency;[155] (8) the award must fall "within the terms of the submission to arbitration";[156] and (9) there should be no other grounds under the law governing the arbitration procedure that would enable a party "to contest the validity of the award in a Court of Law."[157]

The sheer number of conditions for enforcing an award abroad revealed deeper anxieties – in particular, an inability to accept that the arbitral process could be independent of national laws. Formulated as they were in "obscure, restrictive terms,"[158] the conditions led to serious difficulties. The most problematic requirement was that to be enforceable an award had to have become "final" in the country of the seat.[159] In practice, this necessitated "double exequatur" proceedings, which could significantly lengthen the duration of the arbitral process. Another difficulty was the need for awards to conform to the law governing the arbitral procedure, which meant that they could never be fully independent of national laws. Furthermore, the convention set out strict formalities that had to be followed: the party seeking enforcement of the award had to provide numerous documents, such as the original award or "a copy thereof duly authenticated," "documentary or other evidence that the award [had] become final," and a translation of all these documents into the official language of the country where enforcement was sought.[160] These shortcomings were compounded by the fact that many countries failed to ratify the Geneva Convention, including the United States and Soviet Union.[161]

151 Ibid., Article 1(c).
152 Ibid., Article 1(d).
153 Ibid., Article 1(e).
154 Ibid., Article 2(a).
155 Ibid., Article 2(b).
156 Ibid., Article 2(c).
157 Ibid., Article 3.
158 Gaillard and Savage, *Fouchard, Gaillard, Goldman*, ¶ 245, at 121.
159 Ibid.
160 Convention on the Execution of Foreign Arbitral Awards, Article 4.
161 See *ICC News*, 20, no. 3 (April 1954), 3.

To a large extent, then, the Geneva Convention reflected the broader spirit of its time, which was characterized by both multilateralism and strong nationalistic instincts. On the one hand, "[t]he principle of the international validity, and enforcement of arbitration clauses *per se* and the arbitration awards based on them, was established in an official document adopted by the first true international organization, the League of Nations."[162] On the other hand, the convention revealed an underlying miscomprehension – "a false perspective in the conception of the Convention, not seen by its drafters – as the idea was not then current – that, especially internationally, the legal nature of an award was not of the same as a court decision, and that recourse to arbitration was based on virtually none of the concepts that justified recourse to courts."[163] Despite its many imperfections, the Geneva Convention was an important step forward and a cornerstone of the international arbitration regime until replaced by the 1958 New York Convention.

## *6.3.2 From Territorialism to Internationalism: The Genesis of the 1958 New York Convention*

### 6.3.2.1 The ICC's Early Efforts in the Post–World War II Context

During World War II, the Court of Arbitration moved its operations to Stockholm in Sweden, which remained neutral throughout the war. Jarvin, who authored a fascinating study of ICC arbitration during the war (based on original research at the Royal Library of Sweden, where the archives of the Swedish national committee are kept), found that the ICC Court held ten plenary sessions in Stockholm between 1940 and 1943 and administered approximately fifteen arbitration and conciliation cases.[164] After the war, an international conference was convened at the ICC's Paris headquarters between June 13 and 15, 1946.[165] This little-known conference – which foreshadowed the International Council for

162 Tercier, "1927 Geneva Convention," 21.

163 Jean Robert, "La Convention de New York du 10 juin 1958 pour la reconnaissance et l'exécution des sentences arbitrales étrangères," *Revue de l'arbitrage*, 1958, 2.

164 Sigvard Jarvin, "La Cour d'arbitrage de la Chambre de Commerce internationale pendant la seconde guerre mondiale," in Laurent Lévy and Yves Derains (eds.), *Liber amicorum en l'honneur de Serge Lazareff* (Paris: Pedone, 2011), 331–47; and Jarvin, "The Move to Stockholm of the Court of Arbitration of the International Chamber of Commerce (ICC) during the Second World War," *Scandinavian Studies in Law*, 63 (2017), 115–38.

165 International Chamber of Commerce, *Conférence sur l'arbitrage commercial international: Compte rendu des séances destiné aux Membres de la Conférence (June 13–15,*

Commercial Arbitration (ICCA) – brought together representatives of major arbitral bodies.[166] Delegates highlighted the need for "a simplified international procedure of recognition and execution of foreign arbitral awards."[167] The conference expressed the hope

> that the organizations taking part in the Conference immediately start to exchange information with each other on arbitral legislation and practices in arbitration cases;
>
> that the Conference participants exchange the result of their studies with each other through the International Chamber of Commerce in Paris as intermediary; . . .
>
> lastly, that the International Chamber of Commerce forms a Committee to draft a short brochure describing the possibilities for arbitration that exist in different countries, including arbitration clauses, arbitration procedure, and the recognition and execution of foreign arbitral awards.[168]

It was clear that the needs of international commerce could no longer be adequately met by the Geneva framework.[169] At its biennial congresses, the ICC made repeated calls for a new legal instrument that would replace the Geneva Convention. The 1949 congress in Quebec noted as follows:

> The experience which the Court has acquired since its creation more than 25 years ago has shown that an international uniform legislation aimed at simplifying recourse to arbitration would greatly contribute to a widespread use of arbitration procedure. As long as the laws governing arbitration vary from one country to another, there will be uncertainty as to the validity of arbitration clauses and the possibility of enforcing arbitral awards in a foreign country.[170]

*1946).* I thank Jérôme Sgard – who found this document in the Columbia University libraries in New York – for sharing this document with me.

166 Delegates included Pieter Sanders, René Arnaud, Pierre Vasseur, Robert Marx, and Frederic Eisemann of the ICC; Frances Kellor of the American Arbitration Association; and René David of the International Institute for the Unification of Private Law. The guests present included Jean Robert.

167 Algot Bagge, "La situation générale de l'arbitrage commercial international à la fin de la guerre," in International Chamber of Commerce, *Conférence sur l'arbitrage commercial international*, 7.

168 *Conférence sur l'arbitrage commercial international.*

169 See Martin Domke, "The United Nations Conference on International Commercial Arbitration," *American Journal of International Law*, 53 (1959), 414.

170 Resolution 25(A); see International Chamber of Commerce, *Resolutions Adopted by the Twelfth Congress of the ICC* (Quebec, 1949), Brochure No. 141 (Paris: ICC International Headquarters, 1949), 85.

In collaboration with the International Institute for the Unification of Private Law (UNIDROIT) in Rome, the ICC produced a draft Uniform Law on Arbitration in Respect of International Relations of Private Law.[171] As will be seen, this draft was infused with the broader, internationalist spirit of the time. However, it was impracticable in that it sought to regulate all the phases of an arbitration and would have required many provisions of domestic law to be amended.[172] It was soon abandoned.

The ICC/UNIDROIT draft was considered at the ICC's 1937 congress in Berlin.[173] At its 1951 congress in Lisbon, while mentioning the draft, the ICC also contemplated two other possibilities – amending the Geneva Convention and drawing up an entirely new convention:

> The I.C.C. welcomes a continuation of studies for the unification of arbitration laws in all countries, on the basis of the draft proposed by the International Institute for the Unification of Private Law, but recognizes the complexities and difficulties on the subject. The I.C.C. considers that pending completion of these studies an immediate effort should be made (whether by amendment of the Geneva Convention of 1927 or by a new Convention) to remove the main defect which militates against the effectiveness of international arbitration and to permit the immediate enforcement of international arbitral awards. The I.C.C. calls on all governments concerned to cooperate towards that end.[174]

At its 1953 congress in Vienna, the ICC reiterated its demands: "The International Chamber of Commerce once again urges Governments to draw up a new convention providing for the enforcement of international arbitral awards in commercial matters."[175] Thereafter, the ICC

171 Preliminary Draft of a Uniform Law on Arbitration in Respect of International Relations of Private Law, in International Institute for the Unification of Private Law, *Unification of Law: A General Survey of Work for the Unification of Private Law; Drafts and Convention* (Rome: UNIDROIT, 1948), 187.

172 See Paolo Contini, "International Commercial Arbitration: The United Nations Convention on the Recognition and Enforcement of Foreign Arbitral Awards," *American Journal of Comparative Law*, 8 (1959), 286. See also Charles Carabiber, "L'arbitrage international," in *Travaux du Comité français de droit international privé (1951–1954)*, 14–15 (1955), 62.

173 "International Commercial Arbitration," *World Trade*, 9, no. 7–8 (July–August 1937), 38–40.

174 Resolution 22; see International Chamber of Commerce, *Resolutions Adopted at the Thirteenth Congress of the ICC* (Lisbon, 1951), Brochure No. 161 (Paris: ICC International Headquarters, 1951), 75.

175 Resolution 25; see International Chamber of Commerce, *Resolutions Adopted at the Fourteenth Congress of the ICC* (Vienna, 1953), Brochure No. 175 (Paris: ICC International Headquarters, 1953), 90.

continued to monitor the situation and provide regular updates at its biennial congresses.[176]

#### 6.3.2.2 Between Renewal and Anxiety: The ICC and ECOSOC Draft Conventions

In March 1953, the ICC adopted a "Preliminary Draft Convention" (the "ICC Draft Convention") on the enforcement of international arbitral awards.[177] It was the work of a subcommittee chaired by Jean Robert, whose members also included René Arnaud, Ernest Barda, Charles Carabiber, Robert Marx, James Mordan, Pieter Sanders, and Max Shoop.[178] The composition of this committee shows that, well before the "small, closed group of self-regulating artisans" of the 1980s and 1990s,[179] lawyers and arbitration scholars played a key role in constructing the modern ICC arbitration regime.

The ICC Draft Convention was a clear sign of renewal in the field, reflecting a vision of international commercial arbitration that might have been thought of as "revolutionary" at the time.[180] Its boldness stemmed from three notable features: first, it did not require an award to have become final in the country where it was made in order to be enforced elsewhere. This requirement was "burdensome and inadequate in many cases."[181] The ICC Draft Convention simply stated that the award should not have been annulled in its country of origin,[182] thus dispensing with the double exequatur. Second, the ICC Draft Convention abandoned the principle of reciprocity laid down in the Geneva Convention[183] and stated instead that

[176] See, for example, Resolution 44, in International Chamber of Commerce, *Resolutions Adopted at the Fifteenth Congress of the ICC* (Tokyo, 1955), Brochure No. 186 (Paris: ICC International Headquarters, 1955), 81.

[177] International Chamber of Commerce, *Enforcement of International Arbitral Awards: Report and Preliminary Draft Convention Adopted by the Committee on International Commercial Arbitration at Its Meeting on 13th March 1953*, Brochure No. 174 (Paris: ICC International Headquarters, 1953). The brochure was circulated by ECOSOC in UN Doc. E/C.2/373, October 28, 1953. For a useful chart comparing the ICC draft (1953), the ECOSOC draft (1955), and the final text of the New York Convention (1958), see Briner and Hamilton, "History and General Purpose," 24–37.

[178] Florian Grisel, "Treaty Making between Public Authority and Private Interest: The Genealogy of the Convention on the Recognition and Enforcement of Foreign Arbitral Awards," *European Journal of International Law*, 28 (2017), 78.

[179] Dezalay and Garth, *Dealing in Virtue*, 39.

[180] Robert, "La Convention de New York," 73.

[181] International Chamber of Commerce, *Enforcement of International Arbitral Awards*, 10.

[182] ICC Preliminary Draft Convention (1953), Article IV(e).

[183] Convention on the Execution of Foreign Arbitral Awards, Article 1.

it would apply to commercial disputes.[184] In practice, this meant that the convention could be applied in many more situations than was the case under the 1927 framework. Third, the ICC Draft Convention included far fewer references to national law, giving increased importance to the will of the parties. As noted by the Committee on International Commercial Arbitration:

> Since arbitration is always voluntary, it must be based on an agreement between the parties, evidence of which must be given so that the enforcement of the award can be granted. If this is the basic principle, it would seem useless to open the irritating discussion on whether the arbitration agreement should be valid "under the law applicable thereto." It is, on the contrary, far simpler to provide a more general provision under which the judge called upon to enforce the award shall be satisfied that there exists an agreement stipulating settlement of disputes by arbitration, if written evidence is supplied.[185]

Hence, the ICC Draft Convention required the arbitral proceedings to be "in accordance with the agreement of the parties or, failing agreement between the parties in this respect, in accordance with the law of the country where arbitration took place."[186] As Briner and Hamilton explain, this "differed from the Geneva Protocol and Convention, where conformity with national law was an additional rather than an alternative requirement."[187] By giving more weight to the parties' agreement than to national law, the ICC Draft Convention made it possible to conceive of the arbitral process as increasingly "independent of national laws."[188]

The ICC Draft Convention was submitted to member states of the United Nations and various organizations for comments.[189] In April 1954, the United Nations Economic and Social Council (ECOSOC) established an ad hoc committee to discuss the ICC Draft Convention.[190] That committee in turn produced the ECOSOC Draft Convention on the Recognition and Enforcement of Foreign Arbitral Awards (the "ECOSOC Draft Convention"),[191] which was much more

[184] ICC Preliminary Draft Convention (1953), Article I.
[185] International Chamber of Commerce, *Enforcement of International Arbitral Awards*, 10.
[186] ICC Preliminary Draft Convention (1953), Article III(b).
[187] Briner and Hamilton, "History and General Purpose," 10.
[188] International Chamber of Commerce, *Enforcement of International Arbitral Awards*, 7.
[189] Resolution 570 (XIX) adopted by the Economic and Social Council on May 22, 1955.
[190] Domke, "United Nations Conference," 414.
[191] ECOSOC, *Report of the Committee on the Enforcement of International Arbitral Awards*, UN Doc. E/2704, March 28, 1955. The ECOSOC Draft Convention was annexed to this document.

conservative than the ICC Draft Convention, moving the pendulum back toward anxiety (see Figure 6.4).

The ECOSOC Draft Convention's gravitation toward anxiety is seen in its reintroduction of various elements from the Geneva Convention, such as the condition in Article III(b) that awards could be enforced abroad only if they had become "final and operative" in the country where they were made,[192] and the greater weight Article IV(g) gave to the law of the "country where the arbitration took place" compared to the "agreement of the parties."[193] As Grisel notes, "[t]he combined effect of Articles III(b) and IV(g) of the ECOSOC Draft was to reintroduce the two main shortcomings of the Geneva Convention, namely the risk of double exequatur and the lack of autonomy of the arbitration procedure towards domestic laws."[194] The ECOSOC Draft Convention seemed to show that the "[t]he idea of a truly international arbitral award was too progressive for the times."[195] It revealed deeper concerns, a feeling that, desirable as it was to "go further than the

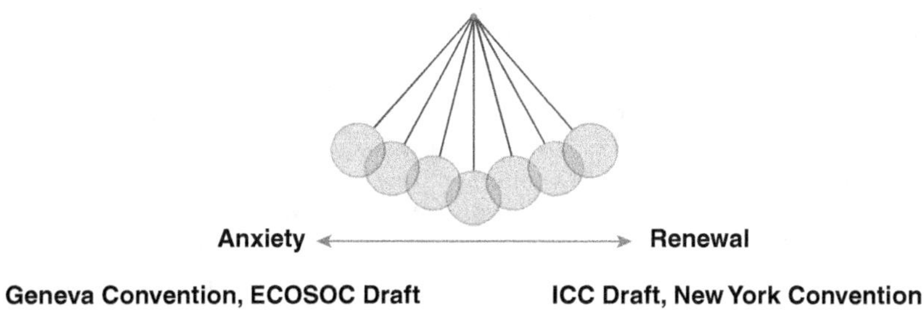


**Figure 6.4** The tension between renewal and anxiety reflected in the preparatory instruments leading to the New York Convention. On the renewal/anxiety spectrum, the Geneva Convention (1927) and the ECOSOC Draft Convention (1955) lean toward anxiety and the ICC Draft Convention (1953) and New York Convention (1958) toward renewal.

192 ECOSOC Draft Convention on the Recognition and Enforcement of Foreign Arbitral Awards, Article III(b).

193 Ibid., Article IV(g).

194 Grisel, "Treaty Making," 80.

195 Pieter Sanders, "The History of the New York Convention," in Albert Jan van den Berg (ed.), *Improving the Efficiency of Arbitration Agreements and Awards 40 Years of Application of the New York Convention*, ICCA Congress Series 9 (The Hague: Kluwer Law International, 1999), 11. See also Pieter Sanders, "The Making of the Convention," in *Enforcing Arbitration Awards under the New York Convention: Experience and Prospects* (New York: United Nations, 1999), 3–5.

Geneva Convention," there was also a need to "maintain generally recognized principles of justice and respect the sovereign rights of States."[196]

In the month before the New York Conference was due to open, the ECOSOC Draft Convention was criticized by the ICC in a special issue of *ICC News*. Noting that it represented "a compromise between the ICC principles and those of the Geneva Convention,"[197] *ICC News* suggested specific amendments to the ECOSOC Draft Convention.[198] One of its major defects was the fact that it did not "prevent the loser from having the award set aside by the courts of the country in which it was rendered on the grounds that the rules of procedure stipulated [did] not comply with the local procedural law."[199] By contrast, the ICC Draft Convention depended on "less rather than more action by governments" and enshrined the principle of "freedom of contract."[200]

The United Nations Conference on International Commercial Arbitration took place in New York from May 20 to June 10, 1958. The standard account of the conference has it that discussions stalled until Sanders miraculously came up with a new idea, known as the "Dutch proposal."[201] Sanders' own account is as follows:

> My review of the Convention's history will deal in particular with what during the Conference was called the "Dutch proposal." It was conceived during the first weekend of the Conference. I spent the weekend at the house of my father-in-law in a suburb of New York. I can still see myself sitting in the garden with a small portable typewriter on my knees. It was there, sitting in the sun, that the "Dutch proposal" was conceived. Upon return to New York on Monday, 26 May, this draft was presented to the Conference.[202]

Over time, this account of the New York Conference has become yet another founding myth of international commercial arbitration[203] – like

[196] ECOSOC, *Report of the Committee on the Enforcement of International Arbitral Awards*, ¶ 14, at 5.

[197] "International Commercial Arbitration," special issue, *ICC News*, 24, no. 3 (1958), 1.

[198] Ibid.

[199] Ibid., 4.

[200] Ibid., 3.

[201] The two components of the Dutch proposal were (i) the removal of the double exequatur and (ii) the requirement that the party *resisting* enforcement should demonstrate its lack of finality (the idea was, therefore, to "switch the burden of proof of the existence of one or more of these grounds to the party against whom the enforcement was sought"). See Sanders, "History of the New York Convention," 12–13.

[202] Ibid., 12

[203] See, for example, Albert Jan van den Berg, "Should an International Arbitrator Apply the New York Convention of 1958," in Jan Schultsz and Albert Jan van den Berg (eds.), *The*

*lex mercatoria* for members of the French school of international arbitration. Yet, what came to be seen as a bold proposal was in fact close to the suggestion made in the ICC Draft Convention. As Grisel contends, Sanders "was not the solitary white knight often praised in . . . arbitration circles but, rather, the acting soldier of an invisible network of experts, with an exact understanding of how the debate had previously developed at the ICC."[204] Indeed, it seems more likely that the Convention was the product of an "epistemic community" of arbitration than the work of a single "founding father."

The New York Convention was signed initially by ten states and by a further thirteen while open for signature.[205] Today, with 168 parties (at the time of writing),[206] it has become "a resounding success."[207] It has led to an unceasing succession of commentaries, monographs, and discussions[208] and has become a sort of "universal constitutional charter for the international arbitral process."[209] In more figurative language, the convention has been described as "the principal, but not the only, star of arbitration's solar system. Planets orbit it and parallel universes can be found."[210]

There have been calls for the New York Convention to be revised.[211] But the stronger view is that the status quo should prevail. Describing "the

*Art of Arbitration: Essays on International Arbitration; Liber Amicorum Pieter Sanders, 12 September 1912–1982* (Deventer: Kluwer Law and Taxation, 1982), 39.

204 Grisel, "Genealogy of the Convention," 82–83.

205 Domke, "United Nations Conference," 415. The ten states were Belgium, Costa Rica, El Salvador, Federal Republic of Germany, India, Israel, Jordan, the Netherlands, the Philippines, and Poland. The thirteen additional states were Argentina, Bulgaria, Belorussian SSR, Ceylon, Czechoslovakia, Ecuador, Finland, Luxembourg, Pakistan, Sweden, Switzerland, Ukrainian SSR, and USSR.

206 UNCITRAL, "Status: Convention on the Recognition and Enforcement of Foreign Arbitral Awards (New York, 1958)," https://uncitral.un.org/en/texts/arbitration/conventions/foreign_arbitral_awards/status2.

207 Gaillard and Savage, *Fouchard, Gaillard, Goldman*, ¶ 248, at 123.

208 For a detailed bibliography on the New York Convention, see, for example, "The 1958 New York Convention. A Bibliography," newyorkconvention1958.org/pdf/NYC1958-Bibliography-130709.pdf.

209 Born, *International Commercial Arbitration*, 1:99.

210 Antonio Remiro Brotóns, "La reconnaissance et l'exécution des sentences arbitrales étrangères," in *Collected Courses of the Hague Academy of International Law*, vol. 184 (Leiden: Brill/Nijhoff, 1984), ¶ 16, at 189.

211 See, for example, Albert Jan van den Berg, "Hypothetical Draft Convention on the International Enforcement of Arbitration Agreements and Awards: Explanatory Note and Annexes," in Albert Jan van den Berg (ed.), *50 Years of the New York Convention*, ICCA Congress Series No. 14 (The Hague: Kluwer Law International, 2009), 649–66. There have also been calls for it not to be revised; see Chapter 1, Section 1.3.2.2 (and n. 109).

urgency of not revising the New York Convention," Gaillard explains that its "genius . . . is to have foreseen the evolution of arbitration law. As per its Art. VII, the Convention sets only a minimum standard. States can always be more liberal. By definition, the Convention cannot freeze the development of arbitration law."[212] Put another way, the conditions laid down in Article VII establish a "'ceiling,' or maximum level of control, which Contracting States may exert over arbitral awards and arbitration agreements," even though states are free to apply more liberal rules if they wish.[213]

But perhaps the reason for the success of the New York Convention lies rather in the fact that it was initially conceived by the very *users* of arbitration and, following intense scrutiny, was adopted in a form very similar to what they had envisioned.[214] In other words, the history of the New York Convention is one of oscillation between renewal and anxiety that finally settled on the former.

### *6.3.3 A New "Internationalist" Legal Consciousness*

The shift from territorialism to internationalism can be seen not only in the instruments developed in the Age of Institutionalization but also in a change of perspective among professionals interested in international commercial arbitration at the time. Whereas scholars and practitioners had previously explored arbitration in relation to specific trades or legal regimes, they now displayed a much more internationalist outlook, turning to comparative law, for instance. In their writings, scholars, jurists, and members of arbitral institutions addressed important topics like the unification of arbitration laws and the private nature of arbitration. Their ideas permeated the legal consciousness of the mercatocracy and, though still embryonic in the 1920s and 1930s, paved the way for later developments in the field, such as the notion that the arbitration process should be detached from national laws.

[212] Emmanuel Gaillard, "The Urgency of Not Revising the New York Convention," in Albert Jan van den Berg (ed.), *50 Years of the New York Convention*, ICCA Congress Series No. 14 (The Hague: Kluwer Law International, 2009), 692.

[213] See also Emmanuel Gaillard and George Bermann (eds.), *UNCITRAL Secretariat Guide on the Convention on the Recognition and Enforcement of Foreign Arbitral Awards (New York, 1958)* (Leiden: Brill/Nijhoff, 2017), 2; Emmanuel Gaillard, "La vision américaine des sentences annulées au siège (Observations sur les arrêts *Pemex* et *Thai-Lao Lignite* de la Cour d'appel fédérale du 2e circuit des 2 août 2016 et 20 juillet 2017)," *Revue de l'arbitrage*, 2017, 1147, 1158–59.

[214] Robert, "La Convention de New York," 81.

#### 6.3.3.1 The Unification of Arbitration Laws

In the Age of Institutionalization, the literature on international commercial arbitration became far more abundant. Legislative reforms in several countries sparked the curiosity of many young scholars and practitioners. In France, they included Jean Robert, who was completing his studies in both law and business around the time the 1925 bill establishing the validity of arbitration clauses was passed;[215] this became the topic of his doctoral thesis, which he published in 1929.[216] As the Italian scholar Pallieri explained in 1935,

> [w]hen practice makes much use of an institution and the questions asked thereby become very numerous and varied, scholars feel called to give their opinion and become more interested in it. That was for the case with arbitration, which has latterly been studied in better ways, more widely and by more authors than before . . . [I]n international law, books on arbitration, which not long ago were still almost inexistent, have suddenly multiplied.[217]

Through these writings, one is able to see the subtle but meaningful shifts in the legal awareness at the time.

A noticeable change was the fact that arbitration scholars became increasingly interested in comparative analysis as a means of revealing the great diversity of arbitration laws and highlighting the need to unify the different systems of arbitration. Some authors felt that "a certain number of provisions are identical, or almost, in all states. The basic features of arbitration are the same everywhere; it is subject to the same rules everywhere."[218] Others, however, emphasized that arbitration laws varied considerably from one country to the next, making it difficult for users to navigate the arbitration system as a whole. The Geneva framework, which had led to undeniable progress, was still too limited; as one Belgian jurist explained, "[p]rogress is under way, but it is far from having reached its culminating point. What obstacles there are to the fast, economic and practical recognition of neglected rights!"[219]

215 Discussion with Me Bertrand Moreau (Paris, September 21, 2016).

216 Jean Robert, *La clause compromissoire et l'organisation de l'arbitrage* (Paris: Sirey, 1929).

217 Giorgio Balladore Pallieri, "L'arbitrage privé dans les rapports internationaux," in *Collected Courses of the Hague Academy of International Law*, vol. 51 (Leiden: Brill/Nijhoff, 1935), 294.

218 Ibid., 298.

219 Sartini van den Kerckhove, "Une juridiction internationale de droit privé," *Journal du droit international*, 1935, 784.

In 1932, René David, from whom the newly founded International Institute for the Unification of Private Law (UNIDROIT)[220] had requested a report on arbitration in comparative law, produced a noteworthy study on arbitration laws in various countries, including France, Germany, Italy, Poland, Spain, Sweden, and the United Kingdom.[221] (The report also contains French translations of the major arbitration laws then applicable in each of those countries – a useful tool even today.) David understood that the spirit of the time was changing:

> The friendly and episodic arbitration of the past has been replaced with arbitration by institutions specially assigned to that task, and with professional arbitration. Powerful institutions have been established, for the purpose of offering their organizations' facilities to private individuals for the settlement of their disputes; an ever-increasing number of professional associations have created arbitration courts that offer their members and people in the profession a system of justice by experts that is capable of gradually creating a new benefit: international case law.[222]

Even though this "international case law" had great appeal, the sheer variety of arbitration laws was a major obstacle to the development of international commercial arbitration. As David explained,

> the development and transformation of arbitration makes a reform of now outdated laws in a good number of countries indispensable. Everywhere, it has become necessary to modernize the laws on arbitration and adapt them its new look. The rules that were suitable for occasional, local and friendly arbitration are not suited to the arbitration that governs international trade relations, which is dispensed by powerful specialized bodies and anonymous arbitrators and has become the normal method of resolving certain disputes.[223]

According to David, it was vital for arbitration to be subject to uniform regulations internationally: "A universal phenomenon based everywhere on

[220] UNIDROIT was set up in 1926 as an auxiliary organ of the League of Nations. See "History and Overview," UNIDROIT, www.unidroit.org/about-unidroit/overview.

[221] René David, *Rapport sur l'arbitrage conventionnel en droit privé: Étude de droit comparé* (Rome: "L'Universale" Tipografia Poliglotta, 1932). For the background to this report, see V. V. Veeder, "Two Arbitral Butterflies: Bramwell and David," in Martin Hunter, Arthur Marriott and V. V. Veeder (eds.), *The Internationalisation of International Arbitration: The LCIA Centenary Conference* (London: Graham & Trotman/Martinus Nijhoff, 1995), 18.

[222] David, *Rapport sur l'arbitrage conventionnel*, 7.

[223] Ibid., 8.

the same causes, arbitration should be subject to identical law, all the more so as it now appears to be the preferred system of justice in international trade."[224]

David's proposals were endorsed by UNIDROIT, which, in April 1933, convened a committee of experts (including David) to produce a draft Uniform Law on Arbitration in Respect of International Relations of Private Law.[225] In its report and explanatory commentary, UNIDROIT praised the work of the League of Nations in connection with the Geneva framework but also noted that "the results recorded in Geneva are without doubt still very inadequate. They must be seen as but a first step on the pathway, as yet poorly marked out and covered with obstacles, to the unification of arbitration laws."[226] According to UNIDROIT, "for interested parties and especially in international relations the current diversity among arbitration laws is a cause of great difficulty. ... The unification of arbitration laws would therefore be tremendously useful for trade. ... It is true that a uniform arbitration regime implies a uniform law on arbitration."[227] David saw the ICC as capable of playing a key role in pursuing this "unification of arbitration law."[228]

Indeed, the ICC attracted much attention at the time because, unlike local trade associations, it did not serve the interests of a specific group of individuals but catered to the wider business community, so its appeal was universal. As already mentioned, the ICC/UNIDROIT project was considered by the ICC at various congresses preceding the New York Convention, but was eventually abandoned. The ICC also played an important role in promoting the unification of arbitration laws by collecting information on various countries. It produced numerous brochures – often enlisting the help of local experts, such as Pozzi in Italy or Molengraaff in the Netherlands – which contained detailed information on the arbitration laws of Belgium, France, Germany, Italy, the Netherlands, and Switzerland.[229] By making the idiosyncrasies of local regimes known to the wider arbitration community, the ICC hoped to

[224] Ibid.

[225] International Institute for the Unification of Private Law, *Avant-projet d'une loi uniforme sur l'arbitrage dans les rapports internationaux en droit privé et rapport explicatif*, U.D.P. 1940 – Projet III (Rome: Tipografia del Senato, 1940).

[226] Ibid., 30.

[227] Ibid., 29.

[228] René David, "Unification des lois relatives à l'arbitrage," in International Chamber of Commerce, *Conférence sur l'arbitrage commercial international*, 41.

[229] See n. 115.

contribute to a better understanding of the different arbitration laws and to their unification.

A related initiative in the Age of Institutionalization was the move to start publishing awards (or excerpts from awards). Based on the belief that lessons could be learned from similar cases in various contexts, it again reflected the outward-looking spirit of the time. In the late 1920s and the 1930s, Arthur Nussbaum, a professor of law in Berlin who escaped to the United States in 1934,[230] edited a four-volume work on international arbitration which contained many decisions, arbitration rules, and other relevant documents.[231] (The first volume was translated into English and published by Oxford University Press in 1928 in conjunction with the American Arbitration Association, which shows that there was a desire to broaden its readership and enable comparisons to be made between legal regimes.)[232]

In 1929 and 1930, the question of the publication of ICC awards became particularly topical, as numerous disputes were submitted to the ICC following the devaluation of the pound sterling during the Great Depression.[233] Within the ICC, there was much debate over whether selected awards should be made available as a source of guidance for traders faced with similar disputes.[234] In 1932, the ICC announced that it would publish some awards "of general interest," while ensuring that "[a]ll necessary precautions will be taken to prevent the parties from being identified. Any details which might enable those in the same trade to identify the firms in the case will be omitted."[235]

Short excerpts from ICC awards, many of them dealing with sterling contracts, were published in successive issues of *World Trade*.[236]

[230] See Elliott Cheatham, Wolfgang Friedmann, Walter Gellhorn, Philip Jessup, Willis Reese, and Schuyler Wallace, "Arthur Nussbaum: A Tribute," *Columbia Law Review*, 57 (1957), 1–7; and Martin Domke, "Arthur Nussbaum: The Pioneer of International Commercial Arbitration," *Columbia Law Review*, 57 (1957), 8–10.

[231] Arthur Nussbaum, *Internationales Jahrbuch für Schiedsgerichtswesen in Zivil- und Handelssachen*, 4 vols. (Berlin: Carl Heymanns, 1926–34).

[232] Arthur Nussbaum, *International Yearbook on Civil and Commercial Arbitration*, vol. 1 (New York: Oxford University Press, 1928).

[233] See "To Avoid Foreign Lawsuits," *World Trade*, 4, no. 2 (January 1932), 6.

[234] See Alec Stone Sweet and Florian Grisel, *The Evolution of International Arbitration: Judicialization, Governance, Legitimacy* (Oxford: Oxford University Press, 2017), 122; Lemercier and Sgard, *Arbitrage privé international*, 83–84.

[235] "Publication of Arbitration Awards," *World Trade*, 4, no. 8 (July–August 1932), 5.

[236] See, for example, "Arbitration Awards Concerning Sterling Contracts" (ICC Cases Nos. 513, 396, and 505), *World Trade*, 4, no. 9 (October 1932), 10–11; "A Case of Forged Letters of Credit" (ICC Case No. 143), *World Trade*, 4, no. 10 (November 1932), 11–15; "A Recent Award Concerning Sterling Contracts" (ICC Case No. 519), *World Trade*, 4, no. 11 (December 1932), 11; "Income Tax Deductions on British Patent Royalties" (ICC

However, these efforts were somewhat limited in scope. As stated in an ICC brochure in 1931:

> It is a matter of regret that the General Secretariat cannot provide the least bit of information on the awards rendered. Indeed, some of them were true monuments and, by establishing precedents, would doubtless have helped to increase awareness of the Chamber's system of arbitration and raise its prestige. There are no doubt reasons for this rule of silence: there was a wish to keep arbitration behind closed doors and prevent initiates from recognizing those who were party to the arbitration even if they were referred to with fictitious initials. There was above all a wish to prevent the creation of a body of international commercial case law. Those arguments certainly carry great weight, but it is nonetheless regrettable that the General Secretariat is handicapped in its propaganda by this inability to provide information about the awards that have been rendered.[237]

This statement illustrates both sides of the debate: the need to ensure confidentiality on the one hand, and the desire to publicize the ICC's most important awards on the other.[238] The wish to prevent the emergence of "a body of international commercial case law" might seem at odds with the prevailing spirit of the time, which was to encourage the unification of arbitration laws. But it shows that, even in the Age of Institutionalization, the internationalist legal consciousness was not shared by all.

#### 6.3.3.2 The Private Nature of International Commercial Arbitration

The issue of the unification of international commercial arbitration laws led many scholars to raise broader questions about the nature of arbitration. What legal principles should inspire a potential uniform arbitration law? And who should be tasked with the drafting of such a law and the regulation of the arbitration process: states or the parties themselves? These were thorny questions in the Age of Institutionalization, when the

Case No. 144), *World Trade*, 5, no. 1 (January 1933), 2; "A Recent Decision in a Sterling Contract Dispute" (ICC Case No. 536), *World Trade*, 5, no. 5 (May 1933), 11; "An Agent's Claim to Commission on Business Effected outside His Area" (ICC Case No. 304), *World Trade*, 5, no. 6 (June 1933), 7; "A Dispute Arising Out of a Contract between a Principal and His Agent" (ICC Case No. 568), *World Trade*, 6, no. 8 (October 1934), 6–7.

[237] International Chamber of Commerce, *Services rendus par le système d'arbitrage de la Chambre de commerce internationale* (Paris: ICC Headquarters, 1931), 6.

[238] On this issue, see Henri Batiffol, "Allocution de M. le Professeur Henri Batiffol, Président du Congrès," in *Travaux du Congrès International de l'Arbitrage (Paris, 11, 12, 13 mai 1961), Revue de l'arbitrage*, 1961, 42.

relationship between states and the mercatocracy was slowly changing, with the latter asserting more forcefully its independence vis-à-vis the former.

The birth of new arbitral institutions led many scholars to insist on the *private* dimension of arbitration and the impact this was having on the reorganization of state sovereignty. As one author explained in 1935, "state sovereignty is a notion that is becoming increasingly nuanced as relations and exchanges between different nations intensify. … In trade and customs agreements and in many other areas, [countries] are making reciprocal undertakings that partially encroach on their sovereignty, amply compensated for by the resulting benefits for public peace and prosperity."[239] The same author – one of the few individuals to express skepticism over the ICC Court of Arbitration at the time[240] – called for "the establishment of an international private-law court for trade and industry. This is bound to happen one day. For me, it is an inevitability."[241]

While such calls for a new international body fit into the internationalist mindset of the era, they also point to a belief that, as a private process, arbitration should be left in the hands of parties and arbitrators. Inquiring into whether arbitration was of a contractual or a jurisdictional nature, Pallieri ruled out the latter, arguing that "[n]owhere do arbitrators receive the power to rule on a dispute from the State itself, nor do they appear as organs of the State"[242] and "in all states arbitrators render their awards as private individuals."[243] For Pallieri, the "private nature of the arbitral mission"[244] meant that states should play a limited role in the arbitration process. Taking the example of the recognition of foreign awards, he argued that "[p]rivate-law effects of an arbitral award … should be recognized everywhere, as the value of a private deeds are not constricted by state boundaries."[245] He further stated that "[t]he arbitration agreement and the award are private deeds which, like any other private deed, have effects even outside the state whose law governs them."[246] To support his views, Pallieri cited an ICC resolution in which it was stated that "[a] judgment handed down in a foreign country is

239 Van den Kerckhove,"Une juridiction internationale."
240 Ibid., 785.
241 Ibid., 776–77.
242 Pallieri, "L'arbitrage privé," 302.
243 Ibid., 302–3.
244 Ibid., 304.
245 Ibid., 368.
246 Ibid., 373.

a deed that derives its authority from the law whose authority ceases at its country's borders. An arbitral award, on the other hand, which originates from the private will of the parties, cannot have its effects confined to a particular territory."[247]

The private nature of arbitration also meant that parties should be free to agree on the procedure to be followed. This point was expressed by various members of the ICC's Commission on International Commercial Arbitration. Its chairman, Sir Edwin Herbert, expressed the view that "for an international award to obtain legal sanction, it should be sufficient for it to conform to the procedure laid down in the parties' contract. Parties who have recourse to international arbitration are exercising rights which spring from the principle of freedom of contract."[248] According to Herbert, "[t]he immediate action to be taken in order to ensure the effectiveness of international arbitration, should . . . be founded upon the will of the parties as the basic principle."[249]

Likewise, Robert Marx, a German lawyer and technical adviser to the commission, argued in a report that

> [t]he essential principle which dominates, or should dominate, all arbitration procedure is the principle of the autonomy of the will of the parties. . . . The autonomy of the will of the parties clashes with a distinct tendency on the part of the State to interfere in contractual matters and thus to lessen the field for the free play of individual will.[250]

According to Marx, this principle was one of a few "essential principles" of arbitration, which even shared "a common point" with "the Rights of Man":

> [L]ike these Rights, which should not remain as a mere theoretical declaration but be incorporated in legislation, the fundamental principles of arbitration should become part of the arbitration rules. It would thus be possible to foster the atmosphere of mutual confidence, indispensable to international commercial arbitration and at the same time develop the proper conditions for legal unification, which is the ultimate goal.[251]

247 "Résolution du Conseil de la Chambre de Commerce internationale (décembre 1925)," quoted in Pallieri, "L'arbitrage privé," 370.

248 Edwin Herbert, "The Prompt Enforcement of International Arbitral Awards," in *International Commercial Arbitration and Freedom of Contract*, Brochure No. 160 (Paris: ICC International Headquarters, 1951), 8.

249 Ibid.

250 Robert Marx, "International Standards of Commercial Practice," in *International Commercial Arbitration and Freedom of Contract*, Brochure No. 160 (Paris: ICC International Headquarters, 1951), 12.

251 Ibid.

To buttress their arguments, Marx and others relied on various decisions from courts and tribunals at the time. For example, they closely scrutinized a decision by the Vaud cantonal tribunal in 1948, which upheld an award rendered under the aegis of the ICC even though the arbitrator had disregarded certain mandatory provisions of the Code of Procedure of the Canton of Vaud. The tribunal stated that

> in international matters, arbitration procedure is regulated above all by the will of the parties, they are free to adopt this or that procedure outside the procedures created by the laws of the country concerned, as the law of the country where the arbitration takes place has merely a default role, coming into play in the absence of party agreement on the matter.[252]

The case, which clearly affirms that the intentions of the parties should prevail over the law of the seat, was cited approvingly by Marx in his report.[253] Writing in the *Arbitration Journal*, Eisemann further noted that, "should the views expressed by the Swiss judges in this instance generally prevail, this would constitute an important step towards the international unification of arbitration proceedings by private organization pending the adoption by governments of a uniform arbitration law."[254] These statements were particularly articulate expressions of the private and even autonomous nature of the arbitration process, and they showed the extent to which an internationalist spirit was already alive in the Age of Institutionalization, decades before the French school of international arbitration took up the subject.[255]

## 6.4 Conclusion

This chapter has looked into the birth and origins of the ICC and of its Court of Arbitration. Those origins – from the Atlantic City Conference (1919) to the creation of the ICC (1920) and its Court of Arbitration (1923) – show how the overlap between public and private interests was

[252] Vaud Cantonal Tribunal (Switzerland), November 24, 1948, *Omnium français des pétroles* v. *Gianotti*, *Journal des Tribunaux*, 3 (1949), 112. For an analysis of this case, see Pierre Lalive, "Problèmes relatifs à l'arbitrage international commercial," in *Collected Courses of the Hague Academy of International Law*, vol. 120 (Leiden: Brill/Nijhoff, 1967), 627–28; and Carabiber,"L'arbitrage international," 70.

[253] Marx, "International Standards," 12.

[254] Frédéric Eisemann, "Local Law and Private Rules of Procedure in Connection with International Commercial Arbitration," *Arbitration Journal*, 4 (1949), 295, repr. in *Arbitration International*, 2 (1986), 73–75.

[255] See Chapter 9.

a key feature of the new organization from the outset. The chapter has also shown the ICC's role in the genesis of key legal instruments, such as the 1927 Geneva Convention and the 1958 New York Convention. These instruments offer a window on the movement between renewal and anxiety in the Age of Institutionalization. They also illustrate the shift from territorialism to internationalism in the broader legal consciousness of that era.

## APPENDIX 6.1

# Members of Foreign Delegations at the Atlantic City International Trade Conference (1919)[256]

### Belgium

M. Florimond Hankar, Chairman; Director, National Bank of Belgium; Honorary Director General, Savings Bank of Belgium.
M. Canon-Legrand, President, Chamber of Commerce, Mons; Construction Engineer; Permanent President, International Congress of Chambers of Commerce.
M. Albert Neve, Departmental Director, Ougree-Marihaye Works, Liège.
Mr. Albert E. Janssen, Director, National Bank of Belgium; Professor, University of Louvain.
Mr. Alexandre de Groote, Vice-President, Antwerp Chamber of Commerce.
Prof. Paul van de Ven, University of Louvain; Delegate of Belgian Minister of Finance at Paris Conference.

### France

M. Eugène Schneider, Chairman of Mission; Head of Creusot Steel Works; President of Iron and Steel Institution of Great Britain; former Member of Chamber of Deputies.
M. Tirman, Councillor of State; Representative of French Ministry of Commerce.
M. le Baron du Marais, Vice-Chairman of Mission; Director of Crédit Lyonnais.
M. André Homberg, Vice-President of the Société Générale.
M. Pellerin de la Touche, President of French Transport-Atlantic Line; President of Paris Subways.
M. Waddington, Textile Manufacturer; Vice-President of Syndicat Normand du Tissage.
M. Roché, Delegate of General Syndicate of Chemical Products; Director of the firm of Poulene Brothers.
M. Julien Potin, Vice-President of Biscuit Syndicate; President of Dry Vegetable Syndicate; President of Potin & Company.

[256] *International Trade Conference* (Chamber of Commerce of the United States of America, 1919), 14–15.

M. Godet, former President of the commercial division of the Tribunal de la Seine; ex-President of the General Association of Textiles; Member of Chamber of Commerce of Paris; Delegate of the Confédération Générale de Production.
M. le Commandant Varaigne, Head of French Mission associated with the American Services in Paris.
M. François-Poncet, Delegate of the Steel Committee in France.
M. Pesson-Didion, Mining Engineer; Delegate of the Union of Metallurgical and Mining Industries; Director of the Société Centrale pour l'Industrie Electrique.
M. Dolléans, Professor of Political Economy at the University of Dijon.
M. Parmentier, Engineer; Delegate to the Ministers of Commerce and Public Works; Assistant to M. Pellerin de la Touche.
M. Loizeau, Engineer of the Crédit Lyonnais; Assistant to M. le Baron du Marais.
M. Collin, Engineer at Schneider establishment; Assistant to the President of the Mission.
M. de Freminville, Engineer at Schneider establishment.
M. Mazot, General Secretary of the French High Commission; General Secretary of the Mission.
M. Boyer, Director of American Services in the Bank of Paris; Assistant General Secretary.
M. Pierre Lehideux, Secretary.

## Great Britain

Sir Arthur Shirley Benn, K.B.E., M.P.; Chairman, London.
Sir James Hope Simpson, Director and General Manager, Bank of Liverpool.
Hon. J. G. Jenkins, Corbiston, London; Member of Finance, General Purposes and Merchants' Committees, London Chamber of Commerce; V.P., British Producers' Association; former Premier, South Australia.
Mr. Marshall Stevels, M.P., Manchester.
Bailie John King, Chairman, National Light Castings Association, Glasgow.
Mr. Frank Moore, Moore, Eady & Murcott Goode, Ltd., Leicester.
Secretaries:
Mr. George Berkes, Assistant Secretary, Federation of British Industries, London; Associate Member, Chartered Institute of Secretaries.
Lieut A. S. Jarratt, Manchester.

## Italy

Commander Engineer Ferdinando Quartieri, Chairman; President of the Italian Corporation for Chemical Industries and other Italian companies.
Commander Prof. Bernardo Attolico.

Commander Engineer Dr. Luigi Luiggi, Member of the State Council of Public Works; Professor at the University of Rome.
Commander Prof. Vittorio Meneghelli, President, Chamber of Commerce of Venice.
Commander Giorgio Mylius, President of the Italian Master Cotton Spinners' and Weavers' Association.
Commander Domenico Guidoni, Delegate of the Italian Treasury.
Commander Pietro Giovanni Lazzerini, Secretary General.
Chevalier Giovanni Fummi, Stock Broker.
Commander Ersilio Baroni, President of the Italian Union for the Manufacture of Explosives.
Commander Dr. Augusto Jaccarino, Representative of the Banco di Napoli.
Chevalier Gaetano Biasutti, Representative of the Banca Italiana di Sconto.
Dr. Ildo Marchisio, Representative of the Banco di Roma.
Chevalier Guido Pedrazzini, Representative of the Banca Commerciale Italiana.
Chevalier Felice Bava, Representative of the Credito Italiano.
Marquis T. Theodoli.
Mr. Antonio Agresti.
Engineer Mario Luigi Luiggi.
Engineer Arturo Anzani.

## APPENDIX 6.2

# Members of the Committee on Permanent Organization at the Atlantic City Conference (1919)[257]

### Belgium

Louis Canon-Legrand
Paul van de Ven
Alexandre de Groote

[257] *International Trade Conference* (Chamber of Commerce of the United States of America, 1919), 459–60.

## France

All members of the Mission[258]

## Great Britain

Sir Arthur Shirley Benn
Sir James Hope Simpson
Marshall Stevens, M.P.
Hon. J. G. Jenkins
Bailie John King
Frank Moore

## Italy

B. Attolico
D. Gidoni
V. Meneghelli
P. G. Lazzerini
G. Fummi
A. Jaccarino
F. Quattrone
G. Granata
L. Solari
L. Perera
G. B. Ceccato
O. Rossati
Sig. Oldrini
Sig. Serrati
P. Decicco

## America

Harry Wheeler, Chairman
S. C. Mead, Vice-Chairman and Secretary

[258] The list of committee members reproduced in the proceedings of the 1920 Paris Congress includes only the following as French members of the Committee on Permanent Organization: Albert Tirman, Julien Potin, Jules Godet, and Édouard Dolléans. *Proceedings: Organization Meeting of the International Chamber of Commerce. Paris, France, June 23 to 30, 1920* (Paris: ICC International Headquarters, 1920), 5.

W. G. G. Benway, Assistant Secretary
John J. Arnold
John J. Carr
John H. Fahey
Edward A. Filene
Myron T. Herrick
Alba B. Johnson
Philip B. Kennedy
Edward G. Miner
George Rublee
F. A. Seiberling
Robert P. Skinner
George Ed. Smith

## APPENDIX 6.3

# Initial Members of the Court of Arbitration of the International Chamber of Commerce[259]

Members marked with an asterisk were present at the inauguration of the ICC on January 19, 1923.

### President

Étienne Clémentel, Président de la Chambre de Commerce Internationale.*

### Vice-Presidents

W. Clare Lees, O.B.E., J.P., President of the Manchester Chamber of Commerce
D. Carlos Prast, Président de la Chambre de Commerce de Madrid, Sénateur, ancien Maire de Madrid.*
K. A. Wallenberg, Ancien Ministre des Affaires Étrangères, Président du Comité Exécutif de l'Union des Chambres de Commerce Scandinaves, Président de la Chambre de Commerce de Stockholm.

[259] International Chamber of Commerce, *Inauguration of the Court of Commercial Arbitration. January 19th 1923*, Brochure No. 22 (Paris: ICC International Headquarters, 1923), 6–12. I have left the members' titles in the language used in the original English brochure.

## United States of America

Owen D. Young, Chairman of the Board, General Electric Company, New York.

Newton D. Baker, President, Chamber of Commerce, Cleveland, Ohio; formerly Secretary of War.

Irving T. Bush, President, Bush Terminal Company, New York; President, Chamber of Commerce of the State of New York.

Edgar Carolan, General European Representative of the International General Electric Company, Paris.*

R. Goodwyn Rhett, President, Peoples National Bank, Charleston, S. C.; formerly President of the Charleston Chamber of Commerce and formerly President of the Chamber of Commerce of the United States.

Henry M. Robinson, President, First National Bank, Los Angeles; Director, Chamber of Commerce of the United States; Member, American Committee, International Chamber of Commerce.

M. J. Sanders, New Orleans, Louisiana.

Frederick S. Snyder, President, Batchelder and Snyder Company, Boston, Massachusetts; President, Chamber of Commerce of Boston.

Thomas E. Wilson, President, Wilson and Company (Meat and Meat Products), Chicago, Illinois.

## Austria

Robert Erhart, Ancien Chef de Section; Vice-Président de l'Association Générale de l'Industrie Autrichienne.

Richard Furth, Représentant de l'Abrechnungsant autrichien auprès de l'Office des Biens et Intérêts privés; Commissaire Administratif pour l'Autriche auprès de la Chambre de Commerce Internationale.*

Dr. Paul Hammerschlag, Vice-Président de la Chambre de Commerce et d'Industrie de Vienne; Directeur du Kredit-Anstalt.

Dr. Franz Klein, Ancien Ministre de la Justice.

Eric Pistor, Ancien Ministre de la Justice.

Josef Vinzl, Vice-Président de la Chambre de Commerce et d'Industrie de Vienne

Emanuel Weissenstein, Directeur Général.

## Belgium

Maurice Despret, Président du Comité National Belge de la Chambre de Commerce Internationale; Président de la Banque de Bruxelles, Bruxelles.*

Jules Carlier, Président du Comité Central Industriel de Belgique, Bruxelles.

Georges Deprez, Administrateur-Délégué de la Société Anonyme des Cristalleries du Val Saint-Lambert, Bruxelles.

Albert Lejeune, Sénateur, Vice-Président du Comité Maritime International et de l'Association Belge de Droit Maritime, Anvers.

Charles Neef, Président de la Chambre de Commerce Belge de Paris, Directeur de la Compagnie Internationale des Wagons-Lits.*

## Denmark

Ernst Meyer, President of the Danish National Committee; and of the Grosserer-Societetets Komite.

Christian Andersen, Member of the Council of Provinshandelskammeret.

Christian Cloos, President of the Provinshandelskammeret.

Aage Dessau, Vice-President of the Industrirådet.*

Harald Kjaer, Member of the Grosserer-Societetets Komite.

F. H. J. Rambusch, Member of the Industrirådet.

Dr. Juris C. Ussing, Director of Nationalbanken, Copenhagen.

## Spain

D. Carlos Prast, Président de la Chambre de Commerce de Madrid.*

Joaquin Cabot y Rovira, Président de la Chambre de Commerce et de Navigation de Barcelone.

Horacio Echevarrieta, Armateur, Industriel, Cadiz et Bilbao.*

José Figueras, Directeur de la Banque de Bilbao, Madrid.*

Vincente Maiquez, Président de la Chambre de Commerce, Industrie et Navigation de Valencia.

José Alvarez Net, Président de la Chambre de Commerce, Industrie et Navigation de Malaga.

Alfonso Sala, Député, Industriel, Barcelone.*

Eugène Lopez Tudela, Président de la Chambre de Commerce d'Espagne, à Paris.*

## France

Étienne Clémentel, Sénateur, Président de la Chambre de Commerce International; Président du Comité National Français.*

H. Darcy, Président de la Confédération Générale de la Production française; Président du Comité Central des Houillères de France.*

René Duchemin, Président de l'Union des Industries Chimiques.*

Maurice Lewandowski, Vice-Président de l'Union Syndicale des Banquiers de France et de Province.*

Eugène Mathon, Président du Comité Central de la Laine.
Du Pasquier, Président de la Chambre de Commerce du Havre.*
Porte, Président du Tribunal de Commerce de la Seine.*
Louis Pradel, Président de la Chambre de Commerce de Lyon.*
Roger, Président de la Chambre de Commerce de Paris.*
Waddington, Président de l'Association Cotonnière Coloniale.*

## Great Britain

Sir Albert J. Hobson, LL.D., J.P., Chairman of the British National Committee; Vice- President of the International Chamber of Commerce, ex-Master Cutler of Sheffield.*
Sir Arthur Shirley Benn, K.B.E., M.P., President of the Association of British Chambers of Commerce.*
Sir Algernon F. Firth, Bart., Vice-President of the Federation of British Industries; ex-President of the Association of British Chambers of Commerce.*
Dr. Walter Leaf, D.Litt., Chairman, London County Westminster and Parr's Bank.
Sir Felix Schuster, Bart., Director of the National Provincial and Union Bank of England; Delegate of the British Bankers Association.*
Hon. J. G. Jenkins, Member of the Council of the London Chamber of Commerce; Hon. Treasurer of the British Imperial Council of Commerce.*
A. Barton Kent, Président du Conseil de l'Entente Cordiale, Member of the Council of the London Chamber of Commerce; Member of the Council of the Federation of British Industries.*
Arthur Balfour, J.P., Deputy President of the Association of British Chambers of Commerce.
W. Clare Lees, O.B.E., J.P., President of the Manchester Chamber of Commerce.*
H. J. Symonds, Chairman of the Council of the London Chamber of Commerce and Deputy Chairman of the London Court of Arbitration.
Sir Henry Whitehead, President of the Bradford Chamber of Commerce.*
O. E. Bodington, Lawyer.*
J. Sandeman Allen, Chairman of the Council of the Liverpool Chamber of Commerce.
James P. Rudolf, ex-Chairman of the Council of the Liverpool Chamber of Commerce.

## Indochina

Marius Borel, Planteur, Président de la Chambre d'Agriculture du Tonkin et du Nord-Annam, Hanoï (Tonkin).
B. Garriguenc, Négociant, Ancien Président de la Chambre de Commerce de Saïgon, Saïgon (Cochinchine).

Louis Jacque, Négociant et Planteur en Cochinchine, Délégué permanent en France du Syndicat des Planteurs de caoutchouc de l'Indochine.

Joseph Mayer, Planteur, Ancien Président de la Chambre d'Agriculture de Cochinchine, Saïgon (Cochinchine).

Léonard Fontaine, Administrateur-Délégué de la Société Française des Distilleries d'Indochine.

## Italy

Gr. Uff. Prof. Dionigi Biancardi, Presidente del Consiglio Centrale dell'Armamento Italiano, Genova; Amministratore Delegato della Navigazione Generale Italiana, Genova; Consigliere della Camera di Commercio e Industria di Genova.*

Comm. Biagio Borriello, Vice Presidente della Camera di Commercio e Industria di Napoli.

On. Gr. Uff. Avv. Marco Cassin, Presidente dell'Unione delle Camere di Commercio e Industria Italiane, Roma; Presidente della Sezione Italiana della Camera di Commercio Internazionale.*

On. Sen. Ing. Ettore Conti, Ex-Ministro, Presidente dell'Associazione fra le Società Italiane per Azioni, Roma.

On. Gr. Uff. Alfredo Fortunati, Presidente della Camera di Commercio e Industria di Roma.

Gr. Uff. Giorgio Mylius, Presidente dell'Associazione Cotoniera Italiana, Milano; Vice-Presidente della Sezione Italiana della Camera di Commercio Internazionale.*

On. Prof. Avv. Empedocle Restivo, Presidente della Camera di Commercio e Industria di Palermo.

Comm. Francesco Sacca, Presidente della Camera di Comercio e Industria di Messina.

On. Sen. Gr. Uff. Ing. Angelo Salmoiraghi, Presidente della Camera di Commercio e Industria di Milano.

Comm. Raimondo Targetti, Presidente della Confederazione Generale dell'Industria Italiana, Roma.

Comm. Vittorio Venezian, Consigliere della Camera di Commercio e Industria di Trieste.

Comm. Dott. Giuseppe Zuccoli, Direttore Generale della Banque Française et Italienne pour l'Amérique du Sud, Paris.*

## Luxemburg

Eugène Dondelinger, Membre de la Chambre de Commerce, Vice-Président de la Chambre des Députés; Président de la Fédération des Commerçants, Kayl.

Auguste Dutreux, Administrateur de la Banque Internationale à Luxembourg; et de la Société des Chemins de Fer Guillaume-Luxembourg, Paris.*

Max Lambert, Administrateur-Directeur de la Société Luxembourgeoise de Crédit et de Dépôts, Walferdange-lez-Luxembourg.*

Léon Laval, Administrateur-Délégué de la Société Luxembourgeoise pour le Commerce des Matériaux de Construction, Luxembourg.*

Albert Reinhard, Industriel, Membre de la Chambre de Commerce, Luxembourg.*

Paul Wurth, Ingénieur-Constructeur, Membre de la Chambre de Commerce; Président de la Fédération des Industriels Luxembourgeois, Luxembourg.*

## Norway

Alfred Bommen, Directeur-Gérant de Viul Traesliberi, Christiania.

Christian A. Hansen, Agent, Christiania.

G. Kamstrup Hegge, Directeur de la Norske Kreditbank, Christiania.

Andreas Moe, Négociant, Consul, Trondhjem.

H. B. Peterson, Directeur-Gérant de la Moss Cellulosefabrik, Moss.

Viktor Plahte, Directeur de la Andresens et Bergens Kreditbank, Christiania-Bergen.

Herman Reimers, Avocat, Commissaire administratif pour la Norvège auprès de la Chambre de Commerce Internationale, Paris.*

## The Netherlands

W. H. Croockewit, Président de la Chambre de Commerce de Rotterdam.*

S. P. Van Eeghen, Ancien Président de la Chambre de Commerce d'Amsterdam.

Dr. J. C. A. Everwijn, Directeur du Nederlandsche Handelmaatschappij; ancien Président du Comité National Néerlandais.

E. Heldring, Président de la Chambre de Commerce d'Amsterdam.

Philip L. von Hemert, Président de la Chambre de Commerce Néerlandaise à Paris.*

E. P. de Monchy, Ancien Président de la Chambre de Commerce de Rotterdam.

Dr. F. E. Posthuma, Ancien Ministre du Commerce, de l'Industrie et de l'Agriculture; Président de l'Association pour le développement de l'Industrie et du Commerce aux Pays-Bas (Maatschappij voor Nijverheid en Handel).

W. G. Wendelaar, Président du Comité de la Bourse d'Amsterdam.

## Poland

Ladislas de Kislanski, Président du Comité National Polonais de la Chambre de Commerce Internationale; Président de l'Union Centrale de l'Industrie, des Mines, du Commerce et des Finances de Pologne.*

Boguslaw Hersé, Membre du Conseil de la Chambre de Commerce Internationale; Président de l'Association des Négociants Polonais.*

Georges Zdziechowski, Vice-Président de l'Union Centrale de l'Industrie, des Mines, du Commerce et des Finances de Pologne; Président de la Compagnie des Industriels Forestiers de Varsovie.

Maurice Poznanski, Vice-Président de l'Association Textile de l'État Polonais.

Jean Zaranski, Président de l'Association des Producteurs et des Raffineurs d'Huiles minérales; Professeur de l'Académie des Mines de Cracovie.*

Comte Ladislas Jezierski, Membre du Conseil de la Chambre de Commerce Internationale; Vice-Président de la Banque Russo-Asiatique, à Paris.*

## Sweden

Thor Carlander, Ancien Avocat, Négociant, Paris.*

Charles Dickson, Directeur-Gérant, Svenska Bankforeningen, Stockholm.

Axel Hultkrantz, Colonel, Directeur-Gérant, Sveriges Industriforbund, Stockholm.

Gösta Huselius, Avocat, Stockholm.

Axel Vennersten, Ancien Ministre des Finances.

K. A. Wallenberg, Ancien Ministre des Affaires Étrangères; Président du Comité Exécutif de l'Union des Chambres de Commerce Scandinaves.

E. Wehtje, Président de la Chambre de Commerce de la Scanie, Malmö.

## Switzerland

Otto Alder, Membre du Comité National Suisse; Membre de la Chambre Suisse du Commerce, St-Gall.

Dr. Hans Dietler, Directeur de la Banque Leu et Co., S. A., Zurich; Représentant de l'Association suisse des banquiers.*

Dr. Alfred Georg, Membre du Comité national suisse; Ex-Président de la Chambre de Commerce de Genève; Membre de la Chambre suisse du Commerce.

John Syz, Président du Comité national suisse; Président de la Chambre de Commerce de Zurich; Membre du Vorort de l'Union Suisse du Commerce et de l'Industrie, Zurich.*

## Czechoslovakia

Dr. François Malinsky, Industriel; Sénateur; Vice-Président de la Chambre de Commerce de Prague.

Dr. B. Marik, Docteur honoraire de la Haute-Ecole technique de Prague; Président de la Fédération des Industriels tchécoslovaques.

Theodor Liebig, Industriel; Président de la Fédération Centrale allemande de l'Industrie textile

Augustin Novak, Directeur en Chef de l'Office Bancaire.

Vojtech Vanicek, Consul Général de la République Tchécoslovaque à Paris.*

# 7

# The Development of the ICC Arbitration System

## 7.1 Introduction

Chapter 6 considered how, in the Age of Institutionalization, new institutions such as the ICC and its Court of Arbitration were created. It also highlighted their contribution to the genesis of new legal instruments such as the Geneva Convention and New York Convention. But it did not explain how international commercial arbitration also developed *within* these institutions – how it was "institutionalized." In other words, how did such organizations codify rules and standards and develop them in response to the demands of their users?

This chapter traces the part the ICC played in the development of a modern, robust, and efficient system of dispute resolution.[1] It explains how, faced with the growing importance of international commercial arbitration and demands from its users, the ICC developed its own rules and methods to deal with arbitration proceedings. The ICC made these rules increasingly precise and sophisticated over time, thereby improving the overall effectiveness of its arbitration system. The ICC arbitration system could be classified as both an "autopoietic system,"[2] closed and

[1] Parts of this chapter have already been published as an article (see Mikaël Schinazi, "The Three Ages of International Commercial Arbitration and the Development of the ICC Arbitration System," *ICC Dispute Resolution Bulletin*, 2020, issue 2, 63–75).

[2] See Gunther Teubner, *Law as an Autopoietic System* (Oxford: Blackwell, 1993). The term "autopoiesis" is used by biologists (e.g., Humberto Maturana and Francisco Varela) to describe the self-organizing and self-referential nature of living systems. Teubner built on the work of Niklas Luhmann, who saw law as a self-referential system of communication; see, for example, Niklas Luhmann, "The Self-Reproduction of Law and Its Limits," in Gunther Teubner (ed.), *The Dilemmas of Law in the Welfare State* (Berlin: De Gruyter, 1985).

increasingly self-regulating, and an open system, adapting itself to user feedback.

This chapter is divided into two sections. The first traces the creation of the ICC dispute resolution system. It shows that some of the founders of the ICC and its Court of Arbitration were familiar with, and may have been inspired by, the arbitration rules of other organizations. Yet the ICC was also innovatory, codifying new rules and practices through a process of "normative densification,"[3] as clearly reflected in the rules used to govern arbitral proceedings (Section 7.2). This chapter refers to all fourteen versions of the ICC Rules of Arbitration (the "Rules") – including the amendments – from 1922 to the present.[4] They have so far never been published together.[5]

The second section explores the *evolution* of the ICC dispute resolution system. It describes the major shifts the system underwent in the 1920s and 1930s: from conciliation to arbitration and from "equity" to "law" (Section 7.3). By showing how the ICC arbitration system "slowly and humbly developed,"[6] continuously adjusting to meet the demands of its users,[7] this chapter qualifies the 1920s and 1930s as a key period for the institutionalization of international commercial arbitration.

[3] The expression is from Thomas Schultz, *Transnational Legality: Stateless Law and International Arbitration* (Oxford: Oxford University Press, 2014), 127.

[4] The latest ICC Rules of Arbitration entered into force on January 1, 2021, applying to cases submitted to the International Court of Arbitration from that date onward. In the words of the ICC Court president at the time, Alexis Mourre, the new Rules "mark a further step towards greater efficiency, flexibility and transparency of the Rules, making ICC Arbitration even more attractive, both for large, complex arbitrations and for smaller cases." See International Chamber of Commerce, "ICC unveils revised Rules of Arbitration," https://iccwbo.org/media-wall/news-speeches/icc-unveils-revised-rules-of-arbitration/.

[5] Current and past versions of the Rules, but not the amendments of 1931, 1933, 1935, and 1939, are freely available online in the ICC Digital Library, (follow "Dispute Resolution" channel, then menu item "Rules") (last visited May 17, 2020). Researchers are not unanimous in their dating of the Rules. Grisel and Stone Sweet state that "[t]he ICC issued its first arbitration rules in 1922, subsequently amended in 1927, 1928, 1932, 1934, 1939, 1947, 1955, 1975, 1988, 1998, and 2012" (Alec Stone Sweet and Florian Grisel, *The Evolution of International Arbitration: Judicialization, Governance, Legitimacy* (Oxford: Oxford University Press, 2017), 87n17), while Lemercier and Sgard mention "four different versions of the Rules" in the interwar years, but not the 1935 amendments (Claire Lemercier and Jérôme Sgard, *Arbitrage privé international et globalisation(s): Rapport final* (March 2015), 48). The bibliography at the end of this book lists all versions of the Rules and amendments with dates and publication details.

[6] Michel Aurillac, "La Cour internationale d'arbitrage de la CCI régulatrice de la mondialisation," in Gerald Aksen et al. (ed.), *Global Reflections on International Law, Commerce and Dispute Resolution: Liber Amicorum in Honour of Robert Briner* (Paris: ICC Publishing, 2005).

[7] Lemercier and Sgard, *Arbitrage privé international*, 47.

## 7.2 Establishment of the ICC Arbitration System

The ICC's arbitration system was not built from scratch; those involved in its creation were aware of the existing arbitration mechanisms in other trades and industries and drew inspiration from them (Section 7.2.1). At the same time, the ICC innovated by developing an increasingly sophisticated system of rules and procedures (Section 7.2.2).

### *7.2.1 Precedents*

Certain aspects of the ICC's dispute resolution system closely resemble other arbitration mechanisms already in existence at the time. The process followed by the ICC might be described as "mimetic isomorphism," a concept coined by sociologists to explain organizational "modeling," whereby the "modeled organization" serves as "a convenient source of practices that the borrowing organization may use."[8] The originators of the ICC's arbitration system sometimes referred expressly to preexisting models while also making key innovations by devising new rules and adjusting to users' practical needs.

A telling example is the report that Roberto Pozzi, an Italian legal scholar,[9] wrote ahead of the ICC's 1921 London congress to prepare the ground for the drafting of the ICC's conciliation and arbitration rules. Pozzi quoted at length a resolution adopted at the 1914 International Congress of Chambers of Commerce in Paris, which stated that

> measures should . . . be adopted for placing at the disposal of traders and manufacturers in all countries the organisms that are necessary to the employment of arbitration in controversies arising between citizens of different countries, and any action taken with this view should conform to the precedents furnished by the Arbitration Rules of the International Cotton Federation and by those [of] the International Publishers' Congress, also taking account of the important results of the inquiry conducted by the Berlin Chamber of Commerce, and of the proposed rules compiled by the

[8] Paul DiMaggio and Walter Powell, "The Iron Cage Revisited: Institutional Isomorphism and Collective Rationality in Organizational Fields," *American Sociological Review*, 48 (1983), 151. In addition to "mimetic isomorphism," DiMaggio and Powell discuss "coercive isomorphism" (when formal and informal pressures are exerted on organizations) and "normative isomorphism" (when normative rules are spread by professional networks). These mechanisms are "not always empirically distinct" and "the three types [of isomorphisms] intermingle in empirical setting."

[9] See, for example, Roberto Pozzi, *Commercial Arbitration under Italian Law*, Brochure No. 62 (Paris: ICC International Headquarters, 1927).

> New York Chamber of Commerce, with a view, that is, to organizing international colleges of arbitrators for all trades or groups of similar trades.[10]

As a legal adviser to the Italian Cotton Association, Pozzi was well acquainted with these arbitration rules adopted during the decade preceding the creation of the ICC. Besides the four "precedents" he designated earlier, Pozzi also mentioned a plan promoting the use of arbitration to settle trade disputes between US and Argentine parties.[11] A product of the Pan-American Financial Conference organized by the Chamber of Commerce of Buenos Aires and the Chamber of Commerce of the United States in Washington in May 1915, the plan sought to "encourage arbitration and make it readily available for all persons engaged in trade between the two countries."[12] The plan included (1) an agreement between the two chambers on the creation of an arbitration system for settling commercial disputes,[13] and (2) accompanying arbitration rules,[14] both of which took effect on April 10, 1916.

Pozzi discerned in the US–Argentine system two features, also present in the cotton industry, that deserved special emphasis. The first was "[a] form of arbitration clause, the use of which is recommended to those engaged in International Commerce and which, once inserted into a contract, becomes obligatory for the parties thereto."[15] The second was the use of moral sanctions, "without prejudice to legal measures, against those who, having accepted the arbitration clause, refuse to admit arbitration at the time when a controversy arises, or refuse to carry out the award of a board of arbitrators."[16]

[10] International Chamber of Commerce, *Commercial Arbitration*, Brochure No. 13 (Paris: ICC International Headquarters, 1921), 6–7.

[11] Ibid., 14.

[12] *Arbitration for Disputes in Trade between the United States and the Argentine Republic* (Chamber of Commerce of the United States, 1919), 1.

[13] Ibid., 9.

[14] Ibid., 18.

[15] International Chamber of Commerce, Brochure No. 13, 14. The US–Argentine plan included a standard clause worded as follows: "All disputed questions which may occasion controversy relating to this contract shall be submitted to arbitration under the rules adopted jointly by the Chamber of Commerce of Buenos Aires and the Chamber of Commerce of the United States of America" (*Arbitration for Disputes in Trade between the United States and the Argentine Republic*, 9–10).

[16] International Chamber of Commerce, Brochure No. 13, 15. The US–Argentine plan stated that "the plan rests wholly upon the voluntary assent of the persons engaged in each particular transaction between the two countries and upon the influence the commercial organizations of the two countries can exert upon any of their members who heedlessly disregard an undertaking to arbitrate" (*Arbitration for Disputes in Trade between the United States and the Argentine Republic*, 2).

These two features became important aspects of the ICC's dispute resolution system as well. The ICC Court of Arbitration drew up an arbitration clause and strongly encouraged traders from different countries to include it in their contracts.[17] And, initially at least, the ICC imposed moral sanctions on parties who refused to comply with an arbitral award – even though, as will be seen, they soon yielded to legal considerations.

Other aspects of the ICC Rules can also be traced to the arbitration rules adopted under the US–Argentine plan. For example, Pozzi acknowledged that Article 10 of his "Proposed Plan for Conciliation and Arbitration Between Traders of Different Countries" – authorizing arbitrators to render a provisional award to protect merchandise[18] – was directly borrowed from the US–Argentine plan,[19] which provided that perishable or seasonal merchandise could be disposed of "to avoid increased loss."[20] Also, the arbitrators' right to order provisional measures found its way into the 1922 Rules, which gave arbitrators "the right to render a provisional decision, providing for such measures of preservation as may be indispensable and, when strictly necessary, disposing of the merchandise or objects in dispute."[21]

These similarities with the US–Argentine plan show that arbitration rules from other organizations sometimes served as precedents for the ICC's dispute resolution system. This is hardly surprising; as Pozzi explained, arbitration rules were already in place in many trades and industries and it was only natural that the ICC should build upon this rich repository of practices. Moreover, some of the individuals involved in the creation of the ICC and its Court of Arbitration had also participated in the drafting of those arbitration rules. For instance, Charles Bernheimer, John Fahey, and Owen Young were members of the Committee on Arbitration of the Chamber of Commerce of the United States, which was involved in both the implementation of the US–Argentine plan and the events that led up to the adoption of

[17] The arbitration clause associated with the 1922 Rules read as follows: "The contracting parties agree to submit to arbitration, in accordance with the Arbitration Rules of the International Chamber of Commerce, the settlement of all disputes in connection with the interpretation or the execution of this contract."

[18] International Chamber of Commerce, Brochure No. 13, 28.

[19] Ibid., 20.

[20] "Agreement for Commercial Arbitration," Article XII, *Arbitration for Disputes in Trade between the United States and the Argentine Republic*, 16. A similar idea was expressed in the arbitration rules of the US–Argentine plan, but using different wording ("Rules of Arbitration," Article 2, *Arbitration for Disputes in Trade between the United States and the Argentine Republic*, 20).

[21] 1922 Rules, Article XVIII/XXXIX.

the ICC Rules. It was indeed Fahey who signed the documents that formed part of the US–Argentine plan as the representative of the US Chamber of Commerce[22] and who also took part in the creation of the ICC and its Court of Arbitration, along with Young.[23] The rapid spread of similar norms and models was thus likely due to the existence of "a pool of almost interchangeable individuals"[24] across a range of organizations. But the ICC did more than "import" rules from other arbitral organizations; it innovated, too, devising its own rules and techniques in key areas of arbitral procedure.

### *7.2.2 The ICC's Codification Efforts*

The ICC's codification efforts manifested above all in the Rules, which "define and regulate the management of cases" referred to the Court of Arbitration.[25] The drafting of the ICC Rules was arguably the clearest instance of the institutionalization of international commercial arbitration during the Age of Institutionalization.

There have been fourteen successive versions (including amendments) of the Rules from the creation of the ICC to the present day. The Rules were first promulgated in 1922. They were recast in 1927, with amendments in 1931, 1933, 1935, 1939, and 1947. New versions then appeared in 1955, 1975, 1988, 1998, 2012, 2017, and, most recently, 2021. The Rules contain essential regulations relating to each stage of the arbitration, from the request for arbitration to the final award, including the constitution of the arbitral tribunal, the arbitral proceedings, and the costs of the arbitration. Analyzing these provisions in full[26] leads to a better understanding of the process of "normative densification" that characterized the creation of the Rules.

#### 7.2.2.1 Request for Arbitration

The submission of a request for arbitration to the secretariat marks the commencement of an ICC arbitration. The request for arbitration is a key part of the proceedings, enabling the opposing party and the ICC Court to

[22] *Arbitration for Disputes in Trade between the United States and the Argentine Republic*, 17.
[23] See, for example, John Fahey, "The International Chamber of Commerce," *The Annals of the American Academy of Political and Social Science*, 94 (1921), 129.
[24] DiMaggio and Powell, "Iron Cage Revisited," 152.
[25] International Chamber of Commerce website, "Arbitration Rules," https://iccwbo.org/dispute-resolution-services/arbitration/rules-of-arbitration/.
[26] Stone Sweet and Grisel undertook such an analysis, but only for certain stages of the arbitration. See Stone Sweet and Grisel, *Evolution of International Arbitration*, 84–107.

become apprised of the principal features of the dispute and make early decisions on the arbitration.[27] The list of particulars to be included in the request for arbitration has progressively expanded over time, as the ICC strove to make the procedural framework increasingly clear from the outset.

Under the "Proposed Plan for Arbitration," the "demand" (as it was then known) consisted of four parts: the parties' names, nationalities, and addresses; the purpose, date, and place of the contract; the questions to be submitted to the arbitrator in relation to the dispute; and the name of a "technical arbitrator." The parties were also required to attach "as complete a file as possible on the matter."[28]

The 1922 Rules, as it turned out, were even simpler, with just three main components: the names and addresses of the parties; a copy of the contract between the parties; and a "brief statement of claims of the applicant for arbitration."[29] Under the 1927 Rules, the procedure for initiating arbitration remained broadly unchanged; in addition to the elements listed earlier, the parties had to include "copies of all contracts and correspondence having passed between the parties, and any other documents or information relied upon."[30]

The list of details to be furnished in the request progressively grew in subsequent versions of the Rules. Under the current 2021 Rules, parties wishing to have recourse to ICC arbitration must include the name, address, and contact details of each party and of the claimant's representatives; a description of the dispute giving rise to the claims; a statement of the relief sought; the arbitration agreement; and any observations or proposals concerning the arbitrators, the place of arbitration, the applicable rules of law, and the language of the arbitration.[31] Hence, the procedure for initiating ICC arbitration became increasingly detailed, showing how exacting the ICC was in this area.

#### 7.2.2.2 Answer to the Request for Arbitration

Upon receipt of a request for arbitration, respondents are given the opportunity to submit an answer in which they respond to the claims

[27] Jason Fry, Simon Greenberg, and Francesca Mazza, *The Secretariat's Guide to ICC Arbitration* (Paris: International Chamber of Commerce, 2012), ¶ 3-80 (regarding the 2012 Rules).

[28] International Chamber of Commerce, Brochure No. 13, 27.

[29] 1922 Rules, Article X/XXX(c). This is mentioned in Grisel and Stone Sweet, *Evolution of International Arbitration*, 91.

[30] 1927 Rules, Article 6(2)(c).

[31] 2021 Rules, Article 4(3)(a)–(h).

brought against them. As with the request for arbitration, the extent of the information to be included in the answer has expanded over time, and the procedure for drafting the answer has likewise grown in complexity.

Under the 1922 Rules, the Court of Arbitration notified the respondent[32] of the request for arbitration "as speedily as possible" and invited him to furnish "similar complete data and information with statement of his case, within a period of fifteen days from the receipt of such notification."[33] There was therefore no clear list of the information to be included in the answer; the respondent was simply asked to provide his statement of the case.

In the 1927 Rules, the time given to the respondent to provide an answer was extended to one month.[34] Like the 1922 Rules, the 1927 Rules did not include a list of information to be included in the answer; Article 7(1) simply stated that the respondent had to include "a statement of the case in answer accompanied by all documents and information in support."

In 1955, the time limit was made more precise – "one month" was replaced with "thirty days"[35] – and the Rules went into greater detail on what was required in the answer, stating that the respondent should reply "to the proposals made to him concerning the number of arbitrators and their choice. He must at the same time and within the same period furnish a statement of the case in answer and any proposals he may wish to make, accompanied by all documents and information in support."[36] Over time, the provisions governing the answer to the request for arbitration became more specific. The current version of the Rules lists six items of information to be supplied by the respondent in the answer within thirty days of receiving the request for arbitration.[37]

#### 7.2.2.3 Written Statements and Counterclaims

Parties to an arbitration usually exchange two rounds of written submissions – the memorial and counter-memorial, then the reply and rejoinder. The 1922 Rules did not contain any detailed provisions on the number of written statements parties were allowed to submit. It was only in 1927 that this was limited to two on each side: "the first being

[32] Respondent parties were referred to as "defendants" in the early versions of the ICC Rules.
[33] 1922 Rules, Article XI/XXXI.
[34] 1927 Rules, Article 7(2).
[35] 1955 Rules, Article 9(1).
[36] Ibid.
[37] 2021 Rules, Article 5(1).

the statement of claims" and "the second being the applicant's rejoinder to the answer of the defendant and the latter's reply to this rejoinder."[38]

This is a clear instance of a rule developed in response to the practical concerns of the Court of Arbitration and its users. As the ICC Court explained when the 1927 Rules were issued, "[t]he Committee considered it necessary to limit the number of statements of case to be presented by the parties so as to prevent a party dragging out the proceedings in bad faith by the presentation of a succession of statements and counter-statements."[39] This rule was not inflexible, however, and arbitrators could still allow parties to submit additional statements if, for example, the last statement filed by the respondent contained new arguments justifying a further rejoinder on the part of the claimant.[40]

Provisions on counterclaims were likewise added to the Rules as they developed. The 1922 Rules did not contain any provisions dealing specifically with counterclaims; Articles XI/XXXI simply stated that the opposing party was to submit, in his answer, "information with statement of his case." Nor were counterclaims specifically mentioned in the 1927 Rules, which simply stated, somewhat more narrowly than in the 1922 Rules, that the respondent was asked to "furnish within the time stipulated a statement of the case in answer accompanied by all documents and information in support."[41]

It was not until the 1939 amendments that the matter of counterclaims was expressly addressed in the Rules. A new paragraph was added to the former Article 17, as follows:

> New claims or counter-claims or new grounds in support of these claims submitted to the arbitrator or arbitrators must be formulated by the parties in writing. The arbitrator or arbitrators will then establish a record of the incident; at the request of the party against whom the new claim or grounds have been submitted, the arbitrator or arbitrators will suspend the proceedings, and, in this case, send the parties before the Court of Arbitration for a decision, and, if necessary, the establishment of an additional submission.[42]

[38] 1927 Rules, Article 18(1).

[39] "Report of the Secretary General Comparing the Old and New Rules and Describing the Principal Amendments," in International Chamber of Commerce, *Arbitration. Revision of the Rules of Conciliation and Arbitration*, Brochure No. 50 (Paris: ICC International Headquarters, 1927), 5.

[40] Ibid.

[41] 1927 Rules, Article 7(1).

[42] 1939 amendments, Article V (relating to Article 17 of the 1927 Rules, not Article 18 as stated in the amendments).

Although clearly describing the procedure to be followed, this amendment did not specify a time limit. It was added in the 1955 Rules, which stated that a respondent putting forward a counterclaim had to do so "within the period laid down for the reply to the claim" and that the other party would then have "thirty days from notification of this counterclaim" to submit a statement in reply.[43] Thus, the provisions on written statements and counterclaims are further examples of rules developed over time in response to the practical needs of users of the ICC system.

#### 7.2.2.4 Appointment of Arbitrators

The issue of how arbitrators should be appointed preoccupied the ICC Court from the very beginning. As Arnaud explained, the choice of the arbitrator was "the keystone of the Rules," since "the Court does not decide any case itself, and merely appoints one or more arbitrators to do so."[44] Under the 1922 Rules, national committees played a key role in selecting arbitrators. They had to compile lists of "technically qualified arbitrators," to which reference would be made when arbitrators were needed for specific disputes.[45] The names of the arbitrators chosen from the list would then be communicated to the parties in dispute.[46] (The difficulty of maintaining up-to-date lists of arbitrators quickly became apparent. As an ICC Court member explained in 1927, "the Committee considered it impossible to draw up and lists for all industries, all trades, and in all countries, and to keep them up to date," even though the Court could always "take into account the lists drawn up by trade federations, as in the silk trade, and by courts."[47])

In the late 1920s and the 1930s, the procedure for selecting arbitrators became more complex. The 1927 Rules stated that "[a]s a general rule the Court, unless for good reason shown, shall apply to National Committees of countries other than those of the parties to the dispute."[48] In other words, as from then, arbitrators had to be of a nationality other than that of the parties.

The 1931 amendments filled another gap by introducing a provision to cover the eventuality of parties failing to nominate an arbitrator. The following provision was added before the last sentence of Article 11(2):

[43] 1955 Rules, Article 10(1).

[44] René Arnaud, "Arbitration in the International Chamber of Commerce," *World Trade*, 1, no. 1 (January 1929), 123.

[45] 1922 Rules, Article VI/XXVI(a).

[46] Ibid., Article XIII/XXXIII.

[47] ICC Archives, "Séance de Groupe du Mardi 28 Juin 1927, Présidence de M. Thor Carlander, assisté du Dr. E. Leslie Burgin," 26.

[48] 1927 Rules, Article 11(1).

"Should one of the parties abstain from nominating his arbitrator within the time set by the Court of Arbitration, the Court shall itself appoint the arbitrator."[49] This new provision meant that parties could no longer delay proceedings by deliberately refraining from appointing an arbitrator.

#### 7.2.2.5 Rules Governing the Proceedings

The rules governing the proceedings come into play once the arbitrators have been seized of the case. For more than a decade after the ICC Court was founded, these rules were left largely undefined, but from the late 1930s onward they were formulated with increasing detail, while nonetheless remaining "extraordinarily flexible."[50]

The 1922 Rules contained no specific provisions on this matter; Articles XIII/XXXIII simply required the national committee or organization member to "determine and regulate the procedure." The 1923 Explanatory Commentary added that "[t]he procedure will necessarily include notice given to the parties or to their representatives who shall be able to furnish verbal explanations or to address documents in writing. The arbitrators will assure the reciprocal communication between the parties of the documents and notes submitted to them." Initially, therefore, national committees were in charge of determining the procedure.

The 1927 Rules provided some additional guidelines, with Article 16(1) authorizing arbitrators to "take such steps as they may in their discretion consider most appropriate for the purpose of ascertaining the facts relating to the case," and Article 16(2) requiring the Court of Arbitration and the arbitrators to "so act as to render an award capable of legal enforcement."

It was in 1939 that the ICC Court took the important step of providing parties and arbitrators with clear rules on the conduct of arbitral proceedings. A new paragraph was added defining a hierarchy in the different provisions that could potentially govern proceedings before the arbitral tribunal: the ICC Rules took priority, followed, in the event that they were silent, by the law of the place of arbitration.[51]

The 1955 Rules added an additional level to the hierarchy defined in the 1939 amendments. Pursuant to Article 16, the proceedings were to be conducted in accordance with the Rules and, where they were silent, the procedural law agreed by the parties or, failing agreement, the rules of "the law of the country in which the arbitrator holds the proceedings."

[49] 1931 amendments, Article III (concerning Article 11(2) of the Rules).

[50] Fry, Greenberg, and Mazza, *Secretariat's Guide*, ¶ 3-709 (regarding the 2012 Rules).

[51] 1939 amendments, Article IV (relating to Article 16 of the 1927 Rules, not Article 17 as stated in the amendments).

The principle of a hierarchy of rules governing the proceedings has become an enduring feature of the Rules and can today be found in Article 19 of the 2021 version.

#### 7.2.2.6 Location of Hearings and Meetings

The (physical) location of hearings and meetings should not be confused with the (legal) place of arbitration, which is the seat of the arbitration and determines the law governing the arbitration proceedings. Although hearings and meetings are often held at the place of arbitration, this is not always the case. The location of hearings may be dictated by considerations such as the place where the parties' counsel, the arbitrators, the parties, or the witnesses are established; or the availability of transport, facilities, and support services, or visa conditions.[52]

Under the 1922 Rules, the "country and town" where the arbitration took place were "determined by the Court of Arbitration, after examination of the request for arbitration and before the appointment of arbitrators."[53] Even though arbitrators were sometimes permitted to take evidence in a country other than that where the arbitration took place by enlisting the help of a "deputy to take such evidence,"[54] the Court of Arbitration played a key role in selecting the location of hearings and meetings.

In 1927, the procedure for choosing the location of meetings became more detailed. Article 12 stated that "[a]rbitration shall take place in the country and place decreed by the Court of Arbitration, unless the parties shall have agreed in advance upon the place of arbitration." Hence, priority was given to party choice. This was an important change because, as explained in an ICC brochure, "parties are given greater freedom of action" and "the Court bows to the will of the parties" if they have agreed in advance upon the place of arbitration.[55] This procedure for selecting the place of arbitration was maintained in both the 1955[56] and the 1975[57] Rules.

#### 7.2.2.7 Legal and Technical Advice

Because arbitrators may not possess all the legal or technical skills relevant to deciding a specific case, they may enlist the help of tribunal-appointed experts, who are often perceived as more neutral than party-appointed

52 Fry, Greenberg, and Mazza, *Secretariat's Guide*, ¶ 3-697 (regarding the 2012 Rules).
53 1922 Rules, Article IX/XXIX(a).
54 Ibid., Article XVI/XXXVII.
55 International Chamber of Commerce, Brochure No. 50, 4.
56 1955 Rules, Article 18.
57 1975 Rules, Article 12.

experts.[58] The 1922 Rules left arbitrators free to "take or obtain any legal or technical advice in reference to a dispute, which they may judge necessary."[59] The 1923 Explanatory Commentary added that they could designate "either a legal expert from among the members of judicial associations of legal constitution or the professors of law of the Universities, or a technical expert, and demand reports from these experts within their competence on the points in dispute."

Further details were added in the ensuing years. Under the 1927 Rules, arbitrators were authorized to hear witnesses directly, with Article 16(1) stating that "[t]he arbitrators or arbitrator shall take such steps as they may in their discretion consider most appropriate for the purpose of ascertaining the facts relating to the case. They shall have power to hear witnesses and may if so decided submit technical or legal matters to experts for report."

The 1931 amendments introduced a new provision allowing the president of the Court of Arbitration to appoint experts even before the file was transmitted to the arbitrators. It stated that "in urgent cases at the request of the parties or of one of them, the President of the Court of Arbitration . . . shall have power to appoint an expert . . . , " who "shall present to the Court of Arbitration or to the arbitrator a detailed report on the accomplishment of his mission."[60] Finally, the requirement that the expert's terms of reference be defined in advance was added in 1955.[61]

#### 7.2.2.8 Timing and Place of Awards

Early ICC cases mostly concerned disputes over simple factual and legal issues such as the quality of goods. In such cases, knowing when and where an award was deemed to have been made was not problematic. This information was considered self-evident – awards were generally made at the arbitrator's office or the place where the goods were inspected – so there was no need to expand on this matter in the 1922 and 1927 Rules.

In 1955, however, the following provision was added: "The arbitral award shall be deemed to be made at the place of the arbitration proceedings and on the date of signature by the arbitrator."[62] This "deeming" provision, which was intended to simplify things for the arbitral tribunal and could also be important in subsequent domestic court proceedings relating to the

[58] See Fry, Greenberg, and Mazza, *Secretariat's Guide*, ¶ 3-967 (regarding the 2012 Rules).
[59] 1922 Rules, Article XIX/XL(b).
[60] 1931 amendments, Article II (adding an Article 11 to the Rules, the former Article 11 becoming Article 12, and so on).
[61] 1955 Rules, Article 20.
[62] 1955 Rules, Article 27.

award, was maintained in the 1975 and subsequent versions of the Rules.[63] Today, it can be found in Article 32(3) of the 2021 version ("The award shall be deemed to be made at the place of the arbitration and on the date stated therein"). The provision was a response to the growing complexity of cases involving parties and arbitrators from multiple countries.

No time limit was set for rendering awards under the 1927 Rules, so the ICC Court was free to decide on a time limit and the date from which it was to run. Internal ICC documentation shows that the Executive Committee spent a vast amount of time tracking individual cases and extending time limits for making awards. Case 66, for example, came before the Executive Committee at least fifteen different times over a two-year period from 1928 to 1929.[64] It was a complex case concerning an "all risks, war included" insurance policy taken out to cover a shipment of iron bars from Glasgow to Bagdad via Basra, which, as it turned out, never reached the claimants. The Executive Committee repeatedly extended the time limit for making the award owing to the complexity of the case and the fact that it would be "materially impossible for the arbitrator to write his award and for the Executive Committee to approve it" during the summer.[65]

In 1955, the Court introduced a time limit of sixty days[66] (which in fact had already been mentioned in the "Proposed Plan for Arbitration"[67] and the 1922 Rules[68]), but it soon proved "hardly realistic" and "necessitated repeated extensions."[69] In 1975, the time limit was therefore extended to six months,[70] which, if it was "necessary to do so," the Court could extend "in exceptional circumstances and pursuant to a reasoned request from the

63 1975 Rules, Article 22.

64 ICC Archives, minutes of meetings of the Executive Committee of the Court of Arbitration: session 40 of January 28, 1928; session 41 of February 29, 1928; session 44 of June 27, 1928; session 46 of September 5, 1928; session 47 of October 3, 1928; session 48 of November 14, 1928; session 49 of December 19, 1928; session 50 of January 30, 1929; session 51 of February 27, 1929; session 52 of March 27, 1929; session 53 of April 24, 1929; session 54 of May 29, 1929; session 55 of June 26, 1929; session 56 of September 25, 1929; and session 58 of November 27, 1929.

65 ICC Archives, minutes of meetings of the Executive Committee of the Court of Arbitration, session 46 of September 5, 1928. Time extensions were also granted in session 48 of November 14, 1928; session 50 of January 30, 1929; session 51 of February 27, 1929; and session 52 of March 27, 1929.

66 1955 Rules, Article 23(1).

67 International Chamber of Commerce, Brochure No. 13, 28.

68 1922 Rules, Article XV/XXXVI.

69 Frédéric Eisemann, "Le nouveau règlement d'arbitrage de la Chambre de Commerce Internationale," *Droit et pratique du commerce international*, 1 (1975), 363.

70 1975 Rules, Article 18(1).

arbitrator, or if need be on its own initiative."[71] Eisemann welcomed the change, explaining that "it lightens the Court's task" and "confirms the parties' entitlement to a serious and thorough examination of their case."[72] Interestingly, the ICC Court had the power to remove an arbitrator who failed to abide by this time limit,[73] a measure designed to encourage efficiency that continues to this day. In what may be described as a "groundbreaking move,"[74] the ICC Court recently decided that arbitrators who submit their draft award later than required under the Rules[75] can expect their fees to be lowered, unless the delay is justified by factors beyond the arbitrators' control or by exceptional circumstances.[76]

#### 7.2.2.9 Costs of Arbitration

Initially, ICC arbitration was a service provided free of charge. Faced with the growing complexity of cases, it soon became clear that arbitrators would need to be paid for their services. This early – and particularly noteworthy – development has already attracted scholars' attention.[77]

Articles XIX/XL(e) of the 1922 Rules stated:

> The arbitrators shall be entitled to reimbursement of all expenses but shall render their services gratuitously, except that, in so far as it is recognized that in such countries and industries fees are customarily provided for arbitrators, the Court of Arbitration may, in its discretion, allow arbitrators' fees to be included in the costs of arbitration at rates customary to such countries or industries.

As noted by Stone Sweet and Grisel, arbitral appointments were largely seen as honorary and "prestige conferring."[78]

71 Ibid., Article 18(2).
72 Eisemann, "Le nouveau règlement," 363.
73 1975 Rules, Articles 18(3) and 2(8).
74 International Chamber of Commerce, "ICC Court announces new policies to foster transparency and ensure greater efficiency," news release, January 5, 2016, https://iccwbo.org/media-wall/news-speeches/icc-court-announces-new-policies-to-foster-transparency-and-ensure-greater-efficiency/.
75 2021 Rules, Articles 27 (Closing of the Proceedings and Date for Submission of Draft Awards) and 31 (Time Limit for the Final Award).
76 International Chamber of Commerce, "Note to Parties and Arbitral Tribunals on the Conduct of the Arbitration under the ICC Rules of Arbitration," practice note, January 1, 2019, ¶¶ 118–22, https://cdn.iccwbo.org/content/uploads/sites/3/2017/03/icc-note-to-parties-and-arbitral-tribunals-on-the-conduct-of-arbitration.pdf.
77 See Grisel and Stone Sweet, *Evolution of International Arbitration*, 91; Eduardo Silva Romero, Emmanuel Jolivet, and Florian Grisel, "Aux origines de l'arbitrage commercial contemporain: L'émergence de l'arbitrage CCI (1920–1958)," *Revue de l'arbitrage*, 2016, 410–11, ¶¶ 14–15; Lemercier and Sgard, *Arbitrage privé international*, 40, 67.
78 Grisel and Stone Sweet, *Evolution of International Arbitration*, 91.

The idea that arbitrators should render their services gratuitously was soon called into question: "Several National Committees have asked that the principle of gratuitous service by arbitrators should be abolished. Experience has shown that in order to secure the services of the really expert arbitrators, it is necessary that there should be fees. So the reference to gratuitous services has been deleted."[79] As a consequence, the 1927 Rules included the following provision: "The costs of arbitration shall include fees of arbitrators, when such fees are allowed, fees of experts if any, and all expenses of the arbitration."[80]

However, determining an appropriate fee structure for arbitrators could be a challenge for the Court of Arbitration, as illustrated by Case 66, filed in the late 1920s. The arbitrator, an American lawyer, spent seventy-nine hours working on the case. After "consulting the authorized persons on this question," the British national committee calculated that the arbitrator should be paid 150 guineas, but that 100 guineas would suffice. The Executive Committee of the Court of Arbitration, on the other hand, unanimously felt that

> fees of this amounts – and even the reduced amount of 100 guineas – seemed out of proportion with the customs of the Court of Arbitration, with precedents in this field, with the costs that would have been incurred had the case been brought to a French court, and with the promises made to parties in the various publications of the Chamber that their disputes will be settled at little expense.[81]

In a letter to Arnaud, Raymond Streat, the secretary of the Manchester Chamber of Commerce, argued that there were cultural reasons for the proposed fee level:

> In your letter you speak of the possibility that your Committee will hesitate in future to have recourse to English arbitrators, or arbitrators living in England, because of the tendency to charge high fees. I think it would be very unjust of your Committee to come to any conclusion about the fees required by the English arbitrators on the basis of this experience of an American arbitrator. As a matter of fact, I believe you will find in a great many cases that an arbitration would be conducted in London at less cost than in, say, Rome, Berlin, etc. It is true that the English arbitrator might charge a small fee, perhaps five or ten guineas for the ordinary commercial case, but the costs incurred by professional and clerical services would be less.

79 International Chamber of Commerce, Brochure No. 50, 6.
80 1927 Rules, Article 22(2).
81 ICC Archives, minutes of the meetings of the Executive Committee of the Court of Arbitration, session 52 of March 27, 1929.

> This particular case, No. 66, is really not a fair example. In the first place, the arbitrator was not chosen by the British Committee, nor was he a British subject. He was an American professional man, and everybody knows that they have ideas about fees which are the envy of European professional men, and the despair of European business men who are obliged to employ them. If you think members of your Committee entertain any mistaken ideas on this subject, I should like you to bring my remarks to their notice.[82]

The American arbitrator finally agreed to a much-reduced figure of sixty guineas.[83]

Another thorny question was who should pay the party-appointed arbitrators. The 1927 Rules stated that the fees of party-appointed arbitrators should be paid "by the parties who appointed them."[84] Because this could give the impression that the arbitrators were acting as the parties' personal representatives, the 1933 amendments provided that arbitrators' fees, instead of being paid directly by the parties, were to be fixed by the Court and included in the costs of arbitration, along with the fees of experts and all the expenses of the arbitration.[85]

In the 1950s, the Court introduced greater predictability through the use of fee schedules to calculate costs based on the amount in dispute. These schedules – one relating to ICC administrative expenses and the other to arbitrators' fees – are today set out in the third appendix III to the Rules. Furthermore, parties can today obtain an estimate of the likely costs of an ICC arbitration using an online "cost calculator."[86] The payment procedure has been clarified, too. Parties wishing to have recourse to ICC arbitration are required to pay fees in three stages: the claimant must pay (1) a nonrefundable filing fee (currently USD 5,000) when it files the request for arbitration, followed by (2) a provisional advance to cover the costs of the arbitration until the Terms of Reference have been drawn up, and then (3) the claimant and respondent must pay an advance on costs when the case is transmitted to the arbitral tribunal.[87]

[82] ICC Archives, minutes of the meetings of the Executive Committee of the Court of Arbitration, session 53 of April 24, 1929.

[83] Ibid.

[84] 1927 Rules, Article 22(3).

[85] 1933 amendments, Article X (relating to Article 22(2) of the 1927 Rules, not Article 23 as stated in the amendments).

[86] International Chamber of Commerce, "Cost Calculator," https://iccwbo.org/dispute-resolution-services/arbitration/costs-and-payments/cost-calculator/.

[87] International Chamber of Commerce, "Costs and Payments," https://iccwbo.org/dispute-resolution-services/arbitration/costs-and-payments/.

#### 7.2.2.10 Scrutiny of Awards

Before signing an award, the arbitral tribunal must submit it to the ICC Court to make sure that it contains no major defects that could diminish its legal effectiveness. The Court's comments on draft awards may range from the correction of typographical errors to remarks on the substance of the award. Scrutiny of the award is a key step in the arbitral process and a "distinctive feature of ICC arbitration."[88] The Court's scrutiny of draft awards is another example of a rule developed over time to improve the efficiency of the ICC's arbitration system.

The 1922 Rules were silent on this matter. Article XIV/XXXV(b) provided that a copy of the arbitrators' decision should be sent to the ICC and that the parties would receive a certified copy of the decision once the requirements relating to fees and charges had been complied with.

It did not take long for the idea of scrutiny to emerge. The 1923 Explanatory Commentary remarked as follows on Article XIV/XXXV: "It is understood that before signing the award, the arbitrators must submit the draft of their award to the Court of Arbitration for the examination of the Court from the point of view of form. No award can be pronounced without having been submitted to the approval of the Court of Arbitration." This language was incorporated into the 1927 Rules, which read "Before completing the award the arbitrators or arbitrator shall submit the same to the Court of Arbitration for examination as to its form. No award shall under any circumstances be issued until approved as to its form by the Court of Arbitration."[89]

Scrutiny of awards by the Court was seen as an important feature of the ICC system at the time. As Clémentel explained at one of the ICC congresses, members of the Executive Committee of the ICC Court

> study with minute care the cases submitted to the Court and see to it that the awards rendered are in due legal form and in case of necessity can be enforced. The parties have but little idea of the large amount of work done with striking impartiality by merchants and manufacturers, traders and bankers, who give their time, out of pure devotion, to the great cause of commercial justice.[90]

[88] Fry, Greenberg, and Mazza, *Secretariat's Guide*, ¶ 3-1181 (regarding the 2012 Rules).

[89] 1927 Rules, Article 21.

[90] "Solemn Session of the Court of Arbitration," proceedings of the Stockholm Congress, June 27–July 2, 1927, *Journal of the International Chamber of Commerce*, no. 15 (September–October 1927), 38.

In the first decade of the ICC's existence, the Court's scrutiny was limited to formal aspects of awards. "It is clearly understood that this examination extends only to the form of the award and that the arbitrator is sole judge of the merits of the case,"[91] an ICC brochure explained, even though it was "essential" that awards should comply with the laws where enforcement might be sought.

As from 1933, the Court was authorized to comment on the substance of awards, too. Article 21 of the 1927 Rules, as amended, read: "The Court of Arbitration is not precluded from calling the attention of the arbitrators or arbitrator even to points connected with the merits of the case, but with due regard to their liberty of decision."[92] Thus, by the 1930s, the principle of scrutiny of draft awards had become firmly established as part of ICC Court practice.

## 7.3 Evolution of the ICC Arbitration System

In the early years of its existence, the ICC's arbitration system underwent some notable changes. Some of these concerned the characteristics of the cases referred to the ICC in the 1920s and 1930s (Section 7.3.1), while others were more fundamental changes of emphasis and perspective – namely, the shift from conciliation to arbitration (Section 7.3.2), and the move from ruling in equity to ruling at law (Section 7.3.3).

### *7.3.1 Changing Trends in Case Characteristics*

The evolution of ICC arbitration in the 1920s and 1930s is a topic of considerable interest to current researchers working on the modern history of international commercial arbitration.[93] The ICC Archives contain forty-seven awards dating from November 22, 1922 (Case 6) to November 25, 1939 (Case 668). Of these, eighteen were rendered in the 1920s and twenty-nine in the 1930s. A detailed examination of the original texts not only confirms the findings of recent research but also reveals new insights.

[91] International Chamber of Commerce, Brochure No. 50, 6.

[92] 1933 amendments, Article IX (relating to Article 21 of the 1927 Rules, not Article 22 as stated in the Amendments).

[93] See especially Lemercier and Sgard, *Arbitrage privé international*, 25–42; Silva Romero, Jolivet, and Grisel, "Aux origines," ¶¶ 38–48. For the purposes of my research, I used a different database from that mentioned by Lemercier and Sgard's on page 31 of their report, and the original arbitral awards from that period kept in the ICC Archives.

#### 7.3.1.1 Length of Awards

Although most awards rendered in the 1920s and 1930s were short, they increased in length with the passage of time. Leaving aside the two longest awards during that period,[94] the average length of arbitral awards was 8.6 pages (with ten awards comprising only three pages, and twelve awards only four pages).

Awards in the 1920s averaged 7.1 pages in length, whereas the 1930s saw the figure rise to 9.2 pages. The two longest awards from that period (Cases 645 and 665) both date from the end of the 1930s (1938 and 1939, respectively). Assuming that longer awards point to more sophisticated factual and legal issues, the increasing length of awards can be taken as a sign of the growing complexity of early ICC cases.

#### 7.3.1.2 Identities of Parties

Who were the users of ICC arbitration in the 1920s and 1930s? If one takes into account both claimants and respondents, the vast majority of parties were French (thirty-four in all, comprising twelve claimants and twenty-two respondents). Other parties were from Belgium (eleven parties), the Netherlands (seven parties), Germany (seven parties), the United Kingdom (five parties), and Spain (three parties), as well as Austria, the Czech Republic, Greece, India, Japan, Luxembourg, Sweden, and the United States (one party each).

Cases in the 1920s mainly involved parties from France and nearby countries in Europe, such as Belgium, England, Germany, Italy, and Spain. (The claimant in Case 163 was from Japan, but that case dates from the late 1920s.) Greater geographical diversity emerged in the 1930s, with arbitrations between a Greek claimant and an Italian respondent (Case 396), a Dutch claimant and a Tunisian respondent (Case 477), a Venezuelan claimant and a Belgian respondent (Case 588), and an Indian claimant and a German respondent (Case 598). This is a clear sign of the ICC's growing renown, bolstered by an intensive "propaganda" drive, to use the term employed at the time.[95]

[94] The award of December 2, 1939 in Case 665 ran to 87 pages and the award of February 11, 1938 in Case 645 to 40 pages. When comparing the length of awards, I used the texts retyped in a standardized format with a uniform font and margins.

[95] See, for example, "Proceedings of the Twelfth Council Meeting," ICC Doc. No. 1214, Paris, July 20, 1923, 27; "Proceedings of the Thirteenth Meeting of the Council," Paris, November 9, 1923, at 48; "Publishing Arbitration Awards," *World Trade*, 4, no. 3 (February 1932), 10.

#### 7.3.1.3 Identities of Arbitrators

Similar trends can be observed in relation to the nationality of arbitrators. French arbitrators were the most numerous (ten served in the 1920s and 1930s), followed by Belgian (eight), Swiss (seven), and Austrian, British, Dutch, German, and Italian arbitrators.

It was rare for arbitrators in the 1920s to be jurists, whereas many in the 1930s had some sort of legal training.[96]

The arbitrators who served in the 1920s included engineers (Cases 6, 111, 247, and 288), members of local chambers of commerce (Cases 67 and 88), a merchant (Case 50), a company director (Case 56), a member of a tobacco journal (Case 115), and an industrialist (Case 265). Most of these arbitrators conducted the proceedings from their homes ("carried out this arbitration at our home" (Case 144); "The arbitrator was tasked with studying the documents relating to the case and rendering his award on the basis of documents at his residence in Basel" (Case 225); "I, the undersigned . . . have carried out this arbitration in my office" (Case 253)).

Toward the end of the 1920s, an increasing number of lawyers and law graduates were acting as arbitrators. The arbitrator in Case 143 (of 1927), which concerned letters of credit, was a Belgian lawyer, as was the arbitrator in Case 304 (of 1929), while an Italian lawyer served as the arbitrator in Case 304 (also of 1929). The arbitrator in Case 144 (of 1927) was both a lawyer and an engineer, and was described in the award as an "ancien élève de l'Ecole Polytechnique, Docteur en droit, Avocat à la Cour de Paris, Secrétaire Général de l'Association française de Propriété Industrielle et Rapporteur-Général de l'Association Internationale de la Propriété Industrielle, Officier de la Légion d'Honneur." Reflecting this development in arbitrators' qualifications, the 1927 Rules referred to the arbitrators whom national committees could nominate as "technical or *legal* experts."[97] Commenting on the 1927 Rules, Arnaud explained: "The Court of Arbitration does not wish to confine its activity to purely technical disputes over the quality of goods or the customs of a particular trade. It feels competent to decide purely legal cases and for these will, of course, seek the collaboration of legal experts."[98]

[96] See Lemercier and Sgard, *Arbitrage privé international*, 36–40; Grisel and Stone Sweet, *Evolution of International Arbitration*, 92.

[97] 1927 Rules, Article 11(1) (emphasis added).

[98] Arnaud, "Arbitration," 123. Arnaud was a key member of the Court of Arbitration; see Comité national français de la Chambre de commerce internationale, *Un demi-siècle au service de la Chambre de commerce internationale: Brochure publiée à l'occasion du départ en retraite de René Arnaud, Directeur Général du Comité* (Paris: International Chamber of Commerce, 1969).

The 1930s saw an increase in the number of arbitrators from the legal world. Many of them were attorneys, as in Cases 380, 381, 382, 383, 387, and 390 (which all involved the same claimant, but different respondents, and were decided by the same English barrister) and Cases 477, 543, and 665. Other arbitrators included law professors and doctors of law (Cases 556, 557, 588, and 667), legal advisers (Cases 536 and 540), and former judges (Cases 536 and 665).

#### 7.3.1.4 Subject Matter of Disputes

As Lemercier and Sgard have shown, arbitration cases in the 1930s differ in nature from those of the 1920s. While in the 1920s, "the ICC Court of Arbitration attracts cases that are similar to those which until then used to be arbitrated by trade associations," the 1930s saw a shift toward disputes of a different kind:

> Corporations, often with share capital, sometimes very large, are more frequently found as parties. The issues in dispute have changed and include problems of exchange, licenses to exploit patents, and agency contracts (representation abroad); new sectors, notably engineering, are present and the amounts in dispute are higher. We are no longer in the sphere of arbitrations concerning raw materials – which of course still exist in other institutions. The ICC Court has started to carve out a particular niche of activity, albeit limited for the moment.[99]

A detailed analysis of arbitral awards from that period reveals that the disputes submitted to arbitration in the 1920s related to the following matters: felt-carding machines (Case 6), rubber (Case 50), creosote oil (Cases 56 and 67), kaolin (Case 91), superheaters (Case 111), tobacco (Case 115), building materials (Case 225), steel-cutting machines (Case 247), mother-of-pearl (Case 265), and railroad materials (Case 1929). In these cases – predominantly concerning quality, which was, and sometimes still is,[100] the purpose of the arbitration offered by trade associations – the arbitrator would often physically inspect the goods. In Case 265, for example, the arbitrator requested a sample of the goods:

> A 7–8 kilo sample of second-quality Florès mother-of-pearl was presented to me as having [been] taken from the two sample baskets . . . ; then, two

[99] Lemercier and Sgard, *Arbitrage privé international*, 31–32.

[100] For example, the International Cotton Association still offers two types of arbitration: quality arbitration ("for disputes arising from the manual examination of the quality of cotton and/or quality characteristics that can only be determined by instrument testing") and technical arbitration ("or all other non-quality disputes"). International Cotton Association, "Arbitration," www.ica-ltd.org/arbitration/.

> full baskets of goods delivered by [the claimant] that were the subject of the discussion were then emptied before me. It was clear to me that this mother-of-pearl was not of a quality and appearance consistent with that of the purported sample and that [the defendant] could not accept these goods in place of what had been sold based on the given sample.[101]

In the 1930s, matters of a different kind began to be referred to ICC arbitration. They included the publication of articles in a sports magazine (Cases 380, 381, 382, 383, 387, and 390), an exclusive license to use a water-softening agent (Case 540), the contracting parties' right to sell products in the territory of the Saar Basin following the Treaty of Versailles (Case 546), agency agreements (Case 556), and licensing agreements (Case 588). Further examples can be found in the short excerpts from ICC awards published in *World Trade*, which covered such topics as "Tax Deductions on British Patent Royalties,"[102] "[a]n Agent's Claim to Commission on Business Effected Outside His Area,"[103] "[a] Dispute Arising Out of a Contract Between a Principal and His Agent,"[104] and "[t]he Validity of Tacit Acceptance."[105] Clearly, these cases involved far more complex legal and factual issues than those of the 1920s.

### *7.3.2 Shift from Conciliation to Arbitration*

#### 7.3.2.1 Early Importance of Conciliation

To understand the development of the ICC's dispute resolution system, it is important to seize the distinction between arbitration and conciliation. Conciliation was aimed at bringing parties together to enable them to reach a "mutual agreement based upon the friendly suggestions" of the Administrative Commission.[106] René Arnaud compared this procedure to that of the French *juge de paix* between 1790 and 1958.[107] Conciliation was a voluntary process; the parties were under no obligation to settle. If conciliation failed, they could proceed to arbitration or initiate court

101 ICC Case No. 265, award, November 6, 1928, 3.

102 "Income Tax Deductions on British Patent Royalties" (ICC Case 144), *World Trade,* 5, no. 1 (January 1933), 2.

103 "An Agent's Claim to Commission on Business Effected outside His Area" (ICC Case 304), *World Trade,* 5, no. 6 (June 1933), 7.

104 "A Dispute Arising Out of a Contract between a Principal and His Agent" (ICC Case 568), *World Trade,* 6, no. 8 (October 1934), 6–7.

105 "The Validity of Tacit Acceptance" (ICC Case 543), *World Trade,* 6, no. 10 (December 1934), 7.

106 1922 Rules, Article I.

107 Arnaud, "Arbitration," 119.

proceedings, with the proviso that "nothing that has been done, said or written" during the conciliation could affect subsequent proceedings.[108]

> In short, the domain of conciliation and the domain of arbitration are completely isolated from each other; under no circumstances can any concessions that a party may have made or any unwise words that a party may at times have uttered in the course of the proceedings undermine its rights in the event that the conciliation fails and it is necessary to resort to arbitration.[109]

In contrast to arbitration, conciliation was conducted at the ICC's Paris headquarters by its Administrative Commission, composed of the secretary general of the ICC and representatives from national member organizations.[110] For example, Basil Miles, an American, presided over one of the very first conciliation cases heard by the Court of Arbitration, a dispute between French and Belgian parties over the quality of a consignment of walnut wood.[111]

The 1922 Rules drew a distinction between conciliation, governed by Section A (Articles I to IV) entitled the "Rules of Procedure for the Conciliation and Good Offices of the International Chamber of Commerce" ("*Règlement de conciliation*"), and arbitration, governed by Sections B (Articles V to XXIV) and C (Articles XXV to XLV) entitled the "Rules of Procedure for Arbitration of the International Chamber of Commerce" ("*Règlement d'arbitrage*").[112] Thus, each procedure was governed by its own set of rules.

[108] 1922 Rules, Article IV.

[109] René Arnaud, "Conciliation et arbitrage," in *Conférence sur l'arbitrage commercial international: Compte rendu des séances destiné aux Membres de la Conférence (June 13–15, 1946)*, 36.

[110] See Arnaud, "Arbitration," 119.

[111] George Ridgeway, *Merchants of Peace: Twenty Years of Business Diplomacy through the International Chamber of Commerce, 1919–1938* (New York: Columbia University Press, 1938), 325–26. Ridgeway describes this case, which was heard on June 22, 1923, as "the first case heard by the newly created court of arbitration and successfully settled according to the rules for conciliation."

[112] Sections B and C were identical, except in respect of two articles, plus an additional article that appeared only in Section C. This explains why we use two numbers when referring to a specific Article of the 1922 Rules. So, for example, Article V of Section B and Article XXV of Section C of the 1922 Rules are the same; they are therefore referred to as Article V/XXV of the 1922 Rules. On the difference between Sections B and C, see "The Settlement of Disputes between Traders of Different Countries," in *Rules of Conciliation (Good Offices) and Arbitration (Fourth Edition)*, Brochure No. 21 (Paris: ICC International Headquarters), 21. Section B was introduced "with special reference to France," whose law did not provide for the legal enforcement of arbitral awards based

Conciliation was essentially a three-step process, with national committees playing a key role throughout.[113] First, a party would request the intervention of the ICC "in writing through his National Committee" and provide a copy of the contract and other relevant documents.[114] The chairman of the Administrative Commission would then reach out to the other party through the ICC national committee in the country where it was resident, "requesting him, provided he accepts the good offices of the Chamber, to submit his statement of the case, supported by a complete documentary record."[115] Finally, the Administrative Commission would study the documents and communicate with the parties (once again, through the relevant national committees), "with a view to arriving at a basis of agreement acceptable to all of the parties."[116]

Largely because of the flexibility it afforded, conciliation proved remarkably successful in the early years of the ICC Court. As stated in an ICC brochure, "the conciliation procedure, so simple and so inexpensive, has had excellent results. When it plays out between two companies of good repute and equally desirous of avoiding chicanery, it can settle what is sometimes a large case in a few weeks."[117] Indeed, data made available in each successive issue of the *Arbitration Report* show that more cases were submitted to conciliation than to arbitration.

As Table 7.1 shows,[118] there were relatively few arbitration proceedings at the ICC in the 1920s (the annual total ranges from two in 1924 to six in 1926). Most cases were settled by mutual agreement of the parties through the unofficial intervention of the ICC. More cases led to conciliation than to arbitration proceedings. As Steuart Hamilton has written, "conciliation, far from being overshadowed by arbitration, was conceived as its equal and in practice was the more prominent of the two services."[119]

upon binding arbitration clauses until 1925; Section B was consequently removed in the 1927 Rules.

113 For a discussion of the ICC conciliation procedure, see also Silva Romero, Jolivet, and Grisel, "Aux origines," ¶ 11.

114 1922 Rules, Article I.

115 Ibid., Article II.

116 Ibid., Article III.

117 International Chamber of Commerce, *Services rendus par le système d'arbitrage de la Chambre de commerce internationale* (Paris: ICC Headquarters, 1931).

118 Additional data are provided in Steuart Hamilton, "ICC Conciliation: A Glimpse into History," in *ADR: International Applications*, special supplement, *ICC International Court of Arbitration Bulletin* (2001).

119 Ibid., 23; Silva Romero, Jolivet, and Grisel, "Aux origines," ¶ 12.

Table 7.1 *Number of disputes submitted to the ICC in the 1920s and method of settlement*

| | | Number of disputes settled | | | |
|---|---|---|---|---|---|
| | Total number of disputes submitted to the ICC | Through arbitration | Through conciliation | Through mutual agreement after unofficial ICC intervention | Through other arbitral institutions after ICC action |
| *Arbitration Report*, no. 3 (June 1924) | 68 | 2 | 6 | 13 | – |
| *Arbitration Report*, no. 4 (March 1925) | 92 | 4 | 7 | 23 | 2 |
| *Arbitration Report*, no. 5 (December 1925) | 100 | 5 | 7 | 10 | 2 |
| *Arbitration Report*, no. 6 (June 1926) | 126 | 6 | 7 | 32 | 2 |

Several examples of conciliation cases can be found in the *Arbitration Reports* (a supplement to the *Journal of the International Chamber of Commerce*) and other sources. For example, on June 22, 1923, a conciliation was conducted between a French seller and a Belgian purchaser. The dispute concerned two questions: the quality of a consignment of walnut wood sold by the French party to the Belgian party, and fluctuating rates on the Belgian exchange. After a discussion lasting approximately an hour, a settlement was reached on the amount to be paid by the Belgian purchaser to the French seller and a formal agreement was signed by the parties in the presence of the Administrative Commission.[120] According to Ridgeway, this was the first case ever heard by the newly created Court of Arbitration.[121]

Another conciliation took place in Paris on December 6, 1923, to resolve a dispute between a Norwegian company and a Swedish company over the deduction of commission on a sale of paper pulp. This time, the parties did not appear and the Administrative Commission issued an opinion on the basis of the documents alone: "The defendant, in deference to the Administrative Commission of the International Chamber, accepted the view adopted by the Commission which was in favour of the plaintiff."[122]

#### 7.3.2.2 The Growing Importance of Arbitration

As time passed, conciliation progressively gave way to arbitration.[123] A practice that was largely informal and uncodified was replaced by a more formalized and court-like procedure. Ironically, conciliation, which enabled parties to avoid "not only the law courts but even the formalities of arbitration,"[124] yielded to the very procedure it was meant to sidestep, "a jurisprudential institution" where arbitrators exercised their function "by an implicit mandate from the State."[125]

120 Ridgeway, *Merchants of Peace*, 326.

121 Ibid., 325. Steuart Hamilton, a former publications manager at the ICC International Court of Arbitration, mentions an earlier conciliation on December 28, 1922, between Dutch and British parties, who agreed that their contract should be canceled and compensation paid to the British party in installments without interest. According to Hamilton, "ICC Conciliation," 27, this was "the earliest decision in the ICC's archives." No record of this case was found in the ICC archival material I consulted.

122 International Chamber of Commerce, *Arbitration Report No. 3* (July 1924), 8.

123 See, for example, Silva Romero, Jolivet, and Grisel, "Aux origines," ¶ 11; Lemercier and Sgard, *Arbitrage privé international*, 25–27.

124 International Chamber of Commerce, *Arbitration Report No. 3*, 8.

125 Roberto Pozzi, "Conciliation and Arbitration between Merchants of Different Countries. Memorandum Submitted by M. Roberto Pozzi," in International Chamber of Commerce, *Commercial Arbitration*, Brochure No. 13, 17.

The shift from conciliation to arbitration was encouraged by the greater prominence the ICC Court started giving to arbitration. In a subtle but telling move, it changed the order in which it referred to the two procedures in various official documents and brochures.[126] But the real change came when the ICC Court made conciliation optional in the 1933 amendments to the Rules, which were adopted at the ICC's congress in Vienna. Section A of the Rules ("Conciliation") was renamed "Optional Conciliation."[127] As explained in the commentary accompanying the 1933 amendments, this change was meant "to underline the fact that it is always open to disputants to proceed straight to arbitration without first submitting the dispute to conciliation."[128]

Several reasons have been advanced to explain this shift. Chief among them is the fact that parties started demanding more legal certainty than conciliation was able to offer.[129] It has also been suggested that the early success of conciliation was due to the fact that France did not recognize the validity of arbitration clauses before 1925, causing many cases that would otherwise have been submitted to arbitration in the early 1920s to be submitted to conciliation instead.[130] More generally, the shift from conciliation to arbitration may reflect a change of mentality. Conciliation was "very much a product of its time, rooted in the will to achieve international understanding through friendship."[131] As proceedings became more adversarial and parties started placing more faith in arbitral institutions, conciliation was downplayed in favor of a more rigid framework.

This change of mentality may help to explain why, even today, arbitration is by far the more prominent of the two services – even though both are still available at the ICC in the form of arbitration and mediation.[132] Some voices in the arbitration community have indeed called for a revival of conciliation. Owen Young's observation that conciliation did not involve

[126] For example, the 1922 Rules mentioned that the ICC's goal was to "encourage the use of conciliation and arbitration," while the 1927 Rules referred to the need to "provide facilities for arbitration and conciliation."

[127] International Chamber of Commerce, "Amendments to the Rules of Conciliation and Arbitration of the International Chamber of Commerce," in *Resolutions Adopted by the Vienna Congress (July 1933)*, 23 (Resolution No. 19).

[128] Algot Bagge, "An Amended Edition of the Rules of Conciliation and Arbitration of the International Chamber of Commerce," *World Trade*, 6, no. 1 (January 1934), 11.

[129] Silva Romero, Jolivet, and Grisel, "Aux origines," ¶ 11.

[130] Ibid., ¶ 13.

[131] Hamilton, "ICC Conciliation," 29–30.

[132] "Foreword," in International Chamber of Commerce, *Arbitration Rules in Force as from 1 March 2017; Mediation Rules in Force as from 1 January 2014* (ICC Publication 880-2; Paris: ICC Publishing, 2017), 1.

"either the expense or the delay of a formal arbitration"[133] would appear to have resonated with users who viewed arbitration as too lengthy and costly, as in the United States for example.[134] In 1988, the ICC revised its conciliation rules; the procedure remained optional, but the conciliation commission was replaced with a sole conciliator.[135] It was suggested at the time that "one of the reasons why there is not more international conciliation today is simply that parties have little idea what it may entail and do not appreciate its extraordinary flexibility."[136] Even though conciliation may never return to the status it enjoyed in the early years of the ICC's existence, it seems to reflect a certain "spirit of arbitration," where parties and arbitrators view themselves as part of "a 'club' of gentlemen trying together to find a peaceful solution to their dispute, according to the rules of a game that they had deliberately chosen to play."[137]

### 7.3.3 *Shift from Equity to Law*

#### 7.3.3.1 From Equitable to Legal Modes of Reasoning

As arbitration acquired greater prominence, recourse to equity and *amiable composition*[138] in the resolution of disputes began to decline. In the early years of the ICC Court of Arbitration, arbitrators relied primarily on equity, not law, when ruling on disputes. It was believed that "in the domain of private law, and especially in that of commercial law, the parties may, by mutual agreement, derogate [from] the strict application of the law."[139] Conversely, as Pozzi explained, "the arbitrators may, as a matter of substantial justice, temper the rigid precepts of the law

133 Quoted in Ridgeway, *Merchants of Peace*, 323.

134 Emmanuel Gaillard and John Savage (eds.), *Fouchard, Gaillard, Goldman on International Commercial Arbitration* (The Hague: Kluwer Law International, 1999), ¶ 17.

135 International Chamber of Commerce, *ICC Rules of Conciliation and Arbitration*, ICC Publication No. 447 (1987); see Gaillard and Savage, *Fouchard, Gaillard, Goldman*, ¶ 17.

136 Eric Schwartz, "International Conciliation and the ICC," *ICC International Court of Arbitration Bulletin*, 5, no. 2 (November 1994), 17.

137 Yves Derains, "New Trends in the Practical Application of ICC Rules of Arbitration," *Northwestern Journal of International Law and Business*, 3, (1981), 44.

138 *Amiable composition*, which is broadly synonymous with *ex aequo et bono*, means that an arbitrator can "disregard any and all provisions of the rules of law governing the merits that are not mandatory and base his or her decisions purely on principles of fairness and justice, regardless of whether the outcome is consistent with the law." Fry, Greenberg, and Mazza, *Secretariat's Guide*, 231 (regarding the 2012 Rules).

139 Pozzi, "Conciliation and Arbitration," 12.

by the principle of equity,"[140] but equity should remain the norm and "strictly legal" arbitration an exception:

> Strictly legal arbitrators constitute an exceptional institution to which litigants rarely have recourse, and then only in the case of controversies which, on account of their material importance or complexity, require judges of exceptional authority and competence. Outside of such extraordinary cases, legal arbitration is little used; and when reduced to the form of an arbitration clause, it becomes in practice an absurdity.[141]

A complete reversal took place, however, in the course of the 1920s and 1930s. As one commentator explained, "as arbitration gradually increased its influence and acquired a stronger foothold in law, ICC conciliation shed something of its original inspiration and yielded to legal considerations."[142] This shift – from equitable to legal modes of reasoning – can be seen in two areas: contemporary arbitral awards and the ICC Rules.

Of the 131 "historical" awards that are still available in the ICC's archives, 18 are from the 1920s and in 15 of these the arbitrator acted as *amiable compositeur.*[143] The arbitrator applied a national law – that of France – in only one case from the 1920s.[144] In another case, the applicable law was not specified,[145] and in a third case the arbitrator referred to the specifications of the stipulations of the parties' contract and to notions of fairness.[146] In the latter case, which concerned the quality of mild steel cutting machines sold by a Belgian engineer to an Italian buyer, the arbitrator requested the opportunity to inspect the allegedly defective machines:

> We requested that the machines be tested regarding the way they cut mild steel (homogeneous iron) based on the promises of the catalog. . . . We found that it was difficult for cutter no. 3 (on page 12 of the catalog) to cleanly cut the pieces of iron as per the catalog. That is why the machines

[140] Ibid.,18.
[141] Ibid., 13.
[142] Hamilton, "ICC Conciliation," 29–30.
[143] Case No. 6, November 22, 1922; Case No. 50, February 12, 1924; Case No. 56, July 9, 1924; Case No. 67, July 22, 1924; Case No. 88, December 19, 1925; Case No. 91, October 28, 1925; Case No. 111, January 24, 1927; Case No. 115, July 27, 1926; Case No. 143, February 19, 1927; Case No. 163, October 26, 1927; Case No. 253, September 18, 1928; Case No. 265, November 6, 1928; Case No. 288, November 25, 1929; Case No. 301, April 24, 1929; Case No. 304, December 9, 1929. The dates mentioned (here and below) are the dates of the awards.
[144] Case No. 225, February 11, 1929.
[145] Case No. 144, February 1, 1927.
[146] Case No. 247, August 8, 1929.

> do not correspond to the sales models. The construction of the machines is too weak and they can furnish only mediocre (cutting) work.[147]

The arbitrator concluded that, "based on the catalog warranty," the machines were unsalable and that it would be "unfair" to force the buyer to keep the defective machines.[148] Despite not acting expressly as *amiable compositeur*, the arbitrator in this case was nonetheless guided by broad notions of "fairness" in reaching his decision.

Further examples of arbitrators acting as *amiable compositeurs* can be found in other contemporary ICC cases. They show that arbitrators in the 1920s referred to their powers of *amiable composition* in various ways.[149] The frequency of these formulations suggests that the use of *amiable composition* powers was widespread and uncontroversial in the 1920s.

In the 1930s, by contrast, an increasing number of awards referred to national laws, including those of Austria, Belgium, France, Germany, and Spain.[150] For example, in Case 380 the respondent, a French individual, contracted to have an engraving of himself in a polo outfit made by the claimant company and printed in a sports magazine, along with a short biography. The claimant company prepared the article and requested payment for half of the overall amount due, but the respondent sought to rescind the contract on the ground that this was higher than what he had previously agreed to.[151] Referring to a provision of the French Civil Code, the arbitrator held that the respondent owed damages to the claimant for breach of contract. The same facts gave rise to other ICC cases (involving

[147] Ibid., 2.

[148] Ibid., 3.

[149] "We, the undersigned, . . . appointed as *amiable compositeur*" (Case No. 111, January 24, 1927); "the arbitrator has the powers of *amiable compositeur*" (Case No. 301, April 24, 1929, 3); "Under the arbitration agreement, it was understood that, as *amiable compositeur*, I would not be bound to follow procedural or legal rules" (Case No. 67, July 22, 1924, 3; Case No. 88, December 19, 1925, 3; Case No. 91, October 28, 1925, 3; Case No. 115, July 27, 1926, 2); "Under the arbitration agreement, I was exempted from all procedural rules as *amiable compositeur*" (Case No. 50, February 12, 1924, 2; Case No. 56, July 9, 1924, 3); "We, the undersigned, . . . deciding in accordance with the terms of the arbitration agreement as *amiable compositeur*, exempted from observing the procedural and legal rules" (Case No. 143, February 19, 1927, 12); "we do not rule according to strict and formal considerations, but equitable grounds are our guide" (Case No. 288, November 25, 1929, 2); the arbitrator's mission is to "determine the amount of money that one party owes in equity to the other" (Case No. 6, November 22, 1922, 2); "the arbitrator was entitled to decide in equity without observing the legal rules of the procedure" (Case No. 163, October 26, 1927, 3).

[150] See Silva Romero, Jolivet, and Grisel, "Aux origines," ¶ 16.

[151] Case No. 380, June 28, 1931.

different respondents) during the same period, with the same English arbitrator again deciding in favor of the claimant.[152]

Changes to the ICC Rules during the 1920s and 1930s likewise testify to a shift from equity to law. Initially, the emphasis was placed on equitable, rather than legal, modes of reasoning. The "Proposed Plan for Arbitration" stated that "[e]xcept where otherwise provided, arbitrators shall render their decisions as *amiable compositeurs*, that is, they shall not be bound to follow the legal rules of procedure or to decide according to law."[153] As the mandatory "shall" indicates, arbitrators were *required* to use equity. The 1922 Rules were slightly more nuanced, dropping the mandatory language while still giving arbitrators broad powers of *amiable composition*.[154]

A turnabout took place in 1933, however, when Article 16(3) of the 1927 Rules was changed to allow parties to object to the exercise of *amiable composition* powers by arbitrators: "The Court of Arbitration shall give to the arbitrators or arbitrator power to act as 'amiable compositeurs' unless one of the parties is opposed thereto and provided that it will not in any way interfere with the legal enforcement of the award."[155] This change thus made it possible to curb the use of *amiable composition* powers.

Finally, the 1947 amendments introduced a number of changes to more clearly define arbitrators' powers. The "Form of Submission" now had to include "[s]pecification of arbitrator's powers (whether they are to act as 'amiable compositeurs' or whether they shall be bound to apply the rules of law)."[156] The 1947 amendments also changed the wording of Article 16 of the 1927 Rules to the effect that the arbitrators were not to act as *amiable compositeurs* "unless *the parties agree* thereto and provided that it will not in any way interfere with the legal enforcement of the award."[157] These provisions were meant to ensure that the parties clearly knew what type of powers the arbitrators were exercising. It is particularly telling that a footnote in the Rules referring to arbitrators as *amiable*

[152] Case No. 381, June 28, 1931; Case No. 382 (n.d.); Case No. 383, June 28, 1931; Case No. 387, June 28, 1931; Case No. 390, June 28, 1931.

[153] International Chamber of Commerce, Brochure No. 13, 26–27.

[154] 1922 Rules, Article VII.

[155] 1933 amendments, Article VI (relating to Article 16(3) of the 1927 Rules, not Article 17(3) as stated in the amendments).

[156] 1947 amendments, Article 6 (relating to Article 14(g) of the 1927 Rules, not Article 15(g) as stated in the amendments).

[157] Ibid., Article 7 (relating to Article 16 of the 1927 Rules, not Article 17 as stated in the amendments) (emphasis in original).

*compositeurs* ("'Amiable compositeurs' are arbitrators who are not bound by rules of law") was deleted as a result of these amendments.

The clear shift from equitable to legal modes of reasoning evidenced in the cases and successive versions of the Rules discussed earlier was accompanied by another related change – an emerging predilection for legal rather than moral sanctions.

### 7.3.3.2 From Moral to Legal Sanctions

As with any legal regime, the efficiency and success of the ICC's arbitration system depended on the ability of a central enforcer, the ICC, to impose sanctions for noncompliant behavior.[158] In the early years of the ICC, the lack of an international instrument providing for the recognition and enforcement of foreign arbitral awards meant that the ICC had to rely mostly on informal sanctions.

However, it soon recognized that a sanctioning mechanism was necessary to ensure that awards were performed. Under Article 12(2) of the "Proposed Plan for Arbitration," the appropriate national committee of the ICC had the power to take "all such measures of discipline" and "such moral and economic penalties as in their discretion may seem appropriate" against the defaulting party.[159] The 1922 Rules did not expand on this, but simply stated that the arbitrators' decision was "binding"[160] and that the parties were "in honour bound to carry out the award of the arbitrators."[161]

[158] The question of how to deal with noncompliant behavior raises many difficulties. Modern legal philosophy has long sought to identify the proper role of sanctions and coercion in general theories of legal systems, from Austin's theory of legal positivism (treating law as consisting in the commands of a sovereign backed by sanctions: see John Austin, *The Province of Jurisprudence Determined* (London: John Murray, 1832)) to Kelsen's sanction-centered account of law (according to which law is a coercive order regulating human behavior: see Hans Kelsen, *Pure Theory of Law*, trans. Max Knight (Berkeley: University of California Press, 1967)) and its rejection by Hart (who considered that law works as a means of social control, not as a series of sanctions that officials must apply if certain circumstances arise: see H. L. A. Hart, *The Concept of Law* (Oxford: Oxford University Press, 2012 [1961])). Other present-day thinkers have also contributed to this debate, with some probing the different types of socially enforced norms. Key among them is Ellickson, who tried to explain why unwritten social norms for dispute resolution have developed (see Robert Ellickson, *Order without Law: How Neighbors Settle Disputes* (Cambridge, MA: Harvard University Press, 1991), arguing that social norms are particularly important in close-knit groups because they have lower transaction costs than legal rules and achieve a similar level of behavior).

[159] International Chamber of Commerce, Brochure No. 13, 29.

[160] 1922 Rules, Article XIV/XXXV(a). The Article referred to "the decision of the umpire," when two arbitrators and an umpire are nominated.

[161] Ibid., Article XX/XLI(a).

Alongside these provisions, the ICC also adopted the practice of publishing the names of the defaulting parties: "The Court of Arbitration of the International Chamber of Commerce shall have the right to request that the name of the defaulting party be published in the official publications of the International Chamber of Commerce, in those of the National Committees, together with the text of the award so remaining unexecuted."[162] This was a form of moral sanction that, as Arnaud explained, relied on

> one of the most characteristic advantages of the arbitral organization of the International Chamber, which is that this organization rests upon a powerful federation having created a network of economic forces in all the countries of the world. One of the advantages of this solidarity is that recalcitrant defendants can always be reached and pressure brought to bear upon to force compliance with arbitral awards rendered against them. ... The International Chamber is convinced that, as a general rule, business firms having signed the arbitration clause will have too high a regard for their commercial reputation and their credit not voluntarily to fulfil their arbitration undertakings and not to cooperate in every way in the procedure.[163]

Arnaud's words reflect the view, prevalent at the time, that arbitration was a "gentleman's game" and commercial reputation could serve as an effective means of pressuring parties to comply with awards. An ICC brochure containing "practical hints" to parties explained that "[i]f you have dealt with a company of a good 'standing', it will willingly and without difficulty comply with the award rendered in the name of the Court of Arbitration of the International Chamber of Commerce," failing which, by "persisting in its ill-will, the recalcitrant party would risk ruining its trade reputation and losing its credit."[164] In the words of a contemporary author, "the blacklisting of the recalcitrant party is ... a sufficient sanction."[165]

To ensure that parties complied with the conciliation decisions reached by the Administrative Commission, despite their having no binding force, the ICC appealed to local chambers of commerce to exert pressure on parties who did not comply with the decisions. For example, in a dispute between Dutch and Algerian parties, compliance with the Administrative Commission's proposal was achieved,

[162] Ibid., Article XX/XLI(c).

[163] Arnaud, "Arbitration," 123.

[164] International Chamber of Commerce, *Arbitrage commercial international: Conseils pratiques* (Paris: ICC International Headquarters, 1935), 7.

[165] J. -P. Palewski, "L'arbitrage commercial en France et la Cour d'Arbitrage de la Chambre de Commerce Internationale," *Journal du droit international*, 1926, 44.

> [t]hanks to the kind intervention of the Chamber of Commerce of Algiers and to the distinguished authority of its President. … In this way, a local Chamber of Commerce was able to come to the assistance of the International Chamber of Commerce and to establish a precedent which will facilitate in the future the settlement of disputes by friendly agreement.[166]

Similarly, in a dispute between a Chinese seller and a Dutch buyer, it was reported:

> The Commission succeeded in obtaining the personal assistance of the President of the French Chamber of Commerce in China, who was requested to approach the French merchant on the matter. The Administrative Commission has frequently solicited the aid of local chambers of commerce, requesting them to make friendly suggestions to the parties concerned, and this moral action has always had the happiest results, as the proposals submitted to the two parties by the Commission of Conciliation have nearly always been accepted. This friendly and inexpensive procedure can therefore be of great use to commerce in general.[167]

In the late 1920s and the 1930s, formal sanctions aimed at achieving enforcement through the application of legal rules began to take the place of moral sanctions. In the 1927 Rules, the notion of honor ("parties are in honour bound to carry out the award") was removed and replaced with the more categoric statement that "[t]he parties shall be bound to comply with the award."[168] Also in the late 1920s, the Geneva framework introduced new legal remedies for parties seeking to enforce arbitral awards. As a result of this increasing insistence on legal as opposed to moral sanctions, the ICC's arbitration system became more robust and effective.

## 7.4 Conclusion

Part II has explored key features of the Age of Institutionalization, situated in the first half of the twentieth century. This period witnessed the emergence of a new class of arbitration scholars and practitioners, who developed specialized knowledge about international commercial arbitration. New organizations were founded, such as the ICC and its Court of Arbitration. These organizations started administering cases and codifying existing rules and practices. Through such codification,

166 International Chamber of Commerce, *Arbitration Report No.* 3, 8.
167 International Chamber of Commerce, *Arbitration Report No.* 4, 2.
168 1927 Rules, Article 25(1).

they played a key role in shaping contemporary international commercial arbitration practice.

The Age of Institutionalization was central to the creation of the modern regime of international commercial arbitration. It saw some notable achievements, such as the Geneva Protocol and Geneva Convention. But these instruments still reflected a highly territorial mindset and could be associated with a sense of anxiety. The situation changed gradually and in the 1950s ultimately gave rise to the New York Convention, which marked the shift from territorialism to internationalism and ushered international commercial arbitration into a new era. This shift from territorialism to internationalism reflected the broader "internationalist" outlook that characterized the legal consciousness of the time. The Age of Institutionalization, can be most aptly described as embodying the "energy aesthetic,"[169] in which the dominant concepts are those of "energy and its manifestations – 'change', 'transformative change', 'reform', 'progress', 'progressive legal change.'"[170] These concepts seem well suited to an age that was marked by the establishment of new arbitral institutions endowed with sophisticated arbitration regimes offering "the allure of change, movement, progress."[171]

[169] See Section 2.1.

[170] Pierre Schlag, "The Aesthetics of American Law," *Harvard Law Review*, 115 (2002), 1070.

[171] Ibid., 1075.

# PART III

# The Age of Autonomy

# 8

# Introduction to the Age of Autonomy

The third period in the modern history of international commercial arbitration is the Age of Autonomy, which started in the late 1950s and extends to the present day. This period has been marked by the "extraordinary fate" of arbitration, as Motulsky wrote in 1963.[1] At least three types of autonomy may be found in this third age. The first is that of the mercatocracy, a distinct class of professionals who, having devoted an increasing amount of time and attention to international commercial arbitration, see themselves as experts in international arbitration. The Age of Autonomy has thus been characterized, to a large extent, by increased expertise and specialization.

A second (and related) type of autonomy is that of the field as a whole. Lawyers, scholars, and professors who had hitherto considered international arbitration as a subcategory of civil procedure or international law started viewing the discipline as a full-fledged field of practice and research. In the Age of Autonomy, academic programs began to include specialist courses providing training in international commercial arbitration for new generations of arbitration students and scholars. Books, monographs, and journals started filling entire shelves in law libraries. New professional associations have been formed. Even law firms have developed practice groups specializing exclusively in international arbitration.

The third kind of autonomy is that of the law expounded by the mercatocracy. A notable feature of the Age of Autonomy is that, in addition to working on actual cases, professionals have developed theories and intellectual constructs *about* international commercial arbitration. One such theory, explored in Chapter 9, is *lex mercatoria* – the notion that an international commercial law was gradually replacing domestic laws. Another theory, explored in Chapter 10, is the arbitral

[1] Henri Motulsky, "L'internationalisation du droit français de l'arbitrage," *Revue de l'arbitrage*, 1963, 110, 110.

legal order – the idea that arbitral awards and the arbitral process as a whole exist in a separate legal order of their own. True to the etymological roots of the word "autonomy" – from the Greek *autos* (self) and *nomos* (law), thus meaning "having its own laws" – the mercatocracy has been demanding its own laws. In more philosophical terms, it has embraced autonomy as a "collective enterprise,"[2] which, to use Castoriadis's term, "institutes" a world of imaginary significations for itself.

Part III is thus concerned not so much with *why* a new class of professionals emerged, but with *what* these professionals did or produced. Chapter 9 traces the intellectual history of *lex mercatoria*, from Clive Schmitthoff's and Berthold Goldman's seminal insights in the 1960s to their application by scholars in a wide range of contexts in the 1970s and thereafter. It also shows how this theoretical exploration coincided with the emergence of a new school of thought: the French school of international arbitration. Chapter 10 explores the work of the second generation of the French school from the 1980s onward. It shows how members of this new generation started to focus less on the "society of merchants" and more on the "autonomy" or "juridicity" of international arbitration.

The theories described in this part – *lex mercatoria* and the arbitral legal order – led to heated debates within the arbitration community. On the renewal side of the spectrum were those who felt that these theories rolled back the frontiers of international arbitration and opened new horizons. Opposing them on the anxiety side were those who felt that the theories were deeply flawed and even dangerous. The two sides clashed frequently in their writings and conferences, often taking issue with the case law in various countries. The opposition between these two camps can still be found in international commercial arbitration today.

In the Age of Autonomy, the tension between the state and the mercatocracy greatly increased. Not only did the mercatocracy become fully organized and homogeneous but, like the *Bürgher* in Hegel's narrative, it asserted its own ends to a remarkable degree. Using Teubner's terminology, the mercatocracy became fully aware of the "autopoietic" – that is, self-organizing and self-referential – nature of the arbitration system.[3] In that respect, the Age of Autonomy has been a period of

[2] Cornelius Castoriadis, *The Imaginary Institution of Society* (1975), trans. Kathleen Blamey (Cambridge, MA: MIT Press, 1987), 107. On Castoriadis's conception of autonomy, see Philippe Caumières, *Castoriadis: Le projet d'autonomie* (Paris: Michalon, 2015).

[3] See Gunther Teubner, *Law as an Autopoietic System* (Oxford: Blackwell, 1993).

closure. Remarkably, however, this moment of closure was short-lived. People outside the arbitration world – in particular, citizens' groups and non-governmental organizations reacting to recent trends and developments in investment treaty arbitration – started to make their voices heard, demanding much more transparency from the arbitration system as a whole. Hence, the dominant discourse in the Age of Autonomy has arguably been cast in the "perspectivist aesthetic," allowing "a variety of different political perspectives and social phenomena to be translated faithfully into the language of the law."[4] Faced with these outside influences, the Age of Autonomy might well be on the decline, opening the possibility of a new age in international commercial arbitration.

This opening chapter of Part III concentrates on the first two types of autonomy mentioned earlier: that of the mercatocracy and of international commercial arbitration as a discipline. It argues that the mercatocracy and the discipline became autonomous through a process of professionalization. After defining the terms "profession" and "professionalization" (Section 8.1), it considers their application in the field of international commercial arbitration (Section 8.2).

## 8.1 Defining Profession and Professionalization

According to the definition of a leading dictionary, a profession is "a calling requiring specialized knowledge and often long and intensive academic preparation."[5] As such, professionals stand in contradistinction to amateurs.[6] The proliferation of professions can be traced back to the late nineteenth and early twentieth centuries, when, under the impact of industrialization, professional activities became increasingly specialized and required special training.[7] In the late Middle Ages, professional callings were limited to the law, the clergy, university teaching, and, to some extent, medicine. In the Renaissance, the military emerged as

[4] Pierre Schlag, "The Aesthetics of American Law," *Harvard Law Review*, 115 (2002), 1049, 1087.

[5] Merriam-Webster Dictionary, "Profession," www.merriam-webster.com/dictionary/profession.

[6] On the idea that arbitration should be kept in the hands of professionals rather than amateurs, see Alan Redfern, "The Changing World of Arbitration," in David Caron, Stephan Schill, Abby Smutny, and Epaminontas Triantafilou (eds.), *Practising Virtue: Inside International Arbitration* (Oxford: Oxford University Press, 2015), 51.

[7] W. J. Reader, *Professional Men: The Rise of the Professional Classes in Nineteenth-Century England* (New York: Basic Books, 1966).

another area of professional activity for members of the aristocracy.[8] As Pound pointed out, "[h]istorically, there are three ideas involved in a profession, organization, learning, and a spirit of public service."[9] In his classic history of the American healthcare system, Starr adopted a sociological definition, describing a profession as "an occupation that regulates itself through systematic, required training and collegial discipline; that has a base in technical, specialized knowledge; and that has a service rather than a profit orientation enshrined in its code of ethics."[10]

The notion of profession should be distinguished from that of professionalization. While the former is static, the latter implies a process, which is shaped by a specific social environment. Wilensky identified five key stages in the process of professionalization: (1) organization around a set of tasks, (2) training within universities, (3) formation of a professional association to advance occupational interests, (4) attainment of state licensure; and (5) formation of a formal code of ethics.[11] This sequence represents the "typical process by which the established professions have arrived,"[12] and it is useful in elucidating international commercial arbitration's acquisition of autonomy.

## 8.2 The Professionalization of International Commercial Arbitration

It seems that most, though not all, of the stages mentioned earlier are found in international commercial arbitration.

### *8.2.1 Technical, Specialized Knowledge*

Few would disagree that the bed of technical, specialized knowledge underlying international commercial arbitration grew enormously in the second half of the twentieth century. A number of key instruments

[8] Harold Wilensky, "The Professionalization of Everyone?," *American Journal of Sociology*, 70 (1964), 141.

[9] Roscoe Pound, "What Is a Profession: The Rise of the Legal Profession in Antiquity," *Notre Dame Law Review*, 19 (1944), 204.

[10] Paul Starr, *The Social Transformation of American Medicine: The Rise of a Sovereign Profession and the Making of a Vast Industry* (New York: Basic Books, 1982), 15.

[11] Wilensky, "Professionalization," 142–46. See also Joseph Hermanowicz and David Johnson, "Professions," in Masamichi Sasaki, Jack Goldstone, Ekkart Zimmerman, and Stephen Sanderson (eds.), *Concise Encyclopedia of Comparative Sociology* (Leiden: Brill, 2014) 213.

[12] Wilensky, "Professionalization," 145.

were developed during the Age of Autonomy to promote the effectiveness of the international arbitration regime. Besides the 1958 Convention on the Recognition and Enforcement of Foreign Arbitral Awards (the New York Convention), such instruments included the 1961 European Convention on International Commercial Arbitration and the 1966 Washington Convention, which has become particularly important in the context of investment treaty disputes. This period was also marked by the entry into force of key domestic laws and statutes, such as the Decrees of May 14, 1980, and January 13, 2011, in France; the Arbitration Acts of 1950, 1975, 1979, 1996, 1979, and 1996 in England; and the 1987 Federal Code on Private International Law in Switzerland.

The task of interpreting these instruments was performed by specialist courts, institutions, scholars, and practitioners. For example, thousands of decisions relating to the New York Convention have been issued in both civil law and common law jurisdictions.[13] They reveal that "the interpretation and application of the Convention has been rather consistent and in conformity with the Convention's policy of favouring recognition and enforcement."[14] One might say that there has been a mutually enriching osmosis between the implementation of the New York Convention and professionalization. By virtue of studying the technicalities of the New York Convention, lawyers, judges, academics, and institutional officials increased their technical knowledge of arbitration, becoming experts in the field, skilled in analyzing and interpreting the convention in increasingly nuanced and sophisticated ways.

### 8.2.2 *Training and Professional Associations*

The Age of Autonomy has also seen the steady development of academic and research programs centered on international commercial arbitration. A hallmark of professionalization,[15] such programs are a relatively new phenomenon. Writing about the 1960s, Aksen recalled that "[i]f you were a law professor at that time, you would not be teaching a course called 'International Arbitration'. In fact, in the basic-level contracts law school class, you would be taught that arbitration clauses in contracts

[13] At the time of writing, more than 3,000 such decisions were available at http://newyorkconvention1958.org/.

[14] Emmanuel Gaillard and George Bermann (eds.), *UNCITRAL Secretariat Guide on the Convention on the Recognition and Enforcement of Foreign Arbitral Awards (New York, 1958)* (Leiden: Brill/Nijhoff, 2017), 4.

[15] Wilensky, "Professionalization," 144.

were considered unconscionable and against public policy since they ousted the courts of jurisdiction."[16] (A notable exception was Domke, who was "teaching international trade arbitration . . . before most of us knew what the subject meant.")[17]

Specialist academic programs in international arbitration have since burgeoned. This can be attributed to the rising tide of cases (and, therefore, job prospects), the perceived advantages of this method of dispute resolution, and the increasing technicality of the rules and issues involved. This has resulted in today's extremely broad offering of academic programs in the field. In Paris alone, a cursory online search revealed fourteen graduate-level programs in international arbitration.[18] Similar programs can be found in most major financial and legal centers, including London, New York, Singapore, and Geneva. Less formal workshops and training sessions are organized, too, by the ICC[19] and other institutions.

Alongside these academic programs, countless professional associations have been formed to advance a specific agenda in relation to international commercial arbitration. Practitioners in the field can choose from a wide range of professional associations based on gender, age, and geography.[20] Most, if not all, of these associations were created in the past few decades, and they reflect the professionalization of the field as a whole. A notable example is ICCA, which started as an informal group of delegates – including Jean Robert, Pieter Sanders, Niel Pearson, and Eugenio Minoli – who met at the Relais de Chambésy, on the road to Lausanne, in the early 1960s.[21] Today, ICCA organizes a biennial congress, which has become

[16] Gerald Aksen, "A Dozen Differences in International Arbitration in the Last Half-Century," in *Liber amicorum en l'honneur de William Laurence Craig* (Paris: LexisNexis, 2016), 3. Aksen played an important part in securing the United States' adoption of the New York Convention in his capacity as general counsel of the American Arbitration Association (AAA).

[17] Gerald Aksen, "Scholar, Practitioner, Internationalist: Dr. Domke Remembered," *New York University Journal of International Law and Politics*, 13 (1981), 421. Martin Domke's life (1892–1980), from his birth in a Jewish family in Berlin to his escape from Nazi Germany in 1933 and subsequent academic career in the United States, has not as yet been fully explored.

[18] In addition, in 2011, an International Academy for Arbitration Law was created in Paris "to address the increasing demand for specialized teaching in international arbitration." See International Academy for Arbitration Law, "Welcome to the Arbitration Academy," http://arbitrationacademy.org/welcome-to-the-arbitration-academy/.

[19] The full list is available at https://iccwbo.org/events/.

[20] Gaillard, "Sociology," 8–9.

[21] See International Council for Commercial Arbitration, *ICCA 50th Anniversary* (Geneva, 2011), 4. The anecdote is worth quoting in full: "ICCA was the result of informal gatherings between friends that took place in 1961. Several years prior, friendships had been formed when a group of delegates assembled to assist in the drafting of the New York Convention of

"the largest regular conference devoted to international arbitration,"[22] and is in charge of the *Yearbook Commercial Arbitration*, which it launched in 1976, as well as the originator of many other publications.[23]

### 8.2.3 A Distinct Culture of International Commercial Arbitration

Finally, a key aspect of a profession appears to be its culture. As Greenwood explained, "[t]he culture of a profession consists of its *values*, *norms*, and *symbols*."[24] The international commercial arbitration community has developed its own set of norms and values.[25] Karton described international commercial arbitrators as sharing powerful ideological commitments expressed in a set of normative values: party autonomy, "the service of business," neutrality, and internationalism.[26] These norms have concrete effects, leading arbitrators to "choose" different laws from those applied by state courts, or to apply laws differently, for example in relation to matters of substantive contract law.[27]

1958. In April 1961, certain delegates of this group again reassembled to negotiate and draft the European Convention on International Commercial Arbitration. That spring, the drafting sessions took place in Geneva at the *Office européen*, as it then was, of the United Nations. At the end of the sessions, a group of delegates, including Jean Robert, Pieter Sanders, Niel Pearson, Eugenio Minoli, would fall into the habit of meeting at Relais de Chambésy, a café near the offices of the international organizations. Pieter Sanders recalls that 'the atmosphere was perfect' at Relais de Chambésy. It created an ideal environment to discuss the development of arbitration and arbitration law. It is there that the founders of ICCA agreed to organize an international congress devoted to raising awareness of, and improving international commercial arbitration."

22 International Council for Commercial Arbitration, "Congresses," www.arbitration-icca.org/conferences-and-congresses.html.

23 International Council for Commercial Arbitration, "Publications," www.arbitration-icca.org/publications.html.

24 Ernest Greenwood, "Attributes of a Profession," *Social Work*, 2, no. 3 (1957), 52. Note that for Greenwood norms are "the guides to behavior in social situations" (such as seeking admittance to the profession), while for Karton, they are "any standard that does or is supposed to guide conduct and may serve as a basis for the assessment of conduct" (Joshua Karton, *The Culture of International Arbitration and the Evolution of Contract Law* (Oxford: Oxford University Press, 2013), 6).

25 For the principal references on the related concept of "epistemic community," see Chapter 1, Section 1.1.1 (and n. 24).

26 Karton, *Culture*, chapter 4.

27 Ibid., chapters 6 (on suspension of performance in response to nonperformance) and 7 (on the admissibility and use of extrinsic evidence to interpret contracts); see also Joshua Karton, "Contract Law in International Commercial Arbitration: The Case of Suspension of Performance," *International and Comparative Law Quarterly*, 58 (2009), 863; Karton, "The Arbitral Role in Contractual Interpretation," *Journal of International Dispute Settlement*, 6 (2015), 1.

In addition to these values, rules and principles peculiar to the transnational arbitration community have been fashioned, resulting in a uniquely "transnational arbitral procedure."[28] These principles bridge different legal systems, as is the case with the so-called negative effect of competence-competence, whereby "arbitrators must be the *first* (as opposed to the *sole*) judges of their own jurisdiction and . . . the courts' control is postponed to the stage of any action to enforce or to set aside the arbitral award rendered on the basis of the arbitration agreement."[29] This negative effect – an expression coined in 1994[30] – is not as widely accepted as its corollary, the positive effect of competence-competence,[31] but it has increasingly been adopted in such jurisdictions as Hong Kong (since 1992), Singapore (since 2005), Colombia (since 2007), Mauritius (since 2008), the Philippines (since 2009), Venezuela (since 2010), and Argentina (since 2015).[32] The growing acceptance of this principle is "one of the most significant indications of how much in favor of arbitration a law can be."[33] But it also suggests that the profession of international commercial

[28] See Marie-Claude Rigaud, "La procédure arbitrale transnationale" (PhD diss., Paris XII University, 2008).

[29] Emmanuel Gaillard and Yas Banifatemi, "Negative Effect of Competence-Competence: The Rule of Priority in Favour of the Arbitrators," in Emmanuel Gaillard and Domenico di Pietro (eds.), *Enforcement of Arbitration Agreements and International Arbitral Awards: The New York Convention in Practice* (London: Cameron May 2008), 259–60. See also, for example, Magali Boucaron-Nardetto, *Le principe compétence-compétence en droit de l'arbitrage* (Presses Universitaires d'Aix-Marseille, 2013); Ibrahim Fadlallah and Dominique Hascher, *Les grandes décisions du droit de l'arbitrage commercial* (Paris: Dalloz, 2019), 36–51.

[30] See Emmanuel Gaillard, "Convention d'arbitrage," *JurisClasseur Droit international*, Fascicle 586-5 (1994), ¶¶ 49–50; Emmanuel Gaillard and John Savage (eds.), *Fouchard, Gaillard, Goldman on International Commercial Arbitration* (The Hague: Kluwer Law International, 1999), 401; Emmanuel Gaillard, "L'effet négatif de la compétence-compétence," in Jacques Haldy, Jean-Marc Rapp, and Phidias Ferrari (eds.), *Études de procédure et d'arbitrage en l'honneur de Jean-François Poudret* (Lausanne: Faculté de droit de l'Université de Lausanne, 1999); Gaillard, "La reconnaissance, en droit suisse, de la seconde moitié du principe d'effet négatif de la compétence-compétence," in Gerald Aksen et al. (eds.), *Global Reflections on International Law, Commerce and Dispute Resolution: Liber Amicorum in Honour of Robert Briner* (Paris: ICC Publishing, 2005).

[31] The positive effect of competence-competence means that arbitrators have jurisdiction to determine their own jurisdiction. It concerns arbitrators, whereas the negative effect concerns courts.

[32] See Emmanuel Gaillard, "Actualité de l'effet négatif de la compétence-compétence," in *Le droit à l'épreuve des siècles et des frontières: Mélanges en l'honneur du Professeur Bertrand Ancel* (Paris: LGDJ/Iprolex, 2018); Gaillard, "Comparative Law in International Arbitration," *Ius Comparatum*, 1 (2020), 12.

[33] Gaillard, "Actualité de l'effet négatif," 681.

arbitration has developed its own values and principles and, in doing so, has become increasingly autonomous.

## 8.3 Conclusion

International commercial arbitration thus satisfies most of the criteria traditionally used to determine the professionalization of a field. Through the process of professionalization, both the mercatocracy and the field as a whole have acquired considerable autonomy. But two of the components of professionalization identified by Wilensky are missing. The first is the "attainment of state licensure": there is no such licensure in international commercial arbitration, nor could there be (other than the qualification of "lawyer") as the discipline is, by essence, supranational. The second is the "formation of a formal code of ethics": there is no single code – like the American Medical Association's *Code of Medical Ethics*, for example – but, rather, several sets of guidelines on the conduct of arbitration proceedings.[34] There have indeed been persistent calls from scholars and practitioners for the creation of a formal, comprehensive code of ethics in international arbitration.[35] To a large extent, it may thus be said that the professionalization – and autonomization – of international commercial arbitration is an ongoing process.

[34] See Gary Born, *International Commercial Arbitration* (The Hague: Kluwer Law International, 2014), 199. For example, in 1977, a joint committee of the American Bar Association (ABA) and the American Arbitration Association (AAA) adopted a code of ethics, which was revised in 2004; the International Bar Association (IBA) has adopted various sets of rules and guidelines since issuing its 1987 *Rules of Ethics for International Arbitrators*; and the International Council for Commercial Arbitration (ICCA) created a task force for the purpose of "promoting minimum civility standards within the international arbitration community and providing practitioners with an official set of guidelines on the subject" (in August 2020, the task force released a consultation draft of its guidelines for public comments). See "ICCA Task Force on Standards of Practice in International Arbitration," www.arbitration-icca.org/projects/Task_Force_on_Standards_of_Practice.html.

[35] See, for example, Catherine Rogers, *Ethics in International Arbitration* (Oxford: Oxford University Press, 2014). It should be noted that Eisemann had formulated the idea of a "*code d'honneur*" for arbitrators as early as 1969. See Frédéric Eisemann, "Déontologie de l'arbitre commercial international," *Revue de l'arbitrage*, 1969, 217.

# 9

# *Lex Mercatoria* and the Birth of the French School of International Arbitration

## 9.1 Introduction

In the late 1950s and early 1960s, the idea that a system of international commercial law was gradually replacing domestic laws in the sphere of international transactions began to interest a group of European scholars. Using a bygone expression,[1] they called this phenomenon *lex mercatoria*, or "law merchant," which harkened to the laws and practices of merchants trading in medieval and early modern Europe. Berthold Goldman, widely considered as the intellectual father of *lex mercatoria* (along with Clive Schmitthoff), described it as "a set of general principles, and customary rules spontaneously referred to or elaborated in the framework of international trade, without reference to a particular national system of law."[2] This was by no means the only definition of the concept, however. As one influential critic of *lex mercatoria* remarked, "there appears to be none which accommodates all opinions as to the nature of the doctrine."[3]

[1] See, for example, Gerard Malynes, "*Lex Mercatoria*: Of Arbitrators and their Awards (London, 1622)," *Arbitration International*, 9 (1993), 323–28 (Malynes was a commissioner of trade in the Low Countries). In 1923, roughly forty years before the new *lex mercatoria* concept was fully articulated, Wyndham Anstis Bewes (barrister at Lincoln's Inn and secretary of the Grotius Society and International Law Association) published *The Romance of the Law Merchant: Being an Introduction to the Study of International and Commercial Law; With Some Account of the Commerce and Fairs of the Middle Ages* (London: Sweet & Maxwell, 1923).

[2] Berthold Goldman, "The Applicable Law: General Principles of Law – the *Lex Mercatoria*," in Julian Lew (ed.), *Contemporary Problems in International Arbitration* (London: Springer Science/Business Media Dordrecht, 1987), 116.

[3] Michael Mustill, "The New *Lex Mercatoria*: The First Twenty-Five Years," *Arbitration International*, 4 (1988), 87.

Over the years, the idea of *lex mercatoria* led to a seemingly endless stream of articles, books, doctoral theses, and conferences.[4] As Gaillard has noted, the scholarship on this topic is both global (with "studies published in many different countries worldwide") and "highly controversial."[5] The subject left few indifferent. When Lord Mustill was invited to review a new book on the subject some thirty years ago, he recalled how his "pulses abruptly ceased to race at the sight of the title of the work which he unwrapped. Not another published exposé of the 'New *lex mercatoria*'!"[6]

Importantly for the modern history of international commercial arbitration, the exploration of *lex mercatoria* also coincided with the emergence of a full-fledged school of thought – what could be described as the French school of international arbitration.[7] As this chapter will show, it was a time of intense renewal – "a period of intellectual effervescence around arbitration"[8] – which carried great appeal and led to bold, cutting-edge research at the "frontiers of law" (the words used in the title of Goldman's seminal article).[9] At the same time, vacillating between renewal and anxiety, many scholars strongly disagreed with the existence of *lex mercatoria* and voiced their disagreement. The first section of this chapter will sketch the intellectual history of *lex mercatoria* (Section 9.2); the second will investigate its relationship with a nascent school of thought in international arbitration (Section 9.3); and the third will

4 For a detailed bibliography, see Filip De Ly, *International Business Law and* Lex Mercatoria (Amsterdam: Elsevier Science, 1992), 217–18n59. See, generally, Philippe Fouchard, Philippe Kahn, and Antoine Lyon-Caen (eds.), *Le droit des relations économiques internationales: Études offertes à Berthold Goldman* (Paris: Litec, 1982); Antoine Kassis, *Théorie générale des usages du commerce (droit comparé, contrats et arbitrages internationaux, lex mercatoria)* (Paris: LGDJ, 1984); Filali Osman, *Les principes généraux de la* lex mercatoria*: Contribution à l'étude d'un ordre juridique anational* (Paris: LGDJ, 1992); and Gilles Cuniberti, "La *lex mercatoria* au XXIe siècle: Une analyse empirique et économique," *Journal du droit international*, 2016, 765–80.

5 Emmanuel Gaillard, "Thirty Years of *Lex Mercatoria*: Towards the Selective Application of Transnational Rules," *ICSID Review – Foreign Investment Law Journal*, 10 (1995), 209.

6 Michael Mustill, "*Lex Mercatoria and Arbitration (A Discussion of the New Law Merchant)* edited by Professor Thomas E. Carbonneau" (book review), *Arbitration International*, 8 (1992), 215.

7 Another name is the "Dijon school," from the name of the town where Goldman taught from 1949 to 1960. That said, not all members of the French school were affiliated with the Dijon school or the University of Burgundy (or even resident in France, some of the school's key insights being due to foreign scholars such as Schmitthoff).

8 Claude Reymond, foreword to Henri Motulsky, *Écrits*, vol. 2, *Études et notes sur l'arbitrage*, 2nd ed. (Paris: Dalloz, 2010), i.

9 Berthold Goldman, "Frontières du droit et '*lex mercatoria*,'" *Archives de philosophie du droit*, vol. 9, *Le droit subjectif en question* (Paris: Sirey, 1964), 177–92.

look at the quarrels over *lex mercatoria* that marked the movement from renewal to anxiety (Section 9.4).

## 9.2 The Intellectual History of *Lex Mercatoria*

Just as the intellectual background to the development of modern sociology has been divided into "forerunners" and "founding fathers,"[10] so the intellectual history of *lex mercatoria* – and the French school of international arbitration more broadly – may be divided into a generation of precursors (Section 9.2.1), followed by a first generation of scholars who developed their insights and tested them in a range of contexts (Section 9.2.2).

### *9.2.1 Clive Schmitthoff's and Berthold Goldman's Inaugural Insights*

Goldman (1913–93) and Schmitthoff (1903–90) – both émigré lawyers who pursued distinguished careers in France and England, respectively – were the first to explore the modern *lex mercatoria* through their writings and research activities. However, they were largely unconcerned with its historical accuracy, which explains why it has been called a "founding myth" of the French school of international arbitration.[11]

#### 9.2.1.1 Laying the Foundations for a New Vision of International Arbitration

The modern intellectual origins of *lex mercatoria* are not to be found in the pages of some arcane medieval treatise but rather – at least as far as France is concerned – in comments caused by a political event of great significance: President Nasser's July 1956 decision to nationalize the Suez Canal Company and transfer its funds and assets to the Egyptian government.[12]

[10] Shmuel Eisenstadt and Miriam Curelaru, *The Form of Sociology: Paradigms and Crises* (New York: Wiley, 1976).

[11] See, for example, Gunther Teubner, "Breaking Frames: The Global Interplay of Legal and Social Systems," *American Journal of Comparative Law*, 45 (1997), 162.

[12] See Philippe Kahn, "La *lex mercatoria*: Point de vue français après quarante ans de controverses," *McGill Law Journal*, 37 (1992), 414. Jean Stoufflet's 1956 doctoral thesis is mentioned as a turning point by Kahn in Habib Gherari and Sandra Szurek (eds.), *L'émergence de la société civile internationale: Vers la privatisation du droit international? Actes du colloque des 2–3 mars 2001*, (Paris: Pedone, 2003), 266. Besides Kahn, Klaus Peter Berger has done much to explain the emergence of the new *lex mercatoria* doctrine and the French school; see Berger, "Introduction," in *The Creeping Codification of the New Lex Mercatoria*, 2nd ed. (The Hague: Kluwer Law International, 2010), esp. 1–8; and Berger,

Officials in the United States and England regarded this act as a violation of international law. Writing in *Le Monde*, French academics and lawyers aired their views on the legal status of the Suez Canal Company. One prominent lawyer argued that the company was of Egyptian nationality and that "[t]he nationalization remained within the limits of Egyptian sovereignty."[13] Berthold Goldman strongly disagreed, however. He contended that the Suez Canal Company was "not solely dependent on the Egyptian legal order, not therefore on all the decisions at the pleasure of successive holders of the Egyptian sovereignty."[14] Rather, the company was, "through the composition of its capital and its management bodies, and through the purpose and the impact of its business activity, an *international company that is directly part of the international legal order* – admittedly a new or nascent concept, but the need for which – to 'inform' a long-standing reality – has been acknowledged for several years."[15] In other words, according to Goldman, the company did not have the nationality of a given state – be it Egypt, France, or the United Kingdom – but was transnational, just as the Bank for International Settlements or the International Red Cross were "legal persons created in Switzerland" but could not "be considered as depending only on Swiss law." Goldman's analysis was novel and, in an article published a few days later, was even described by the Suez Canal Company itself as "interesting."[16]

Goldman was not the only scholar to focus on these issues in the late 1950s and early 1960s. In 1960, Fragistas published an article on the transnationalization of arbitral procedure, in which he stressed that parties to an arbitration may "free arbitration from any legal order and give it a supranational dimension."[17] In a colloquium entitled "New Sources of the Law of International Trade," organized by the International Association of Legal Science in London in 1962, Schmitthoff explained

"The New Law Merchant and the Global Market Place – A 21st Century View of Transnational Commercial Law," www.trans-lex.org/2/pdf/, 3–4.

13 Raymond de Geouffre de La Pradelle, "L'Egypte a-t-elle violé le droit international?," *Le Monde*, September 27, 1956.

14 Berthold Goldman, "La Compagnie de Suez, société internationale," *Le Monde*, October 4, 1956.

15 Berthold Goldman, "The Suez Company – An International Company," trans. Thomas Claeßens and Bernd Scholl, in Klaus Peter Berger, *The Creeping Codification of the New Lex Mercatoria*, 2nd ed. (The Hague: Kluwer Law International, 2010), 368–70, and on the TransLex website, www.trans-lex.org/9/_/goldman-berthold-le-monde-p-3/.

16 "Une mise au point de la Compagnie universelle," *Le Monde*, October 10, 1956.

17 Charalambos Fragistas, "Arbitrage étranger et arbitrage international en droit privé," *Revue critique de droit international privé*, 1960, 14.

that a new law merchant was emerging, marking "the beginning of an autonomous international mercantile law which would no longer be fashioned by the principles of national law."[18] Schmitthoff focused specifically on the work of international agencies, which consisted in formulating "conventions, model laws, standard conditions and forms of contract, uniform customs and practices, definitions of trade terms or other forms." Such instruments were said to evidence "the ultimate emergence of a fully autonomous law of international trade."[19] The conclusion of the colloquium, as expressed by Schmitthoff, could not be clearer: "There can be no doubt that an autonomous law of international trade, a new law merchant, is emerging in our time. That law is of universal character and common to countries of different economic and social order, as well as of different legal tradition."[20]

These contributions helped prepare the ground for the full-scale exploration of the underlying features of *lex mercatoria* that was to follow. The years 1963 and 1964 were crucial in this respect. First, in 1963, Goldman delivered his course at the Hague Academy of International Law (see Figure 9.1). Entitled "Conflicts of Laws in Private Law International Arbitration," it posited a system of determining the law applicable to the merits that would be independent of the law of the seat.[21] This vision of an "autonomous system" was explained by "'legal syncretism' in international relations governed by private law and especially in international commerce: each day the legal relations that are created there increasingly elude national laws and become governed by private international law."[22] In strikingly modern terms, Goldman noted that "any search for a system to which it could be linked and which would correspond to the nature of international arbitration leads to the inescapable need for an autonomous, non-national system."[23] The importance of Goldman's course cannot be

[18] Clive Schmitthoff, "The Law of International Trade, Its Growth, Formulation and Operation," repr. in Chia-Jui Cheng (ed.), *Clive M. Schmitthoff's Select Essays on International Trade Law* (London: Martinus Nijhoff/Graham & Trotman, 1988), chapter 13, at 138.

[19] Ibid., at 168.

[20] Clive Schmitthoff, "The New Sources of the Law of International Trade," repr. in Chia-Jui Cheng (ed.), *Clive M. Schmitthoff's Select Essays on International Trade Law* (London: Martinus Nijhoff/Graham & Trotman, 1988), chapter 12, at 136.

[21] Berthold Goldman, "Les conflits de lois dans l'arbitrage international de droit privé," *Collected Courses of the Hague Academy of International Law*, 109 (1963), ¶ 78, at 480.

[22] Ibid., ¶ 6, at 365.

[23] Ibid., ¶ 14, at 380.

**Figure 9.1** Photograph of Berthold Goldman (1913–1993). Reproduced with kind permission of the Hague Academy of International Law. The photograph was taken on the occasion of Berthold Goldman's Hague Academy course "Les conflits de lois dans l'arbitrage international de droit privé," *Collected Courses of the Hague Academy of International Law*, vol. 109 (1963). Goldman's seminal insights paved the way for the French school of international arbitration's research.

overemphasized: it was "fundamental" since it "laid the foundation for the renewal of the vision of international arbitration."[24]

Second, in 1964, Schmitthoff delivered an address in Gothenburg, in which he stressed that "[o]ur institutional arrangements for global unification have not kept in step with the rapidly growing law of international trade." Schmitthoff called for the creation of "an international agency of the highest order, possible on the level of the United Nations, which should be charged with the task of coordinating the various activities of the present formulating agencies and suggesting to them suitable extensions of their work, without actually interfering with them."[25] As Schmitthoff himself related, his suggestions were taken up at the United Nations by the Hungarian delegation and placed on the agenda for a meeting of the General Assembly.[26] This led to

[24] Gaillard, *Legal Theory*, 1.

[25] Clive Schmitthoff, "The Unification of the Law of International Trade," repr. in Chia-Jui Cheng (ed.), *Clive M. Schmitthoff's Select Essays on International Trade Law* (London: Martinus Nijhoff/Graham & Trotman, 1988), chapter 14, at 186.

[26] Clive Schmitthoff, "The Unification of the Law of International Trade," repr. in Chia-Jui Cheng (ed.), *Clive M. Schmitthoff's Select Essays on International Trade Law* (London:

a comprehensive report on the "progressive development of the law of international trade,"[27] also known as the "Schmitthoff Study," which was submitted to the United Nations General Assembly and would prove instrumental in the subsequent establishment of the United Nations Commission on International Trade Law (UNCITRAL) in 1966.[28]

A third key event was the 1964 publication of Berthold Goldman's seminal article "Frontières du droit et *lex mercatoria*" in the *Archives de philosophie du droit*.[29] Citing Schmitthoff twice in the footnotes and referring to the 1962 London colloquium,[30] Goldman wrote as follows of "the international economic relations":

> each day these relations seem increasingly to escape the grip of state law, and even of the uniform laws that have been incorporated into the legislation of the states that have adopted them, and to become adapted to and governed by rules of professional origin, or customary rules and principles that arbitral awards reveal or even create.[31]

Goldman gave various examples of such rules and principles, which could be found in areas like the international sale of goods, documentary credits, international transportation, or the operation of some international companies.[32] Because the person called upon to interpret these instruments was often the arbitrator, whose role was to "adjudicate international commercial disputes," Goldman then turned his attention to the work of those private arbitrators. He perceptively noted that arbitrators often referred to a "'customary law' of international commerce – *lex mercatoria* – of which there is little point in trying to determine whether they are the recorders or the creators, given that the two activities, as whenever exercised by a judge, are intimately linked."[33]

Martinus Nijhoff/Graham & Trotman, 1988), chapter 17, at 214. Originally published in 1981, this essay bore the same title as Schmitthoff's 1964 lecture.

27 UN General Assembly, 21st session, agenda item 88 ("Progressive development of the law of international trade"), report of the Secretary-General, UN Docs. A/6396 and ADD. 1 and 2 (September 23, 1966).

28 "Establishment of the United Nations Commission on International Trade Law," UN Resolution 2205(XXI) of December 17, 1966, https://documents-dds-ny.un.org/doc/RESOLUTION/GEN/NR0/005/08/IMG/NR000508.pdf?OpenElement.

29 Goldman, "Frontières du droit."

30 Ibid., 177n1, 191n1.

31 Ibid., 177.

32 Ibid., 178–83.

33 Ibid., 183.

Goldman's article was theoretically sophisticated, testifying to the amount of energy and scholarly attention he had devoted to the subject since his 1956 article in *Le Monde*. It was also short, at no more than fifteen pages. Somewhat surprisingly, the article mentions the words "*lex mercatoria*" only four times, even though its goal was to elucidate that very concept.[34] In fact, Goldman was interested not so much in formulating the principles of *lex mercatoria* but in describing some of its occurrences. This explains his references to several arbitral awards. Of particular interest is the 1951 *Trucial Coast* Arbitration, in which, despite acknowledging that the contract was "made in Abu Dhabi and wholly to be performed in that country," Lord Asquith decided to apply "principles rooted in the good sense and common practice of the generality of civilised nations – a sort of 'modern law of nature.'"[35] Awards such as this illustrated "arbitrators' constant search, beyond conflicts of state laws, for a 'transnational law', a repository of principles common to national laws but also of specific rules required by international trade."[36]

True to character, Goldman – "a man of tradition" who nevertheless liked to "move away from the paths marked by certainties"[37] – continued to ruminate on the nature of *lex mercatoria* in the following years and decades.[38] In 1979, fifteen years after his "Frontières du droit" article, he published another seminal piece, "La *lex mercatoria* dans les contrats et l'arbitrage internationaux: Réalités et perspectives,"[39] which originated from a speech he gave to the Comité Français de Droit International Privé. Here, Goldman observes that *lex mercatoria* had become "the object of constant research and reflection": its "topicality is obvious," and a "very partial assessment" now possible, despite its being "greatly questioned and its

[34] Ibid., 183, 189, 192 (twice).

[35] *In the matter of an Arbitration between Petroleum Development (Trucial Coast) Ltd. and the Sheikh of Abu Dhabi*, reported in *International and Comparative Law Quarterly*, 1, no. 2 (1952), 251.

[36] Goldman, "Frontières du droit," 184.

[37] Philippe Fouchard, Philippe Kahn, and Antoine Lyon Caen, "Avant-propos," in Fouchard, Kahn, and Lyon-Caen (eds.), *Études offertes à Berthold Goldman*, xi.

[38] See Berthold Goldman, "Une bataille judiciaire autour de la *lex mercatoria*: L'affaire *Norsolor*," *Revue de l'arbitrage*, 1983, 379–409; Goldman, note on *Société Compañia Valenciana de Cementos Portaland* v. *Société Primary Coal Inc.*, *Journal du droit international*, 1992, 177; Goldman, "Nouvelles réflexions sur la *Lex Mercatoria*," in Christian Dominicé, Robert Patry, and Claude Reymond (eds.), *Études de droit international en l'honneur de Pierre Lalive* (Basel: Helbing & Lichtenhahn, 1993).

[39] Berthold Goldman, "La *lex mercatoria* dans les contrats et l'arbitrage internationaux: Réalités et perspectives," *Journal du droit international*, 1979, 475–505.

future contested."[40] Read in conjunction with the "Frontières du droit" article, this piece shows a notable development in Goldman's thought. After previously stressing that *lex mercatoria* "does not make up a completely autonomous system,"[41] Goldman now acknowledged that "*lex mercatoria* fulfills the function of a set of rules of law,"[42] constituting "a set – if not an entire system – of rules of law."[43] This view suggested that it was now possible to envision *lex mercatoria* as a fully autonomous system. Yet, Goldman was more cautious: he warned that "like some state laws, the rules of *lex mercatoria* could be 'odious' and should in that case rightly be fought and set aside, but that does not enable them, and especially all of them, to be denied their nature as rules of law."[44]

Though proponents of *lex mercatoria* initially worked "rather discreetly,"[45] Goldman's research proved hugely influential. It "undeniably influenced"[46] the *Valenciana* case, in which the French Court of Cassation held that an arbitrator who had relied on "the body of international trade rules arising from practice and affirmed by national courts" had not breached his obligations.[47] Underscoring Goldman's role and influence, Jean-Denis Bredin compared him to a mountaineer, "keeping an eye on the most subtle detail of the path, following a very precise course, careful to foresee all the obstacles, but looking towards the summit, open to wider perspectives. That was an ambitious expedition, the aim of which was to delineate the borders of a new law, or rather to discover, as a pioneer would, a borderless law."[48] In less poetic language, Goldman's research was sending "shock waves" through traditional thinking on the sources of law.[49]

40 Ibid., ¶ 3, at 476–77.

41 Goldman, "Frontières du droit," 189.

42 Goldman, "La *lex mercatoria* dans les contrats et l'arbitrage internationaux," 499.

43 Ibid., 502.

44 Ibid., 500.

45 Kahn, in Gherari and Szurek, *L'émergence de la société civile internationale*, 267.

46 Centre de recherche sur le droit des investissements et des marchés internationaux (CREDIMI), "École de Nice/École de Dijon," *Revue internationale de droit économique*, 27 (2013–14), 470.

47 Court of Cassation (France), First Civil Chamber, October 22, 1991, *Société Compañia Valenciana de Cementos Portland* v. *Société Primary Coal Inc.*, *Yearbook Commercial Arbitration* (1993), 528. See Ibrahim Fadlallah and Dominique Hascher, *Les grandes décisions du droit de l'arbitrage commercial* (Paris: Dalloz, 2019), 235–42.

48 Jean-Denis Bredin, "La loi du juge," in Fouchard, Kahn, and Lyon-Caen (eds.), *Études offertes à Berthold Goldman*, ¶ 2, at 15.

49 Paul Lagarde, "Approche critique de la *lex mercatoria*," in Fouchard, Kahn, and Lyon-Caen (eds.), *Études offertes à Berthold Goldman*, 125, 150.

#### 9.2.1.2 Historical Narratives about *Lex Mercatoria*, or the "Founding Myth" of the French School of International Arbitration

An interesting aspect of Goldman's and Schmitthoff's early research was their attempt to place *lex mercatoria* within a broader historical continuum. As Hatzimihail pointed out, "[h]istorical imagery plays an important part in the *lex mercatoria* discourse" and, according to him, "masks its weak historical validation."[50] In a 1968 lecture in London, Schmitthoff divided the development of the law of international trade into three stages:

> It arose in the Middle Ages in the form of the law merchant, a body of truly international customary rules governing the cosmopolitan community of international merchants who travelled through the civilised world from port to port and fair to fair. The second phase began with the incorporation of the law merchant into the national systems of law, a process which, though universal, was carried out in the various countries at different times and for different reasons. The third phase is contemporary; it aims at the unification of international trade law on an international level and has given rise to a new law merchant which reflects the international spirit of our time in the political and economic sphere.[51]

Schmitthoff's analysis has been aptly described as "an optimistic tale of evolution, a progress narrative."[52] The law merchant developed from (1) a set of rules governing a "community" in the medieval era, to (2) incorporation into domestic legal systems in the early modern era, and culminated in (3) harmonization in the modern era. Schmitthoff referred to the first as being marked by "the law of the fairs which was almost as universal as the law of the church," as well as "the special courts dealing with commercial disputes" and "the courts of piepowder."[53] He identified the second period, which covered the seventeenth to the nineteenth centuries, with various codification efforts, such as the 1673 Ordonnance du Commerce and the 1681 Ordonnance de la Marine in France. Schmitthoff saw himself as living in the third period,

[50] Nikitas Hatzimihail, "The Many Lives – and Faces – of *Lex Mercatoria*: History as Genealogy in International Business Law," *Law and Contemporary Problems*, 71, no. 3 (2008), 172–73.

[51] Clive Schmitthoff, "The Unification of the Law of International Trade," repr. in Chia-Jui Cheng (ed.), *Clive M. Schmitthoff's Select Essays on International Trade Law* (London: Martinus Nijhoff/Graham & Trotman, 1988), chapter 16, at 206–7, quoted in Hatzimihail, "Many Lives," 177.

[52] Hatzimihail, 181.

[53] Schmitthoff, 207.

a phase of rediscovery and synthesis. For him, "[t]he modern law of international trade is not of haphazard and casual provenance but consists of norms, practices or usages expressed in a number of authoritative texts. These texts have been compiled by international organizations and agencies."[54]

Goldman, too, situated *lex mercatoria* in a broader historical narrative. Whereas Schmitthoff's main historical reference was medieval mercantile law, Goldman used the Roman *ius gentium* as "the illustrious precursor" of *lex mercatoria.*[55] In a 1983 conference delivered in English, Goldman compared *lex mercatoria* to "a venerable old lady who has twice disappeared from the face of the earth and twice been resuscitated."[56]

If Schmitthoff's explanation for the development of *lex mercatoria* was a "progress narrative," Goldman's personification of *lex mercatoria* as "a venerable old lady" was part of a "cyclical narrative,"[57] a tale of death and resuscitation. According to Goldman, the Roman *ius gentium* could be "understood as a formally autonomous source of law," which nevertheless fell victim "to the breakup of the Roman world and its legal system, and to the disintegration of international economic relations that characterized the early Middle Ages."[58] The *lex mercatoria* was then reborn, first in the Middle Ages and then in the modern era, as evidenced in a number of arbitral awards. In other words, Goldman was concerned with the spontaneous resuscitation of *lex mercatoria* over time.

While some historical references used by Schmitthoff and Goldman made perfect sense, the validity of others, such as the existence of a medieval *lex mercatoria*, could be questioned. The courts of piepowders, to which Schmitthoff referred in his analysis, did indeed exist. Named after the dusty feet (in French, *pieds poudrés*) of travelers, they were created to settle the disputes of wayfaring merchants.[59] Blackstone described this type of court as follows:

> It was instituted to administer justice for all injuries done in that very fair or market, and not in any preceding one. So that the injury must be done, complained of, heard, and determined, within the compass of one and the same day. The court hath cognizance of all matters that can possibly arise

[54] Ibid., 209.
[55] Hatzimihail, 184.
[56] Berthold Goldman, "*Lex mercatoria*," *Forum Internationale*, 3 (1983).
[57] Hatzimihail, 184.
[58] Goldman, 3.
[59] See Charles Gross, "The Court of Piepowder," *Quarterly Journal of Economics*, 20 (1906), 231–49; John Baker, "Courts of Piepowder," in *The Oxford History of the Laws of England*, vol. 6, *1483–1558* (Oxford: Oxford University Press, 2003), 312–14.

within the precinct of that fair or market; and the plaintiff must make oath that the cause of action arose there.[60]

Likewise, the codification efforts described by Schmitthoff in the second of the three periods he identified have been well documented. As is well known, the 1673 Ordonnance du Commerce (also known as the "Code Savary" or "Code Marchand"), which consisted of 122 articles divided into 12 parts, was indeed the first decisive step toward regulating private commercial law.[61] Savary's 1675 commentary of the ordinance, *Le parfait négociant* (followed, in 1679, by *Les Parères*),[62] was a resounding success, becoming widely used as a source of key formulations and examples of commercial terms and practices.[63]

But the existence of a medieval *lex mercatoria*, which constituted the first stage in the evolution described by Schmitthoff as well as a key part of Goldman's analysis, is harder to demonstrate. Various scholars have referred to the medieval *lex mercatoria* in their research, most notably Milgrom, North, and Weingast in the theoretical model they proposed to explain the growth of long-distance trade in the Middle Ages.[64] (The three economists asserted that, "by the end of the 11th century, the Law Merchant came to govern most commercial transactions in Europe, providing a uniform set of standards across large number of locations.")[65] But many legal historians have expressed great skepticism about the existence of a medieval *lex mercatoria*.[66] Donahue argued that there was no such thing as *lex mercatoria* in the medieval and early modern periods, "at least not in the sense that that term is normally used."[67] For Donahue, "the use of *lex mercatoria* for

[60] William Blackstone, *Commentaries on the Laws of England; Book III: Of Private Wrongs*, Thomas Gallanis (ed.) (Oxford: Oxford University Press, 2016), 21.

[61] See, for example, Romuald Szramkiewicz and Olivier Descamps, *Histoire du droit des affaires*, 3rd ed. (Paris: LGDJ, 2019), 185–93.

[62] Jacques Savary, *Le parfait négociant*, ed. Édouard Richard (Geneva: Droz, 2011 [1675]).

[63] *Le parfait négociant* ran to eight editions between 1675 and 1721 and was translated into several languages.

[64] Paul Milgrom, Douglass North, and Barry Weingast, "The Role of Institutions in the Revival of Trade: The Law Merchant, Private Judges, and the Champagne Fairs," *Economics and Politics*, 2 (1990), 1–23.

[65] Ibid., 5.

[66] See, for example, Jean Bart, "La *lex mercatoria* au Moyen Age: Mythe ou réalité?," in Charles Leben, Eric Loquin, and Mahmoud Salem (eds.), *Souveraineté étatique et marchés internationaux à la fin du 20ème siècle* (Dijon: Litec, 2000); John Baker, "The Law Merchant and the Common Law before 1700," *Cambridge Law Journal*, 38 (1979), 295–322; and the articles cited in notes 67–75.

[67] Charles Donahue, "Medieval and Early Modern *Lex Mercatoria*: An Attempt at the *Probatio Diabolica*," *Chicago Journal of International Law*, 5, (2004), 27.

tendentious purposes goes back a long way,"[68] whereas "[n]o general collection of customs of merchants survives from the medieval or early modern periods."[69] Through a careful examination of the original sources – especially the rolls of the fair courts of St. Ives (1275), "the most extensive surviving records of the period" – Sachs showed that "merchants in medieval England were substantially subject to local control."[70] Many French scholars have adopted a similar position. Halpérin warned that "[t]he fate of *lex mercatoria* – inside or outside the common law, depending on the extent of the influence of Roman law – seems . . . problematic."[71] According to Delmas-Marty, "the concept has nothing to do with Roman law and little to do with the law of the medieval fairs, which was also linked to the development of exchanges and the need to ensure the peace of markets but in a very different context."[72] If one adheres to this view, the whole edifice of the new *lex mercatoria* – and a basic tenet of the French school's early research project – becomes a shaky construction founded on a sort of "nostalgia of a lost and imaginary unity."[73]

How important is it that the medieval *lex mercatoria*, to which many members of the French school referred in their research, did or did not exist? And why did Schmitthoff and Goldman rely so extensively on it without trying to check the historical record or available documents first? One simple explanation could be that they genuinely thought that a medieval *lex mercatoria* did exist, even though this was subsequently questioned by legal historians. Or maybe it was part of a broader strategy (whether deliberate or not) to forestall criticism of the new *lex mercatoria* project by giving it an air of historical respectability. A more convincing explanation, however, is that Schmitthoff and Goldman (and other so-called mercatorists after them) were using the medieval law merchant as a mental image, a "construct,"[74] or a "myth."[75] For Goldman, the medieval law

[68] Ibid., 26

[69] Ibid., 28.

[70] Stephen Sachs, "From St. Ives to Cyberspace: The Modern Distortion of the Medieval 'Law Merchant.'" *American University International Law Review*, 21 (2006), 685–812.

[71] Jean-Louis Halpérin, "L'approche historique et la problématique du *jus commune*," *Revue internationale de droit comparé*, 52 (2000), 717.

[72] Mireille Delmas-Marty, *Les forces imaginantes du droit*, vol. 1, *Le relatif et l'universel* (Paris: Seuil, 2004), 102.

[73] Halpérin, 717.

[74] Emily Kadens, "The Medieval Law Merchant: The Tyranny of a Construct," *Journal of Legal Analysis*, 7 (2015), 251–89.

[75] Emily Kadens, "The Myth of the Customary Law Merchant," *Texas Law Review*, 90 (2012), 1153–206.

merchant or Roman *ius gentium* may have been the precursor of the French school, as Santi Romano was for the generation of Fouchard, Kahn, and Loquin: a background reference, thought experiment, and intellectual window through which they could see their own beliefs and ideas. What mattered was not the supposed existence of a medieval *lex mercatoria*, but rather that the French school of international arbitration had found, to use Teubner's expression, a "founding myth."[76]

### *9.2.2 Expanding the Horizon of* Lex Mercatoria

Regardless of the historical validity of the medieval *lex mercatoria*, the potential applications of Goldman's research were so numerous and wide-ranging that they inspired an entire new generation of scholars: the first generation of the French school of international arbitration. Goldman's influence manifested especially in his doctoral students and has been documented in various writings.[77] Three students, in particular, provided powerful illustrations of the concepts and mechanisms that Goldman had started describing, but never fully articulated, in his articles.

The first, Jean Stoufflet, explained that the documentary letter of credit formed part of a greater system that did not belong to national legal orders. In his thesis, subtitled "A Legal Analysis of an Instrument to Finance International Trade,"[78] he gave great attention to the Uniform Customs and Practice for Documentary Credits (UCP). This set of rules on the issuing and use of letters of credit was adopted by the International Chamber of Commerce in 1933[79] and further revised in 1951 and, most recently, in 2007. The UCP played a key role in encouraging "the establishment of certain customary principles, thereby serving to create objective law, as case law does."[80] But Stoufflet stopped short of claiming that the documentary letter of credit was "completely separated from any state legal system" because, he explained, "eliminating any link to a state law is almost impossible."[81] Goldman nonetheless noted at the time that "a common law

[76] Teubner, "Breaking Frames," 162.

[77] See, for example, Philippe Kahn, "Vers la quête de la *lex mercatoria*: L'apport de l'école de Dijon, 1957–1964," with English trans., app. to Klaus Peter Berger, *The Creeping Codification of the New Lex Mercatoria*, 2nd ed. (The Hague: Kluwer Law International, 2010), 357–67.

[78] Jean Stoufflet, *Le crédit documentaire: Étude juridique d'un instrument financier du commerce international* (Paris: Librairies techniques, 1957).

[79] Ibid., ¶ 103, at 103.

[80] Ibid., ¶ 106, at 105.

[81] Ibid., ¶ 114, at 112.

of nations is here well under way."[82] Stoufflet came to recognize the full implications of his research when he subsequently wrote in a US law journal that "the documentary letter of credit is so completely identified with the UCP that it may be said to belong to an autonomous legal system and that its doctrine is the first manifestation of a *lex mercatoria*; an international commercial law distinct from any national legal systems."[83]

The second doctoral student, Philippe Kahn, looked at the ways in which the international community of merchants, the *societas mercatorum*, created law. His dissertation was on international commercial sales and was heavily influenced by Goldman and Eisemann.[84] In the first part of his work, entitled "L'autonomie de la société internationale des vendeurs et des acheteurs,"[85] Kahn explained:

> The independence of sellers and buyers operating in the international marketplace manifests in the way they regulate their legal relations. Sellers and buyers have constructed a contractual device, an international commercial sale, which, insofar as both the formation of the sales contract and the content of the contractual obligations are concerned, constitutes a true charter, the basis of the international society they form outside states.[86]

Kahn concluded that this nascent international society "has a tendency to be independent of states" insofar as "international economic relations do not sit easily with a national legal framework" and lead to the "formation of a truly autonomous group."[87] Through this analysis – reminiscent of Motulsky's analysis of "the constitution of an interstate community"[88] – Kahn was able to shed light on the mechanisms of the "society of international sellers and buyers outside states."[89] This thesis was a powerful work, a stepping stone to a productive and distinguished career.

The third doctoral student of Goldman's who played a key role in the development of *lex mercatoria* – and of international commercial arbitration more broadly – was Philippe Fouchard (see Figure 9.2). A native of Besançon, Fouchard studied law at the University of Dijon, where he

[82] Berthold Goldman, foreword to Stoufflet, *Le crédit documentaire*, 7.
[83] Jean Stoufflet, "Payment and Transfer in Documentary Letters of Credit: Interaction between the French General Law of Obligations and the Uniform Customs and Practice," *Arizona Law Review*, 24 (1982), 267–68.
[84] Philippe Kahn, *La vente commerciale internationale* (Paris: Sirey, 1961).
[85] Ibid., 17.
[86] Ibid., 17.
[87] Ibid., 365.
[88] Henri Motulsky, "L'évolution récente en matière d'arbitrage international" [1959], in Henri Motulsky, *Écrits*, vol. 2, *Études et notes sur l'arbitrage* (Paris: Dalloz, 2010), 301.
[89] Ibid, 366.

**Figure 9.2** Anonymous photograph of Philippe Fouchard (1937–2004) taken at a conference at the University of Paris II in 1997 or 1998. Private collection of Prof. Charles Jarrosson. Reproduced with kind permission of Prof. Charles Jarrosson and Me David Fouchard. Fouchard was a leading member of the first generation of the French school of international arbitration.

completed his PhD in 1963, two years after Kahn. His dissertation, which focused on international commercial arbitration, was published in 1965,[90] the year in which he also passed the *agrégation* in law and started teaching in Africa.[91] Fouchard's dissertation was highly innovative, even though he had relied on some of the same sources as Kahn.[92] Fouchard was arguably the first person – "and not only in France"[93] – to undertake an exhaustive study of international commercial arbitration as "an arbitration that is free from all the state frameworks, subjected in all respects to really international, that is, though all those words sound somewhat barbaric, supranational, extra-national or even better, anational, standards and authorities."[94] "[T]his is a shocking idea," Fouchard readily acknowledged,[95] and yet it was clear to him that "a complete separation of international commercial arbitration from state laws and authorities" was taking place.[96] With extraordinary prescience, Fouchard predicted that international commercial arbitration

90 Philippe Fouchard, *L'arbitrage commercial international* (Paris: Dalloz, 1965).

91 Fouchard taught at the universities of Abidjan (1965–69) and Tunis (1973–77), as well as at the University of Dijon (1969–73 and 1977–80). In 1980, he moved to the University of Paris II Panthéon-Assas, where he taught until his retirement in 2002.

92 See Kahn, in Gherari and Szurek, *L'émergence de la société civile internationale*, 267.

93 Berthold Goldman, foreword to Fouchard, *L'arbitrage commercial international*, vii.

94 Fouchard, *L'arbitrage commercial international*, ¶ 39, at 23.

95 Ibid., ¶ 40, at 23.

96 Ibid., ¶ 44, at 25.

would fulfill the function of a "real international jurisdiction, which is to state the law. That law will essentially be anational, and, despite being undeveloped, will replace state law, which is generally ill-suited to international trade disputes."[97]

Fouchard's ideas were quickly confirmed in the *Gosset* case, which Motulsky correctly predicted would contribute to "the emergence of an international legal order."[98] According to Clay, Fouchard's research was so important that 1963 – the year of (1) Fouchard's thesis, (2) Goldman's course at the Hague Academy, and (3) the seminal *Gosset* case – has been described as the year of the "birth of modern international commercial arbitration."[99]

Over time, scholars from a wide range of disciplines – including public and private law, economics, and even geography – decided to focus their research on similar issues, the appeal of which had increased with "the explosion of technological advancements, economic expansion, and the political and legal consequences of decolonization."[100] They organized several conferences on such topics as foreign investment and eurobonds.[101] A research team – the Centre de Recherche sur le Droit des Marchés et des Investissements Internationaux, or CREDIMI – was officially constituted and placed under Kahn's direction in January 1972.

The CREDIMI proved a fertile ground for new thinking on *lex mercatoria* and related issues. Scholars included Jacquemont,[102]

97 Ibid., ¶¶ 758–59, at 544.

98 Court of Cassation (France), First Civil Chamber, May 7, 1963, *Etablissements Raymond Gosset* v. *Société Frère Carapelli S.p.A.*, *Revue critique de droit international privé*, 1963, note Motulsky; repr. in Motulsky, *Études et notes sur l'arbitrage*, 343.

99 Discussion with Professor Thomas Clay (Paris, March 22, 2017). See also Thomas Clay and Philippe Pinsolle, "General Introduction: The Major Cases of the French Case Law on International Arbitration," in Thomas Clay and Philippe Pinsolle (eds.), *French International Arbitration Law Reports* (Huntington, NY: JurisNet, 2014), v ("[t]he French law of international arbitration has a beginning (1963) and a culminating point (2007), but fortunately it does not have an ending").

100 Jacques Dehaussy, "Philippe Kahn," in Charles Leben, Eric Loquin, and Mahmoud Salem (eds.), *Souveraineté étatique et marchés internationaux à la fin du 20ème siècle (À propos de 30 ans de recherche du CREDIMI): Mélanges en l'honneur de Philippe Kahn* (Dijon: Litec, 2000), 2.

101 Centre de recherche sur le droit des investissements et des marchés internationaux, *Investissements étrangers et arbitrages entre États et personnes privées; La Convention de la B.I.R.D. du 18 mars 1965* (Paris: Pedone, 1969); Centre de recherche sur le droit des marchés et des investissements internationaux, *Les Euro-obligations: Eurobonds* (Paris: Librairies techniques, 1972).

102 See, for example, André Jacquemont, *L'émission des emprunts euro-obligataires: Pouvoir bancaire et souverainetés étatiques* (Paris: Litec, 1976).

Loquin,[103] and Jehl,[104] all of whom went on to publish key writings and have brilliant careers of their own. Looking back at the CREDIMI's activities over the past forty years, two broad periods can be distinguished: the first concentrated on analyzing the content and existence of *lex mercatoria* in a wide range of contexts, while the second focused on globalization and its impact on international trade and commerce.[105] The CREDIMI still exists to this day and numerous publications have been produced under its auspices. The scope of its activities has continued to expand: in 2012, it merged with the Laboratoire du Droit du Sport, which led to a new branch of research on the so-called *lex sportiva*.[106] Its scholars were not just part of a research team; the importance and coherence of their writings gave every impression that a new school of thought was emerging.

## 9.3 The Emergence of the French School of International Arbitration

New schools of thought – meaning a group of people sharing a relatively stable position on a similar set of questions and theoretical issues over an extended period of time[107] – are relatively infrequent in international law and other disciplines. One must therefore look at schools of thought generally (Section 9.3.1) before trying to understand whether the features that characterize them apply to the French school of international arbitration (Section 9.3.2).

### *9.3.1 Framing the French School of International Arbitration as a School of Thought*

How does one make sense of the struggles through which a set of ideas become dominant at a given time and new schools of thought emerge? Kennedy's answer is that "[d]isciplinary renewal – no less than disciplinary

103 See, for example, Eric Loquin, *L'amiable composition en droit comparé international: Contribution à l'étude du non-droit dans l'arbitrage commercial* (Paris: Librairies Techniques, 1980).

104 Joseph Jehl, *Le commerce international de la technologie: Approche juridique* (Paris: Litec, 1985).

105 CREDIMI, "École de Nice/École de Dijon," 464–65.

106 On the so-called *lex sportiva*, see Franck Latty, *La lex sportiva: Recherche sur le droit transnational* (The Hague: Martinus Nijhoff, 2007).

107 David Kennedy, "When Renewal Repeats: Thinking Against the Box," *NYU Journal of International Law and Politics*, 32 (2000), 373.

stasis – can best be understood as a complex interaction among groups of individuals pursuing intellectual, political, and personal projects."[108] In other words, Kennedy invites us to

> think of the field as a group of people situated in a professional community over time, who share projects and commitments, a common ethos, a practice, and even a character. Across a long period, we find lawyers who think of themselves as internationalists, who relate to one another as part of a discipline or profession, who share points of reference, professional tools, and technical knowledge.[109]

Kennedy's insights, it could be argued, are not far from Cotterrell's law-and-community approach, which emphasizes the meaningful back-and-forth between the people and the institution. A key idea for Cotterrell is the notion that "'the social' – the social environment in which law operates – should be seen as composed of *networks of community*."[110] Cotterrell identifies four types of communities: *instrumental* community (based on "a convergence of the participants' projects"), *traditional* community (based on "shared customs, traditions, physical environment or linguistic or historical heritage"), community of *belief or values* (based on "shared fundamental convictions"), and *affective* community (based on "emotional attractions or rejections, likes or dislikes, loves or hatreds towards others").[111] These four types of community seem to closely match the three sorts of group dynamics identified by Kennedy in the field of international law: "those based on an affinity for ideas" (Cotterrell's community of belief), "those based on professional and personal identity" (Cotterrell's affective and/or traditional communities), and "those based on struggle for domination" (Cotterrell's instrumental community).[112]

Kennedy explored these dynamics in the field of international law in the United States. From the 1960s until the end of the Cold War, that field was largely dominated by two schools of thought: the Yale School (with Harold Lasswell and then Myres McDougal at its helm), which emphasized policy as an alternative to norms; and the Columbia School (dominated by Louis Henkin and Oscar Schachter), which prioritized norms over policy. Kennedy's analysis explains how these two schools of thought embraced different positions on the formal/informal law spectrum and the sovereign

[108] Ibid., 338.
[109] Ibid., 344.
[110] Roger Cotterrell, "Rethinking 'Embeddedness': Law, Economy, Community," *Journal of Law and Society*, 40 (2013), 50–51 (emphasis in original).
[111] Ibid., 55.
[112] Kennedy, 423.

autonomy/international community spectrum. The relative positions of the two schools – one embodying the "mainstream consensus" and the other a set of "methodological counterpoints" – reversed several times.[113] This continued until 1989, when "the basic vocabulary differentiating Columbia and Yale began to break up" and international law in the United States was "brimming over with new angles and methods for renewing and preserving the field by escaping its past limitations."[114]

By contrast, the French school of international arbitration, which also started in the 1960s, still has influential exponents. One could consider Goldman as the precursor of the French school; Fouchard, Kahn, Loquin, and other members of the Dijon school as the first generation; and scholars such as Gaillard, Clay, and Racine as belonging to the second generation. (Table 10.1 provides an overview of the French school in terms of key individuals, key issues, background references, and background cases.) As the next chapter will show, the second generation of the French school benefited from insights offered by the first generation's early research, but strongly renewed the terms of the debate. What seems clear, however, is that the aura of the French school remains undiminished, both in France and elsewhere. As will be seen later, the various types of group dynamics identified by Kennedy and Cotterrell can be found in the French school, and may help explain the enduring success of its vision and appeal.

### 9.3.2 *Key Features of the French School of International Arbitration*

Three key features of the French school deserve emphasis: its members' shared belief in legal pluralism, their strong sense of professional and personal identity, and their similar life experiences, which – for Goldman and Schmitthoff at least – may help explain why they explored such issues as *lex mercatoria* in the first place.

#### 9.3.2.1 A Shared Belief in Legal Pluralism

First, the French school was a "community of belief" (to use Cotterrell's expression), whose members shared a commitment to ideas with which they had a common affinity.[115] The activity of the French school was constructed around two fundamental pillars found in the works of Kahn and Fouchard: "the pluralism of the legal orders (law is not necessarily

113 Ibid., 380–95.
114 Ibid., 386–87.
115 Ibid., 423–28.

created by states) and the capacity of the 'international society of traders' to structure itself into an autonomous legal order that produces its own rules and has them applied by arbitral tribunals."[116] Members of the French school started applying these insights to a wide range of contexts, using both traditional and nontraditional sources. As Goldman pointed out in his preface to Kahn's dissertation, the author's reliance on traditional sources, namely, statutes and case law, was relatively limited.[117] When, in 1974, the ICC started to allow some of its arbitral awards to be published in the *Yearbook Commercial Arbitration* and the so-called *Clunet* (*Journal du droit international*), members of the French school would have even more material to work with.[118] This "originality of sources and solutions"[119] seems to have been a constant feature of the French school.

Another defining trait of the French school was its members' reliance on common intellectual references. A key event in this regard – "a cultural revolution," according to Kahn[120] – was the publication in 1975 of Lucien François and Pierre Gothot's masterly translation of Santi Romano's *L'ordinamento giuridico*, with an introduction by Phocion Francescakis.[121] (Despite its importance, Romano's book was translated into only a handful of languages[122] and it was not until 2017 that an English translation appeared.[123]) Lagarde referred to the French translation in his "Critical Approach to *Lex Mercatoria*,"[124] noting that the translation offered a means of understanding "the strongest expression of the *lex mercatoria* doctrine"[125] and "the benefit that supporters of *lex mercatoria* could draw from that analysis of the legal order."[126]

And benefit they did. Lagarde probably did not realize that he was giving powerful ammunition to the very people whose theories he was seeking to attack. Just as Lord Mustill's list of twenty transnational

116 CREDIMI, "École de Nice/École de Dijon," 460.

117 Goldman, foreword to Philippe Kahn, *La vente commerciale internationale* (Paris: Sirey, 1961), vi.

118 Kahn, in Gherari and Szurek, *L'émergence de la société civile internationale*, 268.

119 Goldman, vii.

120 Kahn, 267.

121 Santi Romano, *L'ordre juridique*, trans. Lucien François and Pierre Gothot (Paris: Dalloz, 1975 [1917]). A second French edition was published in 2002, with a foreword by Pierre Mayer.

122 The work was translated into Spanish in 1963, German in 1975, and Portuguese in 2008.

123 Santi Romano, *The Legal Order*, trans. Mariano Croce (New York: Routledge, 2017).

124 Lagarde, "Approche critique," ¶ 15, at 134.

125 Ibid., 134n31.

126 Ibid., ¶ 17, at 135.

rules[127] – which were intended to illustrate the method's feebleness[128] – was hailed as an achievement by proponents of *lex mercatoria*, so Lagarde's use of Romano's theories opened new perspectives for mercatorists. As Kahn recalls, Romano

> gave what was nonetheless a very pragmatic vision – whether that of Berthold Goldman, or of Philippe Fouchard, Jean Stoufflet, or myself – its theoretical dimension. We had perceived and described a phenomenon but that was all. Santi Romano, plus Phocion Francescakis in his foreword to the translation, ... gave us, as it were, a more philosophical structure, which I term pluralism of legal orders. And it was from then on that our writings became more systematized.[129]

It may be thought surprising that the French school "built an important part of their theoretical edifice on a thinker his own compeers, scholars of the highest caliber, depict as a reactionary author."[130] But it was Romano's theories not his political views that were used by those who sought to describe *lex mercatoria* as an autonomous legal order. As Fontanelli explains in his detailed study on Romano, two major principles underlying Romano's thinking – pluralism and institutionalism – may serve as a theoretical model to explain contemporary debates in international, transnational, and global law.[131] Romano rejected a basic tenet of legal positivism – the Kelsenian idea of law as "an aggregate or system of norms, as a normative order"[132] – and posited an absolute equivalence between an organized social order and law.[133] That view "open[ed] the way for the study of a universe of non-State legal orders, which, in fact, were at that time hardly regarded as fully juridical."[134] As Kahn stated in his comment quoted earlier, Romano provided a sound theoretical framework within which members of the French school could develop their own ideas.

127 Mustill, "New *Lex Mercatoria*," 110–14.
128 See Gaillard, "Thirty Years of *Lex Mercatoria*," 224.
129 Kahn, in Gherari and Szurek, *L'émergence de la société civile internationale*, 268.
130 Thomas Schultz, *Transnational Legality: Stateless Law and International Arbitration* (Oxford: Oxford University Press, 2014), 60–61.
131 Filippo Fontanelli, "Santi Romano and *L'ordinamento giuridico*: The Relevance of a Forgotten Masterpiece for Contemporary International, Transnational and Global Legal Relations," *Transnational Legal Theory*, 2 (2011), 108.
132 Hans Kelsen, "On the Basic Norm," *California Law Review*, 47 (1959), 107.
133 Romano's theory came close to Maurice Hauriou's legal institutionalism, despite some differences between the two.
134 Fontanelli, 74.

#### 9.3.2.2 A Strong Sense of Professional and Personal Identity

Second, the French school could be described – to use Cotterrell's words – as an "affective community." In addition to having common ideas, members of a given school of thought often share a sense of professional and personal identity. According to Kennedy, the profession is "ridden with sociological and political affiliations both internal to the field and part of the broader social context within which international lawyers work and which are not experienced first as intellectual commitments."[135] Kennedy looked at a wide range of affiliations, such as "professional identities," "disciplinary" and "generational" identification, and "social identities from the broader society."[136] Mentor–mentee relations are also "among the strongest sources of professional identification," whereby the mentor offers "information and guidance" and the mentee offers "a temporary fealty in exchange for entrée."[137]

These insights help in identifying some of the key features of the French school. There were, for example, strong "generational identifications" among the early members of the school. Stoufflet was born in 1928, Farjat in 1929, Kahn in 1931, Fouchard in 1937, and Loquin in 1949. Several of these individuals received the same legal training; they also became friends and it seems that at least some of them shared "a common commitment to decolonization."[138] As mentioned earlier, they greatly benefited from Goldman's mentorship. In fact, some of them went on to create their own "schools of thought" (to use the expression loosely). For example, there was a Nice school founded by Gérard Farjat,[139] and what may be described as a Fouchard school with Clay, Racine, and Ben Hamida among its members.[140]

#### 9.3.2.3 "Frontiers of Law" – and of Life

Besides this sense of generational identification, another, less evident reason for considering Goldman and Schmitthoff as the precursors of a new school of thought (and of the *lex mercatoria* project more

[135] Kennedy, "When Renewal Repeats," 428.
[136] Ibid., 428–34.
[137] Ibid., 432.
[138] CREDIMI, "École de Nice/École de Dijon," 460n5. The article concentrates particularly on Farjat and Kahn.
[139] Ibid See also Gilles Martin and Jean-Baptiste Racine, "Gérard Farjat et la doctrine," *Revue internationale de droit économique*, 27 (2013–14), 409–18.
[140] The expression "Fouchard school" ("une école Fouchard") was used by Professor Thomas Clay in discussion with the author, March 22, 2017.

specifically) is the fact that these were people whose lives were lived on the margins or at the intersection of several legal systems. In other words, the theoretical exploration of the "frontiers of law," to quote the title of Goldman's article, was all the more meaningful as these individuals had experienced frontiers of a different kind in their personal lives.

This argument is particularly relevant when one looks at the biography of the early proponents of *lex mercatoria*. Schmitthoff was a German jurist who emigrated to England in 1933 – the same year as Francis Mann.[141] He studied English law at the London School of Economics, was called to the Bar in 1936, and taught at the City of London College from 1948 until his retirement in 1971.[142] Goldman was born in Bucharest in 1913 and moved to Paris in 1930. He received his legal education in France and was naturalized a French citizen in 1937. He received his doctorate in civil law and became a law professor in 1947, starting his teaching career in Indochina; he later taught in Dijon (from 1949 to 1960) and Paris. From 1974 to 1979, he was the president of the University of Paris II. Even there, at the apex of the French academic world, he was confronted with "insults, threats, lewd tags" and other anti-Semitic acts.[143]

The biography of Henri Motulsky is also worth mentioning here as he, too, was an émigré lawyer whose writings provided inspiration for members of the French school (even though his field of research was mainly civil procedure, not arbitration). Motulsky was a German Jew who studied law in Munich.[144] He fled the Nazi regime and moved to Paris in 1933, becoming the last surviving member of his family.[145] Motulsky initially worked for a well-known French lawyer, Me de Segone, and in 1941 joined the Resistance (after a stint in the French

[141] See Lawrence Collins, "F.A. Mann (1907–1991)," in Jack Beatson and Reinhard Zimmermann (eds.), *Jurists Uprooted: German-Speaking Emigré Lawyers in Twentieth Century Britain* (Oxford: Oxford University Press, 2004), 384.

[142] John Adams, "Clive M. Schmitthoff (1903–1990)," in Beatson and Zimmermann (eds.), *Jurists Uprooted*, 368–69.

[143] Jean-Denis Bredin, "Berthold Goldman, toujours vivant," in Philippe Fouchard and Louis Vogel (eds.), *L'actualité de la pensée de Berthold Goldman: Droit commercial international et européen* (Paris: Panthéon-Assas, 2004), 18.

[144] On Motulsky generally, see Georges Bolard, "Motulsky Henri, 1905–1971," in Loïc Cadiet (ed.), *Dictionnaire de la justice* (Paris: Presses Universitaires de France, 2004), 915–17; Loïc Cadiet, "Motulsky Henri," in Patrick Arabeyre, Jean-Louis Halpérin, and Jacques Krynen (eds.), *Dictionnaire historique des juristes français, XII-XXe siècle*, 756–57. The Court of Cassation hosted a daylong conference in memory of Motulsky in 1991 and the University of Caen a colloquium entitled "Qu'est devenue la pensée de Henri Motulsky?" in 2012.

[145] Cadiet, *Dictionnaire*, 915.

Foreign Legion in Africa). He started working on his doctorate in the cellar of his supervisor, Paul Roubier; the thesis, which he defended in 1947, was hailed as a major achievement.[146] Motulsky passed the *agrégation* in 1959, teaching first in Rabat and Casablanca, then in Dijon (from 1961 to 1970) and at Paris X-Nanterre University. Even though the bulk of Motulsky's work was in the field of civil procedure,[147] he left a number of key writings in which he gave impassioned expression to his distinctive vision of international arbitration.[148] He had even started writing a *Traité de l'arbitrage*, which remained unfinished at the time of his death.[149]

The lives of these individuals may go some way to explaining why they became so interested in the idea of a new, supranational legal order in the first place. Bredin's metaphor of the "mountaineer" is particularly apt – someone on the edge, navigating between different worlds and forging a path of his own.[150] As Foucault reminds us, an emergence is always a "'non-place', a pure distance, which indicates that the adversaries do not belong to a common space. Consequently, no one is responsible for an emergence; no one can glory in it, since it always occurs in the interstice."[151] It was indeed largely in the interstices that the lives and research of Goldman, Schmitthoff, and Motulsky unfolded.

In this light, a meaningful connection between *lex mercatoria* and the biography of those who shaped it is not as surprising as it may at first seem. It fits squarely with Grisel's notion of "secant marginals," a term he borrowed from sociologists Crozier and Friedberg and convincingly applied to the field of international commercial arbitration.[152] "Secant marginals" may be defined as "individuals who, while being members of

[146] Henry Motulsky, *Principes d'une réalisation méthodique du droit privé: La théorie des éléments générateurs des droits subjectifs* (Paris: Dalloz, 2002 [1948]). See also Georges Bolard, "Témoignages," in "Qu'est devenue la pensée de Henri Motulsky?," *Procédures*, 3 (2012), 6.

[147] See Henri Motulsky, *Écrits*, vol. 1, *Études et notes de procédure civile* (Paris: Dalloz, 2009 [1973]).

[148] Motulsky, *Études et notes sur l'arbitrage.*

[149] Philippe Fouchard and Berthold Goldman, foreword to Motulsky, *Études et notes sur l'arbitrage*, vi.

[150] Bredin, "La loi du juge," ¶ 2, at 15.

[151] Michel Foucault, "Nietzsche, Genealogy, History," in *Language, Counter-Memory, Practice. Selected Essays and Interviews*, ed. Donald Bouchard, trans. Donald Bouchard and Sherry Simon (New York: Cornell University Press, 1977), 150.

[152] Florian Grisel, "Competition and Cooperation in International Commercial Arbitration: The Birth of a Transnational Legal Profession," *Law and Society Review*, 51 (2017) 790–824.

multiple social groups (national, ethnic, professional), do not develop a sense of primary identity, or exclusive loyalty, with regard to any one of these groups."[153] According to Grisel, they "did not seek to enhance or exploit competition between national approaches; rather, they actively worked to build bridges across legal systems and professions."[154] "Secant marginals" like Goldman and Schmitthoff are familiar figures in international law, belonging more broadly to the class of international lawyers who "seem strongly identified with their own deracinated, confused, multinational, or refugee identities."[155] That they played a key role in shaping new disciplines should come as no surprise; as sociologist Jean-Louis Fabiani reminds us, "most changes to the overall arrangement of disciplines occur at the borders or edges of knowledge."[156] Having experienced frontiers directly in their lives, the modern founders of *lex mercatoria* – and of the French school of international arbitration – were doubtless all the more aware of a need to push back the "edges of knowledge."

## 9.4 From Renewal to Anxiety: The Quarrels over *Lex Mercatoria*

The French school's exploration of *lex mercatoria* was not without its critics. Scholars disagreed on how to ascertain the content and methods of *lex mercatoria* (Section 9.4.1) and expressed their views in unusually strong terms, foreshadowing future debates in the field (Section 9.4.2).

### *9.4.1 Ascertaining the Content and Methods of* Lex Mercatoria

Despite providing a fertile ground for new thinking, *lex mercatoria* was slowly pushing the pendulum back toward anxiety. Some scholars felt that the early French school's research should be abandoned altogether. As with later disputes over the delocalization of arbitral awards and the arbitral legal order, the quarrel over *lex mercatoria* split the arbitration

153 Ibid., 793.

154 Ibid., 821.

155 Kennedy, "When Renewal Repeats," 430. A parallel may be drawn with other Jewish international lawyers who came of age between the two World Wars and who were "both minority outsiders and individual legal insiders, present and absent at the same time" (see James Loeffler and Moria Paz, "Introduction," in James Loeffler and Moria Paz (eds.), *The Law of Strangers: Jewish Lawyers and International Law in the Twentieth Century* (Cambridge: Cambridge University Press, 2019), 3).

156 Jean-Louis Fabiani, "À quoi sert la notion de discipline?," in Jean Boutier, Jean-Claude Passeron, and Jacques Revel (eds.), *Qu'est-ce qu'une discipline?* (Paris: Éditions de l'École des hautes études en sciences sociales, 2006), 20.

community into two camps. As Gaillard explained, "*lex mercatoria* continues to be a hotly debated subject, with a number of extremists on both sides."[157]

Scholars disagreed over how to ascertain both the content and methods of *lex mercatoria.*[158] There were those who maintained that it was sufficiently precise to govern international transactions. As a prominent US arbitration scholar explained, "[t]ogether with Goldman, Lando, and most of its other proponents, I do not view *lex mercatoria* as some arcane mystery, open only to anointed guardians of an ambiguous flame. . . . In fact, in my experience, counsel nearly always do present such evidence and argument, in one guise or another."[159] Awards can indeed be found in which *lex mercatoria* was applied and defended:

> The application of international principles [derived from *lex mercatoria*] offers many advantages. They apply in a uniform fashion and are independent from the peculiarities of each national law. They take into consideration the needs of international relations and allow for a fruitful exchange between systems which are sometimes excessively attached to conceptual distinctions, and systems which seek a just and pragmatic solution to particular situations.[160]

Most awards, however, did not refer to *lex mercatoria* and were decided on the basis of the provisions of the parties' contract.[161] Many scholars displayed skepticism towards the concept. Lord Mustill, one of the most fervent critics of *lex mercatoria*, wondered how it would work in practice:

> The proponents of the *lex mercatoria* claim it to be the law of the international business community: which must mean the law unanimously adopted by all countries engaged upon international commerce. Such a claim would have been sustainable two centuries ago. But the international business community is now immeasurably enlarged. What principles of trade law, apart from those which are so general as to be useless,

157 Gaillard, "Thirty Years of *Lex Mercatoria*," 209.

158 For an excellent overview, see Michael Pryles, "Application of the *Lex Mercatoria* in International Commercial Arbitration," *Mealey's International Arbitration Report*, 18, no. 2 (2003), 1–26.

159 Andreas Lowenfeld, "*Lex Mercatoria*: An Arbitrator's View," *Arbitration International*, 6 (1990), 140.

160 Award in ICC Case No. 8385, quoted in Partial Award in ICC Case No. 14208/14236, in *ICC International Court of Arbitration Bulletin*, 24, no. 2 (2013), 64. Award in ICC Case No. 8385 was published (in French) in Jean-Jacques Arnaldez, Yves Derains, and Dominique Hascher (eds.), *Collection of ICC Arbitral Awards 1996–2000* (New York: Wolters Kluwer, 2003), 479.

161 Yves Derains, "The Application of Transnational Rules in ICC Arbitral Awards," *World Arbitration and Mediation Review*, 5 (2011), 198.

> are common to the legal systems of the members of such a community? How could the arbitrators . . . amass the necessary materials on the laws of, say, Brazil, China, the Soviet Union, Australia, Nigeria, and Iraq?[162]

Lord Mustill compiled a list of twenty principles, which he described as "a modest haul for 25 years of international arbitration."[163] Other scholars created much longer lists; indeed, Berger saw *lex mercatoria* as an ongoing process of "creeping codification,"[164] considering the list as unclosed, unifying "the various sources that have fostered the evolution of a transnational commercial legal system into one single, open-ended set of rules and principles."[165]

Other scholars have argued against the list method, contending that Lord Mustill's questioning was beside the point.[166] Gaillard, who was himself critical of *lex mercatoria*, preferring instead the concepts of "transnational rules" or "general principles of international commercial law," explained that the goal was never to compile a list of principles. Arguing that "transnational rules should not be thought of as a list, but rather as a method,"[167] he explained that, when required to apply transnational rules, arbitrators should first look at the parties' intentions and see whether they explained how the applicable rules should be determined. If they did not, arbitrators and counsel would then be able to carry out a comparative law analysis. Doing so, Gaillard maintained, would be "no more arduous than, say, researching the content of various national laws connected to a dispute, in order to establish what is at stake when the traditional choice of law method is used in the absence of any agreement on the applicable law."[168] As will be seen in the next chapter, it was this move away from *lex mercatoria* that marked the transition from the first to the second generation of the French school of international arbitration.

162 Mustill, "New *Lex Mercatoria*," 92.

163 Ibid., 114.

164 Klaus Peter Berger, *TransLex-Principles with Commentary* (Cologne: Center for Transnational Law, 2019). See also Berger, *The Creeping Codification of the New Lex Mercatoria* (The Hague: Kluwer Law International, 2010 [1999]); "The Concept of the 'Creeping Codification' of Transnational Commercial Law," www.trans-lex.org/4/_/berger-klaus-peter-the-concept-of-the-creeping-codification-of-transnational-commercial-law/.

165 Berger, *Creeping Codification*, 256.

166 See, for example, Gary Born, *International Commercial Arbitration* (The Hague: Kluwer Law International, 2014), 2764.

167 See Gaillard, "Thirty Years of *Lex Mercatoria*," 224.

168 Ibid., 226.

### 9.4.2 *Images of War*

Foreshadowing the intensity of subsequent debates in the field, the debate over *lex mercatoria* was cast in unusually strong terms. Images of wars and battles abound in the literature on *lex mercatoria*. Goldman's analysis of the *Norsolor* case was aptly entitled "a judicial battle on *lex mercatoria*."[169] Lagarde spoke of "trench warfare, during which arguments of varying degrees of acrimoniousness are exchanged, of which it is vain to think they will advance the debate."[170] Asked by a US scholar to write an introduction to a book on *lex mercatoria* along with Mann, Goldman wryly observed: "I guess Thomas Carbonneau likes duels: he asked me and my good old friend Francis Mann to write concurrent introductions to this fascinating book, and no doubt he knew that this choice would result in a fight. To be sure, a very courteous one – the foils are covered with buttons – but still a fight."[171] Images of war and combat have permeated the discourse on *lex mercatoria* so deeply that scholars continue to use them when discussing the topic. In 2014, Schultz noted that French scholars "launched some of the most effective missiles in the intellectual battles that shaped the French tradition in international arbitration."[172]

There may be several reasons for these recurrent references to war. It might be simply that the scholars had a penchant for trenchant analysis and expression. Goldman, for instance, "liked to plead, demonstrate and convince."[173] A more convincing explanation, however, is that the debate over *lex mercatoria* was linked to deeper anxieties about the international legal regime and its implications. Some felt that the research on *lex mercatoria* was disrupting traditional thinking on the sources of law, arousing the "hostility and horror of positivists, be they in private or public law."[174] As Kahn explained, the theory of *lex mercatoria* was "long considered as heretical, as its enunciation contradicted the dominant doctrine on the sources of law and their hierarchy, the legal positivism whereby any legal rule emanates from the state."[175]

169 Goldman, "Une bataille judiciaire," 379–409.

170 Lagarde, "Approche critique," ¶ 2, at 125.

171 Berthold Goldman, "Introduction," in Thomas Carbonneau (ed.), *Lex Mercatoria and Arbitration: A Discussion of the New Law Merchant*, 2nd ed. (Yonkers, NY: Juris and Kluwer Law International, 1988), xix.

172 Schultz, *Transnational Legality*, 153.

173 Bredin, "Berthold Goldman," 16.

174 Kahn, in Gherari and Szurek, *L'émergence de la société civile internationale*, 268.

175 Philippe Kahn, "La *lex mercatoria* et son destin," in Philippe Fouchard and Louis Vogel (eds.), *L'actualité de la pensée de Berthold Goldman: Droit commercial international et européen* (Paris: Panthéon-Assas, 2004), 25.

Various scholars and practitioners saw the theory of *lex mercatoria* as subversive and problematic. Some felt that it was being used by private arbitrators and parties to serve the interests of multinational corporations[176] and that it was essentially "a doctrine of *laissez-faire*."[177] Others saw it as merely a convenient tool, or, in the words of a practitioner interviewed by Dezalay and Garth, "something that can be subject to abuse where an arbitrator doesn't feel like going through a difficult choice of law . . . or simply decides that something is *lex mercatoria* because that's an answer he feels is right."[178] Reisman expressed the same idea in unusually strong terms, describing "the imposition of *lex mercatoria*" as "a violation of [the parties'] wishes and a usurpation of their power."[179] For Reisman, an award based on *lex mercatoria* "would be little more than an equitable decision, rendered by a tribunal without authorization from the parties."[180] As such, "the development of *lex mercatoria* coincide[d] with the breakdown of the international control system"[181] and "[i]ts consequences for democratic political values could be severe."[182]

The debate over *lex mercatoria* shows no signs of abating. Other issues have attracted the attention of the arbitration community, but they have not ousted the quarrel over *lex mercatoria*, which continues to resurface periodically. To give but one example, the late Judge James Crawford delivered a scathing attack on *lex mercatoria* in his 2013 course at the Hague Academy:

> It is true that attempts have been made to "constitute" systems of law divorced from social systems. A notable example is the idea of *lex mercatoria* postulated by French comparatist Berthold Goldman and developed further by institutions such as UNIDROIT. The problem with it is that it is a pure confection, unrelated to any real source of authority or any existing *praxis*. It is a law of and for professors, a *Buchrecht* reduced to a single book, based on the assumption that comparative law techniques can distil

176 Born, *International Commercial Arbitration*, 2761.
177 Mustill, "New *Lex Mercatoria*," 117.
178 Yves Dezalay and Bryant Garth, *Dealing in Virtue: International Commercial Arbitration and the Construction of a Transnational Legal Order* (Chicago: Chicago University Press, 1996), 39.
179 Michael Reisman, *Systems of Control in International Adjudication and Arbitration: Breakdown and Repair* (Durham: Duke University Press, 1992), pt. 4, "Non-Institutional International Commercial Arbitration: The Breakdown of the Control System of the New York Convention," 135.
180 Ibid.
181 Ibid.
182 Ibid., 139.

> a true or real underlying common law – a sort of natural law without the benefit of divinity. The assumption is demonstrably untrue.[183]

Few subjects in international commercial arbitration scholarship have given rise to such impassioned argument as the *lex mercatoria* that lay at the heart of the French school's early research agenda.

## 9.5 Conclusion

The late 1950s and 1960s were characterized by a period of intense renewal in the field of international arbitration. French scholars – including Goldman, Fouchard, Kahn, and Loquin – put forward the idea of a transnational legal system apart from domestic legal systems. This was a radically new insight, renewing the way in which international commercial arbitration was traditionally viewed. It caused much disagreement within the arbitration community, and in time led scholars to shift their attention to a related but analytically distinct concept, the arbitral legal order. As the next chapter will show, their research provoked the same movement between renewal and anxiety that has characterized much of arbitration's history.

183 James Crawford, *Chance, Order, Change: The Course of International Law, General Course on Public International Law*, the Hague Academy of International Law (Leiden: Martinus Nijhoff, 2013), ¶ 232, at 143.

# 10

# The Second Generation of the French School of International Arbitration and the Quarrel over the Arbitral Legal Order

## 10.1 Introduction

In the 1980s and 1990s, a new generation took the helm within the French school of international arbitration. Members of this second generation – who had been the students of leading members of the first generation and envisioned international commercial arbitration as a field of both research and practice – felt that the debates over *lex mercatoria* had led to important insights but did not sufficiently address fundamental questions, such as the source of the arbitrators' power to adjudicate or the "juridicity" of international arbitration.[1] Thus, members of the second generation shifted the focus of the inquiry – from *lex mercatoria* to the arbitral legal order. It may be said, albeit somewhat schematically, that while members of the first generation had focused on the "society of merchants" and "anational rules," members of the second generation were primarily concerned with the "arbitral legal order" and the "autonomy" of international arbitration.

Unlike members of the first generation, who had relatively few cases on which to ground their theories, those of the second generation were able to exchange views on a number of practical issues. One such issue – the enforcement of arbitral awards set aside in the country of the seat – arose in a succession of cases, for the most part in the French courts. The heated discussions they sparked within the international arbitration community pitted so-called *territorialists*, who maintained that an award that had been set aside had ceased to exist and could not be enforced elsewhere, against *internationalists*, who argued that an award was not part of the

[1] Emmanuel Gaillard, *Legal Theory of International Arbitration* (Leiden: Martinus Nijhoff, 2010), ¶ 2, at 2.

legal order of the state where it was rendered and could therefore be enforced elsewhere. As this chapter will show, the debate over the delocalization of awards – both the arguments made and the people involved – foreshadowed the quarrel over the arbitral legal order that began soon thereafter and continues to this day.[2]

This chapter explores the dynamics of renewal and anxiety in the context of the second generation of the French school of international arbitration. It shows how the vacuum left by the first generation was filled by a new generation of scholar-practitioners intent on working on actual cases and renewing the terms of the debate about the nature of international arbitration (Section 10.2). At the same time, arbitration scholars – not just in France but also elsewhere, including England, Switzerland, and the United States – argued vigorously for or against the enforcement of awards set aside in the country of the seat (Section 10.3). The major contribution of the second generation of the French school was to theorize the arbitral legal order, which led to a deeper sense of renewal for some and anxiety for others (Section 10.4).

## 10.2 Renewal in the French School of International Arbitration

Two trends may be observed within the French school from the late 1980s onward. First, a new generation of arbitration scholars rose to prominence (Section 10.2.1). Second, these scholars asked a new set of theoretical questions, shifting the focus of inquiry from the *lex mercatoria* to the arbitral legal order and renewing the terms of the debate about the nature of arbitrators' powers and of international arbitration as a whole (Section 10.2.2).

### *10.2.1 From the First to the Second Generation*

The rise of a new group of scholars within the French school was largely the result of a change of generations (as shown in Table 10.1). The French school mourned the passing of several key figures in the years leading up to and following the millennium. They included Goldman, who died in

[2] Of course, the fact that this chapter devotes so much attention to the debate over the "delocalization" of awards should not give the impression that this was the only key debate taking place in the Age of Autonomy. There were in fact many debates, covering such issues as the scope of arbitrators' freedom to identify the rules governing the merits of the dispute, or how to deal with antisuit injunctions.

Table 10.1 *The French school of international arbitration*

| | Precursors Late 1950s–1970s | First generation 1960s–1990s | Second generation 1980s–present |
|---|---|---|---|
| Key individuals | Goldman (Schmitthoff in England) | Fouchard, Kahn<br>Loquin, Derains | Gaillard<br>Clay, Racine, etc.[1]<br>(Lalive in Switzerland)[2] |
| Key issue(s) | *Lex mercatoria* | *Lex mercatoria* legal order, society of merchants, anational rules | Arbitral legal order, autonomy of international arbitration |
| Background reference(s) | Medieval *lex mercatoria*, Roman *ius gentium* (a formally autonomous source of law) | Romano (legal pluralism) | Gaillard (legal theory of international arbitration),<br>Ost and van de Kerchove (network) |
| Examples of background cases | Suez crisis (international legal entity), *Trucial Coast* Arbitration (1951) | Various ICC awards (published from 1974 onward), *Gosset* (1963), *Norsolor* (1984) | *Dalico* (1993),<br>*Hilmarton* (1994),<br>*Chromalloy* (1997),<br>*Zanzi* (1999),<br>*International Bechtel* (2005), *Nioc* (2005), *Putrabali* (2007) |

1 If the hallmark of the "second generation" is a shared belief in the existence of an arbitral legal order, younger scholars could be added to the list; see, for example, Malik Laazouzi, "L'arbitre international et les rapports entre ordres juridiques," in Baptiste Bonnet (ed.), *Traité des rapports entre ordres juridiques* (Paris: LGDJ, 2016).

2 Lalive was a Swiss national and closer to the first generation in terms of his background, but a strong proponent of the arbitral legal order; see, for example, Pierre Lalive, "L'ordre public transnational et l'arbitre international," in Gabriella Venturini and Stefania Bariatti (eds.), *New Instruments of Private International Law. Liber Fausto Pocar* (Milan: Giuffrè, 2009).

1993,[3] and Fouchard, whose death in 2004 in a plane crash, along with ten members of his family, when returning from Christmas holidays in the Red Sea resort of Sharm el-Sheik, was a particularly tragic moment.[4] The shock waves caused by his passing were felt throughout the arbitration world, from São Paulo[5] to Alexandria.[6] In Paris, more than 400 lawyers, academics, former colleagues, students, and friends gathered for a daylong conference at the Court of Cassation.[7] Its president at the time remarked how moving it was for the Court of Cassation to host a memorial tribute to a great jurist and to have been chosen as the place in which to honor his significant oeuvre.[8] In 2007, the Comité Français de l'Arbitrage (CFA) published Fouchard's *Écrits*, which included his writings on arbitration and international trade law.[9] It was as if Fouchard's death had consolidated the field of international arbitration both in France and abroad and reinforced the intergenerational and interpersonal bonds within it.

Meanwhile, a new generation of international arbitration scholars started emerging in the 1970s and 1980s, which was to change the face of the French school. While the original members of the first generation, such as Kahn and Loquin, were primarily based in Dijon, the new generation chiefly lived and studied in Paris. Its members not only had a sophisticated understanding of private and public international law but also envisioned international commercial arbitration as a full-fledged field of research and practice. In sharp contrast to the precursors of the French school – Goldman or Motulsky, for instance – the new generation

[3] See, for example, Philippe Fouchard and Louis Vogel (eds.), *L'actualité de la pensée de Berthold Goldman: Droit commercial international et européen* (Paris: Panthéon-Assas, 2004); Jean-Marc Bischoff, "In Memoriam: Jean-Louis Bismuth, Berthold Goldman," *Travaux du Comité français de droit international privé*, 11 (1994), 143–44; "*In memoriam* Berthold Goldman," *ASA Bulletin*, 11, no. 2 (1993), 187–89.

[4] See, for example, Hélène Gaudemet-Tallon, "*In Memoriam*: Philippe Fouchard (1937–2004)," *Travaux du Comité français de droit international privé (2002–2004)*, 16 (2005) 195.

[5] See, for example, the conference organized by the Brazilian Arbitration Committee, "Homenagem a Philippe Fouchard" (September 15–16, 2004), http://cbar.org.br/site/en/2004-iv-congresso-cbar-e-i-jornada-icc/.

[6] See the proceedings of the conference organized at the Bibliotheca Alexandrina on April 28, 2005, *L'éthique dans les relations économiques internationales: En hommage à Philippe Fouchard* (Paris: Pedone, 2006).

[7] "Journée d'hommage et d'études à la mémoire de Philippe Fouchard, Paris, 11 mars 2005," *Revue de l'arbitrage*, 2005, 245; and full list of participants, 511–25.

[8] Guy Canivet, "Accueil," in *Journée d'hommage*, 243.

[9] Philippe Fouchard, *Écrits: Droit de l'arbitrage, droit du commerce international* (Paris: Comité français de l'arbitrage, 2007).

were not *émigré* lawyers; most of them had studied in France and had been steeped in the French academic tradition from an early age.[10]

The passing of the first generation left a void in the French arbitration world that was slow to fill. In the early 1990s, Fouchard and Guinchard created a specialized program in litigation, arbitration, and alternative dispute resolution at the University of Paris II, where Fouchard had been teaching since 1980.[11] The program, which exists to this day, trained an entire generation of French arbitration scholars, including Clay, Racine, and Ben Hamida.[12] In many cases, these scholars earned their doctorates under the supervision of leading early members of the French school.[13] Before long, arbitration programs were burgeoning in French universities. As already noted in Chapter 8, the proliferation of these academic programs has strongly marked the professionalization of the field in France since the 1980s and 1990s.

### *10.2.2 From* Lex Mercatoria *to the Quest for an Autonomous Legal Order*

It could be argued that with the emergence of a new class of arbitration scholars the focus of theoretical inquiry within the French school changed. Without denying the value of the work achieved by the previous generation, the second generation felt that the time had come to ask a new set of questions. Members of the second generation behaved like Kuhn's scientist, who, in order to make "new discoveries and theories in the sciences," must "usually rearrange the intellectual ... equipment he has previously relied upon."[14] As Kuhn explains, the successful scientist often has to "simultaneously display the characteristics of the traditionalist and of the

[10] To a large extent, the second generation of the French school drew inspiration from the figure of the scholar-practitioner epitomized by Gaillard, Paulsson, and others. Not only had new members of the French school amassed intellectual prestige and academic habitus, but they also had strong business acumen.

[11] "Biographie de Philippe Fouchard (1937–2004)," in Philippe Fouchard, *Écrits*, xvii.

[12] Discussion with Professor Thomas Clay (Paris, March 22, 2017).

[13] For example, Cohen completed his PhD under Oppetit's supervision: Daniel Cohen, *Arbitrage et société* (Paris: LGDJ, 1993). Racine, Clay, and Ben Hamida all completed their doctorates under Fouchard's supervision: Jean-Baptiste Racine, *L'arbitrage commercial international et l'ordre public* (Paris: LGDJ, 1999); Thomas Clay, *L'arbitre* (Paris: Dalloz, 2001); Walid Ben Hamida, "L'arbitrage transnational unilatéral: Réflexions sur une procédure réservée à l'initiative d'une personne privée contre une personne publique" (PhD diss., Panthéon-Assas (Paris II) University, 2003).

[14] Thomas Kuhn, *The Essential Tension: Selected Studies in Scientific Tradition and Change* (Chicago: University of Chicago Press, 1977), chapter 9, at 226.

iconoclast," in a sort of "'essential tension' implicit in scientific research."[15] In like manner the second generation of the French school of international arbitration built on the insights of the first generation while shifting the focus of theoretical inquiry.

Gaillard has clearly explained that shift. He observed that the quarrel over *lex mercatoria*, which had "dominated most of the theoretical debates in the second half of the twentieth century," had allowed scholars and practitioners to exchange views,[16] thereby "stimulating the thinking concerning the very notion of a legal order."[17] But, "by exclusively focusing on such issues," the reflection on *lex mercatoria* "overlooked the fundamental question regarding the source of the arbitrators' power to adjudicate."[18] For Gaillard, the quarrel over *lex mercatoria* was "outdated": "No longer is it a problem for arbitrators to apply transnational rules. What remains at the heart of the theoretical debate today is in fact the constitutional aspect of the subject: Upon what norm are arbitrators' jurisdictional powers founded?"[19]

Moreover, given that *lex mercatoria* was born of a critical stance toward national legal systems, there was a negative current in the debate. This point was key: whereas *lex mercatoria* implied a degree of disassociation from domestic legal orders, the debate over the arbitral legal order was marked by a more harmonious view of legal orders.[20] As Gaillard concluded, "[t]oday, the debate has refocused on issues of sources and methodology"[21] and "has been strongly renewed."[22]

This *renewal* of the methods and questions raised in relation to the nature of international arbitration manifested at various levels – for example, in the intellectual references used and the topics addressed. Whereas the first generation had relied heavily on Santi Romano's ideas, the new generation felt closer to such thinkers as François Ost and Michel

[15] Ibid., 227.
[16] Gaillard, *Legal Theory*, 3.
[17] Ibid., 37–38. According to Gaillard, the debate was also "productive" in that it contributed to "the movement towards greater internationalization of arbitration" by "freeing arbitrators from the constraints of the choice of law rules of the seat understood as a forum" (ibid.).
[18] Ibid., 38.
[19] Emmanuel Gaillard, "Souveraineté et autonomie: Réflexions sur les représentations de l'arbitrage international," *Journal du droit international*, 2007, 1170.
[20] Emmanuel Gaillard, "Transcending National Legal Orders for International Arbitration," in Albert Jan van den Berg (ed.), *International Arbitration: The Coming of a New Age?*, ICCA Congress Series No. 17 (The Hague: Kluwer Law International, 2013), 373n5.
[21] Emmanuel Gaillard, "Transnational Law: A Legal System or a Method of Decision Making?," *Arbitration International*, 17 (2001), 60.
[22] Ibid.

van de Kerchove.[23] In an important work, these two authors sought to replace Kelsen's "essentially hierarchical, linear and arborescent conception of the structure of a legal system"[24] with a "competing paradigm – that of law as a network."[25] This was a novel conception, inspired by the textile metaphor of a "web" (*maillage*),[26] and conveyed the idea – appealing to proponents of an autonomous legal order – that regulation might involve an "organization that is more flexible, decentralized, adaptive and often negotiated."[27]

In addition, the second generation took the theoretical exploration of an autonomous legal order further in their writings. This can be seen in several works from the late 1980s and 1990s – that is, at the time of the generational change in the French school. For example, in the late 1980s, Goldman – then editor-in-chief of the *Juris-Classeur Droit International* – enlisted Gaillard and Fouchard to assist him in writing a series of fascicles on international commercial arbitration. Hence, the project associated a leading member of each generation of the French school.[28] It soon became clear that the fascicles could serve as a model for an even more comprehensive book about the law and practice of international commercial arbitration at a time when there were relatively few treatises and monographs on the subject.[29] That book – Fouchard,

23 See, for example, Gaillard, *Legal Theory*, 7–8.

24 François Ost and Michel van de Kerchove, *De la pyramide au réseau? Pour une théorie dialectique du droit* (Brussels: Publications des Facultés universitaires Saint-Louis, 2002), 43. See also Ost and van de Kerchove, *Jalons pour une théorie critique du droit* (Brussels: Publications des Facultés universitaires Saint-Louis, 1987), chapter 4.

25 Ost and van de Kerchove, *De la pyramide au réseau?*, 14. But see Mireille Delmas-Marty, *Le pluralisme ordonné: Les forces imaginantes du droit*, vol. 2 (Paris: Seuil, 2006), 278–79 (arguing that this approach might still be ambiguous and that the metaphor of "ordered clouds" (*nuages ordonnés*) might be more apt).

26 Ost and van de Kerchove, *De la pyramide au réseau?*, 23.

27 Ibid., 26.

28 The fascicles appeared from 1989 to 1994. Goldman could be considered a precursor of the French school, Fouchard a member of the first generation, and Gaillard a member of both the first and second generations.

29 For example, Robert's treatise, first published in 1937, reached its sixth edition in 1993 (Jean Robert and Bertrand Moreau, *L'arbitrage: Droit interne, droit international privé*, 6th ed. (Paris: Dalloz, 1993 [1937])). An English translation of the fifth edition appeared in 1983 (Jean Robert and Thomas Carbonneau, *The French Law of Arbitration* (New York: Matthew Bender, 1983)). Fouchard's dissertation was published in 1965 (Philippe Fouchard, *L'arbitrage commercial international* (Paris: Dalloz, 1965)). David's treatise came out in 1982 (René David, *L'arbitrage dans le commerce international* (Paris: Economica, 1982)), Redfern and Hunter's in 1986 (Alan Redfern and Martin Hunter, *Law and Practice of International Commercial Arbitration* (London: Sweet & Maxwell, 1986)), and Lalive, Poudret, and Reymond's in 1989 (Pierre Lalive, Jean-François Poudret, and

Gaillard, and Goldman's *Traité de l'arbitrage commercial international*[30] – was published in 1996, three years after Goldman's death.[31]

The treatise went beyond a mere description of arbitration law and practice; it addressed some of the key preoccupations of both the first and the second generations of the French school. For instance, Gaillard devoted more than thirty pages to the modern controversies surrounding *lex mercatoria*,[32] expressing the view that

> it is essential to recognize that the system of general principles cannot be reduced to the application of a list of rules which have already been formally codified, but that it consists instead of a method enabling the underlying principles of comparative law to be uncovered, if required. It is hard to deny that such a method is an appropriate tool for resolving all disputes liable to arise out of contracts which the parties intended to be governed by transnational rules or to which arbitrators choose to apply transnational rules where the parties fail to elect a governing law.[33]

At the same time, following the path that had been forged by Goldman and members of the first generation, while renewing the terms of the debate somewhat, the treatise sought to highlight the worldwide movement toward an autonomous legal regime. Thus, it referred to "arbitrations entirely detached from national laws and governed solely by autonomous rules constituting a genuine international legal order."[34] While the phrasing "autonomous rules" did not acknowledge the existence of a full-fledged arbitral legal order, several members of the French school soon began to address this question through the study of actual cases.

## 10.3 The Debate over the Delocalization of Arbitral Awards

In the 1980s and 1990s, while the "juridicity" of international arbitration was being discussed in theoretical writings, a succession of judgments, mostly from the French courts, pondered a separate issue – the

Claude Reymond, *Le droit de l'arbitrage interne et international en Suisse* (Lausanne: Payot, 1989)).

30 Philippe Fouchard, Emmanuel Gaillard, and Berthold Goldman, *Traité de l'arbitrage commercial international* (Paris: Litec, 1996).

31 It was subsequently translated into English, revised, and updated as Emmanuel Gaillard and John Savage (eds.), *Fouchard, Gaillard, Goldman on International Commercial Arbitration* (The Hague: Kluwer Law International, 1999).

32 *Fouchard, Gaillard, Goldman*, ¶¶ 1443–99, at 813–47. Part 5 of the treatise, entitled "The Law Applicable to the Merits of the Dispute," was written by Gaillard.

33 *Fouchard, Gaillard, Goldman*, ¶ 1499, at 834.

34 Ibid., ¶ 95, at 50.

enforcement of arbitral awards set aside in the country of the seat. This led to a vigorous debate within the arbitration community over the delocalization of arbitral awards.[35] The debate has been couched in terms of "territorialists" vs. "internationalists"[36] and Ancients vs. Moderns.[37] Before considering the two sides of the debate – clearly reflective of renewal and anxiety (Section 10.3.2) – it is useful to review the judgments that fueled the debate (Section 10.3.1). The debate over the delocalization of awards had a number of key characteristics – both in terms of the actors involved and the language used – and, to a large extent, prefigured the quarrel over the arbitral legal order that was to rage soon thereafter (Section 10.3.3).

### *10.3.1 The Fate of Awards Set Aside in the Country of the Seat*

The question at the core of the debate over the delocalization of arbitral awards is a simple one: Can an award be enforced if it has been set aside by the courts at the seat of arbitration? Starting in the 1980s, French courts – as well as some Belgian,[38] Dutch,[39] and American[40] courts – confirmed that an award that has been set aside in the country of the seat

35 This could be defined as "the idea that parties from different countries, in order to achieve neutrality, wish to avoid as much as possible the intervention of their respective courts, and at the same time the application of the rules of their respective countries." Pierre Mayer, "The Trend Towards Delocalisation in the Last 100 Years," in Martin Hunter, Arthur Marriott, and V. V. Veeder, *The Internationalisation of International Arbitration: The LCIA Centenary Conference* (London: Graham & Trotman/Martinus Nijhoff, 1995), 37. See also Pierre Mayer, "L'insertion de la sentence dans l'ordre juridique français", in Yves Derains (ed.), *Droit et pratique de l'arbitrage international en France* (Paris: Feduci, 1984), 83.

36 David Rivkin, "The Enforcement of Awards Nullified in the Country of Origin: The American Experience," in Albert Jan van den Berg (ed.), *Improving the Efficiency of Arbitration Agreements and Awards: 40 Years of Application of the New York Convention*, ICCA Congress Series No. 9 (The Hague: Kluwer Law International, 1999), 539–40.

37 Pierre Mayer, "Revisiting *Hilmarton* and *Chromalloy*," in Albert Jan van den Berg (ed.), *International Arbitration and National Courts: The Never Ending Story*, ICCA Congress Series No. 10 (The Hague: Kluwer Law International, 2001), 166.

38 See Brussels Court of First Instance, December 6, 1988, *Société Nationale pour la Recherche, le Transport et la Commercialisation des Hydrocarbures (Sonatrach)* v. *Ford, Bacon and Davis Inc.*, *Yearbook Commercial Arbitration*, XV (1990), 370–78. The Brussels court recognized an award rendered in Algiers in 1985 and subsequently annulled by the Court of Appeal of Algiers in 1986. The decision was confirmed by the Brussels Court of Appeal in 1990.

39 Supreme Court of the Netherlands, October 26, 1973, *Société européenne d'études et d'entreprises* v. *Socialist Federal Republic of Yugoslavia*, *Netherlands Yearbook of International Law*, V (1974), 290.

40 See, for example, my discussion of *Chromalloy* later in this section.

could nevertheless be recognized elsewhere. Arbitration scholars and practitioners are familiar with these judgments, which have played a significant role in the modern history and evolution of international commercial arbitration and have already been analyzed in great detail.[41]

The first major case to consider the fate of an international arbitral award that had been set aside in a foreign state was *Norsolor* in 1984. An arbitration between a Turkish company (Pabalk) and a French company (Ugilor, later Norsolor) was held in Austria and resulted in an award in favor of Pabalk. The award was initially recognized in Austria and France, but it was then partially set aside by the Vienna Court of Appeal.[42] In turn, the decision granting recognition of the award in France was reversed by the Paris Court of Appeal, based on Article V(1)(e) of the New York Convention (according to which recognition and enforcement of an award may be refused if the award "has been set aside or suspended by a competent authority of the country in which, or under the law of which, that award was made").[43] The Paris Court of Appeal's decision was overturned by the French Court of Cassation,[44] which held that, under Article VII of the New York Convention, "the judge cannot refuse enforcement when his own national legal system permits it and, by virtue of Article 12 of the New Code of Civil Procedure, he should, even *sua sponte*, inquire into the matter if such is the case."[45] In other words, it was incumbent on the French court to assess whether enforcement of the award would be prohibited under French law. The ground on which the Vienna Court of Appeal based its decision – that the arbitral tribunal, instead of determining which

[41] See, for example, Emmanuel Gaillard, "The Enforcement of Awards Set Aside in the Country of Origin," *ICSID Review – Foreign Investment Law Journal*, 16 (1999), 16–45; Jean-François Poudret and Sébastien Besson, *Comparative Law of International Arbitration* (London: Sweet & Maxwell, 2007), ¶ 927; Benoit Le Bars and Joseph Dalmasso, *Arbitrage commercial international: Les grands arrêts du droit français* (Paris: LexisNexis, 2016), 325–42; Hamid Gharavi, *The International Effectiveness of the Annulment of an Arbitral Award* (The Hague: Kluwer Law International, 2002), ¶¶ 188–95, at 77–80.

[42] The decision of the Vienna Court of Appeal was subsequently overturned; see Supreme Court of Austria, November 18, 1982, *Revue de l'arbitrage*, 1983, 519.

[43] Paris Court of Appeal, November 19, 1982, *Norsolor S.A.* v. *Pabalk Ticaret Limited Sirketi*, *Revue de l'arbitrage*, 1983, 472.

[44] Court of Cassation (France), First Civil Chamber, October 9, 1984, *Société Pabalk Ticaret Limited Sirketi* v. *Norsolor S.A.*, *Revue de l'arbitrage*, 1985, 431, note Goldman; *Journal du droit international*, 1985, 679, note Kahn; *Dalloz* (1985), 101, note Robert. For a key commentary on the decision, see Berthold Goldman, "Une bataille judiciaire autour de la *lex mercatoria*: L'affaire *Norsolor*," *Revue de l'arbitrage*, 1983, 379–409.

[45] Quoted in *Fouchard, Gaillard, Goldman*, ¶ 270, at 134.

national law was applicable, had directly applied *lex mercatoria* – did not justify refusing enforcement under French law.

The principles set out in the *Norsolor* decision were reapplied in 1993 in *Polish Ocean Line*. An arbitration between that Polish company and French company Jolasry resulted in an award in favor of Jolasry. Polish Ocean Line appealed to a Polish court, which suspended enforcement of the award. In France, meanwhile, a decision ordering enforcement of the award was rendered by the Douai Court of Appeal and upheld by the Court of Cassation, which held that

> when an arbitral award has been set aside or suspended by a competent authority in the country in which it was rendered, a French court may not refuse enforcement on this ground, which, although provided for in Art. V(1)(e) of the 1958 New York Convention, is not among those listed in Art. 1502 of the New Code of Civil Procedure.[46]

The Douai Court of Appeal was therefore correct in finding that the action to set aside the award in Poland – and the Polish court's decision to suspend enforcement – was not a reason to refuse enforcement in France.

The French Court of Cassation took another key step forward in its *Hilmarton* decision in 1994, which confirmed *Norsolor* by clearly stating that an award set aside in the country of the seat may be recognized in France. The *Hilmarton* arbitration between a French corporation (Omnium de traitement et de valorisation, or OTV) and an English corporation (Hilmarton) took place in Switzerland. In an award rendered in 1988, the sole arbitrator rejected Hilmarton's claims on the ground that the contract between the parties – a consultancy agreement under which Hilmarton provided services to help OTV win a contract in Algeria – was contrary to *bonos mores* and, therefore, unenforceable. The award was set aside by the Swiss Federal Tribunal. The French Court of Cassation upheld the decision of the Paris Court of Appeal enforcing the award that had been rendered and set aside in Switzerland.[47] The Court of Cassation famously stated that "the award rendered in Switzerland is an international

[46] Court of Cassation (France), First Civil Chamber, March 10, 1993, *Société Polish Ocean Line* v. *Société Jolasry*, *Revue de l'arbitrage*, 1993, 276, note Hascher; *Journal du droit international*, 1993, 360, note Kahn; *Yearbook Commercial Arbitration* (1994), 662.

[47] Court of Cassation (France), First Civil Chamber, March 23, 1994, *Société Hilmarton Ltd.* v. *Société Omnium de traitement et de valorisation (OTV)*, *Journal du droit international*, 1994, 701, note Gaillard; *Revue de l'arbitrage*, 1994, 327, note Jarrosson; *Revue critique de droit international privé*, 1995, 356, note Oppetit.

award which is not integrated into the legal system of that State, so that it remains in existence even if set aside and its recognition in France is not contrary to international public policy."[48] This was a bold statement, in which Goldman's influence was clear,[49] even though some commentators argued that the Court to Cassation had simply affirmed that an international award does not belong to the legal order of the country in which it is rendered. That said, the Court of Cassation left open "the question of whether recognition is possible in every case where an award can be characterized as an international award under French law."[50]

A second award was rendered in Switzerland in 1992, granting Hilmarton the right to collect its commission. In two decisions, the Versailles Court of Appeal approved the decision of the Nanterre Court that had ruled in favor of enforcement of the second award. This led to a conundrum, which could be summarized as follows: "[T]wo conflicting awards concerning the same dispute between the same parties, as well as a judgment setting aside the first award, coexisted within the French legal order. It goes without saying that this situation was unsustainable."[51] It was not until 1997, almost ten years after the first award, that the situation was finally resolved when the Court of Cassation quashed the two decisions of the Versailles Court of Appeal on grounds of *res judicata*, meaning that, ultimately, only the first *Hilmarton* award was recognized in France, despite having been set aside in Switzerland.

As is well known, *Hilmarton* was followed by another key case, *Chromalloy*. In that case, a dispute arose between a US corporation (Chromalloy Aeroservices) and the Air Force of Egypt regarding a military procurement contract providing for the maintenance and repair of helicopters belonging to Egypt. In 1994, a tribunal composed of distinguished arbitrators rendered an award in Egypt, ordering the Egyptian government to pay approximately USD 16 million plus interest to Chromalloy. The Egyptian Court of Appeal annulled the award because it was not "properly grounded under Egyptian law."[52] The award was recognized by the District Court for the District of

[48] English translation in Gaillard, *Legal Theory*, 61.
[49] See Goldman, "Une bataille judiciaire," 389.
[50] Gaillard, "Enforcement of Awards," 23.
[51] Ibid.
[52] The arbitrators had applied Egyptian *civil* law instead of *administrative* law, even though neither party had argued that the application of administrative law would lead to a different result.

Columbia in 1996[53] and by the Paris Court of Appeal in 1997,[54] despite having been set aside in Egypt.

Reiterating the French position on the recognition and enforcement of awards set aside in the country of the seat, the Paris Court of Appeal stated that "the award rendered in Egypt was *an international award which by definition was not integrated into the legal order of that country* such that its existence continues despite its nullification and . . . its recognition in France is not contrary to international public policy."[55] This was a forceful restatement of the French approach and a "welcome clarification concerning the fate of an international award rendered in a foreign state which, from the French point of view, is, 'by definition', not integrated in the legal order of the state in which it was rendered."[56]

Over the years, the French approach was followed in a number of other cases, including *Zanzi* (1999),[57] *International Bechtel* (2005),[58] *Nioc* (2005),[59]

53 *Matter of Arbitration between Chromalloy Aeroservices* v. *Arab Republic of Egypt*, July 31, 1996, 939 F. Supp. 907 (D.D.C. 1996). The US *Chromalloy* case led to abundant literature: see, for example, Hamid Gharavi, "*Chromalloy*: Another View," *Mealey's International Arbitration Report*, 12, no. 1 (1997), 21–27; Jan Paulsson, "Rediscovering the N.Y. Convention: Further Reflections on *Chromalloy*," *Mealey's International Arbitration Report*, 12, no. 4 (1997), 20–34; Rivkin, "Enforcement of Awards," 528–43; Gary Sampliner, "Enforcement of Foreign Arbitral Awards after Annulment in their Country of Origin," *Mealey's International Arbitration Report*, 11, no. 9 (1996), 22–34; Gary Sampliner, "Enforcement of Nullified Foreign Arbitral Awards: *Chromalloy* Revisited," *Journal of International Arbitration*, 14, no. 3 (1997), 141–65; Eric Schwartz, "A Comment on *Chromalloy*: Hilmarton, *à l'américaine*," *Journal of International Arbitration*, 14, no. 2 (1997), 125–36; Philipp Wahl, "Enforcement of Foreign Arbitral Awards Set Aside in their Country of Origin: The *Chromalloy* Case Revisited," *Journal of International Arbitration*, 16, no. 4 (1999), 131–40.

54 Paris Court of Appeal, January 14, 1997, *Arab Republic of Egypt* v. *Chromalloy Aero Services*, *Revue de l'arbitrage*, 1997, 395, note Fouchard; *Journal du droit international*, 1998, 750, note Gaillard; *Yearbook Commercial Arbitration*, 22 (1997), 691.

55 Gaillard, "Enforcement of Awards," 25 (emphasis added).

56 Ibid., 25.

57 Court of Cassation (France), First Civil Chamber, January 5, 1999, *M. Zanzi* v. *J. De Coninck and others*, *Revue de l'arbitrage*, 1999, 260, note Fouchard. See also Ibrahim Fadlallah and Dominique Hascher, *Les grandes décisions du droit de l'arbitrage commercial* (Paris: Dalloz, 2019), 33–51.

58 Paris Court of Appeal, September 29, 2005, *Directorate General of Civil Aviation of the Emirate of Dubai* v. *International Bechtel Co. Limited*, *Revue de l'arbitrage*, 2006, 695, note Muir Watt; *Juris-Classeur Périodique*, 2006, 1174, commentary Seraglini; *Revue critique de droit international privé*, 2006, 387, note Szekely.

59 Court of Cassation (France), First Civil Chamber, February 1, 2005, *État d'Israël* v. *Société NIOC*, *Revue de l'arbitrage*, 2005, 693. See also Fadlallah and Hascher, *Les grandes décisions*, 151–56.

*Putrabali* (2007), and *Ryanair* (2015).[60] The *Putrabali* case was particularly important since it pushed even further the logic of the *Hilmarton* decision.[61] An arbitration between an Indonesian company (Putrabali) and a French company (Est Epices, later Rena Holding) was held in London and resulted in an award in favor of Rena Holding.[62] The award was partially set aside by the English High Court, which held that there had been a breach of contract on the part of Rena Holding. A second award was then rendered in favor of Putrabali. In enforcement proceedings in France, the Court of Cassation[63] upheld the decision of the Paris Court of Appeal, which ruled that the setting-aside of an arbitral award in a foreign country did not prevent the award from being enforced in France. Using language that was almost identical to that used twenty-seven years earlier in *Norsolor*,[64] the Court of Cassation reasoned that "[a]n international arbitral award, which is not anchored in any national legal order, is *a decision of international justice* whose validity must be ascertained with regard to the rules applicable in the country where its recognition and enforcement are sought."[65] Rena Holding was therefore allowed to seek enforcement of the first award rendered in London pursuant to the parties' arbitration agreement.

Recent developments show that the issue of the enforcement of arbitral awards set aside in the country of the seat is far from settled and that courts and commentators still disagree on this issue. In the United States, for example, *Chromalloy* was followed by various cases that adopted a much more restrictive approach. In *Baker Marine*, the Court of Appeals for the Second Circuit stated that it would enforce an award that had been annulled only if there were "adequate reason[s] for refusing

60 Court of Cassation (France), First Civil Chamber, July 8, 2015, *Société Ryanair Ltd et Société Airport Marketing Services Ltd* v. *Syndicat Mixte des Aéroports de Charente (SMAC)*, *Revue de l'arbitrage*, 2015, 1131.

61 Le Bars and Dalmasso, *Arbitrage commercial international*, 336.

62 The arbitration was conducted in accordance with the Rules of Arbitration and Appeal of the International General Produce Association (IGPA).

63 Court of Cassation (France), First Civil Chamber, June 29, 2007, *Société PT Putrabali Adyamulia* v. *Société Rena Holding et Société Moguntia Est Epices*, *Yearbook Commercial Arbitration* (2007), 299. See Fadlallah and Hascher, *Les grandes décisions*, 323–42; Dominique Hascher, "The Review of Arbitral Awards by Domestic Courts: France," in Emmanuel Gaillard (ed.), *The Review of Arbitral Awards*, IAI Series on International Arbitration No. 6 (Huntington: Juris, 2010), 97.

64 Thomas Clay and Philippe Pinsolle, "General Introduction: The Major Cases of the French Case Law on International Arbitration," in Thomas Clay and Philippe Pinsolle (eds.), *French International Arbitration Law Reports* (Huntington: JurisNet, 2014), xxi.

65 See Gaillard, *Legal Theory*, ¶ 65, at 62–63 (emphasis added).

to recognize the set-aside judgments of the Nigerian court."[66] The US court held that these reasons were not satisfied on the facts of the case. A few months later, the US court followed similar reasoning in *Spier*.[67]

In *TermoRio*, the Court of Appeals for the District of Columbia distinguished *Chromalloy* and refused to enforce a Colombian award that had been set aside in Colombia.[68] The court set a high threshold, stating that a foreign set-aside judgment should be respected unless it was "repugnant to the fundamental notions of what is decent and just in the state where enforcement is sought."[69] The court explained that enforcement of an award that had been set aside abroad should not be refused "absent extraordinary circumstances."[70]

In *Pemex*, "the first U.S. federal *appellate* decision to confirm a foreign Convention award that has been set aside at the seat,"[71] the Court of Appeals for the Second Circuit adopted "a new framework."[72] Commisa, the Mexican subsidiary of a US corporation, had concluded two contracts with the Mexican state-owned petroleum company Pemex. Following contractual disagreements, Commisa initiated arbitration proceedings under the aegis of the ICC. In 2009, Commisa was awarded USD 300 million in damages. The award was then set aside by a Mexican court on the ground that a newly enacted Mexican law barred the action.

Notwithstanding this annulment, the New York federal district court confirmed the award in 2013, holding that the Mexican court's retroactive application of a prohibition on arbitrability violated basic notions of justice.[73] The decision was confirmed by the Court of Appeals for the Second Circuit, which relied on the concept of comity, stating that foreign judgments are "generally conclusive" except where recognition and enforcement "would offend the public policy of the state in which enforcement is

[66] *Baker Marine (Nig.) Ltd.* v. *Chevron (Nig.) Ltd.*, August 12, 1999, 191 F.3d 194 (2d Cir. 1999).

[67] *Spier* v. *Calzaturificio Tecnica, S.p.A.*, October 22, 1999, 71 F. Supp. 2d 279 (S.D.N.Y. 1999).

[68] *TermoRio S.A. E.S.P.* v. *Electranta S.P.*, 487 F.3d 928 (D.C. Cir. 2007), 935.

[69] Ibid., 937–38 (quoting *Tahan* v. *Hodgson*, 662 F.2d 862, 864 (D.C. Cir. 1981)).

[70] Ibid.

[71] Linda Silberman and Nathan Yaffe, "The US Approach to Recognition and Enforcement of Awards after Set-Asides: The Impact of the *Pemex* Decision," *Fordham International Law Journal*, 40, no. 3 (2017), 799.

[72] Ibid., 812.

[73] *Corporación Mexicana de Mantenimiento Integral* v. *Pemex-Exploración y Producción*, 962 F. Supp. 2d 642 (S.D.N.Y. August 27, 2013).

sought."[74] Thus, the court used a different standard than *Baker Marine* ("adequate reason") and *TermoRio* ("extraordinary circumstances"). While the decision of the District Court for the Southern District of New York was a "welcome development"[75] and "an important step in the right direction"[76] for some, others felt that "it is in fact but another illustration of the restrictive approach adopted by US courts on this matter."[77]

In *Thai-Lao Lignite*, the court came to a finding that was the opposite of *Pemex*. *Thai-Lao* concerned a mining contract between two companies and the government of Laos. The companies brought claims for improper termination and damages and were awarded USD 60 million in arbitration proceedings. The award was confirmed by the District Court for the Southern District of New York,[78] whose decision was affirmed by the Court of Appeals for the Second Circuit.[79]

The government of Laos then successfully challenged the award in Malaysia on the ground that the arbitral tribunal had exceeded its jurisdiction by allowing nonparties to join the proceedings. The government sought to have the case reopened pursuant to the Federal Rules of Civil Procedure. The motion was granted by the district court, which held that the Malaysian proceedings, unlike those in *Pemex*, did not violate basic notions of justice. Even though the court in *Thai-Lao Lignite* reached a finding that was the opposite of *Pemex*, it displayed "the same timid and conservative approach to the enforcement of awards annulled at the seat."[80]

[74] *Corporación Mexicana de Mantenimiento Integral* v. *Pemex-Exploración y Producción*, No. 13–4022 (2d Cir. August 2, 2016), 27 (citing *Ackermann* v. *Levine*, 788 F.2d 830, 837 (2d Cir. 1986)).

[75] Silberman and Yaffe, "US Approach," 812.

[76] Luca Radicati di Brozolo, "The Enforcement of Annulled Awards: An Important Step in the Right Direction," *Cahiers de l'arbitrage/Paris Journal of International Arbitration* (2013), 1027–40.

[77] Coralie Darrigade, "États-Unis: La sentence annulée dans son pays d'origine, approche américaine, note sous District Court Southern District of New York, 27 août 2013," *Revue de l'arbitrage*, 2015, 185, ¶ 3.

[78] *Thai-Lao Lignite (Thailand) Co. Ltd. et al.* v. *Government of the Lao People's Democratic Republic*, February 6, 2014, 997 F. Supp. 2d 214 (S.D.N.Y. 2014).

[79] *Thai-Lao Lignite (Thailand) Co. Ltd. et al.* v. *Government of the Lao People's Democratic Republic*, July 20, 2017, 864 F.3d 172 (2d Cir. 2017).

[80] Luca Radicati di Brozolo, "The Fate of Awards Annulled at the Seat in Light of *Thai-Lao Lignite*," *Transnational Notes* (March 19, 2014), https://blogs.law.nyu.edu/transnational/2014/03/the-fate-of-awards-annulled-at-the-seat-in-light-of-thai-lao-lignite/; Luca Radicati di Brozolo, "The Enforcement of Annulled Awards: Further Reflections in Light of *Thai-Lao Lignite*," *American Review of International Arbitration*, 25, no. 1 (2014), 47–61.

Courts in other countries, too, have had to grapple with the same issues. A striking example was provided by the *Yukos Capital* case, in which the Amsterdam Court of Appeal enforced awards that had been set aside by a Russian court.[81]

Yukos Capital, a Luxembourg finance company that was part of the Yukos group, made various loans to its subsidiary Yuganskneftegaz (YNG, later acquired by the Russian state oil company Rosneft). In 2005, Yukos Capital initiated arbitration proceedings, claiming repayment of the loans with interest. In 2006, Yukos Capital was awarded a total of USD 425 million in four separate decisions under the rules of the International Commercial Arbitration Court of the Russian Chamber of Commerce and Industry in Moscow. Yukos Capital sought enforcement of the awards in the Netherlands. Meanwhile, the Russian courts, seized by Rosneft, set them aside.

The Dutch court ruled that the Russian decision annulling the awards should not be recognized, as it was "the result of a partial and dependent judicial process," so the awards should be enforced.[82] Yukos Capital then brought further proceedings in England to seek recovery of interest of over USD 160 million. The key question was whether the Dutch decision gave rise to an issue estoppel. The English Court of Appeal found that there was no issue estoppel due to differing public policy standards.[83]

While some US commentators described the Dutch *Yukos* case as "probably an 'easy' case for a 'judgments approach' because the need for impartial tribunals and fairness of proceedings is a universal ground for non-recognition of a judgment,"[84] others disagreed. In particular, Gaillard referred to the "chaos likely to be caused by replacing the logic of recognizing awards themselves with that of recognizing foreign court decisions on the awards" and the "embarrassment a national court is likely to be caused by having to assess the independence or partiality of another national court."[85] These divergent views reveal the division that still exists among commentators on such difficult issues.

[81] See, generally, Emmanuel Gaillard, "La vision américaine des sentences annulées au siège: Observations sur les arrêts *Pemex* et *Thai-Lao Lignite* de la Cour d'appel fédérale du 2e circuit des 2 août 2016 et 20 juillet 2017," *Revue de l'arbitrage*, 2017, 1162–64, ¶ 14.

[82] Amsterdam Court of Appeal, April 28, 2009, *Yukos Capital Sarl* v. *OAO Rosneft*, *Yearbook Commercial Arbitration* (2009), esp. 713.

[83] *Yukos Capital S.a.r.l.* v. *OJSC Rosneft Oil Company* [2012] EWCA Civ 855. The court also considered the act-of-state doctrine, but held that the doctrine did not apply to allegations of impropriety against foreign court decisions.

[84] Silberman and Yaffe, "US Approach," 810.

[85] Gaillard, "La vision américaine," ¶ 14, at 1163–64.

### *10.3.2 Renewal and Anxiety in the Debate over the Delocalization of Awards*

The case law on the enforcement of awards set aside in the country of the seat split the arbitration community into two camps. On the one hand, the so-called territorialists argued that an award annulled in the country of the seat ceases to exist and, as such, cannot be enforced elsewhere. On the other hand, the so-called internationalists argued that an award does not belong to the legal order of the state in which it is rendered and can therefore be enforced in another country. The two sides clashed on a number of points. While the internationalist approach was associated with a broad sense of renewal, the territorialists did "not always feel that to be 'floating in the transnational firmament' – to use the famous words of Lord Justice Kerr – is an exciting experience; it rather generates anxiety."[86] Each of these positions will be examined in turn.

#### 10.3.2.1 The Territorialist Approach

The territorialist approach was voiced in particularly forceful terms around the time of the *Hilmarton* and *Chromalloy* decisions. Gharavi pointed to the "potential deleterious consequences"[87] of enforcing awards that had been set aside in the country of the seat: it could worryingly result in the "the coexistence of two conflicting awards concerning the same issues between the same parties, and thus violate the intended uniformity of the [New York] Convention and damage the image of international arbitration."[88] Gharavi attributed much of the blame to the New York Convention, which, he wrote, contained "outdated" and "unpredictable" provisions.[89] Gharavi further defended his views in his doctoral thesis.[90] He described the "malfunctioning" of international arbitration,[91] which was "threatened by the insecurity, unpredictability and tension caused by the present international legal regime of control over arbitral awards."[92]

[86] Mayer, "Trend Towards Delocalisation," 46. Kerr LJ's famous expression can be found in *Bank Mellat* v. *Helliniki Techniki SA* [1984] 1 Q.B. 291.

[87] Gharavi, "*Chromalloy*: Another View," 24.

[88] Ibid., 23.

[89] Ibid., 24.

[90] Gharavi, *International Effectiveness.*

[91] Ibid., ¶ 15, at 5

[92] Ibid., ¶ 456, at 192. Gharavi divided the measures that would improve the regime for dealing with foreign awards into two categories: "solutions of continuity" (e.g., harmonization through the UNCITRAL Model Law on International Commercial Arbitration) and "solutions of rupture" (e.g., a new multilateral convention and a supranational court

Schwartz, while not as extreme as Gharavi in his views, shared his "fear" that *Chromalloy* may "undercut the efforts of those who have been labouring for years to restore confidence in the international arbitration process in Egypt and elsewhere in the Middle East, where international arbitration has long been viewed with suspicion."[93] Using a classic territorialist argument, Schwartz referred to a "modern international arbitration 'compact'" founded on a "system of dual State control, first at the place of the arbitration and secondly at the place of enforcement of the award."[94] For Schwartz, this system of dual control, which was "rooted in a 'territorial' conception of arbitration," had already "achieved the broadest international acceptance."[95] His attitude toward the *Hilmarton* decision was not so much one of anxiety as bemusement and incredulity:

> Although consistent with a conception of international arbitration that has a noble and prestigious heritage in France, this pronouncement, I might timidly venture to ask, is nevertheless just a little bit presumptuous, is it not? For on what authority can a French court decide what does or does not form part of the Swiss legal order? I would have thought that this is a matter for Swiss legislators and courts, and not the French Court of Cassation, to decide.[96]

To buttress their claims, some territorialists found a powerful ally in Francis Mann. In 1967, Mann had written an article entitled "*Lex Facit Arbitrum*," published in the *Liber Amicorum for Martin Domke*.[97] Mann's goal was to rebut the view – expressed by Goldman and others[98] – that arbitrators should be free to base their decisions on "what the arbitrator believes to be custom or usage, good sense, fairness, justice, *aequitas* or, as it is sometimes wrongly put, 'equity.'"[99] He claimed instead that "arbitration, like any other institution of municipal law, requires a firm legal basis which can only be found in the recognition and implementation of the idea of *lex facit arbitrum*"[100] – literally, "the law makes the arbitrator." In the course of his analysis, Mann made the following argument:

of control vested with exclusive jurisdiction over the annulment of an award, creating a harmonious framework of control over awards).

93 Schwartz, "Comment on *Chromalloy*," 135.

94 Ibid., 128.

95 Ibid., 129.

96 Ibid., 131.

97 Francis Mann, "Lex Facit Arbitrum," in Pieter Sanders (ed.), *International Arbitration: Liber Amicorum for Martin Domke* (The Hague: Martinus Nijhoff, 1967).

98 See Goldman, "Les conflits de lois," ¶ 14, at 380.

99 Mann, "Lex Facit Arbitrum," 158.

100 Ibid., 159. As Bollée reminds us, the territorialist approach had even more distant precursors in France, for example, Armand Lainé, "De l'exécution en France des

> In the legal sense no international commercial arbitration exists. Just as, notwithstanding its notoriously misleading name, every system of private international law is a system of national law, every arbitration is a national arbitration, that is to say, subject to a specific system of national law. ... [E]very arbitration is necessarily subject to the law of a given State. No private person has the right or the power to act on any level other than that of municipal law.[101]

Mann's concern was not the "juridicity" or nature of international arbitration, but rather what law arbitrators would apply.[102] However, his statement above was taken to mean that international arbitration as a whole could not be detached from the law of a given state and that, consequently, the existence of an independent legal order was an impossibility. While a handful of internationalists nonetheless gave credence to some of Mann's ideas,[103] "*lex facit arbitrum*" became the slogan of the territorialist camp, and Mann its "champion"[104] and "inflexible proponent."[105]

In addition to Mann's article, territorialists turned to leading authorities and commentators on the New York Convention for support. They often quoted from Sanders, one of the "founding fathers" of the New York Convention, who explained that: "Courts will ... refuse the enforcement as there does no longer exist an arbitral award and enforcing a non-existing arbitral award would be an impossibility or even go against the public policy of the country of enforcement."[106] They also frequently cited Van den Berg, who argued: "When an award has been annulled in the country of origin, it has become non-existent in that country. ... How then is it possible that courts in another country can consider the same award as still valid? Perhaps some theories of legal philosophy may provide an answer to this question, but for a legal practitioner this phenomenon is inexplicable."[107] As Van den Berg stated in his important commentary on

sentences arbitrales étrangères," *Journal du droit international*, 1899, 641–54; see Sylvain Bollée, *Les méthodes du droit international privé à l'épreuve des sentences arbitrales* (Paris: Economica, 2004), ¶ 19, at 17.

101 Mann, "Lex Facit Arbitrum," 159–60.

102 On this point, see Paulsson's subtle reading of Mann's article in Jan Paulsson, *The Idea of Arbitration* (Oxford: Oxford University Press, 2013), 33.

103 See, for example, Le Bars and Dalmasso, *Arbitrage commercial international*, ¶ 12, at 337.

104 Bollée, *Les méthodes du droit international privé*, ¶ 23, at 19.

105 Paulsson, *Idea of Arbitration*, 33.

106 Pieter Sanders, "New York Convention on the Recognition and Enforcement of Foreign Arbitral Awards," *Netherlands International Law Review*, 6, no. 1 (1959), 55.

107 Albert Jan van den Berg, "Annulment of Awards in International Arbitration," in Richard Lillich and Charles Brower (eds.), *International Arbitration in the 21st Century: Towards "Judicialization" and Uniformity?* (New York: Transnational, 1994), 161. See also Albert

the New York Convention: "A losing party must be afforded the right to have the validity of the award finally adjudicated in one jurisdiction. If that were not the case, in the event of a questionable award a losing party could be pursued by a claimant with enforcement actions from country to country until a court is found, if any, which grants the enforcement."[108]

The internationalists would be quick to observe that such arguments reflected a mindset akin to that which prevailed up until the middle of the twentieth century: "the purest localizing logic which conceives the judicial nature of arbitration exclusively through the judicial order of the seat."[109]

#### 10.3.2.2 The Internationalist Approach

The internationalists took the opposite stance, arguing that awards did not belong to any one legal system. Gaillard – one of the members of the arbitral tribunal in the *Chromalloy* case, along with Briner and El Sharkawy – explained that the Paris Court of Appeal's reasoning in that case provided "a perfect summary of the position of French law on the question of recognition and enforcement of an award set aside in the country of the seat."[110] Gaillard felt that the French courts were favoring "the universalist conception of arbitration," which "tended to reduce as much as possible the role of local idiosyncrasies, even those of French law itself."[111]

But Gaillard acknowledged that "the binding nature of arbitral awards does come from the legal orders of states, the community of states willing to recognize the fundamentally private act that an arbitral award is."[112] He tried to categorize the contrasting views, which he had already described as "philosophies of arbitration."[113] On the one hand was the view put forward by Mann that "the law of the seat necessarily governs the arbitration agreement, either directly or by designating the applicable law,"[114] and on the other hand the position espoused by Goldman and Lalive: "[a]rbitrators do not derive their powers from the state in which they have their seat but rather from the sum of all the legal orders that recognize, under certain conditions, the validity of the arbitration

Jan van den Berg, "Enforcement of Annulled Awards?," *ICC International Court of Arbitration Bulletin*, 9, no. 2 (1998), 15.

108 Albert Jan van den Berg, *The New York Convention of 1958: Towards a Uniform Judicial Interpretation* (Deventer: Kluwer Law and Taxation, 1981), 355.

109 Gaillard, "La vision américaine," ¶ 1, at 1148.

110 Gaillard, "Enforcement of Awards," ¶ 14, at 25.

111 Ibid., 19.

112 Gaillard, "L'exécution des sentences annulées," 646.

113 Gaillard, "Enforcement of Awards," 17.

114 Ibid.

agreement and the award."[115] Gaillard – whose own views on the "arbitral legal order" were yet to be fully articulated – did not give labels to these contrasting views. Identifying just two, rather than three, categories, he associated them with geographic areas: the first view "ha[d] long been dominant and still remain[ed] strong in England," while the second view was "dominant in France and other countries with civil law traditions."[116]

Another key proponent of the internationalist approach – though he later disagreed with Gaillard over the existence of an arbitral legal order – was Paulsson, who had already written on the subject[117] and considered himself "vindicated" by the *Chromalloy* decisions in France and the United States.[118] He criticized Van den Berg's "prudential perception of the orderly administration of justice," noting that "it is not obvious that we cannot live with occasional situations of inconsistent decisions."[119] Writing in the same journal as Gharavi, Paulsson explained that he did "not share Mr. Gharavi's ominous comments about foreign apprehensions of U.S. judicial chauvinism."[120] As Paulsson pointed out, *both* the Paris Court of Appeal and the US district court had treated the Egyptian annulment in the same way. Paulsson further referred to another case, which involved the enforcement by a US court of an ICC award rendered in favor of an Egyptian

115 Ibid., 18

116 Ibid., 17–18.

117 See Jan Paulsson, "Arbitre et juge en Suède: Exposé général et réflexions sur la délocalisation des sentences arbitrales," *Revue de l'arbitrage*, 1980, 441–87; Paulsson, "France and the Arbitral Process in 1980: A New Law and a Major Court Decision," *Svensk och internationell skiljedom* [Yearbook of the Arbitration Institute of the Stockholm Chamber of Commerce] (1981), 40; Paulsson, "The Role of Swedish Courts in Transnational Commercial Arbitration," *Virginia Journal of International Law*, 21 (1981), 211; Paulsson, "Arbitration Unbound: Award Detached from the Law of its Country of Origin," *International and Comparative Law Quarterly*, 30, no. 2 (1981), 358; Paulsson, "Delocalisation of International Commercial Matters: When and Why It Matters," *International and Comparative Law Quarterly*, 32, no. 1 (1983), 53–61; Paulsson, "Arbitration Unbound in Belgium," *Arbitration International*, 2 (1986), 68–73; Paulsson, "The Extent of Independence of International Arbitration from the Law of the *Situs*," in Julian Lew (ed.), *Contemporary Problems in International Arbitration* (Dordrecht: Springer, 1987), 141–48.

118 Paulsson, "Rediscovering the N.Y. Convention," 26.

119 Ibid., 28. See also Jan Paulsson, "Enforcing Arbitral Awards Notwithstanding Local Standard Annulments," *Asia Pacific Law Review*, 6 (1998), 14 (describing *Hilmarton* as "a two-headed white rhinoceros which might give us a thrill in the cinema but does not really endanger our daily walk to work"); Jan Paulsson, "The Case for Disregarding LSAs (Local Standard Annulments) under the New York Convention," *American Review of International Arbitration*, 7 (1996), 99–114.

120 Paulsson, "Rediscovering the N.Y. Convention," 26.

corporation.[121] According to Paulsson, "in today's world injustice will result if too great credence is given to the law of the place of arbitration, because in some places this appears to incite courts to assist the losing party's attempt to overcome the arbitrator's decision on the merits."[122]

Some arbitration scholars made concrete proposals to improve the relationship between the setting-aside of arbitral awards and their possible enforcement abroad. For instance, Fouchard mentioned two possibilities for international action: setting up an international court with exclusive jurisdiction to review arbitral awards – an idea already expressed in some detail by Holtzmann[123] – or revising the New York Convention.[124] Acknowledging that these options would be hard to implement, Fouchard focused instead on domestic action. One solution, he wrote, would be to "do away with set-aside actions against international arbitration awards. The only judicial review they would undergo would take place when their recognition or enforcement is sought in a given country."[125]

This proposal – which Fouchard himself admitted was somewhat "ludicrous"[126] and "revolutionary"[127] – was derided by members of the territorialist camp, who believed it would insulate the respondent's defense arguments from scrutiny while "depriv[ing] the claimant – whose claim was wrongfully rejected – of all possibility of disputing the award."[128] As Poudret repeatedly asserted, "the neutrality and consequently the objectivity of the review of the award are better ensured by the judge of the seat who has been chosen by the

121 *Parsons & Wittlemore Overseas Co.* v. *Société Générale de l'Industrie du Papier (RAKTA)*, December 23, 1974, 508 F.2d 969 (2d Cir. 1974).

122 Paulsson, "Rediscovering the N.Y. Convention," 26.

123 See Howard Holtzmann, "A Task for the 21st Century: Creating a New International Court for Resolving Disputes on the Enforceability of Arbitral Awards," in Martin Hunter, Arthur Marriott and V. V. Veeder, *The Internationalisation of International Arbitration: The LCIA Centenary Conference* (London: Graham & Trotman/Martinus Nijhoff, 1995), 112. See also Howard Holtzmann, "L'arbitrage et les tribunaux: Des associés dans un système de justice internationale," *Revue de l'arbitrage*, 1978, 253–303.

124 Philippe Fouchard, "La portée internationale de l'annulation de la sentence arbitrale dans son pays d'origine," *Revue de l'arbitrage*, 1997, 349–50, ¶¶ 36–37; see also Philippe Fouchard, "Suggestions pour accroître l'efficacité internationale des sentences arbitrales," *Revue de l'arbitrage*, 1998, 671–72, ¶¶ 49–51.

125 Fouchard, "La portée internationale," ¶ 40, at 350–51.

126 Ibid.

127 Fouchard, "Suggestions," ¶ 47, at 670.

128 Jean-François Poudret and Sébastien Besson, *Comparative Law of International Arbitration* (London: Sweet & Maxwell, 2007), ¶ 930, at 854.

parties."[129] Poudret saw the French approach as "more hegemonist than coherent,"[130] since it would risk imposing on the losing party a "perpetual threat" of the award being enforced by a more "sympathetic judge" elsewhere.[131] Some internationalists, meanwhile, agreed with Fouchard that the creation of an international court, while still a "utopia," might be "inescapable in the medium term because of the globalisation of law that we are currently witnessing."[132]

### 10.3.3 *Salient Features of the Delocalization Controversy*

Three key aspects of the debate over the delocalization of awards are noteworthy and deserve further emphasis: its geographical reach, the language used, and the fact that it was framed as a combat.

First, unlike the *lex mercatoria* debate – which originated mostly in French legal circles in the 1960s – the debate over the delocalization of arbitral awards transcended France's borders. Whereas the former was tied to the rather amorphous concept of a "society of merchants," the latter was a response to actual cases and situations encountered in a number of countries. The fact that an award set aside at the seat was recognized by a US court in *Chromalloy* – despite a more restrictive approach in subsequent cases, as explained earlier – meant that scholars on both sides of the Atlantic contributed to the debate. Similar cases involving the recognition of awards set aside in the country of the seat were also brought in Belgium and other countries,[133] which gave the debate a truly international dimension.

A second notable aspect of the debate was its intensity – and even, at times, violence and acrimony. The arguments made by internationalists and territorialists have been described as "sharply contrasting reactions in France and throughout the world,"[134] "harsh and often impressive

[129] Philippe Fouchard and Jean-François Poudret, "Quelle solution pour en finir avec l'affaire *Hilmarton*? Réponse à Philippe Fouchard," *Revue de l'arbitrage*, 1998, 12.

[130] Ibid., 10.

[131] Sébastien Besson and Luc Pittet, "La reconnaissance à l'étranger d'une sentence annulée dans son État d'origine: Réflexions à la suite de l'affaire *Hilmarton*," *ASA Bulletin*, 16, no. 3 (1998), 515.

[132] Jean-Baptiste Racine, "Réflexions sur l'autonomie de l'arbitrage commercial international," *Revue de l'arbitrage*, 2005, 333, ¶ 37.

[133] For other examples of awards set aside in the country of the seat that were enforced elsewhere, see, for example, Fouchard, "La portée internationale," ¶¶ 11–15, at 333–36; Gharavi, *International Effectiveness*, 87–104.

[134] Gaillard, "Enforcement of Awards," 31.

criticisms,"[135] and "fierce controversies."[136] Paulsson, for example, described Van den Berg's arguments as "specious"[137] and compared him to a "dormant Homer."[138] When assessing Reisman's notions of "a primary or secondary control function under Article V" of the New York Convention,[139] Paulsson called them "pure products of [Reisman's] own reflections."[140] Van den Berg responded by likening Paulsson's views to "old wine in new wineskins,"[141] adding that "[i]f Mr. Paulsson's proposals were accepted, a court may wonder whether there is now a Paris Arbitration Convention for Distressed Awards."[142] Meanwhile, Park described Paulsson's theories as nothing less than a "dangerous heresy."[143]

That the debate over the delocalization of awards was so impassioned is perhaps unsurprising. It coincided with a change of generations in international arbitration and, as Kennedy reminds us, "[g]enerational change within a field is rarely smooth."[144] Kennedy's description of "international law as a series of professional performances rather than an edifice of ideas, doctrines, and institutions" is particularly illuminating in this respect.[145] It may help explain why members of the new generation used such strong language to express their project of affiliation or disaffiliation with the

135 Fouchard, "La portée internationale," ¶ 22, at 341.

136 Matthias Audit, Sylvain Bollée, and Pierre Callé, *Droit du commerce international et des investissements étrangers*, 2nd ed. (Paris: LGDJ, 2016), ¶ 948, at 732.

137 Jan Paulsson, "Enforcing Arbitral Awards Notwithstanding a Local Standard Annulment (LSA)," *ICC International Court of Arbitration Bulletin*, 9, no. 1 (1998), 28.

138 Ibid., 23.

139 Michael Reisman, *Systems of Control in International Adjudication and Arbitration: Breakdown and Repair* (Durham: Duke University Press, 1992), pt. 4, "Non-Institutional International Commercial Arbitration: The Breakdown of the Control System of the New York Convention." According to Reisman, the New York Convention "establishes two tiers of review competence" (ibid., 113). "Primary" jurisdictions refer to "the state where the arbitration took place," while "secondary" or "enforcement" jurisdictions include "any other jurisdiction, subject to the convention, in which enforcement is sought." According to Reisman, "[t]he distinction between primary and secondary jurisdictions is . . . central to the control system of the New York Convention and has been an important reason for the attractiveness of the regime to its various consumers" (ibid., 116).

140 Paulsson, "Enforcing Arbitral Awards Notwithstanding a Local Standard Annulment (LSA)," 21.

141 Van den Berg, "Enforcement of Annulled Awards," 20.

142 Ibid., 21.

143 William Park, "The *Lex Loci Arbitri* and International Commercial Arbitration," *International and Comparative Law Quarterly*, 31, no. 1 (1983), 25.

144 David Kennedy, "When Renewal Repeats: Thinking Against the Box," *NYU Journal of International Law and Politics*, 32 (2000), 447.

145 Ibid., 337.

former generation – why, for example, Paulsson confessed to a sense of "iconoclastic exhilaration" when "demonstrat[ing] that the leading commentator on the New York Convention, Prof. van den Berg, is wrong" in his interpretation of Article V(1)(e) of the New York Convention.[146]

Discussing mentor–mentee relations, which are a key aspect of groups based on professional and personal identity, Kennedy further notes that, often, "[m]entoring ends when the mentee has successfully navigated a rebellion against the artificial centrality of the mentor to enter the broader profession and survives, if at all, as a sort of nostalgia."[147] Once again, this insight is particularly relevant when discussing the debates and controversies that agitated the arbitration community in the 1980s and 1990s. It may help explain why, before criticizing Reisman's "misguided view of the [New York] Convention,"[148] Paulsson mentioned his "great respect for an eminent scholar – all the more sincere as it comes from an indebted former student."[149] Through the debate over the delocalization of arbitral awards – and, later, the existence of an arbitral legal order – a new generation of arbitration scholars and practitioners was striving, more or less overtly, to make its voice heard.

The third aspect of the debate that merits attention is the combative language in which it was couched, with each side claiming victory. Schwartz claimed that "it is the more 'territorial' view … that has generally taken hold,"[150] and Besson that "the delocalization theory is currently losing momentum,"[151] while Paulsson maintained the exact opposite: "As we reach the end of the century, I do not believe that much wind is left in the sails of die-hard territorialists, who cling to the abstract notion that nothing of legal significance can happen anywhere if it is not either approved or tolerated by the local sovereign."[152] Sampliner, who was counsel for Chromalloy in both the arbitration and the subsequent US enforcement proceedings, noted that the case was "a major victory for supporters of binding international arbitration."[153] It was as if everyone in the arbitration community felt it necessary to take sides and zealously defend their

[146] Paulsson, "Rediscovering the N.Y. Convention," 24
[147] Kennedy, "When Renewal Repeats," 432.
[148] Paulsson, "Enforcing Arbitral Awards Notwithstanding Local Standard Annulments," 23.
[149] Ibid.
[150] Schwartz, "Comment on *Chromalloy*," 130.
[151] Besson and Pittet, "La reconnaissance," 504.
[152] Paulsson, "Rediscovering the N.Y. Convention," 27.
[153] Sampliner, "Enforcement of Foreign Arbitral Awards," 22. See also Sampliner, "*Chromalloy* Revisited," 149.

respective positions. The combat remained unsettled, with both sides clinging to their positions, until it gave way to a new, but related, debate over the existence of a full-fledged arbitral legal order.

## 10.4 The Theorization of – and Quarrel over – the Arbitral Legal Order

The theoretical inquiry into the nature of the arbitral legal order was the work of several scholars, most of whom were French (Section 10.4.1). It was hailed as an important achievement by some, but criticized by others (Section 10.4.2).

### *10.4.1 The Theorization of the Arbitral Legal Order*

Although undertaken largely by the second generation of the French school of international arbitration, the theoretical exploration of the arbitral legal order also built on insights from the previous generation. Retracing its history,[154] Gaillard points out that, as early as 1986, Loquin had referred to an "anational legal order," which could "provide a theoretical foundation for the application of anational rules in arbitration."[155] Cohen then used the expression "arbitral legal order" in his 1993 work *Arbitrage et société*.[156] Clay devoted a section of his important work *L'arbitre* to the notion of an arbitral legal order.[157] Acknowledging the French school's role in developing this concept,[158] Clay described the arbitral legal order as both "autonomous" and "transnational."[159] Finally, Racine inquired into the "autonomy" of international arbitration – a somewhat "mysterious" and "expansionist" notion that could be explained by the existence of an arbitral legal order.[160]

Yet the scholar who gave the theory of the arbitral legal order its most definitive features – and who has become most closely associated with it – is undoubtedly Gaillard (see Figure 10.1), who imparted his views in

[154] See Gaillard, *Legal Theory*, ¶ 43, at 38–39.

[155] Eric Loquin, "L'application de règles anationales dans l'arbitrage commercial international," in *L'apport de la jurisprudence arbitrale*, ICC Publication No. 440/1 (1986), 72.

[156] Cohen, *Arbitrage et société*, pt. 2.

[157] Clay, *L'arbitre*, esp. 211–28.

[158] Ibid., ¶ 260, at 214.

[159] Ibid.,¶¶ 261–62, at 215–18.

[160] Racine, "Réflexions."

a number of key writings and conferences.[161] From the two conceptions of international arbitration identified in his earlier writings, Gaillard now passed to three, which he called "representations"[162] and categorized as "monolocal," "multilocal" ("Westphalian"), and "transnational" (the "arbitral legal order").[163]

Gaillard explained that each representation had its own proponents and theoretical postulates – although he believed that only the third representation was capable of standing up to rigorous scrutiny for internal consistency and efficiency.[164] The monolocal representation equates the law governing the arbitration to the law of the seat and the arbitrator to "a national judge exercising his or her function within a single national legal order, that of the seat of the arbitration."[165] This view was expressed by Mann (in the so-called "objectivist" strand) and Poudret and Besson (in the "subjectivist" strand).[166] It finds its main philosophical justification in a Kelsenian "form of State positivism and in an exacerbated quest for legal harmony."[167] For Gaillard, this hardly reflects the situation of international arbitration, where practice shows "a double, contradictory, trend," with "the modernization of laws" on the one hand, and "the judicial exacerbation of idiosyncrasies" on the other.[168]

The multilocal theory, which anchored the arbitral process in a plurality of local legal orders and viewed the law of the seat as "one legal order among others," was also based on a form of "State positivism," as reflected in a lecture given by von Mehren in Tel Aviv in 1986.[169] But, in contrast to the first representation, it often implied a "retrospective assessment" of the validity of the arbitral process and of the arbitration

[161] Gaillard's first major public presentation of the theory of the arbitral legal order was his keynote address at the 2006 congress of the Brazilian Arbitration Committee, in which he explained what he meant by the "autonomy" of international arbitration.

[162] See Section 10.4.2.1 for more details about Gaillard's use of the term.

[163] Gaillard, *Legal Theory*.

[164] Ibid., ¶ 35, at 31.

[165] Ibid., 15.

[166] The "objectivist" view draws the law governing the arbitration from the place of the seat; the "subjectivist" view looks to the free choice of the parties (or, in the absence of an agreement between them, the arbitral institution or the arbitrators).

[167] Gaillard, *Legal Theory*, 21.

[168] Ibid., 23.

[169] Arthur von Mehren, "Limitations on Party Choice and the Governing Law: Do They Exist for International Commercial Arbitration?" (Mortimer and Raymond Sackler Institute of Advanced Studies, Tel Aviv University, 1986), quoted in Gaillard, *Legal Theory*.

agreement on which the award was based.[170] Thus, according to the second view, "[i]t is the recognition of the award that retrospectively validates the entire process."[171] In a somewhat grandiloquent formula he had used before,[172] Gaillard described this reversal – approaching the arbitral process and the arbitral award from the "end result," rather than from its "starting point" – as a "Copernican revolution."[173] One problem with the multilocal theory, Gaillard explained, was that

> [i]n a system in which the State where enforcement is sought may, in any event, refuse to grant enforcement to an award that is not compatible with its international public policy requirements, the insistence by certain scholars to ground the juridicity of the award in the sole legal order of the seat results in cumulating the requirements of the seat and those of the State of enforcement.[174]

According to Gaillard, this came dangerously close to the Geneva Convention's double exequatur requirement, which the drafters of the New York Convention had sought to abolish.[175]

For Gaillard, therefore, the transnational approach was to be preferred – which might be thought to amount to yet another "Copernican revolution." This representation was based on "the idea that the juridicity of arbitration is rooted in a distinct transnational legal order, that could be labeled as the arbitral legal order, and not in a national legal system, be it that of the country of the seat or that of the place of enforcement."[176] This vision of arbitration was different from the second representation in that it shifted the focus from the "plurality of States" to the "collectivity of States."[177] In addition, whereas the first two approaches were based on "State positivism," the arbitral legal order embraced a "natural law perspective," such as espoused by David and Oppetit,[178] or a positivist trend, according to which

> the arbitral legal order is not to be understood as a collection of pre-existing rules whose source is wholly extraneous to national laws. To the contrary, it is entirely based on the normative activity of States, which it

170 Gaillard, *Legal Theory*, 28.

171 Ibid., 25. For an earlier presentation of this idea, see also Emmanuel Gaillard, "L'interférence des juridictions du siège dans le déroulement de l'arbitrage," in *Liber amicorum Claude Reymond: Autour de l'arbitrage* (Paris: LexisNexis, 2004), ¶ 7, at 89.

172 See, for example, Gaillard, "Souveraineté et autonomie," 1173.

173 Gaillard, *Legal Theory*, 25.

174 Ibid., 32–33.

175 Ibid.

176 Ibid., 35.

177 Ibid., 37.

178 Ibid., 41–42.

> apprehends in its entirety and not as a juxtaposition of national laws, one of which would be declared applicable through a choice of law process.[179]

It also took into account the "arbitrators' perspective"[180] – the idea that they are acting in a distinct transnational legal order rather than any single domestic order.

A major strength of Gaillard's description of the three representations was that it could explain a wide range of issues arising in international arbitration. For example, it was possible to account for the quasi-systematic opposition between territorialists and internationalists described earlier by seeing it as a clash between different mental representations of international arbitration.[181] Many of the issues arising in international arbitration practice could be explained through whichever representation of international arbitration practitioners espoused.

Gaillard's views proved highly influential in France and, more widely, throughout Continental Europe.[182] In order to further explain and disseminate his views – or, some would say, to make them more palatable to a more practically minded (mostly Anglo-American) readership – Gaillard published shorter articles containing key insights and illustrations relating to the theory,[183] replacing "*philosophie*" with the less daunting "legal

[179] Ibid., 45–46. As Gaillard explained, "in the same way that one can conceive of international law as an autonomous legal order without being a jusnaturalist, one does not need to be a jusnaturalist to accept the idea of an arbitral legal order" (ibid., 40).

[180] Ibid., 35

[181] In another example – the pervasive issue of antisuit injunctions in international arbitration – he demonstrated that only arbitrators who embraced the transnational approach could issue an award when faced with an antisuit injunction that they deemed unfounded. See Gaillard, *Legal Theory*, 70–86; Gaillard, "Reflections on the Use of Anti-Suit Injunctions in International Arbitration," in Loukas Mistelis and Julian Lew (eds.), *Pervasive Problems in International Arbitration* (The Hague: Kluwer, 2006).

[182] See, for example, Pierre Lalive, "*Aspects philosophiques du droit de l'arbitrage international*" (book review), *ASA Bulletin*, 26, no. 4 (2008), 602. Lalive pointed out that, without knowing it, "like Molière's Bourgeois Gentilhomme who was unknowingly creating prose," he had been practicing arbitration with a combination of the Westphalian and transnational approaches in mind.

[183] See, for example, Emmanuel Gaillard, "The Representations of International Arbitration," *New York Law Journal*, 238, no. 67 (2007); Gaillard, "Three Philosophies of International Arbitration," in Arthur Rovine (ed.), *Contemporary Issues in International Arbitration and Mediation: The Fordham Papers 2009* (Leiden: Martinus Nijhoff, 2010); Gaillard, "L'ordre juridique arbitral: réalité, utilité et spécificité," *McGill Law Journal*, 55 (2010), 891–907; Gaillard, "The Representations of International Arbitration," *Journal of International Dispute Settlement*, 1 (2010), 271–81; Gaillard, "International Arbitration as a Transnational System of Justice," in Albert Jan van den Berg (ed.), *Arbitration: The Next Fifty Years*, ICCA Congress Series No. 16 (The Hague: Kluwer Law International, 2012); Gaillard, "The Arbitral Legal Order: Evolution and

theory" in the English title of the book. In 2015, the French Court of Cassation appeared to endorse Gaillard's views when, in its *Ryanair* judgment, it described the award as an "international award, which is not attached to any national legal order" but is rather a "decision of international justice."[184] In many quarters, however, such bold views were met with some skepticism on account of the reservations and objections that could be raised in relation to the theory of the arbitral legal order.

**Figure 10.1** Photograph of Emmanuel Gaillard (1952–2021) taken by Ms. Amélie Debray in 2014 and reproduced with kind permission of the photographer and Prof. Gaillard's family. Gaillard became identified with the French school of international arbitration and was the leading proponent of the theory of the arbitral legal order.

Recognition," in Thomas Schultz and Frederico Ortino (eds.), *The Oxford Handbook of International Arbitration* (Oxford: Oxford University Press, 2020), 554–68.

184 See Court of Cassation (France), First Civil Chamber, July 8, 2015, *Société Ryanair Ltd et Société Airport Marketing Services Ltd* v. *Syndicat mixte des aéroports de Charente (SMAC)*, *Revue de l'arbitrage*, 2015, 1131.

### 10.4.2 *Critical Examination of the Theory of the Arbitral Legal Order*

There appear to be two possible approaches to critically examining the theory of the arbitral legal order. The first – to which the present author subscribes – is to agree with the theory and acknowledge the existence of an arbitral legal order with reservations. The second, and more radical, approach is to refute the existence of an arbitral legal order outright.

#### 10.4.2.1 Reservations about the Theory

First, one might well harbor doubts about the concept of "mental representation," on which so much of the edifice of the arbitral legal order depends. One could argue that this concept is perhaps too malleable and subjective to provide a solid foundation for the theory. Gaillard uses the terms "visions," "philosophies," "mental representations," and "construct" interchangeably, and it is not always clear what, if anything, distinguishes these notions from each other. But can we truly reduce a set of positions – even when they manifest themselves in a "quasi-systematic" way[185] – to a cognitive phenomenon or a set of "mental representations" – which, as Gaillard himself recognizes, "are by definition rarely articulated as such and only appear implicitly"?[186] And doesn't this seductively ordered vision of a field as composed of three distinct representations impose an artificially neat structure on what is in fact – to borrow Delmas-Marty's formulation – "plural" and "disorderly"?[187] These reflections are particularly relevant to the third "mental representation" (of the arbitral legal order), since Gaillard points out that it "corresponds to the international arbitrators' strong perception that they do not administer justice on behalf of any given State, but that they nonetheless play a judicial role for the benefit of the international community."[188] One may feel some unease about giving so much weight and credence to arbitrators' subjective viewpoints and deriving such a coherent framework from an untidy reality.

A second, lesser objection could be raised at a semantic level over Gaillard's use of the notion of a "Westphalian" system to illustrate one of the three "representations" of international arbitration. Gaillard insists that

185 Gaillard, *Legal Theory*, ¶ 7, at 11.

186 Ibid., ¶ 8, at 13.

187 Mireille Delmas-Marty, *Le relatif et l'universel: Les forces imaginantes du droit*, vol. 1 (Paris: Seuil, 2004), 109.

188 Gaillard, *Legal Theory*, 35.

the "multilocal" representation of international arbitration "can be labeled as 'Westphalian' by analogy to the world order based on a juxtaposition of sovereign power established for the international community after the 1648 Peace of Westphalia."[189] Yet, this overlooks the extensive scholarship that has challenged the "Westphalian myth."[190] In an important book, Teschke rejected 1648 as the foundational moment of the modern interstate system, describing it as a "false caesura" in the history of international relations.[191] Like *lex mercatoria*, perhaps the Westphalia idea – which, according to Gaillard, symbolizes the second representation of international arbitration – belongs to the "poetics of law,"[192] rather than historical facts. It is a weak basis on which to discuss the "Copernican revolution" and the complete "reversal" from the first to the second representation of international arbitration.[193]

#### 10.4.2.2 Denying the Existence of an Arbitral Legal Order

A far stronger criticism is to deny the existence of an arbitral legal order altogether. Such an objection to the theory has been raised – more or less convincingly – by a minority of scholars in France and, more vociferously, in the English-speaking world.

[189] Ibid., 29.

[190] See, for example, Randall Lesaffer, "The Westphalia Peace Treaties and the Development of the Tradition of Great European Peace Treaties prior to 1648," *Grotiana*, 18, no. 1 (1997), 71–95; Lesaffer, "Peace Treaties from Lodi to Westphalia," in Randall Lesaffer (ed.), *Peace Treaties and International Law in European History: From Late Middle Ages to World War One* (Cambridge: Cambridge University Press, 2004). See also Koskenniemi's description of Westphalia as the "founding myth of the system" (Martti Koskenniemi, "What is International Law For?," in Malcolm Evans (ed.), *International Law* (Oxford: Oxford University Press, 2003), 60) and Tourme-Jouannet's call to "demystify Westphalia once and for all" (Emmanuelle Tourme-Jouannet, *Le droit international libéral-providence: Une histoire du droit international* (Brussels: Bruylant/Éditions de l'Université de Bruxelles, 2011), 17).

[191] Benno Teschke, *The Myth of 1648: Class, Geopolitics, and the Making of Modern International Relations* (London: Verso, 2003). Other scholars have taken the same line. Lesaffer, while agreeing that the treaties constituted an important episode in European legal history, contested the notion that they "laid down the basic principles of the modern law of nations, such as sovereignty, equality, religious neutrality and the balance of power" (Lesaffer, "Peace Treaties from Lodi to Westphalia," 9). After carefully examining the treaties, Croxton came away "disappointed, without finding a clear statement of the principle of sovereignty" (Derek Croxton, "The Peace of Westphalia of 1648 and the Origins of Sovereignty," *International History Review*, 21, no. 3 (1999), 569).

[192] Peter Fitzpatrick, "Taking Place: Westphalia and the Poetics of Law," *London Review of International Law*, 2, no. 1 (2014), 155–65.

[193] Gaillard, *Legal Theory*, 25.

Some scholars in France have criticized the theory of the arbitral legal order from a somewhat abstract and theoretical perspective.[194] For example, Mayer insisted that, unlike judicial decisions, arbitral awards are *private* acts and, as such, do not belong to *any* legal order.[195] His argument reflects a highly positivist vision that sees law as the command of a sovereign backed up by force:

> A legal system is formed not only of rules, but, even more importantly, of judges and of organs exercising a power of coercion. *Lex mercatoria* lacks both. In particular, contrary to what has been suggested by some authors, arbitrators are not empowered to adjudicate disputes by the society of merchants and do not render their awards in the name of that society: they receive their powers only from the parties in the particular dispute; and only State courts and State organs of coercion are able to enforce arbitral awards. It is even doubtful that there is a society of international merchants; it requires more than doing business together to form a society.[196]

For Mayer, then, an arbitral legal order or a *lex mercatoria* legal system is a contradiction in terms because it lacks sufficiently clear rules. Echoing Lagarde's critique of the *lex mercatoria* as nothing more than "pockets of organization" ("*îlots d'organisation*"),[197] Mayer questioned the existence of the *societas mercatorum* for want of distinguishing features. As he explained: "I personally do not believe that a legal system corresponding to the definition of *lex mercatoria* exists. . . . I think that

[194] An interesting criticism – which will not be discussed here – is that reliance on comparative law techniques in constructing the theory of the arbitral legal order is misplaced. It has been most cogently expressed by Pfersmann, who argued that comparative law has a weak epistemological basis (see Otto Pfersmann, "Le droit comparé comme interprétation et comme théorie du droit," *Revue internationale de droit comparé*, 53 (2001), 275–88). According to Pfersmann, "comparative law is not a legal order at all, but a discipline" (ibid., 277). This view is hardly compatible with the existence of an arbitral legal order, because such a legal order would be merely an amalgamation of elements bearing no relation to one another – "a set of several unrelated elements" (ibid.).

[195] Mayer, "L'insertion," 83 ("It is possible to talk of the *legal delocalization* of the awards in that they are not considered as acts that belong to a given legal order but as private acts." (emphasis in original)).

[196] Pierre Mayer, "Effect of International Public Policy in International Arbitration?," in Loukas Mistelis and Julian Lew (eds.), *Pervasive Problems in International Arbitration* (The Hague: Kluwer Law International, 2006), ¶ 2-16, at 64.

[197] Paul Lagarde, "Approche critique de la *lex mercatoria*," in Philippe Fouchard, Philppe Kahn, and Antoine Lyon-Caen (eds.), *Le droit des relations économiques internationales: Études offertes à Berthold Goldman* (Paris: Litec, 1982), ¶ 21, at 139.

*lex mercatoria* may well be the name given to a set of legal rules, but does not constitute a legal system."[198]

Since, according to Mayer, there is no arbitral legal order, it would be impossible for arbitrators to act "on behalf" of all the constituent states of a transnational legal order that transcends their individuality. Arbitrators should be viewed as private individuals who derive their authority from the parties themselves, not from the legal order of any given state.[199] Even though arbitral awards are "very close to judgments," they differ insofar as they "do not come from a state body: arbitrators act as representatives of the parties, not as organs of states":[200] "Arbitrators, being private persons, have no inherent power to decide; a state rule is needed to give legal effect to their awards, which are no more than facts in the broad sense of the term."[201]

Mayer's views were further developed by Bollée, who insisted that an arbitrator's mandate derives not from the state's authority but from the parties' agreement.[202] Bollée contended that arbitrators could be viewed simply as private individuals,[203] and that arbitral awards are completely "extrinsic" to any legal order.[204] He explained that "far from reaching the heights of a legal norm, an award is purely and simply a *fact* which, like a contract or a tort, *is situated not at the bottom of but outside the legal order.*"[205] As an externality, an arbitral award cannot have its legal existence determined by any given legal system.[206] Its existence is a universal fact, over which states have no control and to which, at least logically, they are all equally entitled to attach legal consequences. Thus, no state legal system is fundamental to an award.[207] According to Bollée's

[198] Mayer, "Effect of International Public Policy," ¶ 2-15, at 64. See also Bollée, *Les méthodes*, ¶ 111, at 81 and ¶ 113, at 83.

[199] Mayer, "L'insertion," 81. See also Pierre Mayer, "Reflections on the International Arbitrators' Duty to Apply the Law: The 2000 Freshfields Lecture," *Arbitration International*, 17 (2001), 235–48.

[200] Pierre Mayer, *La distinction entre règles et décisions et le droit international privé* (Paris: Dalloz, 1973), 12.

[201] Pierre Mayer, "Les méthodes de la reconnaissance en droit international privé," in *Le droit international privé: Esprit et méthodes; Mélanges en l'honneur de Pierre Lagarde* (Paris: Dalloz, 2005), 558.

[202] See Bollée, *Les méthodes*, 25.

[203] Ibid., 657.

[204] Ibid., 37.

[205] Ibid., 37–38 (emphasis in original).

[206] Ibid., 38.

[207] Ibid.

account, therefore, arbitral awards do not emanate from any legal system, be it a state or a non-state system.[208]

In addition to these interesting, though somewhat isolated, voices in France, the theory of an arbitral legal order was criticized by some scholars, practitioners, and judges in the English-speaking world.[209] One of the most vocal critics of the theory was Paulsson, who dismissed it as a "false start,"[210] "diaphanous abstractions,"[211] and "Parisian poetry."[212] According to Paulsson, it is not because French courts have acknowledged the existence of an arbitral legal order that this legal order truly exists:

> Gaillard seeks support in various French judicial pronouncements to the effect that arbitrators are not "integral parts of the judicial organisation of the State" of the legal seat of arbitration. Such comments, however, prove nothing more than that the *French* legal order is willing to give effect to arbitral awards when enforcement is sought *in France* without concerning itself with the views of the courts of the seat. It does not demonstrate the existence of an autonomous "arbitral legal order." It is but the reaction of a single national legal order of the multiplicity of orders which may have the occasion to play a role in the life of an arbitration.[213]

Paulsson describes his own approach as a "revised conception [that] does not depend directly either on law or judges" and, as such, "does not seek to attach itself, in the manner of the Parisian thesis, to the somewhat dreamy and self-contradictory premise of an 'autonomous' order *recognized* by the very state orders from which it purports to be free."[214]

This "fourth conception," described by Paulsson as arbitration "in three dimensions," is based on the idea that the "horizonal" notion of pluralism – the idea that states exercise control over their respective territories – is insufficient to explain the reality or complexity of social life. One needs to take into account the "*vertical* dimension," which "reveals itself when more than one legal order occupies the same space."[215] Thus, "the

208 Ibid., 105.

209 Of course, the theory also had, and continues to have, supporters in the English-speaking world; see, for example, Julian Lew, "Achieving the Dream: Autonomous Arbitration," *Arbitration International*, 22 (2006), 179–204.

210 Paulsson, *Idea of Arbitration*, 39.

211 Ibid., 44.

212 Jan Paulsson, "Arbitration in Three Dimensions," LSE Law, Society and Economy Working Papers 2/2010, 2.

213 Ibid., 13.

214 Paulsson, *Idea of Arbitration*, 45 (emphasis in original).

215 Ibid., 48 (emphasis in original).

pluralistic model, expanded to include non-state legal orders, must be seen as three-dimensional. The dimension of depth is required to account for the fact that legal orders in modern international society overlap."[216] According to Paulsson, this vision of a "[t]hree-dimensional reality"[217] provides "[a]n apter model for a fluid world."[218]

It is hard to see where the true novelty of Paulsson's model lies, for its origins can be traced back to Santi Romani's theory, which Paulsson repeatedly quotes in support of the idea that "every organized social group is a kind of legal order."[219] This leads Paulsson to claim that social groups as diverse as "business entities, labour unions, economic cooperatives, sports federations, political parties, [and] criminal associations"[220] are capable of "generating legal systems, be they admirable or grotesque."[221] Yet this is not a new idea as far as arbitration is concerned. As shown in Chapter 9, Santi Romano's theories were well understood and discussed by members of the first generation of the French school of international arbitration.[222] It is not because he "remained, broadly speaking, an Italian secret for half a century," to the "considerable loss" of the anglophone world,[223] that his theories remained unexplored by others. It is rather ironic that Paulsson dismisses the "Parisian thesis" in favor of an "apter" model that yet draws inspiration from the very thinker on which so much of the French school's research is based. Paulsson's own theory may be framed as a grand narrative – a "revised conception"[224] – but it is hard to see how it adds anything new to the French school's earlier research.

Regardless of whether one agrees or disagrees with Paulsson's views, his book, full of illuminating insights, stimulated discussion on this and related issues. Paulsson's ideas were quoted approvingly by Lord Mance in his 2015 Freshfields lecture, which provided a robust defense of the territorial thesis.[225] Mance spoke about the "unfortunate difference in

216 Ibid., 199.
217 Ibid., 48.
218 Ibid., 193.
219 Ibid., 46.
220 Ibid., 195.
221 Ibid.
222 See Chapter 9, Section 9.3.2.
223 Paulsson, *Idea of Arbitration*, 46.
224 Ibid.
225 Jonathan Mance, "Arbitration: A Law unto Itself?" (2015 School of International Arbitration/30th Freshfields lecture, London, November 4, 2015), *Arbitration International*, 32 (2016), 223–41, also at www.supremecourt.uk/docs/speech-151104.pdf. The references below are to the online text.

attitude" between common law countries and French civil law with regard to "the fundamental basis of arbitration."[226] He felt there was "something noble, as well as bold, about a decision taken in the higher interests of justice and of the parties' agreement to ignore a court order made by the court of the seat."[227] But he voiced deep concern about the French approach, which he saw as "a mix of parochialism and universalism – parochialism since French law looks at international arbitration only through its own eyes, universalism since it insists that its own standards apply to all international arbitration."[228]

Lord Mance's lecture demonstrated that the quarrel over the arbitral legal order was far from over. Moreover, unlike the earlier debate over *lex mercatoria*, it reverberated widely across different communities – the judiciary, academics, and practitioners alike – and played out in the open along what appeared to be standard lines: a keynote speech by an eminent judge generally championing the territorialist thesis, followed by a public challenge from a leading practitioner and ardent proponent of the transnational approach.[229]

At a deeper level, such debates about the existence of an arbitral legal order were further confirmation that the quarrel over the arbitral legal order – much like that over *lex mercatoria* decades earlier – mobilized individuals to defend their convictions about the international arbitration system as a whole. Perhaps this is what made them so enduring.

## 10.5 Conclusion

The chapters in this part explored a key dimension of the Age of Professionalization: the quest to push international commercial arbitration beyond the frontiers of the state and justify its theoretical foundations. They have explained how, in the second half of the twentieth century, a new class of arbitration experts worked on increasingly abstract theories and models, such as *lex mercatoria* and the arbitral legal order.

226 Ibid., 24.

227 Ibid., 8.

228 Mance, "Arbitration," 11.

229 Gaillard, for instance, responded to Lord Mance's 2015 Freshfields lecture by proposing they debate in public, which they did a year later in the Grand'chambre of the French Court of Cassation. A similar scenario unfolded the same year in Singapore, with a keynote speech by Chief Justice Menon espousing the territorialist viewpoint, followed by a challenge from Born in defense of the transnational thesis.

On the second generation of the French school of international arbitration, this chapter explained how, in the late 1980s and beyond, a younger group of arbitration scholars explored novel issues such as the "juridicity" of international arbitration. These scholars examined concrete cases, such as the *Chromalloy–Hilmarton* saga, which considered the enforcement of awards set aside in the country of the seat. These cases revealed a sharp division within the arbitration community between territorialists and internationalists. Drawing on these and other cases, the second generation developed a novel theory – the arbitral legal order, which saw arbitration as transcending national legal systems and constituting a transnational legal order. This led to fervent disagreement between the territorialist and internationalist camps, which manifested in a series of key writings and conferences. The controversy is far from settled, as recent debates have shown.

Like the other ages described in this book, the Age of Autonomy tended to oscillate between periods of renewal and anxiety. The proponents of *lex mercatoria* and the arbitral legal order felt that they were putting forth a new *vision* of international commercial arbitration, which pushed the pendulum in the opposite direction, inspiring anxiety in those who felt that these theories went too far and could even be dangerous. As shown in Chapter 11, this tension between renewal and anxiety still exists today and we might even be entering a new age in the modern history of international commercial arbitration.

# 11

# General Conclusion

## 11.1 The Tripartite Division of the Modern History of International Commercial Arbitration

It has been claimed that "[t]here is as yet no general history of arbitration. Indeed, writing such a history would be like trying to put together an immense jigsaw puzzle, with many of the pieces missing and lost forever."[1] The goal of this book has never been to complete the jigsaw puzzle entirely – doing so would be impossible – but to identify key units within it. As discussed in Chapter 1, three broad phases or periods have been identified: the Age of Aspirations, the Age of Institutionalization, and the Age of Autonomy. The chronological markers used to delimit the three periods – 1780s–1920s for the first age, 1920s–1950s for the second, and 1950s to the present time for the third – are intentionally imprecise, as the periods tend to overlap.

Chapter 2 explained how, in the Age of Aspirations (*ca.*1780s–1920), arbitration was used in a range of contexts, relating to both in private law and public international adjudication, where it contributed to the development of various defining features of modern international arbitration practice. Chapter 3 focused on two such contexts – the commodity markets and interstate relations – and analyzed them as threads in the genealogy of international arbitration. Commercial arbitration was widely used in such cities as London or Liverpool, where specialized trade associations (the London Corn Trade Association, the Liverpool Cotton Association, etc.) played an important role in settling disputes

[1] Nigel Blackaby, Constantine Partasides, Alan Redfern, and Martin Hunter, *Redfern and Hunter on International Arbitration*, 5th ed. (Oxford: Oxford University Press, 2009), ¶ 1-08, at 4.

between merchants. Meanwhile, arbitration was also used in the international arena, where many state-to-state disputes were settled through mixed commissions, such as those created under the Jay Treaty of 1794, or through arbitration by sovereign, as between the Suez Canal Company and Egypt in 1864.

As Chapter 3 showed, while these arbitration mechanisms were marked by a number of features peculiar to each of them, they influenced modern international arbitration practice in numerous ways. For example, they showed the advantages of entrusting the dispute resolution process to an arbitral tribunal and also provided a "template" for international arbitration. Additionally, these mechanisms raised a general "arbitral consciousness," an awareness that peace and stability could be achieved through arbitration. The discourse on "peace through arbitration" permeated the arbitration world and was still very present in the early decades of the twentieth century and beyond.

Finally, the Age of Aspirations was marked by the establishment of a special regime for international commercial arbitration in some countries. Chapter 4 discussed the example of France, where the courts' hostility toward arbitration clauses, clearly visible in the *Prunier* decision (1843), was counterbalanced by the willingness of some judges to uphold arbitration agreements in some circumstances. This led to many debates in the French legal community over the distinction between national and international arbitration. In time, a distinct regime for international arbitration emerged under French law, culminating in the *Pélissier du Besset* (1927) and *Mardelé* (1930) decisions, both of which occurred in the transition period between the Age of Aspirations and the Age of Institutionalization.

As described in Chapter 5, the Age of Institutionalization (1920s–1950s) witnessed the creation of key institutions, such as the Court of Arbitration of the International Chamber of Commerce in 1923 and the American Arbitration Association in 1926, and the establishment of coherent and effective institutional arbitration systems. Chapter 6 traced the origins of the ICC and its Court of Arbitration, from the Atlantic City Conference (1919) to the foundation of the ICC (1920) and its Court of Arbitration (1923). These early developments are illuminating in many respects, explaining how the ICC both administered cases and contributed to the development of the law and practice of international arbitration, outliving its contemporary the League of Nations. Moreover, the ICC's early history suggests that the key "builders" of the current regime of international commercial arbitration were not the "grand old men" described by Dezalay and Garth in their seminal book *Dealing in Virtue*, but predominantly private business leaders and members of arbitral institutions.

The Age of Institutionalization was marked not only by the birth of new arbitral institutions but also by the establishment, under their auspices, of sophisticated arbitration systems. Focusing again on the ICC, Chapter 7 looked at how international commercial arbitration developed from *within* the ICC – how it was *institutionalized*. Through an analysis of the successive versions of the ICC Rules of Arbitration since 1922, as well as a wide range of sources, it traced the development of the ICC's arbitration system, paying close attention to how the institution codified existing rules and practices. It showed that these codification efforts were a prime example of the institutionalization of international commercial arbitration that took place in the 1920s and thereafter. The chapter also explored the series of changes or shifts that occurred in the early years of the ICC's existence: from conciliation to arbitration, and from equity to law. These changes reflected the ICC's increasingly important role in the administration of international disputes.

As explained in Chapter 8, the Age of Autonomy (1950s–present) was marked by increased specialization and the attempt to create a separate body of law and justify the theoretical foundations of the arbitration system as a whole. At least two claims of autonomy should be distinguished in the third age: the autonomy of the mercatocracy, the community of increasingly specialized professionals who saw themselves as international arbitration experts; and the autonomy of the body of law they sought to create, the so-called *lex mercatoria*. These claims of autonomy impelled renewal in the field, such that the exploration of *lex mercatoria* coincided with the emergence of a full-fledged school of thought – the French school of international arbitration. Chapter 9 sketched the intellectual history of that school – from Clive Schmitthoff's and Berthold Goldman's inaugural insights to the application of those insights in a wide range of contexts – and explored some of the school's key features: a shared belief in legal pluralism, a strong sense of professional and personal identity, and the fact that some of its members seemed to be operating "on the margins," in both their personal and professional lives.

Chapter 10 explained how, in the 1980s and 1990s, a new generation took the helm within the French school, with scholar-practitioners asking a new set of theoretical questions and shifting the focus of inquiry from *lex mercatoria* to the arbitral legal order. The chapter charted the vigorous debate over the delocalization of arbitral awards that marked the arbitration community in the 1980s and 1990s. It then considered the theorization of, and quarrel over, the arbitral legal order, which continues to this day. In taking up increasingly complex and theoretical issues such as *lex mercatoria* and the arbitral legal order, members of the French school sought to justify the theoretical foundations of the international arbitration system. Their theories had strong appeal and have been accepted in some quarters (including by French courts) and rejected, in whole or in part, in others.

## 11.2 Renewal and Anxiety

A central claim of this book is that the history of international commercial arbitration has witnessed broad phases of renewal and anxiety. This oscillatory movement is clearly visible in each of the three ages. For example, Chapter 4 explored legislative and judicial attitudes toward arbitration in the Age of Aspirations. It explained how the French Revolution initially saw arbitration as a fundamental way of settling disputes between private citizens; provisions on arbitration were even incorporated in the constitutions of 1793 and 1795. Soon enough, however, there was a backlash, with arbitration being described as a "parody of judicial administration."[2] Such hostility toward arbitration lasted for several decades until, at the end of the Age of Aspirations, the validity of arbitration clauses was firmly established in French law.

In the Age of Institutionalization, as Chapter 6 showed, the swing toward anxiety was apparent in the Geneva Protocol on Arbitration Clauses (1923) and the Geneva Convention on the Execution of Foreign Awards (1927), both of which reflected a highly territorial mindset. The movement was reversed with the Convention on the Recognition and Enforcement of Foreign Arbitral Awards (1958), which took international commercial arbitration into a new era, in which territorialism superseded to internationalism, and the Age of Institutionalization to the Age of Autonomy. The genesis of the New York Convention is in itself illuminating. Both the ICC and the United Nations Economic and Social Council (ECOSOC) produced draft conventions; the ICC's was distinctly progressive, while the ECOSOC's was much more conservative and reintroduced various features of the Geneva framework. The New York Convention thus oscillated between

[2] See Chapter 4, Section 4.2.2.1.

renewal (the ICC draft) and anxiety (the ECOSOC draft), and finally settled on the former.

The dynamics of renewal and anxiety also drove many of the debates that stirred members of the French school in the 1980s and thereafter. For example, the case law on the enforcement of awards set aside in the country of the seat – with such important cases as *Norsolor* (1984), *Hilmarton* (1994), *Chromalloy* (1997), and *Putrabali* (2007) – split the arbitration community into two camps. The territorialists, moved by anxiety, maintained that an award annulled in the country of the seat could not be enforced elsewhere, while the internationalists, thirsting for renewal, argued that an award was not integrated into the legal order of the state in which it was rendered and could therefore be enforced in another country. Recent developments – cases such as *Pemex* and *Thai-Lao Lignite*[3] – have shown that the issue of the enforcement of arbitral awards set aside in the country of the seat is far from settled and it is an issue with which state courts, too, are having to grapple.

The idea of a pendulum movement between renewal and anxiety is not simply a heuristic device for ordering historical material; it is also a way of explaining the forces that give coherence and an inner structure to the field as a whole. What does this tell us about the current state of international commercial arbitration? There is clear evidence of a similar oscillation continuing today.

On the one hand, international commercial arbitration, as well as its sibling investment treaty arbitration, is widely practiced throughout the world; arbitral institutions continue to receive new requests for arbitration and to open new offices; books in the field (including this one) abound; and new generations of lawyers, students, and academics are drawn to international arbitration like moths to a flame. Yet, on the other hand, there are also palpable signs of anxiety, which have so far been largely confined to investor-state dispute settlement (ISDS),[4] reaching an apex with the 2018 *Achmea* decision of the Court of Justice of the European Union.[5] Will the anxiety surrounding ISDS have spillover

[3] See, for example, Emmanuel Gaillard, "La vision américaine des sentences annulées au siège: Observations sur les arrêts *Pemex* et *Thai-Lao Lignite* de la Cour d'appel fédérale du 2e circuit des 2 août 2016 et 20 juillet 2017," *Revue de l'arbitrage*, 2017, ¶ 14, at 1162–64.

[4] See, generally, David Caron and Esmé Shirlow, "Dissecting Backlash: The Unarticulated Causes of Backlash and Its Unintended Consequences," in Andreas Follesdal and Geir Ulfstein (eds.), *The Judicialization of International Law: A Mixed Blessing?* (Oxford: Oxford University Press, 2018), 159–82.

[5] In the *Achmea* decision, the Court of Justice of the European Union ruled that an arbitration clause contained in an intra-EU bilateral investment treaty was incompatible

effects, affecting international commercial arbitration as well? A flurry of recent news articles about international arbitration – which put international commercial arbitration and investment treaty arbitration in the same basket – convey the tension that exists in the field between renewal and anxiety. To take a few examples from the French press, the ISDS system has been described as "casting an increasingly worrying shadow over the capacity of nations to legislate on the environment, health or working conditions";[6] while another article asked, "are arbitral tribunals a threat to democracy?"[7] At the same time, pro-arbitration authors have sought to instill a renewed sense of optimism into arbitration, adopting such evocative titles as "Restoring the enchantment of international arbitration";[8] "Arbitration, a jewel in Paris's crown";[9] and "Paris, stronghold of international arbitration."[10] Whether the pendulum continues its swing toward anxiety or stops midway remains to be seen.

## 11.3 The Ongoing Tension between the State and the Mercatocracy

Another way of reading this book is to focus on the grand narrative, or "metanarrative," that weaves together its various parts, namely, the constant tension between the state and the mercatocracy, defined as the transnational community of merchants and arbitration experts seeking to expand the reach of international commercial arbitration. Indeed, the history of international commercial arbitration may be seen as the search for a compromise between, on the one hand, states seeking to assert their power and authority, and, on the other hand, the mercatocracy seeking to create its own norms, rules, and institutions. This tension was hardly palpable in the Age of Aspirations, since the mercatocracy was not yet fully organized. Arbitration worked well in a range of contexts, but it remained largely local (in British trade associations, for instance); hence, truly *international* arbitration was more a set of aspirations than a clear legal or political project.

with EU law (Case C-284/16, *Slowakische Republik* v. *Achmea BV*, March 6, 2018). The decision was roundly criticized by many arbitration practitioners.

6 Maxime Vaudano, "L'arbitrage international, une justice sur la sellette," *Le Monde*, August 24, 2018.

7 Marta Orosz, Justus von Daniels, and Maxime Vaudano, "'Au cœur du CETA', épisode 1: Les tribunaux d'arbitrage menacent-ils la démocratie?," *Le Monde*, October 31, 2016.

8 Philippe Sarrailhé, "Réenchanter l'arbitrage international," *Les Echos*, May 15, 2017.

9 Vincent Bouquet, "L'arbitrage, joyau de la place parisienne," *Les Echos*, April 24, 2017.

10 Lisa Vignoli, "Paris, place forte de l'arbitrage international," *Le Monde*, January 15, 2016.

The situation changed over time, with the mercatocracy growing stronger and forming its own epistemic community, thereby asserting its power and leaving its mark on the broader landscape of international arbitration. In the Age of Institutionalization, private business leaders and some political figures joined hands to create new arbitral institutions, developing their own rules, methods, and practices. The mercatocracy sought to enlist the support of states, often successfully; it is telling that the first president of the ICC and of its Court of Arbitration was Étienne Clémentel, a key figure in the Third Republic, and that the Court of Arbitration was inaugurated at a ceremony in a state court, the Tribunal de Commerce de la Seine. State influence nonetheless remained very strong in the Age of Institutionalization, as illustrated by the Geneva Convention, which made the enforcement of awards abroad subject to nine conditions that were strongly colored by nationalistic instincts. The dawning of the Age of Autonomy was marked by emboldened demands from the mercatocracy, which became increasingly specialized and attempted to create its own body of law.

As these examples show, there were times when the compromise between the state and the mercatocracy failed and times when it was more successful. But even when the mercatocracy seemed to have achieved its goals, the state, in its manifold forms, was always present in the background. In that respect, the state could be compared to the unconscious in psychoanalytic theory: "its memory-traces are present in all their freshness"[11] and it is "indestructible," that is, always ready to return. Or perhaps Freud's notion of the "return of the unconscious"[12] would be more fitting: the state always reappears in more or less recognizable forms throughout the history of international commercial arbitration.

## 11.4 A New "Age of Disruption" in the History of International Commercial Arbitration?

One may wonder whether we are entering a new age in the modern history of international commercial arbitration – an Age of Disruption,

[11] Sigmund Freud, *The Standard Edition of the Complete Psychological Works of Sigmund Freud*, vol. 23, *Moses and Monotheism* (London: Hogarth Press, 1964 [1939]), 94.

[12] See Sigmund Freud, "The Dissection of the Psychical Personality," in *The Standard Edition of the Complete Psychological Works of Sigmund Freud*, vol. 22, *New Introductory Lectures on Psycho-Analysis and Other Works* (London: Hogarth Press, 1964 [1933]), 73.

where the tension between the mercatocracy and the state will be exacerbated by unfamiliar circumstances that could threaten the integrity of the arbitration system as a whole. These circumstances include the rise of nationalism, the reemergence of protectionism, and broader fears about globalization. They are illustrated by, for example, the United Kingdom's vote to exit the European Union and the United States' withdrawal from the Trans-Pacific Partnership (TPP) and attempts to fundamentally overhaul its legal framework for trade and investment. While some analysts predict that these circumstances will not radically alter the current arbitration landscape – that, for example, Brexit will have little impact on the status of London as a key center of international arbitration – it remains to be seen whether the status quo will prevail.

Pessimists will contend that these events threaten to disrupt the entire landscape of international arbitration, marking a shift from the Age of Autonomy to the Age of Disruption. Borrowing from Schlag, law in this fourth age would be cast in the "dissociative aesthetic," in which "[t]he crucial contributions of the prior aesthetics – the grid (and its fixed identities), energy (and its quantifiable magnitudes), and perspective (and its identifiable relations) – have all collapsed. No determinable identities, relations, or perspectives survive."[13] As such, a key feature of the Age of Disruption would be the dissolution of legal identities in an age where law and politics are so intertwined that no amount of legal or conceptual work can separate them.

Crawford's discussion of the political discourse concerning international law is illuminating in this respect. In the course of his analysis, Crawford used the image of international law as a sedimentary formation:

> At its base is a solid set of principles, norms and institutions: the fundamentals of the post-War global legal structure. It would be difficult for any state to effect a wholesale withdrawal from this solid base. It has survived the worst of the Cold War and many other international crises. We can have faith in those foundational layers. But our situation requires a combination of faith and action. The top layers, at least, are at risk of erosion in the current political climate.[14]

This "erosion" could signal a shift from the Age of Autonomy to the Age of Disruption. Indeed, the foundational layers of international

[13] Pierre Schlag, "The Aesthetics of American Law," *Harvard Law Review*, 115, no. 4 (2002), 1052.

[14] James Crawford, "The Current Political Discourse Concerning International Law," *Modern Law Review*, 81, no. 1 (2018), 21–22.

commercial arbitration, its key legal instruments and principles, like those of international law more broadly, are firmly established. But the top layers – charged with the rhetoric of backlash and anxiety – may jeopardize the current system. Let us hope that the pendulum's perpetual motion will enable a new balance to be found between these ever-competing forces, so that the threat of disruption does not transform into a full-blown Age of Disruption.

# BIBLIOGRAPHY

This bibliography lists the main items that have been consulted for this book. It follows the customary distinction between primary sources (including court decisions, national legislation, and the archives and records of institutions) and secondary sources (such as treatises, monographs, and journal articles).[1] Primary sources are mostly listed in chronological order, and secondary sources in alphabetical order.

Given the great variety of primary sources used, it would have been awkward, if not confusing for the reader, to present such a variety of materials in a single continuous alphabetical list. I have therefore divided the first part into sections, allowing readers and those interested in the history of international commercial arbitration to easily apprehend the range and form of the available materials. The sections relating to the International Chamber of Commerce – Sections 1.A (ICC arbitral awards) and 1.G (archives and records of the ICC) – should be all the more useful as there is currently no inventory of the ICC's archives.

## 1 Primary Sources

### *A Arbitral Awards*

#### ICC[2]

ICC Case No. 6 of November 22, 1922
ICC Case No. 50 of February 12, 1924

[1] While some sources belong to a single category, others could be assigned to more than one category (e.g., a newspaper article written about an event immediately after its occurrence is a primary source, but if the article contains opinions or interpretations of events, it is a secondary source). When this is the case, I have included the item in the section that best corresponds to its use for the purposes of this book (as a firsthand account or interpretive documentation).

[2] The date mentioned is the date of the award. See Chapter 7, Section 7.3 for more information on these awards, most of which remain unpublished. The gaps in this list are explained by the fact that no other awards from the period were found in the ICC's archives.

ICC Case No. 56 of July 9, 1924
ICC Case No. 67 of July 22, 1924
ICC Case No. 88 of December 19, 1925
ICC Case No. 91 of October 28, 1925
ICC Case No. 111 of January 24, 1927
ICC Case No. 115 of July 27, 1926
ICC Case No. 143 of February 19, 1927
ICC Case No. 144 of February 1, 1927
ICC Case No. 163 of October 26, 1927
ICC Case No. 225 of February 11, 1929
ICC Case No. 247 of August 8, 1929
ICC Case No. 253 of September 18, 1928
ICC Case No. 265 of November 6, 1928
ICC Case No. 288 of November 25, 1929
ICC Case No. 301 of April 24, 1929
ICC Case No. 304 of December 9, 1929
ICC Case No. 380 of June 28, 1931
ICC Case No. 381 of June 28, 1931
ICC Case No. 382 (n.d.)[3]
ICC Case No. 383 of June 28, 1931
ICC Case No. 387 of June 28, 1931
ICC Case No. 388 of March 11, 1932
ICC Case No. 390 of June 28, 1931
ICC Case No. 396 of January 8, 1932
ICC Case No. 477 of March 21, 1932
ICC Case No. 498 of March 20, 1933
ICC Case No. 513 of April 11, 1932
ICC Case No. 536 of February 11, 1933
ICC Case No. 540 of March 4, 1933
ICC Case No. 543 of March 10, 1934
ICC Case No. 546 of October 14, 1933
ICC Case No. 550 of December 13, 1933
ICC Case No. 556 of November 29, 1933
ICC Case No. 557 of July 12, 1933
ICC Case No. 575 of February 28, 1933
ICC Case No. 585 of June 2, 1932
ICC Case No. 586 of July 28, 1934
ICC Case No. 588 of November 7, 1935
ICC Case No. 589 of November 29, 1932

[3] The date is most likely June 28, 1931, as cases 380–83 and 387 involved the same claimant and sole arbitrator, and the hearing in each of these cases took place in April 1931 at the International Chamber of Commerce.

ICC Case No. 592 of March 12, 1934
ICC Case No. 598 of May 18, 1935
ICC Case No. 645 of February 11, 1938
ICC Case No. 665 of December 2, 1939
ICC Case No. 667 of August 4, 1939
ICC Case No. 668 of November 25, 1939
ICC Case No. 682 of March 21, 1946
ICC Case No. 710 of January 22, 1948
ICC Case No. 734 of January 20, 1948
ICC Case No. 742 of January 11, 1952
ICC Case No. 752 of December 30, 1950
ICC Case No. 756 of November 25, 1949
ICC Case No. 759 of July 12, 1951
ICC Case No. 762 of March 21, 1955
ICC Case No. 763 of March 21, 1955
ICC Case No. 764 of March 21, 1955
ICC Case No. 768 (n.d.)[4]
ICC Case No. 769 (n.d.)
ICC Case No. 770 (n.d.)
ICC Case No. 781 of April 5, 1951
ICC Case No. 787 of December 22, 1951
ICC Case No. 804 (n.d.)[5]
ICC Case No. 809 of October 22, 1952
ICC Case No. 816 of March 19, 1953
ICC Case No. 834 of December 15, 1952
ICC Case No. 848 of March 4, 1953
ICC Case No. 850 of September 24, 1953
ICC Case No. 861 of September 22, 1953
ICC Case No. 865 of October 15, 1953
ICC Case No. 889 of April 1, 1955
ICC Case No. 890 of August 6, 1954
ICC Case No. 892 of May 24, 1954
ICC Case No. 893 of April 6, 1955
ICC Case No. 895 of July 28, 1954
ICC Case No. 899 of July 1, 1955
ICC Case No. 904 of October 28, 1954
ICC Case No. 907 of January 24, 1956
ICC Case No. 909 of November 19, 1954

[4] In Cases 768–70, the hearing took place on January 18, 1954, at the International Chamber of Commerce.

[5] The award states “14 January” only; the year was most likely 1952 as the arbitrator was appointed on November 21, 1951.

ICC Case No. 914 (n.d.)[6]
ICC Case No. 919 of March 21, 1956
ICC Case No. 925 of November 28, 1955
ICC Case No. 927 of October 21, 1955
ICC Case No. 949 of December 19, 1955
ICC Case No. 953 of January 25, 1956
ICC Case No. 954 of November 24, 1955
ICC Case No. 958 of May 5, 1956
ICC Case No. 967 of September 11, 1957
ICC Case No. 968 of May 24, 1956
ICC Case No. 969 of November 26, 1957
ICC Case No. 974 of February 2, 1958
ICC Case No. 982 of July 18, 1958
ICC Case No. 983 of February 3, 1958
ICC Case No. 985 of April 28, 1958
ICC Case No. 986 of March 31, 1957
ICC Case No. 987 of March 18, 1957
ICC Case No. 988 of June 15, 1957
ICC Case No. 998 of June 20, 1957
ICC Case No. 1007 of February 19, 1959
ICC Case No. 1010 of February 22, 1958
ICC Case No. 1012 of June 30, 1958
ICC Case No. 1018 of June 16, 1958
ICC Case No. 1024 of October 14, 1959
ICC Case No. 1030 of May 19, 1959
ICC Case No. 1037 of May 23, 1960
ICC Case No. 1052 of September 30, 1959
ICC Case No. 1073 of December 30, 1961
ICC Case No. 1082 of June 16, 1960
ICC Case No. 1110 of May 27, 1963
ICC Case No. 1116 of October 2, 1961
ICC Case No. 1124 of January 16, 1961
ICC Case No. 1144 of February 8, 1965
ICC Case No. 1151 of October 14, 1963
ICC Case No. 1156 of September 29, 1962
ICC Case No. 1158 of May 28, 1962
ICC Case No. 1175 of July 8, 1962
ICC Case No. 1205 of December 27, 1963
ICC Case No. 1267 of March 20, 1964
ICC Case No. 1281 of August 17, 1964

[6] The arbitration agreement was signed by the parties on January 19, 1954.

ICC Case No. 1309 of July 16, 1965
ICC Case No. 1315 of September 27, 1965
ICC Case No. 1341 of March 10, 1964
ICC Case No. 1373 of September 29, 1969
ICC Case No. 1383 of June 6, 1966
ICC Case No. 1408 of July 30, 1969
ICC Case No. 1443 of June 17, 1968
ICC Case No. 1448 of December 6, 1966
ICC Case No. 1453 of June 17, 1968
ICC Case No. 1468 of April 26, 1968
ICC Case No. 1473 of July 23, 1969
ICC Case No. 1489 of August 30, 1967
ICC Case No. 8385, in Jean-Jacques Arnaldez, Yves Derains, and Dominique Hascher, *Collection of ICC Arbitral Awards 1996–2000* (New York: Wolters Kluwer, 2003), 479

## ICJ

*Fisheries Case (United Kingdom* v. *Norway),* December 18, 1951, Dissenting Opinion of Sir Arnold McNair, *I.C.J. Reports 1951*, 116, 181
*Nottebohm Case (Liechtenstein* v. *Guatemala),* Judgment of November 18, 1953 (Preliminary Objection), *I.C.J. Reports 1953*, 111, 119

## UNCITRAL

*Yukos Universal Limited (Isle of Man)* v. *Russian Federation* (PCA Case No. AA 227), Final Award, July 18, 2014

## Other

Napoléon III, *Sentence arbitrale rendue par Sa Majesté l'Empereur des Français sur les réclamations réciproques de Son Altesse le Bey de Tunis et du général Benaïad* (Paris: Eugène Penaud, 1857)
"Sentence arbitrale rendue par l'Empereur Napoléon III, le 6 juillet 1864, entre le Vice-Roi d'Egypte et la Compagnie universelle du canal de Suez," Final Award, April 21, 1864, in Henri La Fontaine, *Pasicrisie Internationale 1794–1900: Histoire documentaire des arbitrages internationaux* (The Hague: Martinus Nijhoff, 1997 [1902]), 122–29

"Award Rendered on 14 September 1872 by the Tribunal of Arbitration Established by Article I of the Treaty of Washington of May 8, 1871," in John Bassett Moore, *History and Digest of the International Arbitrations to Which the United States Has Been a Party, Together with Appendices Containing the Treaties Relating to Such Arbitrations, and Historical and Legal Notes on other International Arbitrations Ancient and Modern, and on the Domestic Commissions of the United States for the Adjustment of International Claims* (Washington: Government Printing Office, 1898), 1: 653

*In the matter of an Arbitration between Petroleum Development (Trucial Coast) Ltd. and the Sheikh of Abu Dhabi*, reported in *International and Comparative Law Quarterly*, 1 (1952), 247–61

## *B Arbitration Rules*

Rules of Procedure for the Conciliation and Good Offices of the International Chamber of Commerce (1922), in International Chamber of Commerce, *Rules of Conciliation (Good Offices) and Arbitration (Fourth Edition)*, Brochure No. 21 (Paris: ICC International Headquarters [1922])[7]

ICC Rules of Conciliation and Arbitration (1927), in International Chamber of Commerce, *Arbitration: Revision of the Rules of Conciliation and Arbitration*, Brochure No. 50 (Paris: ICC International Headquarters, 1927)

Amendments to the ICC Rules of Conciliation and Arbitration (1931), in International Chamber of Commerce, *Resolutions Adopted by the Washington Congress*, Brochure No. 77 (Paris: ICC International Headquarters, 1931)

Amendments to the ICC Rules of Conciliation and Arbitration (1933), in International Chamber of Commerce, *Resolutions Adopted by the Seventh Congress of the ICC* [Vienna], Brochure No. 83 (Paris: ICC International Headquarters, 1933)

Amendments to the ICC Rules of Conciliation and Arbitration (1935), in International Chamber of Commerce, *Resolutions Adopted by the Eighth Congress of the ICC* [Paris], Brochure No. 89 (Paris: ICC International Headquarters, 1935)

Amendments to the ICC Rules of Conciliation and Arbitration (1939), in International Chamber of Commerce, *Resolutions Adopted by the Tenth Congress of the ICC* [Copenhagen], Brochure No. 100 (Paris: ICC International Headquarters, 1939)

Amendments to the ICC Rules of Conciliation and Arbitration (1947), in International Chamber of Commerce, *Resolutions Adopted by the Eleventh Congress of the ICC* [Montreux], Brochure No. 117 (Paris: ICC International Headquarters, 1947)

[7] The dates of Brochures Nos. 21 and 77 are not mentioned on the documents themselves; they are most likely 1922 and 1931, respectively.

ICC Rules of Conciliation and Arbitration (1955), in International Chamber of Commerce, *Rules of Conciliation and Arbitration in Force on 1st June 1955*, 5th ed. (Paris: ICC International Headquarters, 1967)

ICC Rules of Conciliation and Arbitration (1975), in International Chamber of Commerce, *Rules for the ICC Court of Arbitration*, Brochure No. 291 (Paris: ICC International Headquarters, 1975)

ICC Rules of Conciliation and Arbitration (1988), in International Chamber of Commerce, *ICC Rules of Conciliation and Arbitration*, Brochure No. 447 (Paris: ICC International Headquarters, 1988)

ICC Rules of Arbitration (1998), in International Chamber of Commerce, *ICC Rules of Arbitration – ICC Rules of Conciliation*, Brochure No. 581 (Paris: ICC International Headquarters, 1998)

ICC Rules of Arbitration (2012), in International Chamber of Commerce, *ICC Rules of Arbitration – ICC Rules of Conciliation*, Brochure No. 850 (Paris: ICC International Headquarters, 2012)

ICC Arbitration Rules (2017) and Mediation Rules (2014), in International Chamber of Commerce, *Arbitration Rules in Force as from 1 March 2017; Mediation Rules in Force as from 1 January 2014*, Brochure No. 880 (Paris: ICC International Headquarters, 2018)

ICC Arbitration Rules (2021) and Mediation Rules (2014), in International Chamber of Commerce, *Arbitration Rules in Force as from 1 January 2021; Mediation Rules in Force as from 1 January 2014*, Brochure No. 892 (Paris: ICC International Headquarters, 2020)

## *C International Instruments*

"Treaty of Amity Commerce and Navigation, between His Britannic Majesty; and The United States of America, by Their President, with the advice and consent of Their Senate," November 19, 1794, http://avalon.law.yale.edu/18th_century/jay.asp ("Jay Treaty")

Treaty between the United States and Great Britain, May 8, 1871, https://archive.org/details/cihm_27720/page/n15 ("Treaty of Washington")

"Projet de règlement pour la procédure arbitrale internationale," August 28, 1875, www.idi-iil.org/app/uploads/2017/06/1875_haye_01_fr.pdf

Convention for the Pacific Settlement of International Disputes, July 29, 1899, http://avalon.law.yale.edu/19th_century/hague01.asp ("1899 Hague Convention")

Convention for the Pacific Settlement of International Disputes, October 18, 1907, http://avalon.law.yale.edu/20th_century/pacific.asp ("1907 Hague Convention")

Protocol on Arbitration Clauses, September 24, 1923 ("Geneva Protocol"), 27 L.N.T.S. 157

Convention on the Execution of Foreign Arbitral Awards, September 26, 1927, 92 L.N.T.S. 301 ("Geneva Convention")

Statute of the International Court of Justice, June 26, 1945, www.icj-cij.org/en/statute

United Nations Economic and Social Council (ECOSOC), Draft Convention on the Recognition and Enforcement of Foreign Arbitral Awards, March 28, 1955, in *Report of the Committee on the Enforcement of International Arbitral Awards*, UN Doc. E/2704 ("ECOSOC Draft Convention")

Convention on the Recognition and Enforcement of Foreign Arbitral Awards, June 10, 1958, 330 U.N.T.S. 3 ("New York Convention")

Convention on the Settlement of Investment Disputes between States and Nationals of Other States, March 18, 1965, 575 U.N.T.S. 160

Establishment of the United Nations Commission on International Trade Law, G. A. Res. 2205(XXI), December 17, 1966

United Nations Economic and Social Council (ECOSOC), Res. 1996/31, July 25, 1996 (Consultative relationship between the United Nations and nongovernmental organizations)

## *D Court Decisions*

### Austria

Supreme Court of Austria, November 18, 1982, *Revue de l'arbitrage*, 1983, 519

### Belgium

Court of Cassation (Belgium), First Chamber, February 17, 1888, *Dugniolle* v. *Ceulemans*, *Recueil Dalloz*, 1889, II, 168

*Société Nationale pour la Recherche, le Transport et la Commercialisation des Hydrocarbures (Sonatrach)* v. *Ford, Bacon and Davis Inc.*, Brussels Court of First Instance, December 6, 1988, *Yearbook Commercial Arbitration*, 15 (1990), 370–78

### England

*Bank Mellat* v. *Helliniki Techniki SA* [1984] 1 Q.B. 291

*Yukos Capital S.a.r.l.* v. *OJSC Rosneft Oil Company* [2012] EWCA Civ 855

### Europe – Court of Justice of the European Union

Grand Chamber, March 6, 2018, Case C-284/16, *Slowakische Republik* v. *Achmea BV*, EU:C:2018:158,

## France

Court of Cassation, Civil Chamber, July 10, 1843, *Compagnie L'Alliance* v. *Prunier, Sirey*, 1843, I, 561, note Devilleneuve, conclusions Advocate General Hello

Court of Cassation, Civil Chamber, February 21, 1844, *Compagnie du Soleil* v. *Lorents, Journal du palais*, 1844, I, 596

Court of Cassation, Civil Chamber, December 2, 1844, *Compagnie d'assurances du Phénix* v. *Perret, Journal du palais*, 1844, II, 567

Rouen Court of Appeal, January 18, 1845, *Journal du palais*, 1845, I, 271

Court of Cassation (*Chambre des requêtes*), July 17, 1899, *Ospina* v. *Ribon, Revue des sociétés*, 1899, 497

Court of Cassation (*Chambre des requêtes*), June 21, 1904, *Georges Bernard* v. *General Mercantile Company, Dalloz*, 1906, I, 395

Court of Cassation, May 17, 1927, *Pélissier du Besset* v. *The Algiers Land and Warehouse Co. Ltd., Dalloz*, 2 (1928), 25, conclusions Matter, note Capitant

Court of Cassation, February 19, 1930, *Mardelé* v. *Muller, Sirey*, 1933, I, 41

Court of Cassation, January 27, 1931, *Dambricourt* v. *Rossard, Sirey*, 1933, I, 41, note Jean-Paulin Niboyet

Court of Cassation, First Civil Chamber, May 7, 1963, *Etablissements Raymond Gosset* v. *Société Frère Carapelli S.p.A., Revue critique de droit international privé*, 1963, note Motulsky; reprinted in Henri Motulsky, *Écrits*, vol. 2, *Études et notes sur l'arbitrage* (Paris: Dalloz, 2010), 343

Paris Court of Appeal, November 19, 1982, *Norsolor S.A.* v. *Pabalk Ticaret Limited Sirketi, Revue de l'arbitrage*, 1983, 472

Court of Cassation, First Civil Chamber, October 9, 1984, *Société Pabalk Ticaret Limited Sirketi* v. *Norsolor S.A., Revue de l'arbitrage*, 1985, 431, note Goldman; *Journal du droit international*, 1985, 679, note Kahn; *Dalloz*, 1985, 101, note Robert

Court of Cassation, First Civil Chamber, October 22, 1991, *Société Compañia Valenciana de Cementos Portaland* v. *Société Primary Coal Inc., Yearbook Commercial Arbitration* 18 (1993), 528; *French International Arbitration Law Report* (1963–2007), Thomas Clay and Philippe Pinsolle (eds.), case no. 23, at 177

Court of Cassation, First Civil Chamber, March 10, 1993, *Société Polish Ocean Line* v. *Société Jolasry, Revue de l'arbitrage*, 1993, 276, note Hascher; *Journal du droit international*, 1993, 360, note Kahn; *Yearbook Commercial Arbitration*, 19 (1994), 662

Court of Cassation, First Civil Chamber, March 23, 1994, *Société Hilmarton Ltd.* v. *Société Omnium de traitement et de valorisation (OTV), Journal du droit international*, 1994, 701, note Gaillard; *Revue de l'arbitrage*, 1994, 327–28, note Jarrosson; *Revue critique de droit international privé*, 1995, 356, note Oppetit

Paris Court of Appeal, January 14, 1997, *Arab Republic of Egypt* v. *Chromalloy Aero Services, Revue de l'arbitrage*, 1997, 395–98, note Fouchard; *Journal du droit international*, 1998, 750, note Gaillard; *Yearbook Commercial Arbitration*, 22 (1997), 691

Court of Cassation, First Civil Chamber, January 5, 1999, *M. Zanzi* v. *J. De Coninck and others*, *Revue de l'arbitrage*, 1999, 260–61, note Fouchard

Court of Cassation, First Civil Chamber, February 1, 2005, *Etat d'Israël* v. *Société NIOC*, *Revue de l'arbitrage*, 2005, 693–95

Paris Court of Appeal, September 29, 2005, *Directorate General of Civil Aviation of the Emirate of Dubai* v. *International Bechtel Co. Limited*, *Revue de l'arbitrage*, 2006, 695, note Muir Watt; *Juris-Classeur Périodique*, 2006, 1174, commentary Seraglini; *Revue critique de droit international privé*, 2006, 387, note Szekely

Court of Cassation, First Civil Chamber, June 29, 2007, *Société PT Putrabali Adyamulia* v. *Société Rena Holding et Société Moguntia Est Epices*, *Yearbook Commercial Arbitration*, 32 (2007), 299

Court of Cassation, First Civil Chamber, July 8, 2015, *Société Ryanair Ltd et Société Airport Marketing Services Ltd* v. *Syndicat Mixte des Aéroports de Charente (SMAC)*, *Revue de l'arbitrage*, 2015, 1131–33

Court of Cassation, First Civil Chamber, September 30, 2020, *PWC Landwell-PricewaterhouseCoopers Tax & Legal Services* v. *Mme L . . . Y . . . ; et autres*, *Journal du droit international*, 2020, 1327, note Gaillard; *Hebdo édition privée*, October 15, 2020, note Vidal; *Dalloz actualité*, October 21, 2020, note Jourdan-Marques

## Netherlands

Supreme Court of the Netherlands, October 26, 1973, *Société européenne d'études et d'entreprises* v. *Socialist Federal Republic of Yugoslavia*, *Netherlands Yearbook of International Law*, 5 (1974), 290

Amsterdam Court of Appeal, April 28, 2009, *Yukos Capital Sarl* v. *OAO Rosneft*, *Yearbook Commercial Arbitration*, 34 (2009), 703

## Switzerland

Vaud Cantonal Tribunal, November 24, 1948, *Omnium français des pétroles* v. *Gianotti*, *Journal des Tribunaux*, 3 (1949), 112

## United States

*Parsons & Wittlemore Overseas Co.* v. *Société Générale de l'Industrie du Papier (RAKTA)*, December 23, 1974, 508 F.2d 969 (2d Cir. 1974)

*Matter of Arbitration between Chromalloy Aeroservices* v. *Arab Republic of Egypt*, July 31, 1996, 939 F. Supp. 907 (D.D.C. 1996)

*Baker Marine (Nig.) Ltd.* v. *Chevron (Nig.) Ltd.*, August 12, 1999, 191 F.3d 194 (2d Cir. 1999)

*Spier* v. *Calzaturificio Tecnica, S.p.A.*, October 22, 1999, 71 F. Supp. 2d 279 (S.D.N. Y. 1999)

*TermoRio S. A. E.S.P. and LeaseCo Group LLC* v. *Electranta S. P. et al.*, May 25, 2007, 487 F. 3d 928 (D.C. Cir. 2007)

*Corporación Mexicana de Mantenimiento Integral* v. *Pemex-Exploración y Producción*, August 27, 2013, 962 F. Supp. 2d 642 (S.D.N.Y. 2013)

*Corporación Mexicana de Mantenimiento Integral* v. *Pemex-Exploración y Producción*, August 2, 2016, No 13-4022 (2d Cir. 2016)

*Thai-Lao Lignite (Thailand) Co. Ltd. et al.* v. *Government of the Lao People's Democratic Republic*, February 6, 2014, 997 F. Supp. 2d 214 (S.D.N.Y. 2014)

*Thai-Lao Lignite (Thailand) Co. Ltd. et al.* v. *Government of the Lao People's Democratic Republic*, July 20, 2017, 864 F.3d 172 (2d Cir. 2017)

## *E Miscellaneous Collections of Decisions*

Coussirat-Coustère, Vincent and Pierre Michel Eisemann, *Répertoire de la jurisprudence arbitrale internationale* vol. 1 *1794–1918*, vol. 2 *1919–1945*, vol. 3 *1946–1988* (Dordrecht: Martinus Nijhoff, 1989 [vols. 1, 2], 1991 [vol. 3])

Crépet Daigremont, Claire, Arnaud De Nanteuil, Jean-Louis Iten, Guillaume Le Floch, and Régis Bismuth, *Les grandes décisions de la jurisprudence internationale* (Paris: Dalloz, 2018)

La Fontaine, Henri, *Pasicrisie Internationale 1794–1900: Histoire documentaire des arbitrages internationaux* (The Hague: Martinus Nijhoff, 1997)

Lapradelle, Albert de, and Nicolas Politis, *Recueil des arbitrages internationaux* (Paris: Pedone, 1905 and 1923)

Miller, Hunter (ed.), *Treaties and Other International Acts of the United States of America*, vol. 2 (Washington: Government Printing Office, 1931)

Moore, John Bassett, *History and Digest of the International Arbitrations to Which the United States Has Been a Party, Together with Appendices Containing the Treaties Relating to Such Arbitrations, and Historical and Legal Notes on Other International Arbitrations Ancient and Modern, and on the Domestic Commissions of the United States for the Adjustment of International Claims*, 6 vols. (Washington: Government Printing Office, 1898)

Nussbaum, Arthur, *Internationales Jahrbuch für Schiedsgerichtswesen in Zivil-und Handelssachen* (Berlin: Carl Heymanns, 1926–34)

*International Yearbook on Civil and Commercial Arbitration*, vol. 1 (New York: Oxford University Press, 1928)

United Nations, Codification Division, *Reports of International Arbitral Awards*, http://legal.un.org/riaa/

Wharton, Francis, *Digest of the International Law of the United States; Taken from Documents Issued by Presidents and Secretaries of State, and from Decisions of Federal Courts and Opinions of Attorneys-General*, 3 vols. (Washington: W. H. Lowdermilk, 1886)

## *F Archives of the French National Assembly*

### Chamber of Deputies

"Exposé des motifs et texte de la proposition de loi, présentée par M. Louis Dreyfus, relative à la clause compromissoire en matière commerciale" (May 7, 1907), *Documents parlementaires, session ordinaire*, 73 (1908), 283

"Adoption d'une proposition de loi relative à la clause compromissoire en matière commerciale," *Annales de la Chambre des députés* (July 2, 1908, second session), 620

### Senate

"Transmission de propositions de loi," *Annales du Sénat* (July 3, 1908), 1066

"Proposition de loi ayant pour objet de modifier les articles 1003, 1004, 1005, 1006, 1007 et 1023 du code de procédure civile en déclarant valable la clause compromissoire ou engagement de soumettre à l'arbitrage les difficultés à naître de l'interprétation ou de l'exécution d'un contrat, présentée par M. Étienne Flandin, sénateur," *Documents parlementaires – Sénat* (1921), app. 4, at 2

"Proposition de loi tendant à modifier l'article 1006 du code de procédure civile en vue de reconnaître la validité de la clause compromissoire en matière commerciale, présentée au nom de M. Alexandre Millerand, Président de la République française, par M. Aristide Briand, président du conseil, ministre des affaires étrangères . . ., " *Documents parlementaires – Sénat* (1921), app. 566, at 1019

"Proposition de loi sur l'arbitrage commercial dans les rapports internationaux, présentée par M. Clémentel, sénateur," *Documents parlementaires – Sénat* (1923), app. 168, at 134

"Scrutin sur l'article unique de la proposition de loi relative à la clause compromissoire en matière commerciale," *Annales du Sénat*, December 8, 1925, at 144

## G Archives and Records of the International Chamber of Commerce

### Arbitration Reports

Arbitration Report No. 3, *Supplement to Journal of the International Chamber of Commerce*, July 1924

Arbitration Report No. 4, *Supplement to Journal of the International Chamber of Commerce*, April 1925

Arbitration Report No. 5, *Supplement to Journal of the International Chamber of Commerce*, December 1925

Arbitration Report No. 6, *Supplement to Journal of the International Chamber of Commerce*, June 1926

Arbitration Report No. 7, *Supplement to Journal of the International Chamber of Commerce*, January 1927

Arbitration Report No. 8, *Supplement to Journal of the International Chamber of Commerce*, July 1927

### Brochures[8]

*Proceedings: Organization Meeting of the International Chamber of Commerce, Paris, France, June 23 to 30, 1920* (Paris: ICC International Headquarters, 1920)

*Résolutions adoptées et résolutions renvoyées pour examen au Conseil d'Administration par la Chambre de Commerce Internationale à son Congrès Constitutif tenu à Paris du 23 au 30 juin 1920* (Paris: ICC International Headquarters, 1920)

*Resolutions Adopted* [London Congress] (Paris: ICC International Headquarters, 1921)

*Commercial Arbitration*, Brochure No. 13 (Paris: ICC International Headquarters, 1921)

*Constitution and Rules of Procedure*, Brochure No. 17 (Paris: ICC International Headquarters, 1920)

*Proceedings of the First Congress*, Brochure No. 18 (Paris: ICC International Headquarters, n.d.)

*Select Committees: List of Members*, Brochure No. 19 (Paris: ICC International Headquarters, n.d.)

*The Organization of the International Chamber of Commerce*, Brochure No. 20 (Paris: ICC International Headquarters, 1922)

[8] Some of these pamphlets were numbered, while others were unnumbered leaflets.

*Rules of Conciliation (Good Offices) and Arbitration (Fourth Edition)*, Brochure No. 21 (Paris: ICC International Headquarters, n.d.)

*Inauguration of the Court of Commercial Arbitration: January 19th 1923*, Brochure No. 22 (Paris: ICC International Headquarters, 1923)

*Programme of the Rome Congress and Resolutions*, Brochure No. 23 (Paris: ICC International Headquarters, 1923)

*Resolutions Adopted at the Second Congress (Rome, March 1923)*, Brochure No. 31 (Paris: ICC International Headquarters, 1923)

*Proceedings of the Second Congress*, Brochure No. 32 (Paris: ICC International Headquarters, 1923)

*Proceedings of the Third Congress of the ICC (Brussels, 21–27 June 1925)* (Paris: ICC International Headquarters, 1925)

*Resolutions Passed at the Third Congress*, Brochure No. 40 (Paris: ICC International Headquarters, 1925)

*Constitution and Rules of Procedure (1925 Edition)*, Brochure No. 41 (Paris: ICC International Headquarters, 1925)

*Arbitration. Revision of the Rules of Conciliation and Arbitration*, Brochure No. 50 (Paris: ICC International Headquarters, 1927)

*Exequatur (Enforcement of Foreign Judgments)*, Brochure No. 51 (Paris: ICC International Headquarters, 1927)

*Resolutions Passed at the Stockholm Congress*, Brochure No. 60 (Paris: ICC International Headquarters, 1927)

*Commercial Arbitration under Swiss Law*, Brochure No. 61 (Paris: ICC International Headquarters, 1927)

*Commercial Arbitration under Italian Law*, Brochure No. 62 (Paris: ICC International Headquarters, 1927)

*Commercial Arbitration under Dutch Law*, Brochure No. 63 (Paris: ICC International Headquarters, 1927) (with W. L. P. A. Molengraaff)

*Commercial Arbitration under French Law*, Brochure No. 65 (Paris: ICC International Headquarters, 1927) (with Jean Duchenois)

*Commercial Arbitration under German Law*, Brochure No. 72 (Paris: ICC International Headquarters, 1930) (with the German National Committee of the International Chamber of Commerce)

*Resolutions Adopted by the Washington Congress*, Brochure No. 77 (Paris: ICC International Headquarters, 1931)

*Services rendus par le système d'arbitrage de la Chambre de commerce internationale* (Paris: ICC Headquarters, 1931), https://gallica.bnf.fr/ark:/12148/bpt6k1412857k.image

*Constitution and Rules of Procedure (1932 Edition)*, Brochure No. 79 (Paris: ICC International Headquarters, 1932)

*Resolutions Adopted by the Seventh Congress of the ICC* [Vienna], Brochure No. 83 (Paris: ICC International Headquarters, 1933)

*Commercial Arbitration under Belgian Law*, Brochure No. 88 (Paris: ICC International Headquarters, 1934) (with E. Huysmans)

*Resolutions Adopted by the Eighth Congress of the ICC* [Paris], Brochure No. 89 (Paris: ICC International Headquarters, 1935)

*Arbitrage Commercial International : Conseils pratiques* (Paris: ICC International Headquarters, 1935)

*Commercial Arbitration under British Law (England and Wales, Scotland and Northern Ireland)*, Brochure No. 91 (Paris: ICC International Headquarters, 1936) (with J. E. James)

*Resolutions Adopted by the Ninth Congress of the ICC* [Berlin], Brochure No. 98 (Paris: ICC International Headquarters, 1937)

*Resolutions Adopted by the Tenth Congress of the ICC* [Copenhagen], Brochure No. 100 (Paris: ICC International Headquarters, 1939)

*Revised Constitution of the ICC*, Brochure No. 110 (Paris: ICC International Headquarters, 1945)

*Resolutions Adopted by the Eleventh Congress of the ICC* [Montreux], Brochure No. 117 (Paris: ICC International Headquarters, 1947)

*Constitution of the International Chamber of Commerce*, Brochure No. 119 (Paris: ICC International Headquarters, 1947)

*Commercial Arbitration under Swedish Law*, Brochure No. 122 (Paris: ICC International Headquarters, 1947) (with Swedish National Committee of the International Chamber of Commerce)

*A Charter for World Trade. Report to the United Nations Conference on Trade and Employment*, Brochure No. 124 (Paris: ICC International Headquarters, 1947)

*ICC Arbitration and National Law: Draft Resolution and Report*, Brochure No. 137 (Paris: ICC International Headquarters, 1949)

*Resolutions Adopted at the Twelfth Congress of the ICC* [Quebec], Brochure No. 141 (Paris: ICC International Headquarters, 1949)

*International Commercial Arbitration and Freedom of Contract*, Brochure No. 160 (Paris: ICC International Headquarters, 1951)

*Resolutions Adopted at the Thirteenth Congress of the ICC* [Lisbon], Brochure No. 161 (Paris: ICC International Headquarters, 1951)

*Enforcement of International Arbitral Awards: Report and Preliminary Draft Convention Adopted by the Committee on International Commercial Arbitration at its Meeting on 13th March 1953*, Brochure No. 174 (Paris: ICC International Headquarters, 1953)

*Resolutions of the Fourteenth Congress of the ICC* [Vienna], Brochure No. 175 (Paris: ICC International Headquarters, 1953)

*Resolutions of the Fifteenth Congress* [Tokyo], Brochure No. 186 (Paris: ICC International Headquarters, 1955)

*Sixteenth Congress of the ICC: Statements and Resolutions*, Brochure No. 193 (Paris: ICC International Headquarters, 1957)

*Seventeenth Congress of the ICC: Statements and Resolutions*, Brochure No. 207 (Paris: ICC International Headquarters, 1959)

*World Peace through World Trade*, Brochure No. 342 (Paris: ICC International Headquarters, 1979) (with Nigel Blackburn)

*60 Years of ICC Arbitration: A Look at the Future*, ICC Publication No. 412 (Paris: ICC International Headquarters, 1984)

## *ICC News*

*ICC News*, vol. 20, no. 3 (April 1954), 3

"International Commercial Arbitration," special issue, *ICC News*, 24, no. 3 (1958)

"Arbitration and the ICC," *ICC News*, 29, no. 3 (1958), 2

## *Journal of the International Chamber of Commerce*

"International Commercial Arbitration," *Journal of the International Chamber of Commerce*, no. 1 (July 1924), 3

"Owen D. Young, Étienne Clémentel, Alberto Pirelli," *Journal of the International Chamber of Commerce*, no. 2 (October 1924), 2–6

Oliver Bodington, "Is a General Arbitration Clause Valid in England When One of the Parties Is a Foreigner?," *Journal of the International Chamber of Commerce*, no. 2 (October 1924), 8

"Court of Arbitration," *Journal of the International Chamber of Commerce*, no. 4 (April 1925), 10

"Walter Leaf, Willis H. Booth," *Journal of the International Chamber of Commerce*, nos. 5–6 (July–October 1925), 1–5

"Commercial Arbitration," *Journal of the International Chamber of Commerce*, nos. 5–6 (July–October 1925), 13–14

"International Commercial Arbitration," *Journal of the International Chamber of Commerce*, no. 7 (December 1925), 14–15

"Administrative Bodies and Committees of the ICC," *Journal of the International Chamber of Commerce*, no. 9 (April 1926), 8–11

"Enforcement of Judgments and Legal Decisions. Convention between Belgium and the Netherlands," *Journal of the International Chamber of Commerce*, no. 10 (June–July 1926), 12–13

"Inauguration of New Building," *Journal of the International Chamber of Commerce*, no. 13 (March–April 1927), 4–8

"The New Rules of Conciliation and Arbitration," *Journal of the International Chamber of Commerce*, no. 16 (January 1928), 11

"Commercial Arbitration and the League of Nations," *Journal of the International Chamber of Commerce*, no. 17 (May 1928), 20

"Basil Miles (1877–1928)," *Journal of the International Chamber of Commerce*, no. 18 (July 1928), 3

"International Commercial Arbitration," *Journal of the International Chamber of Commerce*, no. 19 (October 1928), 11

## *World Trade / L'Économie internationale*[9]

Arnaud, René "Arbitration in the International Chamber of Commerce," *World Trade*, 1, no. 1 (January 1929), 116–30

"Court of Arbitration," *World Trade*, 1, no. 2 (April 1929), 320

Arnaud, René, "Report on the Work of the Court of Arbitration," *World Trade*, 1, no. 3 (July 1929), 492–98

"Classification of Countries in Order of the Importance of Their Membership to the ICC," *World Trade*, 1, no. 3 (July 1929), 516

Arnaud, René, "England and International Arbitration," *World Trade*, 2, no. 5 (January 1930), 33–91

Arnaud, René, "Practical Hints of International Commercial Arbitration," *World Trade*, 2, no. 8 (October 1930), 381–91

Marx, Robert, "The Court of Arbitration of the International Chamber of Commerce: Revision of the Rules," *World Trade*, 3, no. 11 (August 1931), 301–8

"To Avoid Foreign Lawsuits," *World Trade*, 4, no. 2 (January 1932), 6

"Publishing Arbitration Awards," *World Trade*, 4, no. 3 (February 1932), 10

"Publication of Arbitration Awards," *World Trade*, 4, no. 8 (July–August 1932), 5

"Arbitration Awards Concerning Sterling Contracts" [ICC Cases Nos. 513, 396, and 505], *World Trade*, 4, no. 9 (October 1932), 10–11

"A Case of Forged Letters of Credit" [ICC Case No. 143], *World Trade*, vol. IV, no. 10 (November 1932), 11–15

"A Recent Award Concerning Sterling Contracts" [ICC Case No. 519], *World Trade*, 4, no. 11 (December 1932), 11

"Income Tax Deductions on British Patent Royalties" [ICC Case No. 144], *World Trade*, 5, no. 1 (January 1933), 2

"Determining the Law Applicable to an International Contract," *World Trade*, 5, no. 3 (March 1933), 9

"The Application of Arbitration Clauses in France," *World Trade*, 5, no. 4 (April 1933), 9

[9] Articles published anonymously in *World Trade* are listed by their title.

"A Recent Decision in a Sterling Contract Dispute" [ICC Case No. 536], *World Trade*, 5, no. 5 (May 1933), 11

"An Agent's Claim to Commission on Business Effected outside His Area" [ICC Case No. 304], *World Trade*, 5, no. 6 (June 1933), 7

Bagge, Algot, "An Amended Edition of the Rules of Conciliation and Arbitration of the International Chamber of Commerce," *World Trade*, 6, no. 1 (January 1934), 11

"The Enforcement of Foreign Arbitral Awards: A Franco-Italian Convention," *World Trade*, 6, no. 2 (February 1934), 9–10

"Insurance and ICC Arbitration," *World Trade*, 6, no. 3 (March 1934), 9

"A Selection of ICC Publications," *World Trade*, 6, no. 4 (April 1934), 11

"A Dispute Arising Out of a Contract between a Principal and His Agent" [ICC Case No. 568], *World Trade*, 6, no. 8 (October 1934), 6–7

"The Validity of Tacit Acceptance" [ICC Case No. 543], *World Trade*, 6, no. 10 (December 1934), 7

"The Arbitration Court of the ICC," *World Trade*, 7, no. 4 (April 1935), 2

"The Settlement of International Commercial Disputes by the Arbitration of the International Chamber of Commerce," *World Trade*, 7, nos. 7–8 (July–August 1935), 24

"Practical Hints on International Commercial Arbitration," *World Trade*, 7, no. 9 (October–November 1935), 4–5

"Court of Arbitration," *World Trade*, 8, no. 4 (April 1936), 7

"Commercial Arbitration," *World Trade*, 8, no. 6 (June 1936), 9

"Commercial Arbitration," *World Trade*, 8, no. 10 (December 1936), 4

"Validity of Arbitration Clause in Sweden: Tacit Acceptance Held to Be Binding," *World Trade*, 9, no. 1 (January 1937), 4

"Étienne Clémentel," *World Trade*, 9, nos. 3–4 (March–April 1937), 1–2

Roché, Georges, "Atlantic City: Birthplace of the International Chamber," *World Trade*, 9, nos. 3–4 (March–April 1937), 2–3

"Commercial Arbitration," *World Trade*, 9, no. 5 (May 1937), 5

"International Commercial Arbitration," *World Trade*, 9, nos. 7–8 (July–August 1937), 38–40

Bagge, Algot, "The Conciliation Procedure of the International Chamber of Commerce: An Inexpensive and Effective Means of Settling Commercial Disputes," *World Trade*, 10, no. 2 (April 1938), 22–23

"A Biography of Étienne Clémentel," *World Trade*, 10, no. 3 (June 1938), 24

Boissier, André, "International Commercial Arbitration: Twenty Years of Growth," *World Trade*, 11, no. 2 (April 1939), 64–69

"Amendments to the I.C.C.'s Rules of Conciliation and Arbitration," *World Trade*, 11, no. 4 (August 1939), 47–48

"International Commercial Arbitration," *World Trade*, 13, no. 2 (August 1947), 10

## H Clémentel Papers[10]

"Discours et toasts de Clémentel. 1911–1915," 5 J art. 3
"Activité de Clémentel au Sénat de 1920 à 1924. 1920–1924," 5 J art. 21
"Activité de Clémentel au Sénat de 1925 à 1932. 1925–1932," 5 J art. 22
"Chambre de commerce internationale (C.C.I.). 1919–1923," 5 J art. 92
"Chambre de commerce internationale (C.C.I.). 1924–1935," 5 J art. 93
"Projets d'ouvrages sur l'économie. [vers 1920] – [vers 1935]," 5 J art. 97
"Collection de lettres reçues de personnalités nationales et internationales. 1915–1940," 5 J art. 105
"La mort d'Étienne Clémentel: coupures de presse, condoléances. 1936–1937," 5 J art. 112
"La mort d'Étienne Clémentel: condoléances. 1936–1937," 5 J art. 113

## I Proceedings of Meetings

Bergasse, Nicolas, "Rapport par M. Bergasse sur l'organisation du pouvoir judiciaire, lors de la séance du 17 août 1789," in Jérôme Mavidal and Emile Laurent (eds.), *Archives parlementaires de 1787 à 1860 – Première série (1787–1799)*, vol. 8 (Paris: Librairie Administrative P. Dupont, 1875), 440–50

Chamber of Commerce of the State of New York, *International Arbitration of Individual Commercial Disputes: Tentative Plan Suggested by the Chamber of Commerce of the State of New York* (New York: Chamber of Commerce of the State of New York, 1914)

*Conférence sur l'arbitrage commercial international: Compte rendu des séances destiné aux Membres de la Conférence* (June 13–15, 1946)

*Fifth International Congress of Chambers of Commerce and Commercial and Industrial Associations* (Boston: Boston Chamber of Commerce, 1912)

*International Trade Conference* (Chamber of Commerce of the United States of America, 1919)

Louis-Dreyfus, Louis, "La clause compromissoire," *Courrier du commerce (Organe national du commerce, de l'agriculture, de l'industrie et maritime)*, July 7, 1926 (no. 5.204), July 10, 1926 (no. 5.205), July 14, 1926 (no. 5.206)[11]

*La clause compromissoire et l'arbitrage commercial: Conférence faite par M. Louis Louis-Dreyfus à Troyes, le 27 juin 1927* (Paris: Imprimerie de publications périodiques, 1927)

[10] The Clémentel papers are kept in the Archives départementales du Puy-de-Dôme in Clermont-Ferrand, France. They are listed here in order of their reference numbers.

[11] Louis-Dreyfus's article appeared in three consecutive issues of *Courrier du commerce*. See Chapter 4, Section 4.3.2 (and n. 66).

Mallarmé, Claude-Joseph, "Discours prononcé par M. Mallarmé, orateur du Tribunat, dans la séance du Corps législatif du 29 avril 1806, pour motiver le vœu d'adoption émis par la section de législation du Tribunat" (April 26, 1806), in Jean-Guillaume Locré, *La législation civile, commerciale et criminelle de la France, ou commentaire et complément des codes français*, vol. 23 (Paris: Treuttel et Würtz, 1830), 433

"Proceedings of the Twelfth Council Meeting," ICC Doc. No. 1214 (Paris, July 20, 1923)

"Proceedings of the Thirteenth Meeting of the Council" (Paris, November 9, 1923),

"Procès-verbaux du Conseil d'État: Séance du 25 prairial an XIII (14 juin 1805), tenue sous la présidence de M. L'Archichancelier," in Jean-Guillaume Locré, *La législation civile, commerciale et criminelle de la France, ou commentaire et complément des codes français*, vol. 23 (Paris: Treuttel et Würtz, 1830)

*Réimpression de l'Ancien Moniteur depuis la réunion des États-Généraux jusqu'au Consulat (Mai 1789–Novembre 1799)*, vol. 5 (Paris: Plon Frères, 1847)

"Séance de Groupe du Mardi 28 Juin 1927, Présidence de M. Thor Carlander, assisté du Dr. E. Leslie Burgin"

United Nations Economic and Social Council (ECOSOC), *Report of the Committee on the Enforcement of International Arbitral Awards*, UN Doc. E/2704, March 28, 1955

## *J Newspaper Articles*[12]

"A propos des traités d'arbitrage," *Journal des débats politiques et littéraires*, January 27, 1904, 1

"Adopts World Court for Trade Disputes. International Chamber of Commerce Plan to Be Put in Effect at Once," *New York Times*, May 27, 1922[13]

"Commerce Chamber to Discuss Prices. Delegates to Go to Paris," *New York Times*, April 26, 1920

"De l'arbitrage," *Le Matin*, August 15, 1905, 2

"Delegates Sail for Commerce Meeting," *New York Times*, May 24, 1920

"Form World Court for Arbitration of Trade Disputes. United States and 27 Other Nations to Be Represented on International Tribunal," *New York Times*, November 6, 1922

"Frances Kellor, 78, Arbitration Aide," *New York Times*, January 5, 1952

[12] Articles published anonymously are listed by their title.

[13] The titles of *New York Times* articles are reproduced verbatim.

Geouffre de La Pradelle, Raymond de, "L'Egypte a-t-elle violé le droit international?," *Le Monde*, September 27, 1956

Goldman, Berthold, "La Compagnie de Suez, société internationale," *Le Monde*, 4 October 1956

"Inauguration de la Chambre de commerce internationale," *Le Temps*, June 30, 1920, 4

"May be a World Centre: Atlantic City Hopes to be Permanent Home of Business League," *New York Times*, October 27, 1919

"Memorials. George Loveland Ridgeway," *Princeton Alumni Weekly*, November 26, 1968, 21

"Ready for New Trade Body. Plans Drawn for First Meeting of International Chamber of Commerce," *New York Times*, May 22, 1920

"Steel Men Coming to Trade Meeting," *New York Times*, October 12, 1919

"To Start World's Business League. Committee of Trade Leaders Adopts Plan for International Chamber of Commerce," *New York Times*, October 22, 1919

"Une mise au point de la Compagnie universelle," *Le Monde*, October 10, 1956

"Vers une politique économique interalliée," *Le Matin*, July 25, 1919, 1

"Wants a Business League for World. Eugène Schneider of Creusot Works Urges a Great Chamber of Commerce," *New York Times*, October 15, 1919

## 2 Secondary Sources

Abi-Saab, Georges, "De l'arbitrage dans ses rapports avec la justice internationale," in Christian Dominicé, Robert Patry, and Claude Reymond (eds.), *Études de droit international en l'honneur de Pierre Lalive* (Basel: Helbing & Lichtenhahn, 1993), 377–84

Adams, John, "Clive M. Schmitthoff (1903–1990)," in Jack Beatson and Reinhard Zimmermann (eds.), *Jurists Uprooted: German-Speaking Emigré Lawyers in Twentieth Century Britain* (Oxford: Oxford University Press, 2004), 367–80

Aksen, Gerald, "A Dozen Differences in International Arbitration in the Last Half-Century," in *Liber amicorum en l'honneur de William Laurence Craig* (Paris: LexisNexis, 2016), 3–15

"Scholar, Practitioner, Internationalist: Dr. Domke Remembered," *New York University Journal of International Law and Politics*, 13 (1981), 421–23

Aksen, Gerald, Karl-Heinz Böckstiegel, Michael J. Mustill, Paolo Michele Patocchi, and Anne Marie Whitesell (eds.), *Global Reflections on International Law, Commerce and Dispute Resolution: Liber Amicorum in Honour of Robert Briner*, ICC Publication No. 693 (Paris: ICC Publishing, 2005)

Ancel, Bertrand, *Eléments d'histoire du droit international privé* (Paris: Editions Panthéon-Assas, 2017)

Anghie, Antony, *Imperialism, Sovereignty and the Making of International Law* (Cambridge: Cambridge University Press, 2004)

Arizzoli, Louise, "Autochromes by Étienne Clémentel (1864–1936): An Enlightened Approach to Early Color Photography," *Études photographiques*, 35 (2017), http://journals.openedition.org/etudesphotographiques/3613

"Clémentel photographe: les autochromes," in Marie-Christine Kessler and Guy Rousseau (eds.), *Étienne Clémentel: Politique et action publique sous la Troisième République* (Brussels: Peter Lang, 2018), 97–105

Armitage, David, *Foundations of Modern International Thought* (Cambridge: Cambridge University Press, 2013)

"The International Turn in Intellectual History," in Darrin McMahon and Samuel Moyn (eds.), *Rethinking Modern European Intellectual History* (New York: Oxford University Press, 2014), 232–52

Armitage, David and Jo Guldi, *The History Manifesto* (Cambridge: Cambridge University Press, 2014)

"The Return of the *Longue Durée*: An Anglo-American Perspective," *Annales: Histoire, Sciences Sociales*, 70 (2015), 289–318

Arnaud, René, "Conciliation et arbitrage," in *Conférence sur l'arbitrage commercial international. Compte rendu des séances destiné aux Membres de la Conférence (June 13–15, 1946)*, 35–37

"Le nouveau Règlement de conciliation et d'arbitrage de la Chambre de commerce internationale," *Journal du droit international*, (1928), 340–46

Aspremont, Jean d', *Epistemic Forces in International Law: Foundational Doctrines and Techniques of International Legal Argumentation* (Cheltenham: Edward Elgar, 2015)

Audit, Matthias, Sylvain Bollée, and Pierre Callé, *Droit du commerce international et des investissements étrangers*, 2nd ed. (Paris: LGDJ, 2016)

Audren, Frédéric, Anne-Sophie Chambost, and Jean-Louis Halpérin, *Histoires contemporaines du droit* (Paris: Dalloz, 2020)

Aurillac, Michel, "La Cour internationale d'arbitrage de la CCI régulatrice de la mondialisation," in Gerald Aksen, Karl-Heinz Böckstiegel, Michael J. Mustill, Paolo Michele Patocchi, and Anne Marie Whitesell (eds.), *Global Reflections on International Law, Commerce and Dispute Resolution: Liber Amicorum in Honour of Robert Briner* (Paris: ICC Publishing, 2005)

Austin, John, *The Province of Jurisprudence Determined* (London: John Murray, 1832)

Badel, Laurence, *Un milieu libéral et européen: le grand commerce français 1925–1948* (Vincennes: Institut de la gestion publique et du développement économique, Comité pour l'histoire économique et financière de la France, 1999)

Badinter, Robert, "Formal Opening," in *60 Years of ICC Arbitration: A Look at the Future* (Paris: ICC Publishing, 1984)

Bagge, Algot, "La situation générale de l'arbitrage commercial international à la fin de la guerre," in *Conférence sur l'arbitrage commercial international: Compte rendu des séances destiné aux Membres de la Conférence (June 13–15, 1946)*, 1–9

Baker, John, "Courts of Piepowder," in *The Oxford History of the Laws of England* (Oxford: Oxford University Press, 2003), 6 (1483–1558), 312–14

"The Law Merchant and the Common Law before 1700," *Cambridge Law Journal*, 38 (1979), 295–322

Bart, Jean, "La *lex mercatoria* au Moyen Age: mythe ou réalité?," in Charles Leben, Eric Loquin, and Mahmoud Salem (eds.), *Souveraineté étatique et marchés internationaux à la fin du 20ème siècle: À propos de 30 ans de recherche du CREDIMI; Mélanges en l'honneur de Philippe Kahn* (Dijon: Litec-CREDIMI, 2000), 9–22

Barty-King, Hugh, *Food for Man and Beast: The Story of the London Corn Trade Association, the London Cattle Food Trade Association, and the Grain and Feed Trade Association, 1878–1978* (London: Hutchinson Benham, 1978)

Batiffol, Henri, "Allocution de M. le Professeur Henri Batiffol, Président du Congrès," in *Travaux du Congrès International de l'Arbitrage (Paris, 11, 12, 13 mai 1961)*, special issue, *Revue de l'arbitrage*, 1961, 41–44

"Le Comité Français de l'Arbitrage," *Revue de l'arbitrage*, (1955), 2–3

Becker Lorca, Arnulf, "Eurocentrism in the History of International Law," in Bardo Fassbender and Anne Peters (eds.), *The Oxford Handbook of the History of International Law* (Oxford: Oxford University Press, 2012), 1034–57

*Mestizo International Law: A Global Intellectual History 1842–1933* (Cambridge: Cambridge University Press, 2015)

Ben Hamida, Walid, "L'arbitrage transnational unilatéral: Réflexions sur une procédure réservée à l'initiative d'une personne privée contre une personne publique" (PhD diss., Université Panthéon-Assas, 2003)

Berger, Klaus Peter, *The Creeping Codification of the New Lex Mercatoria*, 2nd ed. (The Hague: Kluwer Law International, 2010)

*TransLex-Principles with Commentary* (Cologne: Center for Transnational Law, 2019)

Berman, Frank, "Book Report: *The History of ICSID* by Antonio R Parra," *ICSID Review – Foreign Investment Law Journal*, 28 (2013), 144–51

Bernard, Nadine, "Henri La Fontaine (1854–1943) ou la paix par le droit," *Revue belge de droit international*, 28 (1995), 342–56

Bernardini, Piero, Sébastien Besson, Matthieu de Boisséson, and Jean-Denis Bredin (eds.), *Liber amicorum Claude Reymond: Autour de l'arbitrage* (Paris: LexisNexis/Litec, 2004)

Bernstein, Lisa, "Private Commercial Law in the Cotton Industry: Creating Cooperation through Rules, Norms, and Institutions," *Michigan Law Review*, 99 (2001), 1724–90

Besson, Sébastien and Luc Pittet, "La reconnaissance à l'étranger d'une sentence annulée dans son Etat d'origine: Réflexions à la suite de l'affaire *Hilmarton*," *ASA Bulletin*, 16 (1998), 498–527

Bewes, Wyndham, *The Romance of the Law Merchant: Being an Introduction to the Study of International and Commercial Law; With Some Account of the Commerce and Fairs of the Middle Ages* (London: Sweet & Maxwell, 1923)

Bianchi, Andrea, "Epistemic Communities in International Arbitration," in Thomas Schultz and Frederico Ortino (eds.), *The Oxford Handbook of International Arbitration* (Oxford: Oxford University Press, 2020), 569–90

Bingham, Tom, "Alabama Arbitration," in Rüdiger Wolfrum (ed.), *The Max Planck Encyclopedia of Public International Law* (Oxford: Oxford University Press, 2006)

"The *Alabama* Claims Arbitration," *International and Comparative Law Quarterly*, 54 (2005), 1–25

*Lives of the Law: Selected Essays and Speeches: 2000–2010* (Oxford: Oxford University Press, 2011)

Bischoff, Jean-Marc, "*In Memoriam*: Jean-Louis Bismuth, Berthold Goldman," *Travaux du Comité français de droit international privé*, 11 (1994), 143–44

Blackaby, Nigel, Constantine Partasides, Alan Redfern, and Martin Hunter, *Redfern and Hunter on International Arbitration*, 6th ed. (Oxford: Oxford University Press, 2015)

Blackstone, William, *Commentaries on the Laws of England; Book III: Of Private Wrongs*, ed. Thomas Gallanis (Oxford: Oxford University Press, 2016)

Bloch, Marc, *Apologie pour l'histoire ou métier d'historien* (Paris: Armand Colin, 2018)

Boisséson, Matthieu de, *Le droit français de l'arbitrage interne et international* (Paris: Joly, 1990)

Boisson de Chazournes, Laurence, and Danio Campanelli, "Mixed Commissions," *Max Planck Encyclopedia of Public International Law* (December 2006)

Bolard, Georges, "Motulsky Henri, 1905-1971," in Loïc Cadiet (ed.), *Dictionnaire de la justice* (Paris: Presses Universitaires de France, 2004), 915–17

"Témoignages," "Qu'est devenue la pensée de Motulsky?," *Procédures*, 18 (2012), 6–7

Bollée, Sylvain, *Les méthodes du droit international privé à l'épreuve des sentences arbitrales* (Paris: Economica, 2004)

Bonnitcha, Jonathan, Lauge Poulsen, and Michael Waibel, *The Political Economy of the Investment Treaty Regime* (Oxford: Oxford University Press, 2017)

Born, Gary, *International Commercial Arbitration*, 2nd ed. (The Hague: Kluwer Law International, 2014)

*International Commercial Arbitration: Cases and Materials*, 2nd ed. (The Hague: Kluwer Law International, 2015)

*International Commercial Arbitration: Commentary and Materials*, 2nd ed. (The Hague: Kluwer Law International, 2001)

Boucaron-Nardetto, Magali, *Le principe compétence-compétence en droit de l'arbitrage* (Presses Universitaires d'Aix-Marseille, 2013)

Bourdieu, Pierre, "The Force of Law: Toward a Sociology of the Juridical Field," trans. Richard Terdiman, *The Hastings Law Journal*, 38 (1987), 805–53

"Foreword," in Yves Dezalay and Bryant Garth, *Dealing in Virtue: International Commercial Arbitration and the Construction of a Transnational Legal Order* (Chicago: Chicago University Press, 1996), vii–viii

"Foreword," in Yves Dezalay and David Sugarman, trans. Berenice Cleeve and Sol Picciotto (eds.), *Professional Competition and Professional Power: Lawyers, Accountants and the Social Construction of Markets* (London: Routledge, 1995), x–xiii

Bourdieu, Pierre, and Loïc Wacquant, *An Invitation to Reflexive Sociology* (Chicago: University of Chicago Press, 1992)

Brachet, Paul, *De l'exécution internationale des sentences (étude de droit comparé et de droit international privé)* (Paris: Rousseau, 1928)

Braudel, Fernand, *Civilization and Capitalism: 15th–18th Century*, vol. 2, *The Wheels of Commerce*, trans. Siân Reynolds (Berkeley: University of California Press, 1992 [1979])

"Histoire et Sciences sociales: La longue durée," *Annales: Economies, Sociétés, Civilisations*, 13 (1958), 725–53; trans. as Braudel, "History and the Social Sciences," in Braudel, *On History*, trans. Sarah Matthews (University of Chicago Press, 1982), 25–54

"Preface to the First Edition" (1946), in *The Mediterranean and the Mediterranean World in the Age of Phillip II*, trans. Siân Reynolds (Berkeley: University of California Press, 1995), 17–22

Bredin, Jean-Denis, "Berthold Goldman, toujours vivant," in Philippe Fouchard and Louis Vogel (eds.), *L'actualité de la pensée de Berthold Goldman: Droit commercial international et européen* (Paris: Editions Panthéon-Assas, 2004), 15–18

"La loi du juge," in Philippe Fouchard, Philippe Kahn, and Antoine Lyon-Caen (eds.), *Le droit des relations économiques internationales: Études offertes à Berthold Goldman* (Paris: Litec, 1982), 15–27

Brekoulakis, Stavros, "International Arbitration Scholarship and the Concept of Arbitration Law," *Fordham International Law Journal*, 36 (2013), 745–87

Brierly, James, *Brierly's Law of Nations: An Introduction to the Role of International Law in International Relations* (Oxford: Oxford University Press, 2012)

Briner, Robert, and Virginia Hamilton, "The History and General Purpose of the Convention. The Creation of an International Standard to Ensure the Effectiveness of Arbitration Agreements and Foreign Arbitral Awards," in Emmanuel Gaillard and Domenico di Pietro (eds.), *Enforcement of Arbitration Agreements and International Arbitral Awards: The New York Convention in Practice* (London: Cameron May, 2008), 3–36

Brinton, Jasper, *The Mixed Courts of Egypt* (New Haven: Yale University Press, 1930)

Brotóns, Antonio Remiro, "La reconnaissance et l'exécution des sentences arbitrales étrangères," *Collected Courses of the Hague Academy of International Law*, vol. 184 (Leiden: Brill/Nijhoff, 1984)

Brower, Charles, "Arbitration," in Rüdiger Wolfrum (ed.), *The Max Planck Encyclopedia of Public International Law* (Oxford: Oxford University Press, 2007)

"The Global Court: The Internationalization of Commercial Adjudication and Arbitration," *University of Baltimore Law Review*, 26 (1996), 9–13

Brown, Chester, and Kate Miles (eds.), *Evolution in Investment Treaty Law and Arbitration* (Cambridge: Cambridge University Press, 2011)

Cadiet, Loïc, "Motulsky Henri," in Patrick Arabeyre, Jean-Louis Halpérin, and Jacques Krynen (eds.), *Dictionnaire historique des juristes français, XII–XXe siècle*, 2nd ed. (Paris: Presses Universitaires de France, 2015), 756–57

Camara, Fatou, and Abdoullah Cissé, "Arbitrage et médiation dans les cultures juridiques négro-africaines: Entre la prédisposition à dénouer et la mission de trancher," *Revue de l'arbitrage*, 2009, 285–316

Canivet, Guy, "Accueil," in "Journée d'hommage et d'études à la mémoire de Philippe Fouchard, Paris, 11 mars 2005," *Revue de l'arbitrage*, 2005, 243–45

Carabiber, Charles, "L'arbitrage international," *Travaux du Comité français de droit international privé (1951–1954)*, 14–15 (1955), 61–83

"Les centres d'arbitrage: leur rôle dans le développement de l'arbitrage," *Revue de l'arbitrage*, 1955, 4–7

Carbonneau, Thomas (ed.), Lex Mercatoria *and Arbitration: A Discussion of the New Law Merchant*, 2nd ed. (Yonkers: Juris and Kluwer Law International, 1988)

Caron, David, "War and International Adjudication: Reflections on the 1899 Peace Conference," *American Journal of International Law*, 94 (2000), 4–30

Caron, David, and Esmé Shirlow, "Dissecting Backlash: The Unarticulated Causes of Backlash and Its Unintended Consequences," in Andreas Follesdal and Geir Ulfstein (eds.), *The Judicialization of International Law: A Mixed Blessing?* (Oxford: Oxford University Press, 2018), 159–82

Caron, David, Stephan Schill, Abby Smutny, and Epaminontas Triantafilou (eds.), *Practising Virtue: Inside International Arbitration* (Oxford: Oxford University Press, 2015)

Castoriadis, Cornelius, *The Imaginary Institution of Society*, trans. Kathleen Blamey (Cambridge, MA: MIT Press, 1987 [1975])

Caumières, Philippe, *Castoriadis: Le projet d'autonomie* (Paris: Michalon, 2015)

Cavaré, Louis, *Le droit international public positif*, vol. 2, *Les modalités des relations juridiques internationales, les compétences respectives des États* (Paris: Pedone, 1962)

Centre de recherche sur le droit des investissements et des marchés internationaux (CREDIMI), "Ecole de Nice/Ecole de Dijon," *Revue internationale de droit économique*, 27 (2013), 459–473

*Les Euro-obligations - Eurobonds* (Paris: Librairies techniques, 1972)

*Investissements étrangers et arbitrages entre Etats et personnes privées: La Convention de la B.I.R.D. du 18 mars 1965* (Paris: Pedone, 1969)

Certeau, Michel de, *The Writing of History*, trans. Tom Conley (New York: Columbia University Press, 1988)

Chamber of Commerce of the United States, *Arbitration for Disputes in Trade between the United States and the Argentine Republic* (Chamber of Commerce of the United States, 1919)

Chambre de commerce internationale, *Hommage à Frédéric Eisemann: Liber amicorum* (Paris: ICC Publication No. 321, 1978)

Chattaway, Chris, "Arbitration in the Foreign Corn Trade in London," *Economic Journal*, 17 (1907), 428–31

Chatriot, Alain, *La politique du blé: Crises et régulation d'un marché dans la France de l'entre-deux-guerres* (Paris: Institut de la gestion publique et du développement économique, Comité pour l'histoire économique et financière de la France, 2016)

Cheatham, Elliott, Wolfgang Friedmann, Walter Gellhorn, Philip Jessup, Willis Reese, and Schuyler Wallace, "Arthur Nussbaum: A Tribute," *Columbia Law Review*, 57 (1957), 1–7

Cheng, Chia-Jui, "Biography," in Chia-Jui Cheng (ed.), *Clive M. Schmitthoff's Select Essays on International Trade Law* (London: Martinus Nijhoff/ Graham & Trotman, 1988), xiii–xvi

Claringbould, J. E. , "La Chambre de commerce internationale et son Comité national néerlandais," in *Grotius, Annuaire International pour l'année 1926* (The Hague: Martinus Nijhoff, 1926), 27–42

Clay, Thomas, "Arbitre," in Loïc Cadiet (ed.), *Dictionnaire de la justice* (Paris: Presses Universitaires de France, 2004), 58–61

*L'arbitre* (Paris: Dalloz, 2001)

*Code de l'arbitrage commenté* (Paris: LexisNexis, 2021)

"Liberté, égalité, efficacité: La devise du nouveau droit français de l'arbitrage; Commentaire article par article," *Journal du droit international*, 2012, reprinted in expanded form in *Code de l'arbitrage commenté* (Paris: LexisNexis, 2021), 1–24

"Qui sont les arbitres internationaux? Approche sociologique," in Centre français de droit comparé, *Les arbitres internationaux*, vol. 8 (Paris: Editions de la Société de législation comparée, 2005), 13–32

Clay, Thomas, and Carine Jallamion, "Justice publique et arbitrage: hier et aujourd'-hui," in Loïc Cadiet, Serge Dauchy, and Jean-Louis Halpérin (eds.), *Itinéraires d'histoire de la procédure civile* (Paris: IRJS Editions, 2014), 177–221

Clay, Thomas, and Philippe Pinsolle, "General Introduction: The Major Cases of the French Case Law on International Arbitration," in Thomas Clay, Philippe Pinsolle, and Thomas Voisin (eds.), *French International Arbitration Law Report: 1963–2007* (Huntington: Juris, 2014), v–xxviii

Clémentel, Étienne, *La France et la politique économique interalliée* (Paris: Presses Universitaires de France, 1931)

Clère, Jean-Jacques, "L'arbitrage révolutionnaire: Apogée et déclin d'une institution (1790-1806)," *Revue de l'arbitrage*, 1981, 3–28

Cohen, Daniel, *Arbitrage et société* (Paris: LGDJ, 1993)

Cohen, Julius Henry, *Commercial Arbitration and the Law* (New York: D. Appleton, 1918)

Collins, Lawrence, "F.A. Mann (1907–1991)," in Jack Beatson and Reinhard Zimmermann (eds.), *Jurists Uprooted: German-Speaking Emigré Lawyers in Twentieth-Century Britain* (Oxford: Oxford University Press, 2004), 381–440

Comité national français de la Chambre de commerce internationale, *Un demi-siècle au service de la Chambre de commerce internationale: Brochure publiée à l'occasion du départ en retraite de René Arnaud, Directeur Général du Comité* (Paris: International Chamber of Commerce, 1969)

Connerty, Anthony, "International Cotton Arbitration," *Arbitration International*, 29 (2013), 295–318

Contini, Paolo, "International Commercial Arbitration: The United Nations Convention on the Recognition and Enforcement of Foreign Arbitral Awards," *American Journal of Comparative Law*, 8 (1959), 283–309

Cook, Adrian, *The Alabama Claims: American Politics and Anglo-American Relations, 1865-1872* (Ithaca: Cornell University Press, 1975)

Cotterrell, Roger, "Rethinking 'Embeddedness': Law, Economy, Community," *Journal of Law and Society*, 40 (2013), 49–67

Craig, Laurence, "Uses and Abuses of Appeal from Awards," *Arbitration International*, 4 (1988), 174–227

Craig, Laurence, William Park, and Jan Paulsson, *International Chamber of Commerce Arbitration* (New York: Oceana Publications, 1990)

Cranston, Ross, "Law through Practice: London and Liverpool Commodity Markets c.1820–1975," *Society and Economy Working Papers* (London: LSE Law, 2007), 1–35

Craven, Matthew, "Introduction: International Law and Its Histories," in Matthew Craven, Malgosia Fitzmaurice, and Maria Vogiatzi (eds.), *Time, History and International Law* (Leiden: Martinus Nijhoff, 2007), 1–26

"Theorizing the Turn to History in International Law," in Anne Orford, Florian Hoffmann, and Martin Clark (eds.), *The Oxford Handbook of the Theory of International Law* (Oxford: Oxford University Press, 2016), 21–37

Crawford, James, *Chance, Order, Change: The Course of International Law, General Course on Public International Law*, Hague Academy of International Law (Leiden: Martinus Nijhoff, 2013)

"The Current Political Discourse Concerning International Law," *Modern Law Review*, 81 (2018), 1–22

Croxton, Derek, "The Peace of Westphalia of 1648 and the Origins of Sovereignty," *International History Review*, 21 (1999), 569–852

Cuniberti, Gilles, "La *lex mercatoria* au XXIe siècle: – Une analyse empirique et économique," *Journal du droit international*, 2016, 765–80

Cutler, Claire, *Private Power and Global Authority: Transnational Merchant Law in the Global Political Economy* (Cambridge: Cambridge University Press, 2003)

D'Silva, Magdalene, "Dealing in Power: Gatekeepers in Arbitrator Appointment in International Commercial Arbitration," *Journal of International Dispute Settlement*, 5 (2014), 605–34

Darby, William, *International Arbitration. International Tribunals: A Collection of the Various Schemes Which Have Been Propounded; and of Instances in the Nineteenth Century* (London: J. M. Dent and Co., 1899)

Darrigade, Coralie, "États-Unis: La sentence annulée dans son pays d'origine, approche américaine, note sous District Court Southern District of New York, 27 août 2013," *Revue de l'arbitrage*, 2015, 183–92

Darwazeh, Nadia, "The Jerusalem Arbitration Centre: From Tradition to Innovation," *Journal of International Arbitration*, 31 (2014), 121–38

Dauchy, Serge, "Le recours contre les décisions arbitrales en perspective historique: Aux origines des articles 1481–1491 NCPC," *Revue de l'arbitrage*, 1999, 763–84

David, René, *L'arbitrage dans le commerce international* (Paris: Economica, 1982)

"Arbitrage du XIXe et arbitrage du XXe siècle," in *Mélanges offerts à René Savatier* (Paris: Dalloz, 1965), 219–33.

*Les avatars d'un comparatiste* (Paris: Economica, 1982)

*Rapport sur l'arbitrage conventionnel en droit privé: Étude de droit comparé*, U. D.P. – Études III – S.D.N. 1932 – C.D. 1932 (Rome: L'Universale Tipografia Poliglotta, 1932)

"Unification des lois relatives à l'arbitrage," in *Conférence sur l'arbitrage commercial international: Compte rendu des séances destiné aux Membres de la Conférence (June 13–15, 1946)*, 38–42

De la Rasilla, Ignacio, "The Turn to the History of International Adjudication," in Ignacio de la Rasilla and Jorge Viñuales (eds.), *Experiments in International Adjudication: Historical Accounts* (Cambridge: Cambridge University Press, 2019), 32–52

De Ly, Filip, *International Business Law and* Lex Mercatoria (Amsterdam: Elsevier Science, 1992)

Decorzant, Yann, "Internationalism in the Economic and Financial Organisation of the League of Nations," in Daniel Laqua (ed.), *Internationalism Reconfigured: Transnational Ideas and Movements between the World Wars* (London: I. B. Tauris, 2011), 115–34

Dehaussy, Jacques, "Philippe Kahn," in Charles Leben, Philippe Kahn, and Mahmoud Salem (eds.), *Souveraineté étatique et marchés internationaux à la fin du 20ème siècle: À propos de 30 ans de recherche du CREDIMI; Mélanges en l'honneur de Philippe Kahn* (Dijon: Litec-CREDIMI, 2000), 1–4

Delmas-Marty, Mireille, *Les forces imaginantes du droit*, vol. 1, *Le relatif et l'universel* (Paris: Seuil, 2004)

*Les forces imaginantes du droit*, vol. 2, *Le pluralisme ordonné* (Paris: Seuil, 2006)

Derains, Yves, "The Application of Transnational Rules in ICC Arbitral Awards," *World Arbitration and Mediation Review*, 5 (2011), 173–99

"New Trends in the Practical Application of ICC Rules of Arbitration," *Northwestern Journal of International Law and Business*, 3 (1981), 39–55

Dezalay, Yves, *Marchands de droit: La restructuration de l'ordre juridique international par les multinationales du droit* (Paris: Fayard, 1992)

Dezalay, Yves, and Bryant Garth, "Constructing a Transatlantic Marketplace of Disputes on the Symbolic Foundations of International Justice," in Grégoire Mallard and Jérôme Sgard (eds.), *Contractual Knowledge: One Hundred Years of Legal Experimentation in Global Markets* (Cambridge: Cambridge University Press, 2016), 185–214

*Dealing in Virtue: International Commercial Arbitration and the Construction of a Transnational Legal Order* (Chicago: University of Chicago Press, 1996)

"International Commercial Arbitration: The Creation of a Legal Market," in Thomas Schultz and Frederico Ortino (eds.), *The Oxford Handbook of International Arbitration* (Oxford: Oxford University Press, 2020), 769–91

"Merchants of Law as Moral Entrepreneurs: Constructing International Justice from the Competition for Transnational Business Disputes," *Law and Society Review*, 29 (1995), 27–64

Dezalay, Yves, Didier Bigo, and Antonin Cohen, "Enquêter sur l'internationalisation des noblesses d'Etat: Retour réflexif sur des stratégies de double jeu; Entretien avec Yves Dezalay," *Cultures et Conflits* (2015), 15–52

Diggelmann, Oliver, "The Periodization of the History of International Law," in Bardo Fassbender and Anne Peters (eds.), *The Oxford Handbook of the History of International Law* (Oxford: Oxford University Press, 2012), 997–1011

DiMaggio, Paul, and Walter Powell, "The Iron Cage Revisited: Institutional Isomorphism and Collective Rationality in Organizational Fields," *American Sociological Review*, 48 (April 1983), 147–60

Djelic, Marie-Laure, and Sigrid Quack, "Conclusion: Globalization as a Double Process of Institutional Change and Institution Building," in Marie-Laure Djelic and Sigrid Quack (eds.), *Globalization and Institutions: Redefining the Rules of the Economic Game* (Cheltenham: Edward Elgar, 2003), 302–34

Dolléans, Edouard, *Histoire du mouvement ouvrier* (Paris: Armand Colin, 1948 [vol. 1 and 2] and 1953 [vol. 3])

Domke, Martin, "Arthur Nussbaum: The Pioneer of International Commercial Arbitration," *Columbia Law Review*, 57 (1957), 8–10

"The United Nations Conference on International Commercial Arbitration," *American Journal of International Law*, 53 (1959), 414–26

Donahue, Charles, "Medieval and Early Modern *Lex Mercatoria*: An Attempt at the *Probatio Diabolica*," *Chicago Journal of International Law*, 5 (2004), 21–36

Dreyfus, Ferdinand, *L'arbitrage international* (Paris: Calmann Lévy, 1892)

Druelle-Korn, Clotilde, "De la pensée à l'action économique: Étienne Clémentel (1864–1936), un ministre visionnaire," *Histoire@Politique* (2012), 40–54

"Étienne Clémentel président-fondateur de la Chambre de commerce internationale," in Marie-Christine Kessler and Guy Rousseau (eds.), *Étienne Clémentel: Politique et action publique sous la Troisième République* (Brussels: Peter Lang, 2018), 419–34

"The Great War: Matrix of the International Chamber of Commerce, a Fortunate Business League of Nations," in Andrew Smith, Kevin Tennent, and Simon Mollan (eds.), *The Impact of the First World War on International Business* (London: Routledge, 2016)

"Un laboratoire réformateur, le département du commerce en France et aux États-Unis de la Grande Guerre aux années vingt" (PhD diss., Institut d'études politiques de Paris, 2004)

Druelle-Korn, Clotilde, Marie-Christine Kessler, and Guy Rousseau, "Étienne Clémentel président-fondateur de la Chambre de commerce internationale," in Marie-Christine Kessler and Guy Rousseau (eds.), *Étienne Clémentel: Politique et action publique sous la Troisième République* (Brussels: Peter Lang, 2018), 419–34

Dunham, Arthur, *The Anglo-French Treaty of Commerce of 1860 and the Progress of the Industrial Revolution in France* (Ann Arbor: University of Michigan Press, 1930)

Eck, Jean-François, "La Chambre de commerce internationale: les positions des représentants français," in Sylvain Schirmann (ed.), *Organisations internationales et architectures européennes 1929–1939: Actes du colloque de Metz (31 mai – 1er juin 2001); En hommage à Raymond Poidevin* (Metz: Centre de recherche histoire et civilisation, 2003), 303–24

Eisemann, Frédéric, "Arbitrations under the International Chamber of Commerce," *International and Comparative Law Quarterly*, 15 (1966), 726–36

"The Court of Arbitration: Outline of Its Changes from Inception to the Present Day," in *60 Years of ICC Arbitration: A Look at the Future* (Paris: ICC Publishing, 1984), 391–98

"Déontologie de l'arbitre commercial international," *Revue de l'arbitrage*, 1969, 217–33

"Local Law and Private Rules of Procedure in Connection with International Commercial Arbitration," *Arbitration Journal* (1949); reprinted in *Arbitration International*, 2 (1986), 73–75

"Le nouveau règlement d'arbitrage de la Chambre de Commerce Internationale," *Droit et pratique du commerce international*, 1 (September 1975), 355–65

Eisenstadt, Shmuel, and Miriam Curelaru, *The Form of Sociology: Paradigms and Crises* (New York: Wiley, 1976)

Ellenbogen, Gershon, "English Arbitration Practice," *Law and Contemporary Problems*, 17 (1952), 656–78

Ellickson, Robert, *Order without Law: How Neighbors Settle Disputes* (Cambridge, MA: Harvard University Press, 1991)

Elsen, Albert, *All the Masks Fall Off: Rodin's Last Sculpture; The Portrait of Clémentel* (Memphis: Memphis Brooks Museum of Art, 1988)

Fabiani, Jean-Louis, "À quoi sert la notion de discipline?," in Jean Boutier, Jean-Claude Passeron, and Jacques Revel (eds.), *Qu'est-ce qu'une discipline?* (Paris: Éditions de l'École des hautes études en sciences sociales, 2006), 11–34

Fadlallah, Ibrahim, and Dominique Hascher, *Les grandes décisions du droit de l'arbitrage commercial* (Paris: Dalloz, 2019)

Fahey, John, "The International Chamber of Commerce," *Annals of the American Academy of Political and Social Science*, 94 (March 1921), 126–30

Fassbender, Bardo, and Anne Peters, "Introduction: Towards a Global History of International Law," in Bardo Fassbender and Anne Peters (eds.), *The Oxford Handbook of the History of International Law* (Oxford: Oxford University Press, 2014), 1–24

Faure, J. C. A., "Commodity Market Arbitrations with Special Reference to the Incorporated Oil Seed Association Rules," *International and Comparative Law Quarterly*, 15 (1966), 736–742

Findlay, Ronald, and Kevin O'Rourke, *Power and Plenty: Trade, War, and the World Economy in the Second Millennium* (Princeton: Princeton University Press, 2007)

Fitzpatrick, Peter, "Taking Place: Westphalia and the Poetics of Law," *London Review of International Law*, 2 (2014), 155–65

Fontanelli, Filippo, "Santi Romano and *L'ordinamento giuridico*: The Relevance of a Forgotten Masterpiece for Contemporary International, Transnational and Global Legal Relations," *Transnational Legal Theory*, 2 (2011), 67–117

Foucault, Michel, "Nietszche, la généalogie, l'histoire" (1971), in Daniel Defert, François Ewald, and Jacques Lagrange (eds.) *Dits et écrits I: 1954–1988* (Paris: Gallimard, 2001)

"Nietszche, Genealogy, History," in *Language, Counter-Memory, Practice: Selected Essays and Interviews*, ed. Donald Bouchard, trans. Donald Bouchard and Sherry Simon (New York: Cornell University Press, 1977), 139–64

Fouchard, Philippe, *L'arbitrage commercial international* (Paris: Dalloz, 1965)

*Écrits: Droit de l'arbitrage, droit du commerce international* (Paris: Comité Français de l'Arbitrage, 2007)

"Où va l'arbitrage international?," *McGill Law Journal*, 34 (1989), 436–53

"La portée internationale de l'annulation de la sentence arbitrale dans son pays d'origine," *Revue de l'arbitrage*, 1997, 329–52

"Suggestions pour accroître l'efficacité internationale des sentences arbitrales," *Revue de l'arbitrage*, 1998, 653–72

Fouchard, Philippe, and Berthold Goldman, "Préface," in Henri Motulsky, *Écrits*, vol. 2, *Études et notes sur l'arbitrage* (Paris: Dalloz, 2010), v–x

Fouchard, Philippe, and Jean-François Poudret, "Quelle solution pour en finir avec l'affaire *Hilmarton*? Réponse à Philippe Fouchard," *Revue de l'arbitrage*, 1998, 7–24

Fouchard, Philippe, and Louis Vogel (eds.), *L'actualité de la pensée de Berthold Goldman: droit commercial international et européen* (Paris: Editions Panthéon-Assas, 2004)

Fouchard, Philippe, Emmanuel Gaillard, and Berthold Goldman, *Traité de l'arbitrage commercial international* (Paris: Litec, 1996)

Fouchard, Philippe, Philippe Kahn, and Antoine Lyon-Caen, "Avant-propos," in Philippe Fouchard, Philippe Kahn, and Antoine Lyon-Caen (eds.), *Le droit des relations économiques internationales: Études offertes à Berthold Goldman* (Paris: Litec, 1982), xi–xvi

Fragistas, Charalambos, "Arbitrage étranger et arbitrage international en droit privé," *Revue critique de droit international privé*, 1960, 1–20

Franke, Ulf, Annette Magnusson, and Joel Dahlquist (eds.), *Arbitrating for Peace: How Arbitration Made a Difference* (The Hague: Kluwer Law International, 2016)

Freud, Sigmund, "The Dissection of the Psychical Personality," in *The Standard Edition of The Complete Psychological Works of Sigmund Freud*, vol. 22, *New Introductory Lectures on Psycho-Analysis and Other Works* (London: Hogarth, 1964 [1933]), 57–80

"Moses and Monotheism," in *The Standard Edition of The Complete Psychological Works of Sigmund Freud*, vol. 23 (London: Hogarth, 1964 [1939])

Fry, Jason, Simon Greenberg, and Francesca Mazza, *The Secretariat's Guide to ICC Arbitration* (Paris: International Chamber of Commerce, 2012)

Gaillard, Emmanuel, "Actualité de l'effet négatif de la compétence-compétence," in *Le droit à l'épreuve des siècles et des frontières: Mélanges en l'honneur du Professeur Bertrand Ancel* (Paris: LGDJ/IPROLEX, 2018), 679–707

"L'apport de la pensée juridique française à l'arbitrage international," *Journal du droit international*, 2017, 529–42

"The Arbitral Legal Order: Evolution and Recognition," in Thomas Schultz and Frederico Ortino (eds.), *The Oxford Handbook of International Arbitration* (Oxford: Oxford University Press, 2020), 554–68

"Comparative Law in International Arbitration," *Ius Comparatum*, 1 (2020), 1–35

"Convention d'arbitrage," *Juris-Classeur Droit International*, Fascicle 586-5 (1994)

"L'effet négatif de la compétence-compétence," in Jacques Haldy, Jean-Marc Rapp, and Phidias Ferrari (eds.), *Études de procédure et d'arbitrage en l'honneur de Jean-François Poudret* (Lausanne: Faculté de droit de l'Université de Lausanne, 1999), 387–402

"The Enforcement of Awards Set Aside in the Country of Origin," *ICSID Review – Foreign Investment Law Journal*, 16 (1999), 16–45

"L'interférence des juridictions du siège dans le déroulement de l'arbitrage," in Piero Bernardini, Sébastien Besson, Matthieu de Boisséson, and Jean-Denis Bredin (eds.), *Liber amicorum Claude Reymond: Autour de l'arbitrage* (Paris: LexisNexis, 2004), 83–96

"International Arbitration as a Transnational System of Justice," in Albert Jan van den Berg (ed.), *Arbitration: The Next Fifty Years*, ICCA Congress Series No. 16 (The Hague: Kluwer Law International, 2012), 66–73

"La jurisprudence de la Cour de cassation en matière d'arbitrage international," *Revue de l'arbitrage*, 2007, 697–720

*Legal Theory of International Arbitration* (Leiden: Martinus Nijhoff, 2010)

"Nouvelles réflexions sur la sociologie de l'arbitrage," *Procédures*, 2 (2020), 35–37

"L'ordre juridique arbitral: réalité, utilité et spécificité," *McGill Law Journal*, 55 (2010), 891–907

"La reconnaissance, en droit suisse, de la seconde moitié du principe d'effet négatif de la compétence-compétence," in Gerald Aksen, Karl-Heinz Böckstiegel, Michael J. Mustill, Paolo Michele Patocchi, and Anne Marie Whitesell (eds.), *Global Reflections on International Law, Commerce and Dispute Resolution: Liber Amicorum in Honour of Robert Briner* (Paris: ICC Publishing, 2005), 311–26

"Reflections on the Use of Anti-Suit Injunctions in International Arbitration," in Loukas Mistelis and Julian Lew (eds.), *Pervasive Problems in International Arbitration* (The Hague: Kluwer Law International, 2006), 203–15

"The Representations of International Arbitration," *Journal of International Dispute Settlement*, 1 (2010), 271–81

"Sociology of International Arbitration," *Arbitration International*, 31 (2015), 1–17

"Souveraineté et autonomie: Réflexions sur les représentations de l'arbitrage international," *Journal du droit international*, 2007, 1163–73

"Thirty Years of *Lex Mercatoria*: Towards the Selective Application of Transnational Rules," *ICSID Review – Foreign Investment Law Journal*, 10 (1995), 208–31

"Three Philosophies of International Arbitration," in Arthur Rovine (ed.), *Contemporary Issues in International Arbitration and Mediation: The Fordham Papers 2009* (Leiden: Martinus Nijhoff, 2010), 305–10

"Transcending National Legal Orders for International Arbitration," in Albert Jan van den Berg (ed.), *International Arbitration: The Coming of a New Age?*, ICCA Congress Series No. 17 (The Hague: Kluwer Law International, 2013), 371–77

"Transnational Law: A Legal System or a Method of Decision Making?," *Arbitration International*, 17 (2001), 59–72

"The Urgency of Not Revising the New York Convention," in Albert Jan van den Berg (ed.), *50 Years of the New York Convention*, ICCA Congress Series No. 14 (The Hague: Kluwer Law International, 2009), 689–707

"La vision américaine des sentences annulées au siège (Observations sur les arrêts *Pemex* et *Thai-Lao Lignite* de la Cour d'appel fédérale du 2e circuit des 2 août 2016 et 20 juillet 2017)," *Revue de l'arbitrage*, 2017, 1147–65

Gaillard, Emmanuel, and George Bermann (eds.), *UNCITRAL Secretariat Guide on the Convention on the Recognition and Enforcement of Foreign Arbitral Awards (New York, 1958)* (Leiden: Brill/Nijhoff, 2017)

Gaillard, Emmanuel, and John Savage (eds.), *Fouchard, Gaillard, Goldman on International Commercial Arbitration* (The Hague: Kluwer Law International, 1999)

Gaillard, Emmanuel, and Pierre de Lapasse, "Le nouveau droit français de l'arbitrage interne et international," *Dalloz*, 2011, 175–92

Gaillard, Emmanuel, and Yas Banifatemi, "Negative Effect of Competence-Competence: The Rule of Priority in Favour of the Arbitrators," in Emmanuel Gaillard and Domenico di Pietro (eds.), *Enforcement of Arbitration Agreements and International Arbitral Awards: The New York Convention in Practice* (London: Cameron May, 2008), 257–73

"The Representations of International Arbitration," *New York Law Journal*, 238 (2007)

Garth, Bryant, "One Window into the State of Insiders' Arbitration Scholarship," *Journal of World Investment and Trade*, 19 (2018), 155–64

Gaudemet-Tallon, Hélène, "*In Memoriam*: Philippe Fouchard (1937–2004)," *Travaux du Comité français de droit international privé (2002–2004)*, 16 (2005), 195–98

Gaurier, Dominique, *Histoire du droit international: De l'Antiquité à la création de l'ONU* (Rennes: Presses Universitaires de Rennes, 2014)

"Le règlement privé des conflits dans la Chine impériale: Arbitrage ou médiation?," *Revue de l'arbitrage*, 2004, 189–223

Gharavi, Hamid, "*Chromalloy*: Another View," *Mealey's International Arbitration Report*, 12 (1997), 21–27

*The International Effectiveness of the Annulment of an Arbitral Award* (The Hague: Kluwer Law International, 2002)

Gherari, Habib, and Sandra Szurek (eds.), *L'émergence de la société civile internationale: vers la privatisation du droit international? Actes du colloque des 2–3 mars 2001*, Cahiers du CEDIN, vol. 18 (Paris: Pedone, 2003)

Ginsburg, Tom, "The Culture of Arbitration," *Vanderbilt Journal of Transnational Law*, 36 (2003), 1335–45

Godron, Jacques, "La clause compromissoire dans les rapports internationaux devant les Tribunaux français," *Journal du droit international*, 1919, 47–62 (pt. 1) and 658–59 (pt. 2)

*La clause compromissoire: Étude de droit comparé (jurisprudences française et belge, droit anglais) et de droit international privé* (Paris: Arthur Rousseau, 1916)

Goldman, Berthold, "The Applicable Law: General Principles of Law – the *Lex Mercatoria*," in Julian Lew (ed.), *Contemporary Problems in International Arbitration* (London: Springer Science/Business Media Dordrecht, 1987), 113–25

"Une bataille judiciaire autour de la *lex mercatoria*: L'affaire *Norsolor*," *Revue de l'arbitrage*, 1983, 379–409

"Les conflits de lois dans l'arbitrage international de droit privé," *Collected Courses of the Hague Academy of International Law*, vol. 109 (Dordrecht: Martinus Nijhoff, 1963)

Foreword to Jean Stoufflet, *Le crédit documentaire: Étude juridique d'un instrument financier du commerce international* (Paris: Librairies techniques, 1957)

Foreword to Philippe Fouchard, *L'arbitrage commercial international* (Paris: Dalloz, 1965)

Foreword to Philippe Kahn, *La vente commerciale internationale* (Paris: Sirey, 1961)

"Frontières du droit et '*lex mercatoria*,'" in *Archives de philosophie du droit*, no. 9, *Le droit subjectif en question* (Paris: Sirey, 1964), 177–92

"Introduction," in *Lex Mercatoria and Arbitration: A Discussion of the New Law Merchant* (Yonkers: Juris and Kluwer Law International, 1998), xix–xxii

"*Lex mercatoria*," *Forum Internationale*, 3 (1983), 3–24

"La *lex mercatoria* dans les contrats et l'arbitrage internationaux: Réalité et perspectives," *Journal du droit international*, 1979, 475–505

Note on *Société Compañia Valenciana de Cementos Portaland* v. *Société Primary Coal Inc.*, *Journal du droit international*, 1992, 177–83

"Nouvelles réflexions sur la *Lex Mercatoria*," in Christian Dominicé, Robert Patry, and Claude Reymond (eds.), *Études de droit international en l'honneur de Pierre Lalive* (Basel: Helbing & Lichtenhahn, 1993), 241–55

"The Suez Company – An International Company," in Klaus Peter Berger, *The Creeping Codification of the New Lex Mercatoria*, trans. Thomas Claeßens and Bernd Scholl, 2nd ed. (The Hague: Kluwer Law International, 2010), 368–70

Gordon, Robert, "The Past as Authority and as Social Critic: Stabilizing and Destabilizing Functions of History in Legal Argument," in *Taming the Past: Essays on Law in History and History in Law* (Cambridge: Oxford University Press, 2017), 282–316

Greenwood, Ernest, "Attributes of a Profession," *Social Work*, 2 (1957), 45–55

Grisel, Florian, *L'arbitrage international ou le droit contre l'ordre juridique* (Paris: LGDJ, 2011)

"Competition and Cooperation in International Commercial Arbitration: The Birth of a Transnational Legal Profession," *Law and Society Review*, 51 (2017), 790–824

"Droit et non-droit dans les sentences arbitrales CCI: Une perspective historique," *ICC International Court of Arbitration Bulletin*, 25, no. 2 (2014), 13–20

"Marginals and Elites in International Arbitration," in Thomas Schultz and Frederico Ortino (eds.), *The Oxford Handbook of International Arbitration* (Oxford: Oxford University Press, 2020), 260–82

"Treaty Making between Public Authority and Private Interest: The Genealogy of the Convention on the Recognition and Enforcement of Foreign Arbitral Awards," *European Journal of International Law*, 28 (2017), 73–87

Grisel, Florian, and Alec Stone Sweet, "L'arbitrage international: Du contrat dyadique au système normatif," *Archives de philosophie du droit*, 52 (2009), 75–95

Gross, Charles, "The Court of Piepowder," *Quarterly Journal of Economics*, 20 (1906), 231–49

Guillet, Léon, "Notice biographique. Eugène Schneider (1868–1942)," *Revue de métallurgie* (May 1943), 156–60

Haas, Peter, "Epistemic Communities and International Policy Coordination," *International Organization*, 46 (1992), 1–35

Hale, Thomas, *Between Interests and Law: The Politics of Transnational Commercial Disputes* (Cambridge: Cambridge University Press, 2015)

"What Is the Effect of Commercial Arbitration on Trade?," in Walter Mattli and Thomas Dietz (eds.), *International Arbitration and Global Governance: Contending Theories and Evidence* (Oxford: Oxford University Press, 2014), 196–213

Hall, Nigel, "The Governance of the Liverpool Raw Cotton Market, c.1840–1914," *Northern History*, 53 (2016), 98–115

"The Liverpool Cotton Market: Britain's First Futures Market," *Transactions of the Historical Society of Lancashire and Cheshire*, 49 (2000), 99–117

Halpérin, Jean-Louis, "L'approche historique et la problématique du *jus commune*," *Revue internationale de droit comparé*, 52 (2000), 717–731

*Histoire des droits en Europe de 1750 à nos jours* (Paris: Flammarion, 2006 [2004])

*Histoire du droit privé français depuis 1804*, 2nd ed. (Paris: Presses Universitaires de France 2012)

"Le juge et le jugement en France à l'époque révolutionnaire," in Robert Jacob (ed.), *Le juge et le jugement dans les traditions juridiques européennes: Études d'histoire comparée* (Paris: LGDJ, 1996), 257–71

"Portalis Joseph-Marie," in Patrick Arabeyre, Jean-Louis Halpérin, and Jacques Krynen (eds.), *Dictionnaire historique des juristes français, XII–XXe siècle* (Paris: Presses Universitaires de France, 2015), 831–32

Hamel, Joseph, "La clause compromissoire dans les rapports de commerce internationaux: À propos de quelques récents projets et propositions de loi," *Revue de droit international privé*, 18 (1923), 721–40 (pt. 1) and 19 (1924), 15–30 (pt. 2)

Hamilton, Steuart, "ICC Conciliation: A Glimpse into History," in *ADR: International Applications*, special supplement, *ICC International Court of Arbitration Bulletin* (Paris: ICC Publishing, 2001), 23–30

Hammond, Nicholas, "Arbitration in Ancient Greece," *Arbitration International*, 1 (1985), 188–90

Haraucourt, Edmond, *L'œuvre artistique d'Étienne Clémentel* (Paris: Editions Lapina, 1927)

Hart, H. L. A., *The Concept of Law*, ed. Joseph Raz and Penelope Bulloch (Oxford: Oxford University Press, 2012 [1961])

Hascher, Dominique, "The Review of Arbitral Awards by Domestic Courts: France," in Emmanuel Gaillard (ed.), *The Review of Arbitral Awards*, IAI Series on International Arbitration No. 6 (Huntington: Juris, 2010), 97–110

Hatzimihail, Nikitas, "The Many Lives – and Faces – of *Lex Mercatoria*: History as Genealogy in International Business Law," *Law and Contemporary Problems*, 71 (2008), 169–90

Hebié, Mamadou, *Souveraineté territoriale par traité: Une étude des accords entre puissances coloniales et entités politiques locales* (Paris: Presses Universitaires de France, 2015)

Hegel, Georg Wilhelm Friedrich, *Elements of the Philosophy of Right*, ed. Allen Wood, trans. Hugh Barr Nisbet (Cambridge: Cambridge University Press, 2003 [1821])

Herbert, Edwin (Lord Tangley), "International Arbitration Today," *International and Comparative Law Quarterly* (1966), 719–25

"The Prompt Enforcement of International Arbitral Awards," in *International Commercial Arbitration and Freedom of Contract*, ICC Brochure No. 160 (Paris: ICC International Headquarters, 1951), 7–9

Hermanowicz, Joseph, and David Johnson, "Professions," in Masamichi Sasaki, Jack Goldstone, Ekkart Zimmerman, and Stephen Sanderson (eds.), *Concise Encyclopedia of Comparative Sociology* (Leiden: Brill, 2014), 213

Hilaire, Jean, "L'arbitrage dans la période moderne (XVIe–XVIIIe siècle)," *Revue de l'arbitrage*, 2000, 187–226

Hobsbawm, Eric, *The Age of Revolution: Europe 1789–1848* (New York: Vintage, 1996 [1962])

Holtzmann, Howard, "L'arbitrage et les tribunaux: Des associés dans un système de justice internationale," *Revue de l'arbitrage*, 1978, 253–303

"A Task for the 21st Century: Creating a New International Court for Resolving Disputes on the Enforceability of Arbitral Awards," in Martin Hunter, Arthur Marriott, and V. V. Veeder (eds.), *The Internationalisation of International Arbitration: The LCIA Centenary Conference* (London: Graham & Trotman/Martinus Nijhoff)

Hoyle, Mark, *Mixed Courts of Egypt* (London: Graham & Trotman, 1991)

Hueck, Ingo, "The Discipline of the History of International Law: New Trends and Methods on the History of International Law," *Journal of the History of International Law*, 3 (2001), 194–217

Hull, James, "From Rostow to Chandler to You: How Revolutionary Was the Second Industrial Revolution?," *Journal of European Economic History*, 25 (1996), 194–96

Hunt, Lynn, *Writing History in the Global Era* (New York: Norton, 2014)

Hyam, Ronald, *Britain's Imperial Century, 1815–1914: A Study of Empire and Expansion* (New York: Palgrave Macmillan, 2002)

"*In Memoriam* Berthold Goldman," *ASA Bulletin*, 11, no. 2 (1993), 187–89

International Chamber of Commerce, *2019 ICC Dispute Resolution Statistics, in ICC Dispute Resolution Bulletin*, 2020, issue 2, 15–40

International Council for Commercial Arbitration, *ICCA 50th Anniversary* (Geneva, 2011)

International Institute for the Unification of Private Law, *Avant-projet d'une loi uniforme sur l'arbitrage dans les rapports internationaux en droit privé et rapport explicatif*, U.D.P. 1940 – Projet III (Rome: Tipografia del Senato, 1940)

*Unification of Law: A General Survey of Work for the Unification of Private Law; Drafts and Convention* (Rome: UNIDROIT, 1948)

Ishikazi, Masaichiro, *Le droit corporatif international de la vente des soies: Les contrats-types américains et la codification lyonnaise dans leurs rapports avec les usages des autres places* (Paris: Marcel Giard, 1928)

Jacquemont, André, *L'émission des emprunts euro-obligataires: Pouvoir bancaire et souverainetés étatiques* (Paris: Litec, 1976)

Jaffe, James, "Industrial Arbitration, Equity, and Authority in England, 1800–1850," *Law and History Review*, 18 (2000), 525–58

Jallamion, Carine, "L'arbitrage en matière civile du XVIIe au XIXe siècle: L'exemple de Montpellier" (PhD diss., Université de Montpellier 1, 2004)

"Arbitrage et pouvoir politique en France du XVIIe au XIXe siècle," *Revue de l'arbitrage*, 2005, 3–62

"Arbitrage forcé et justice d'état pendant la Révolution française d'après l'exemple de Montpellier," *Annales historiques de la Révolution française* (2007), 69–85

"Le juge français au service de l'investissement: Le développement en France de l'arbitrage commercial international (XIXe–XXe siècle)," in Luisa Brunori, Serge Dauchy, Olivier Descamps, and Xavier Prévost (eds.), *Le droit face à l'économie sans travail*, vol. 1, *Sources intellectuelles, acteurs, résolution des conflits* (Paris: Classiques Garnier, 2019)

"La jurisprudence française et l'arbitrage de 1843 à 1958: De la défaveur à la faveur jusqu'à l'avènement de l'arbitrage international," *Revue de l'arbitrage*, 2015, 739–80 (pt. 1) and 1037–101 (pt. 2)

Jarrosson, Charles, "L'actualité de la pensée de Henri Motulsky sur l'arbitrage," "Qu'est devenue la pensée de Motulsky?," *Procédures*, 18 (2012), 51–55

"La clause compromissoire (art. 2061 C. civ)," *Revue de l'arbitrage*, 1992, 259–78

"Les frontières de l'arbitrage," *Revue de l'arbitrage*, 2001, 5–41

"Lecture entre les lignes: Philippe Fouchard à travers ses écrits," in "Journée d'hommage et d'études à la mémoire de Philippe Fouchard, Paris, 11 mars 2005," *Revue de l'arbitrage*, 2005, 291–304

*La notion d'arbitrage* (Paris: LGDJ, 1987)

"Note – Cour de cassation (1re Ch. civ.) 23 mars 1994 – *Société Hilmarton* v. *Société OTV*," *Revue de l'arbitrage*, 1994, 329–36

"Le nouvel essor de la clause compromissoire après la loi du 15 mai 2001," *JCP – La Semaine Juridique Edition Générale*, issue 27 (2001)

Jarvin, Sigvard, "La Cour d'arbitrage de la Chambre de Commerce internationale pendant la seconde guerre mondiale," in Laurent Lévy and Yves Derains (eds.), *Liber amicorum en l'honneur de Serge Lazareff* (Paris: Pedone, 2011), 331–47

"The move to Stockholm of the Court of Arbitration of the International Chamber of Commerce (ICC) during the Second World War," *Scandinavian Studies in Law*, 63 (2017), 115–38

Jeanclos, Yves, "La pratique de l'arbitrage du XIIe au XVe siècle: Éléments d'analyse," *Revue de l'arbitrage*, 1999, 417–74

Jehl, Joseph, *Le commerce international de la technologie: Approche juridique* (Paris: Litec, 1985)

Jolivet, Emmanuel, *Les Incoterms: Étude d'une norme du commerce international* (Paris: Litec, 2003)

"Témoignage d'Emmanuel Jolivet," in "Journée d'hommage et d'études à la mémoire de Philippe Fouchard, Paris, 11 mars 2005," *Revue de l'arbitrage*, 2005, 277–82

"Journée d'hommage et d'études à la mémoire de Philippe Fouchard, Paris, 11 mars 2005," *Revue de l'arbitrage*, 2005, 243–509

Kadens, Emily, "The Medieval Law Merchant: The Tyranny of a Construct," *Journal of Legal Analysis*, 7 (2015), 251–89

"The Myth of the Customary Law Merchant," *Texas Law Review*, 90 (2012), 1153–206

Kahn, Philippe, "La *lex mercatoria*: Point de vue français après quarante ans de controverses," *McGill Law Journal*, 37 (1992), 413–27

"La *lex mercatoria* et son destin," in Philippe Fouchard and Louis Vogel (eds.), *L'actualité de la pensée de Berthold Goldman: Droit commercial international et européen* (Paris: Editions Panthéon-Assas, 2004), 25

*La vente commerciale internationale* (Paris: Sirey, 1961)

"Vers la quête de la *lex mercatoria*: L'apport de l'Ecole de Dijon, 1957-1964," in Klaus Peter Berger, *The Creeping Codification of the New Lex Mercatoria*, 2nd ed. (The Hague: Kluwer Law International, 2010), app. 1, at 357–67

Kantorowicz, Ernst, *The King's Two Bodies: A Study in Medieval Political Theology* (Princeton: Princeton University Press, 2016 [1957])

Karton, Joshua, "The Arbitral Role in Contractual Interpretation," *Journal of International Dispute Settlement*, 6 (2015), 1–38

"Contract Law in International Commercial Arbitration: The Case of Suspension of Performance," *International and Comparative Law Quarterly*, 58 (2009), 863–96

*The Culture of International Arbitration and the Evolution of Contract Law* (Oxford: Oxford University Press, 2013)

"International Arbitration as Comparative Law in Action," *Journal of Dispute Resolution*,, 2 (2020), 293–325

"International Arbitration Culture and Global Governance," in Walter Mattli and Thomas Dietz (eds.), *International Arbitration and Global Governance: Contending Theories and Evidence* (Oxford: Oxford University Press, 2014), 74–116

Kassis, Antoine, *Théorie générale des usages du commerce (droit comparé, contrats et arbitrages internationaux, lex mercatoria)* (Paris: LGDJ, 1984)

Kelly, Dominic, *The International Chamber of Commerce as a Diplomatic Actor* (Leicester: Centre for the Study of Diplomacy, University of Leicester, 2000)

Keller, Alexis, "Inter-State Arbitration in Historical Perspective," in Thomas Schultz and Frederico Ortino (eds.), *The Oxford Handbook of International Arbitration* (Oxford: Oxford University Press, 2020), 843–73

Kellor, Frances, *American Arbitration: Its History, Functions, and Achievements* (Washington, DC: Beard Books, 1999)

*Arbitration and the Legal Profession: A Report Prepared for the Survey of the Legal Profession* (New York: American Arbitration Association, 1952)

*Arbitration in Action: A Code for Civil, Commercial and Industrial Arbitrations* (New York: Harper, 1941)

"La coordination des systèmes d'arbitrage commercial," in *Conférence sur l'arbitrage commercial international: Compte rendu des séances destiné aux Membres de la Conférence (June 13–15, 1946)*, 24–27

Kellor, Frances, and Antonia Hatvany, *The United States and the International Court* (New York: Thomas Seltzer, 1925)

Kellor, Frances, and Martin Domke, *Arbitration in International Controversy* (New York: Commission to Study the Organization of Peace and American Arbitration Association, 1944)

"Western Hemisphere Systems of Commercial Arbitration," *University of Toronto Law Journal*, 6 (1946), 307–30

Kelsen, Hans, "On the Basic Norm," *California Law Review*, 47 (1959), 107–10

*Pure Theory of Law*, trans. Max Knight (Berkeley: University of California Press, 1967)

Kennedy, David, "When Renewal Repeats: Thinking against the Box," *NYU Journal of International Law and Politics*, 32 (2000), 335–500

Kennedy, Duncan, *The Rise and Fall of Classical Legal Thought* (Washington, DC: Beard Books, 2006)

"Savigny's Family/Patrimony Distinction and Its Place in the Global Genealogy of Classical Legal Thought," *American Journal of Comparative Law*, 58 (2010), 811–41

Kessler, Amalia, "Arbitration and Americanization: The Paternalism of Progressive Procedural Reform," *Yale Law Journal*, 124 (2015), 2680–3203

Kessler, Marie-Christine, "Introduction," in Marie-Christine Kessler and Guy Rousseau (eds.), *Étienne Clémentel: Politique et action publique sous la Troisième République* (Brussels: Peter Lang, 2018), 19–23

Kessler, Marie-Christine, and Guy Rousseau (eds.), *Étienne Clémentel: Politique et action publique sous la Troisième République* (Brussels: Peter Lang, 2018)

Kidane, Won, *The Culture of International Arbitration* (New York: Oxford University Press, 2017)

Koskenniemi, Martti, *From Apology to Utopia: The Structure of International Legal Argument* (Cambridge: Cambridge University Press, 2005)

"Expanding Histories of International Law," *American Journal of Legal History*, 56 (2016), 104–12

*The Gentle Civilizer of Nations: The Rise and Fall of International Law 1870–1960* (Cambridge: Cambridge University Press, 2001)

"Histories of International Law: Dealing with Eurocentrism," *Rechtsgeschichte*, 19 (2011), 152–76

"What Is International Law For?," in Malcolm Evans (ed.), *International Law* (Oxford: Oxford University Press, 2003), 89–114

"Why History of International Law Today?," *Rechtsgeschichte*, 4 (2004), 61–66

Krasner, Stephen, "State Power and the Structure of International Trade," *World Politics*, 28 (1976), 317–47

Kuhn, Thomas, *The Essential Tension: Selected Studies in Scientific Tradition and Change* (Chicago: University of Chicago Press, 1977), chap. 9, 225–39

Kuisel, Richard, *Le capitalisme et l'État en France: Modernisation et dirigisme au XXe siècle* (Paris: Gallimard, 1984)

*L'éthique dans les relations économiques internationales: En hommage à Philippe Fouchard: colloque, Alexandrie, 28 avril 2005* (Paris: Pedone, 2006)

Lafont, Sophie, "*L'arbitrage en Mésopotamie*," *Revue de l'arbitrage*, 2000, 557–90

La Fontaine, Henri, and Paul Otlet, "La Vie Internationale et l'effort pour son organisation," *La Vie Internationale*, 1 (1912), 9

Lagarde, Paul, "Approche critique de la *lex mercatoria*," in Philippe Fouchard, Philippe Kahn, and Antoine Lyon-Caen (eds.), *Le droit des relations économiques internationales: Études offertes à Berthold Goldman* (Paris: Litec, 1982), 125–50

Lainé, Armand, "De l'exécution en France des sentences arbitrales étrangères," *Journal du droit international privé,* 1899, 641–54

Lalive, Pierre, "Aspects philosophiques du droit de l'arbitrage international" (book review), *ASA Bulletin*, 26 (2008), 700–4

"L'ordre public transnational et l'arbitre international," in Gabriella Venturini and Stefania Bariatti (eds.), *New Instruments of Private International Law: Liber Fausto Pocar* (Milan: Giuffrè, 2009), 599–611

"Problèmes relatifs à l'arbitrage international commercial," *Collected Courses of the Hague Academy of International Law,* vol. 120 (Leiden: Brill/Nijhoff, 1967)

"Sur une 'commercialisation' de l'arbitrage international," in Piero Bernardini, Sébastien Besson, Matthieu de Boisséson, and Jean-Denis Bredin (eds.), *Liber amicorum Claude Reymond: Autour de l'arbitrage* (Paris: LexisNexis, 2004), 167–72

Lalive, Pierre, Jean-François Poudret, and Claude Reymond, *Le droit de l'arbitrage interne et international en Suisse* (Lausanne: Payot, 1989)

Laazouzi, Malik, "L'arbitre international et les rapports entre ordres juridiques," in Baptiste Bonnet (ed.), *Traité des rapports entre ordres juridiques* (Paris: LGDJ, 2016), 1025–44

Lamont, Edward M., *The Ambassador from Wall Street: The Story of Thomas W. Lamont, J. P. Morgan's Chief Executive* (Lanham: Madison Books, 1994)

Latty, Frank, *La lex sportiva: Recherche sur le droit transnational* (The Hague: Martinus Nijhoff, 2007)

Lipson, Charles, *Standing Guard: Protecting Foreign Investment in the Nineteenth and Twentieth Centuries* (Berkeley: University of California Press, 1985)

Le Bars, Benoît, and Joseph Dalmasso, *Arbitrage commercial international: Les grands arrêts du droit français* (Paris: LexisNexis, 2016)

Le Goff, Jacques, *Faut-il vraiment découper l'histoire en tranches?* (Paris: Seuil, 2014)

"Les mentalités: Une histoire ambiguë," in Jacques Le Goff and Pierre Nora (eds.), *Faire l'Histoire: Nouveaux problèmes, nouvelles approches, nouveaux objets* (Paris: Gallimard, 2011), 728–51

Leben, Charles, "L'arbitrage par un tribunal rabbinique appliquant le droit hébraïque," *Revue de l'arbitrage,* 2011, 87–98

Lefebvre-Teillard, Anne, "Arbiter, Arbitrator Seu Amicabilis Compositor," *Revue de l'arbitrage,* 2008, 369–87

"L'arbitrage en droit canonique," *Revue de l'arbitrage,* 2006, 5–34

Legrand, Pierre, "On the Singularity of Law," *Harvard International Law Journal,* 47 (2006), 517–30

Lemercier, Claire, and Jérôme Sgard, *Arbitrage privé international et globalisation-(s): Rapport final* (March 2015)

*Waiting for the Markets to Catch Up: The Construction of International Commercial Arbitration between Two Global Eras (1920–1960)*, Conference on Law and Globalization in Historical Perspective: The Inter-War and the Post-Cold War Eras Compared (Paris: Sciences Po, 5 December 2013)

Leray, René, "L'arbitrage et la loi nouvelle sur la clause compromissoire," *Revue des ventes et transports* (1926), 301–37

Lesaffer, Randall, "Peace Treaties from Lodi to Westphalia," in Randall Lesaffer (ed.), *Peace Treaties and International Law in European History: From Late Middle Ages to World War One* (Cambridge: Cambridge University Press, 2004), 9–44

"The Westphalia Peace Treaties and the Development of the Tradition of Great European Peace Treaties Prior to 1648," *Grotiana*, 18 (1997), 71–95

Lew, Julian, "Achieving the Dream: Autonomous Arbitration," *Arbitration International*, 22 (2006), 179–203

Loeffler, James, and Moria Paz, "Introduction," in James Loeffler and Moria Paz (eds.), *The Law of Strangers: Jewish Lawyers and International Law in the Twentieth Century*, (Cambridge: Cambridge University Press, 2019), 1–20.

Loquin, Eric, *L'amiable composition en droit comparé international: Contribution à l'étude du non-droit dans l'arbitrage commercial* (Paris: Librairies techniques, 1980)

"L'application de règles anationales dans l'arbitrage commercial international," in *L'apport de la jurisprudence arbitrale*, ICC Publication No. 440/1 (Paris: International Chamber of Commerce, 1986), 67–122

"Arbitrage – Aperçu historique – Aperçu de droit comparé," *Juris-Classeur Procédure Civile*, fascicle 1010 (Paris: LexisNexis, 2013)

"Louis-Dreyfus (Louis)," in Jean Jolly (ed.), *Dictionnaire des Parlementaires français: Notices biographiques sur les ministres, députés, et sénateurs français de 1889 à 1940* (Paris: Presses Universitaires de France, 1970), 6: 2306

Louis-Dreyfus, Louis, "La clause compromissoire," *Revue politique et parlementaire* (1925), 370–87

Lowenfeld, Andreas, "*Lex Mercatoria*: An Arbitrator's View," *Arbitration International*, 6 (1990), 133–50

Loynes de Fumichon, Bruno de, "La passion de la Révolution française pour l'arbitrage," *Revue de l'arbitrage*, 2014, 3–52

Loynes de Fumichon, Bruno de, and Michel Humbert, "L'arbitrage à Rome," *Revue de l'arbitrage*, 2003, 185–348

Loynes de Fumichon, Bruno de, and William Park, "Retour sur l'affaire de l'*Alabama*: de l'utilité de l'histoire pour l'arbitrage international," *Revue de l'arbitrage*, 2019, 743–834

Luhmann, Niklas, "The Self-Reproduction of Law and Its Limits," in Gunther Teubner (ed.), *The Dilemmas of Law in the Welfare State* (Berlin: De Gruyter, 1985)

Lyotard, Jean-François, *Heidegger and "the jews,"* trans. Andreas Michel and Mark Roberts (Minneapolis: University of Minnesota Press, 1990 [1988])

*The Postmodern Condition: A Report on Knowledge*, trans. Geoff Bennington and Brian Massumi (Manchester: Manchester University Press, 1984 [1979])

Madsen, Mikael, and Yves Dezalay, "The Power of the Legal Field: Pierre Bourdieu and the Law," in Reza Banakar and Max Travers (eds.), *An Introduction to Law and Social Theory* (Oxford: Hart, 2002), 189–207

Magnier, Léon, *La Chambre de commerce internationale* (Paris: Arthur Rousseau, 1928)

Malynes, Gerard, "*Lex Mercatoria*: Of Arbitrators and Their Awards (London, 1622)," *Arbitration International*, 9 (1993), 323–28

Mance, Jonathan, "Arbitration: A Law unto Itself?," *Arbitration International*, 32 (2016), 223–41

Mann, Francis, "Introduction," in Lex Mercatoria *and Arbitration: A Discussion of the New Law Merchant* (Yonkers: Juris/Kluwer Law International, 1998), xxiii–xxv

"Lex Facit Arbitrum," in Pieter Sanders (ed.), *International Arbitration: Liber Amicorum for Martin Domke* (The Hague: Martinus Nijhoff, 1967), 157–83

Mantica, Margit, "Arbitration in Ancient Egypt," *Arbitration Journal*, 12 (1957), 155–63

Marrella, Fabrizio, "L'arbitrage à Venise (XIIe–XVIe siècles)," *Revue de l'arbitrage*, 2002, 263–300

Martin, Gilles, and Jean-Baptiste Racine, "Gérard Farjat et la doctrine," *Revue internationale de droit économique*, 27 (2013), 409–18

Martineau, Anne-Charlotte, "A Forgotten Chapter in the History of International Commercial Arbitration: The Slave Trade's Dispute Settlement System," *Leiden Journal of International Law*, 31 (2018), 219–41

Marx, Karl, *Grundrisse: Foundations of the Critique of Political Economy* (1939), trans. Martin Nicolaus (London: Penguin, 1993)

Marx, Robert, "International Standards of Commercial Practice," in *International Commercial Arbitration and Freedom of Contract*, ICC Brochure No. 160 (Paris: ICC International Headquarters, 1951), 10–15

Mattli, Walter, and Thomas Dietz (eds.), *International Arbitration and Global Governance: Contending Theories and Evidence* (Oxford: Oxford University Press, 2014)

Mayer, Pierre, *La distinction entre règles et décisions et le droit international privé* (Paris: Dalloz, 1973)

"Effect of International Public Policy in International Arbitration?," in Loukas Mistelis and Julian Lew (eds.), *Pervasive Problems in International Arbitration* (The Hague: Kluwer Law International, 2006)

"L'insertion de la sentence dans l'ordre juridique français," in Yves Derains (ed.), *Droit et pratique de l'arbitrage international en France* (Paris: Feduci, 1984), 81–104

"Les méthodes de la reconnaissance en droit international privé," in *Le droit international privé: Esprit et méthodes; Mélanges en l'honneur de Pierre Lagarde* (Paris: Dalloz, 2005), 547–73

"Préface," in Sylvain Bollée, *Les méthodes du droit international privé à l'épreuve des sentences arbitrales* (Paris: Economica, 2004)

"Reflections on the International Arbitrators' Duty to Apply the Law: The 2000 Freshfields Lecture," *Arbitration International*, 17 (2001), 235–48

"Revisiting *Hilmarton* and *Chromalloy*," in Albert Jan van den Berg (ed.), *International Arbitration and National Courts: The Never Ending Story*, ICCA Congress Series No. 10 (The Hague: Kluwer Law International, 2001), 165–76

"The Trend Towards Delocalisation in the Last 100 Years," in Martin Hunter, Arthur Marriott, and V. V. Veeder (eds.), *The Internationalisation of International Arbitration: The LCIA Centenary Conference* (London: Graham & Trotman/Martinus Nijhoff, 1995), 37–46

Mezghani, Ali, "Le droit musulman et l'arbitrage," *Revue de l'arbitrage*, 2008, 211–25

Miles, Kate, *The Origins of International Investment Law: Empire, Environment, and the Safeguarding of Capital* (Cambridge: Cambridge University Press, 2013)

Milgrom, Paul, Douglas North, and Barry Weingast, "The Role of Institutions in the Revival of Trade: The Law Merchant, Private Judges, and the Champagne Fairs," *Economics and Politics*, 2 (1990), 1–23

Montesquieu, *De l'esprit des lois* (1748), in *Œuvres complètes*, ed. Roger Caillois, vol. 2 (Paris: Gallimard, 1951)

Morel, René, "La clause compromissoire en matière commerciale," *Revue critique de législation et jurisprudence*, 46 (1926), 486–540

Motulsky, Henri, "L'évolution récente en matière d'arbitrage international," in *Écrits*, vol. 2, *Études et notes sur l'arbitrage* (Paris: Dalloz, 2010), 295–303

*Écrits*, vol. 1, *Études et notes de procédure civile* (Paris: Dalloz, 2009)

*Écrits*, vol. 2, *Études et notes sur l'arbitrage* (Paris: Dalloz, 2010)

"L'internationalisation du droit français de l'arbitrage," *Revue de l'arbitrage*, 1963, 110–22

*Principes d'une réalisation méthodique du droit privé: La théorie des éléments générateurs des droits subjectifs* (Paris: Dalloz, 2002)

Moynier, Gustave, "Note sur la création d'une institution judiciaire internationale propre à prévenir et à réprimer les infractions à la Convention de Genève," *Bulletin international des Sociétés de secours aux militaires blessés*, vol. 11 (Geneva: Soullier et Wirth, 1872)

Muir Watt, Horatia, "International Arbitration: A Critical Private International Law Perspective," in Thomas Schultz and Frederico Ortino (eds.), *The*

*Oxford Handbook of International Arbitration* (Oxford: Oxford University Press, 2020), 513–36

"Private International Law Beyond the Schism," *Transnational Legal Theory*, 2 (2011), 347–427

"Private International Law's Shadow Contribution to the Question of Informal Transnational Authority," *Indiana Journal of Global Legal Studies*, 25 (2018), 37–60

Mustill, Michael, "Arbitration: History and Background," *Journal of International Arbitration*, 6 (1989), 43–56

"The History of International Commercial Arbitration: A Sketch," in Lawrence Newman and Richard Hill (ed.), *The Leading Arbitrators' Guide to International Arbitration*, 3rd ed. (Huntington: Juris, 2014), 3–32

"Is It a Bird . . . ?," in Piero Bernardini, Sébastien Besson, Matthieu de Boisséson, and Jean-Denis Bredin (eds.), *Liber amicorum Claude Reymond: Autour de l'arbitrage* (Paris: LexisNexis, 2004), 205–18

"*Lex Mercatoria and Arbitration" (A Discussion of the New Law Merchant)* edited by Professor Thomas E. Carbonneau" (book review), *Arbitration International*, 8 (1992), 215–16

"The New *Lex Mercatoria*: The First Twenty-Five Years," *Arbitration International*, 4 (1988), 86–119

Mustill, Michael, and Stewart Boyd, *Commercial Arbitration*, 2nd ed. (London: Butterworths, 1989)

Nietzsche, Friedrich, *On the Genealogy of Morality*, ed. Keith Ansell-Pearson, trans. Carol Diethe, rev. ed. (Cambridge: Cambridge University Press, 2007)

Nordon, Charles, "British Experience with Arbitration," *University of Pennsylvania Law Review*, 83 (1935), 314–25

Northedge, F. S., *The League of Nations, Its Life and Times, 1920–1946* (Leicester: Leicester University Press, 1986)

O'Connell, Mary, "Arbitration and Avoidance of War: The Nineteenth-Century American Vision," in Cesare Romano (ed.), *The United States and International Courts and Tribunals* (New York: Cambridge University Press, 2009), 30–45

O'Connell, Mary, and Lenore VanderZee, "The History of International Adjudication," in Cesare Romano, Karen Alter, and Yuval Shany (eds.), *The Oxford Handbook of International Adjudication* (Oxford: Oxford University Press, 2013), 40–62

Oppetit, Bruno, "Eléments pour une sociologie de l'arbitrage," *L'Année sociologique*, 27 (1976), 179–95

*Théorie de l'arbitrage* (Paris: Presses Universitaires de France, 1998)

O'Rourke, Kevin, "The European Grain Invasion, 1870–1913," *Journal of Economic History*, 57 (1997), 775–801

O'Rourke, Kevin, and Jeffrey Williamson, *Globalization and History: The Evolution of a Nineteenth-Century Atlantic Economy* (Cambridge, MA: MIT Press, 1999)

Orford, Anne, "On International Legal Method," *London Review of International Law*, 1 (2013), 166–97

"What Is the Place of Anachronism in International Legal Thinking" (lecture, Panthéon-Sorbonne University, Paris, January 23, 2013)

Osman, Filali, *Les principes généraux de la* lex mercatoria*: Contribution à l'étude d'un ordre juridique anational* (Paris: LGDJ, 1992)

Ost, François, and Michel van de Kerchove, *De la pyramide au réseau? Pour une théorie dialectique du droit* (Brussels: Publications des Facultés universitaires Saint-Louis, 2002)

*Jalons pour une théorie critique du droit* (Brussels: Publications des Facultés universitaires Saint-Louis, 1987)

Paillat, Claude, *Dossiers secrets de la France contemporaine*, vol. 1, *1919: Les illusions de la gloire* (Laffont, 1979)

Palewski, J. -P., "L'Arbitrage commercial en France et la Cour d'Arbitrage de la Chambre de Commerce Internationale," *Journal du droit international*, 1926, 43–47

Pallieri, Giorgio Balladore, "L'arbitrage privé dans les rapports internationaux," *Collected Courses of the Hague Academy of International Law*, vol. 51 (Leiden: Brill/Nijhoff, 1935)

Papadatou, Daphné, "L'arbitrage byzantin," *Revue de l'arbitrage*, 2000, 349–76

Park, William, "The *Lex Loci Arbitri* and International Commercial Arbitration," *International and Comparative Law Quarterly*, 31 (1983), 21–52

Parra, Antonio, "'Black's Bank' and the Settlement of Investment Disputes," in David Caron, Stephan Schill, Abby Smutny, and Epaminontas Triantafilou (eds.), *Practising Virtue: Inside International Arbitration* (Oxford: Oxford University Press, 2015), 150–58

*The History of ICSID*, 2nd ed. (Oxford: Oxford University Press, 2017)

Paulsson, Jan, "The *Alabama Claims Arbitration*: Statecraft and Stagecraft," in Ulf Franke, Annette Magnusson, and Joel Dahlquist (eds.), *Arbitrating for Peace: How Arbitration Made a Difference* (The Hague: Kluwer Law International, 2016)

"Arbitration in Three Dimensions," LSE Law, Society and Economy Working Papers 2/2010, https://papers.ssrn.com/sol3/papers.cfm?abstract_id=1536093, reprinted in *International and Comparative Law Quarterly*, 60 (2011), 291–323

"Arbitration Unbound: Award Detached from the Law of Its Country of Origin," *International and Comparative Law Quarterly*, 30 (1981), 358–87

"Arbitration Unbound in Belgium," *Arbitration International*, 2 (1986), 68–73

"Arbitre et juge en Suède: Exposé général et réflexions sur la délocalisation des sentences arbitrales," *Revue de l'arbitrage*, 1980, 441–87

"The Case for Disregarding LSAs (Local Standard Annulments) under the New York Convention," *American Review of International Arbitration*, 7 (1996), 99–114

"Delocalisation of International Commercial Matters: When and Why it Matters," *International and Comparative Law Quarterly*, 32 (1983), 53–61

"Enforcing Arbitral Awards Notwithstanding a Local Standard Annulment (LSA)," *ICC International Court of Arbitration Bulletin*, 9, no. 1 (1998), 14–31

"Enforcing Arbitral Awards Notwithstanding Local Standard Annulments," *Asia Pacific Law Review*, 6 (1998), 1–28

"The Extent of Independence of International Arbitration from the Law of the *Situs*," in Julian Lew (ed.), *Contemporary Problems in International Arbitration* (Dordrecht: Springer, 1987), 141–48

"France and the Arbitral Process in 1980: A New Law and a Major Court Decision," *Svensk Och Internationell Skiljedom* [Yearbook of the Arbitration Institute of the Stockholm Chamber of Commerce], 1981, 40

*The Idea of Arbitration* (Oxford: Oxford University Press, 2013)

"Rediscovering the N.Y. Convention: Further Reflections on *Chromalloy*," *Mealey's International Arbitration Report*, 12 (1997), 20–34

"The Role of Swedish Courts in Transnational Commercial Arbitration," *Virginia Journal of International Law*, 21 (1981), 211

"Third World Participation in International Investment Arbitration," *ICSID Review – Foreign Investment Law Journal*, 2 (1987), 19–65

Paxton, Robert, *French Peasant Fascism: Henry Dorgères' Greenshirts and the Crises of French Agriculture, 1929–1939* (Oxford: Oxford University Press, 1997)

Pfersmann, Otto, "Le droit comparé comme interprétation et comme théorie du droit," *Revue internationale de droit comparé*, 53 (2001), 275–88

Philippe, Mirèze, "Autant en emporte le vent . . . de l'arbitrage," in Nassib Ziadé (ed.), *Liber Amicorum Samir Saleh: Reflections on Dispute Resolution with Particular Emphasis on the Arab World* (Alphen aan den Rijn: Wolters Kluwer, 2020), 249–76

Picard, Maurice, "La clause compromissoire et l'arbitrage dans les rapports internationaux," *Journal du droit international*, 1923, 508–19

Politis, Nicolas, *La justice internationale* (Paris: Éditions Panthéon-Assas, 2017)

Poudret, Jean-François, "Deux aspects de l'arbitrage dans les pays romands du Moyen Age: l'arbitrabilité et le juge-arbitre," *Revue de l'arbitrage*, 1999, 3–20

Poudret, Jean-François, and Sébastien Besson, *Comparative Law of International Arbitration* (London: Sweet & Maxwell, 2007)

Pound, Roscoe, "What Is a Profession? The Rise of the Legal Profession in Antiquity," *Notre Dame Law Review*, 19 (1944), 203–28

Pozzi, Roberto, "Conciliation and Arbitration between Merchants of Different Countries. Memorandum Submitted by M. Roberto Pozzi," in *Commercial Arbitration*, ICC Brochure No. 13 (Paris: ICC International Headquarters, 1921)

Press, John, "Frances Kellor, Americanization, and the Quest for Participatory Democracy" (PhD diss., New York University, 2009)

Prudhomme, André, "The Present Position of the Arbitration Clause under the Law of France," in Arthur Nussbaum (ed.), *International Yearbook on Civil and Commercial Arbitration* (New York: Oxford University Press, 1928), 74–75

Pryles, Michael, "Application of the *Lex Mercatoria* in International Commercial Arbitration," *Mealey's International Arbitration Report*, 18 (2003), 1–26

"Application of the *Lex Mercatoria* in International Commercial Arbitration," *UNSW Law Journal*, 31 (2008), 319–29

Puig, Sergio, "Social Capital in the Arbitration Market," *European Journal of International Law*, 25 (2014), 387–424

Racine, Jean-Baptiste, "L'arbitrage: Propos liminaire sur un droit pragmatique," in Yves Strickler and Jean-Baptiste Racine (eds.), *L'arbitrage: Questions contemporaines* (Paris: L'Harmattan, 2012), 11–12

*L'arbitrage commercial international et l'ordre public* (Paris: LGDJ, 1999)

*Droit de l'arbitrage* (Paris: Presses Universitaires de France, 2016)

"Eléments pour une sociologie de l'arbitrage: Actes de la Journée d'étude du Groupe Sociologie de l'arbitrage du Comité français de l'arbitrage," *Revue de l'arbitrage*, 2012, 709–16

"Réflexions sur l'autonomie de l'arbitrage commercial international," *Revue de l'arbitrage*, 2005, 305–60

Radicati di Brozolo, Luca, "The Enforcement of Annulled Awards: An Important Step in the Right Direction," *Cahiers de l'arbitrage/Paris Journal of International Arbitration* (2013), 1027–40

"The Enforcement of Annulled Awards: Further Reflections in Light of *Thai-Lao Lignite*," *American Review of International Arbitration*, 25 (2014), 47–61

"The Fate of Awards Annulled at the Seat in Light of *Thai-Lao Lignite*," *Transnational Notes* (March 19, 2014), https://blogs.law.nyu.edu/transnational/2014/03/the-fate-of-awards-annulled-at-the-seat-in-light-of-thai-lao-lignite/

Ralston, Jackson, *International Arbitration from Athens to Locarno* (Stanford: Stanford University Press, 1929)

Reader, W. J., *Professional Men: The Rise of the Professional Classes in Nineteenth-Century England* (New York: Basic Books, 1966)

Redfern, Alan, "The Changing World of Arbitration," in David Caron, Stephan Schill, Abby Smutny, and Epaminontas Triantafilou (eds.),

*Practising Virtue: Inside International Arbitration* (Oxford: Oxford University Press, 2015), 45–51

Redfern, Alan, and Martin Hunter, *Law and Practice of International Commercial Arbitration* (London: Sweet & Maxwell, 1986)

Refort, Charles, *Les difficultés soulevées par l'application de la loi du 31 décembre 1925 sur la clause compromissoire* (Paris: M. Lavergne, 1939)

Reisman, Michael, "Sovereignty and Human Rights in Contemporary International Law," *American Journal of International Law*, 84 (1990), 866–76

*Systems of Control in International Adjudication and Arbitration: Breakdown and Repair* (Durham: Duke University Press, 1992), pt. 4, "Non-Institutional International Commercial Arbitration: The Breakdown of the Control System of the New York Convention," 107–41

Renault, Louis, "Préface," in Albert de Lapradelle and Nicolas Politis, *Recueil des arbitrages internationaux* (Paris: Pedone, 1905), 1: xi

Ricœur, Paul, "Le retour de l'événement," *Mélanges de l'école française de Rome*, 104 (1992), 29–35

Ridgeway, George, *Merchants of Peace: The History of the International Chamber of Commerce* (Boston: Little, Brown and Company, 1959)

*Merchants of Peace: Twenty Years of Business Diplomacy through the International Chamber of Commerce, 1919–1938* (New York: Columbia University Press, 1938)

Rigaud, Marie-Claude, "La procédure arbitrale transnationale" (PhD diss., Université de Paris-XII, 2008)

Rivkin, David, "The Enforcement of Awards Nullified in the Country of Origin: The American Experience," in Albert Jan vanden Berg (ed.), *Improving the Efficiency of Arbitration Agreements and Awards: 40 Years of Application of the New York Convention*, ICCA Congress Series No. 9 (The Hague: Kluwer Law International, 1999), 528–43

Robert, Jean, *La clause compromissoire et l'organisation de l'arbitrage* (Paris: Sirey, 1929)

"La Convention de New York du 10 juin 1958 pour la reconnaissance et l'exécution des sentences arbitrales étrangères," *Revue de l'arbitrage*, 1958, 70–82

Robert, Jean, and Bertrand Moreau, *L'arbitrage: Droit interne, droit international privé*, 6th ed. (Paris: Dalloz, 1993)

Robert, Jean, and Thomas Carbonneau, *The French Law of Arbitration* (New York: Matthew Bender, 1983)

Roebuck, Derek, *Ancient Greek Arbitration* (Oxford: Holo Books, Arbitration Press, 2001)

"L'arbitrage en droit anglais avant 1558," *Revue de l'arbitrage*, 2002, 535–77

*Arbitration and Mediation in Seventeenth-Century England* (Oxford: Holo Books, Arbitration Press, 2017)

*Early English Arbitration* (Oxford: Holo Books, Arbitration Press, 2008)

*The Golden Age of Arbitration: Dispute Resolution under Elizabeth I* (Oxford: Holo Books, Arbitration Press, 2015)

*Mediation and Arbitration in the Middle Ages: England 1154 to 1558* (Oxford: Holo Books, Arbitration Press, 2013)

"Sources for the History of Arbitration: A Bibliographical Introduction," *Arbitration International*, 14 (1998), 237–343

Roebuck, Derek, and Bruno de Loynes de Fumichon, *Roman Arbitration* (Oxford: Holo Books, Arbitration Press, 2004)

Roelofsen, Cornelis, "International Arbitration and Courts," in Bardo Fassbender and Anne Peters (eds.), *The Oxford Handbook of the History of International Law* (Oxford: Oxford University Press, 2012), 145–69

Rogers, Catherine, *Ethics in International Arbitration* (Oxford: Oxford University Press, 2014)

Romano, Santi, *The Legal Order*, trans. Mariano Croce (New York: Routledge, 2017)

*L'ordre juridique*, ed. Pierre Mayer, trans. Lucien François and Pierre Gothot (Paris: Dalloz, 2002)

*L'ordre juridique*, trans. Lucien François and Pierre Gothot (Paris: Dalloz, 1975)

Romano, Cesare, "Trial and Error in International Judicialization," in Cesare Romano, Karen Alter, and Yuval Shany (eds.), *The Oxford Handbook of International Adjudication* (Oxford: Oxford University Press, 2013), 111–34

Ronit, Karsten, and Volker Schneider, "Global Governance through Private Organizations," *Governance: An International Journal of Policy and Administration*, 12 (July 1999), 243–66

"Private Organizations and Their Contribution to Problem-Solving in the Global Arena," in Karsten Ronit and Volker Schneider (eds.), *Private Organizations in Global Politics* (London: Routledge, 2000), 1–33

Rosenbaum, Samuel, *A Report on Commercial Arbitration in England*, Bulletin 12 (Chicago: American Judicature Society, 1916)

Rosengarten, Monika, "Die Internationale Handelskammer: Wirtschaftspolitische Empfehlungen in der Zeit der Weltwirtschaftskrise 1929–1939" (PhD diss., Freie Universität Berlin, 1999)

Rothé, Otto, *La clause compromissoire et l'arbitrage depuis la loi de 1925* (Paris: Domat/Montchrestien,1934)

Rothstein, Morton, "Centralizing Firms and Spreading Markets: The World of International Grain Traders, 1846–1914," *Business and Economic History*, 17 (1988), 103–13

Rousseau, Guy, *Étienne Clémentel (1864–1936): Entre idéalisme et réalisme, une vie politique* (Clermont-Ferrand: Archives départementales du Puy-de-Dôme, 1998)

Royer, Jean-Pierre, Jean-Paul Jean, Nicolas Derasse, Jean-Pierre Allinne, and Bernard Durand, *Histoire de la justice en France du XVIIIe siècle à nos jours*, 5th ed. (Paris: Presses Universitaires de France, 2016)

Rudler, Jean, *La clause compromissoire et l'arbitrage civil* (Nancy: A. Suzaine, 1927)

Sachs, Stephen, "From St. Ives to Cyberspace: The Modern Distortion of the Medieval 'Law Merchant,'" *American University International Law Review*, 21 (2006), 685–812

Saleilles, Raymond, "Loi du 26 août 1889 pour amender et codifier les dispositions légales relatives à l'arbitrage," in Société de législation comparée, *Annuaire de législation étrangère* (1889), 39–47

Sampliner, Gary, "Enforcement of Foreign Arbitral Awards after Annulment in Their Country of Origin," *Mealey's International Arbitration Report*, 11 (1996), 22–34

"Enforcement of Nullified Foreign Arbitral Awards: *Chromalloy* Revisited," *Journal of International Arbitration*, 14 (1997), 141–66

Sanders, Pieter, "The History of the New York Convention," in Albert Jan van den Berg (ed.), *Improving the Efficiency of Arbitration Agreements and Awards: 40 Years of Application of the New York Convention*, ICCA Congress Series No. 9 (The Hague: Kluwer Law International, 1999), 11–14

"The Making of the Convention," in *Enforcing Arbitration Awards under the New York Convention: Experience and Prospects* (New York: United Nations, 1999), 3–5

"New York Convention on the Recognition and Enforcement of Foreign Arbitral Awards," *Netherlands International Law Review*, 6 (1959), 43

Sanders, Pieter (ed.), *International Arbitration: Liber Amicorum for Martin Domke* (The Hague: Martinus Nijhoff, 1967)

Sassen, Saskia, "The Global Inside the National. A Research Agenda for Sociology," *Sociopedia.Isa* (2010), 1–10

*Losing Control? Sovereignty in an Age of Globalization* (New York: Columbia University Press, 1996)

*Territory, Authority, Rights: From Medieval to Global Assemblages* (Princeton: Princeton University Press, 2006)

Savary, Jacques, *Le parfait négociant*, ed. Edouard Richard (Geneva: Droz, 2011 [1675])

Scarfi, Juan Pablo, *The Hidden History of International Law in the Americas: Empire and Legal Networks* (Oxford: Oxford University Press, 2017)

Schill, Stephan, Christian Tams, and Rainer Hofmann (eds.), *International Investment Law and History* (Cheltenham: Edward Elgar, 2018)

Schinazi, Mikaël, "The Three Ages of International Commercial Arbitration and the Development of the ICC Arbitration System," *ICC Dispute Resolution Bulletin*, 2020, issue 2, 63–75

Schlag, Peter, "The Aesthetics of American Law," *Harvard Law Review*, 115 (2002), 1047–18

Schmitthoff, Clive, "The Law of International Trade, Its Growth, Formulation and Operation," repr. in Chia-Jui Cheng (ed.), *Clive M. Schmitthoff's Select Essays on International Trade Law*, chap. 13 (London: Martinus Nijhoff/ Graham & Trotman, 1988), 137–69

"The New Sources of the Law of International Trade," repr. in Chia-Jui Cheng (ed.), *Clive M. Schmitthoff's Select Essays on International Trade Law*, chap. 12 (London: Martinus Nijhoff/Graham & Trotman, 1988), 131–36

"The Unification of the Law of International Trade," repr. in Chia-Jui Cheng (ed.), *Clive M. Schmitthoff's Select Essays on International Trade Law*, chap. 14 (London: Martinus Nijhoff/Graham & Trotman, 1988), 170–87

"The Unification of the Law of International Trade," repr. in Chia-Jui Cheng (ed.), *Clive M. Schmitthoff's Select Essays on International Trade Law*, chap. 16 (London: Martinus Nijhoff/Graham & Trotman, 1988), 206–18

"The Unification or Harmonization of Law by Means of Standard Contracts and General Conditions," *International and Comparative Law Quarterly*, 17 (1968), 551–70

Schneider, Eugène, *Le voyage des missions économiques des pays alliés aux États-Unis et le Congrès d'Atlantic-City, octobre-novembre 1919* (Paris: Imprimerie Chaix, 1919)

Schultz, Thomas, "Celebrating 20 Years of 'Dealing in Virtue,'" *Journal of International Dispute Settlement*, 7 (2016), 531–33

*Transnational Legality: Stateless Law and International Arbitration* (Oxford: Oxford University Press, 2014)

Schultz, Thomas, and Niccolò Ridi, "Arbitration Literature," in Thomas Schultz and Frederico Ortino (eds.), *The Oxford Handbook of International Arbitration* (Oxford: Oxford University Press, 2020), 1–32

Schultz, Thomas, and Robert Kovacs, "The Rise of a Third Generation of Arbitrators? Fifteen Years after Dezalay and Garth," *Arbitration International*, 28 (2012), 161–71

Schwartz, Eric, "A Comment on *Chromalloy*: Hilmarton, *à l'américaine*," *Journal of International Arbitration*, 14(2) (1997), 125–36

"International Conciliation and the ICC," *ICC International Court of Arbitration Bulletin*, 5, no. 2 (November 1994), 5–17

Schwob, Georges, *Les contrats de la London Corn Trade Association (Vente CAF)* (Paris: Arthur Rousseau, 1928)

Seraglini, Christophe, and Jérôme Ortscheidt, *Droit de l'arbitrage interne et international*, 2nd ed. (Paris: LGDJ, 2019)

Sgard, Jérôme, "Global Economic Governance during the Middle Ages: The Jurisdiction of the Champagne Fairs," *International Review of Law and Economics*, 42 (2015), 174–84

"A Tale of Three Cities: The Construction of International Commercial Arbitration," in Jérôme Sgard and Grégoire Mallard (eds.), *Contractual Knowledge: One Hundred Years of Legal Experimentation in Global Markets* (Cambridge: Cambridge University Press, 2016), 153–84

Shalakany, Amr, "Arbitration and the Third World: A Plea for Reassessing Bias under the Specter of Neoliberalism," *Harvard International Law Journal*, 41 (2000), 419–68

Silberman, Linda, and Nathan Yaffe, "The US Approach to Recognition and Enforcement of Awards after Set-Asides: The Impact of the *Pemex* Decision," *Fordham International Law Journal*, 40 (2017), 799–812

Silva Romero, Eduardo, Emmanuel Jolivet, and Florian Grisel, "Aux origines de l'arbitrage commercial contemporain: L'émergence de l'arbitrage CCI (1920–1958)," *Revue de l'arbitrage*, 2016, 403–44

Skinner, Quentin, "Meaning and Understanding in the History of Ideas," *History and Theory*, 8 (1969), 3–53

Skouteris, Thomas, "The Turn to History in International Law," Oxford Bibliographies of International Law, www.oxfordbibliographies.com/view/document/obo-9780199796953/obo-9780199796953-0154.xml (last modified June 27, 2017)

Smit, Robert, "Remembrance and Reminiscence: Thoughts on Arbitrator Selection: Why My Father Was (Usually) a Good Choice," *American Review of International Arbitration*, 23 (2012), 575–93

Smith, Steven, "At the Crossroads: Hegel and the Ethics of *bürgerliche Gesellschaft*," *Laval théologique et politique*, 51 (1995), 345–62

Sornarajah, Muthucumaraswamy, "The Climate of International Arbitration," *Journal of International Arbitration*, 8 (1991), 47–86

St. John, Taylor, "The Creation of Investor-State Arbitration," in Thomas Schultz and Frederico Ortino (eds.), *The Oxford Handbook of International Arbitration* (Oxford: Oxford University Press, 2020), 792–814

*The Rise of Investor-State Arbitration: Politics, Law, and Unintended Consequences* (Oxford: Oxford University Press, 2018)

Starr, Paul *The Social Transformation of American Medicine: The Rise of a Sovereign Profession and the Making of a Vast Industry* (New York: Basic Books, 1982)

Stone Sweet, Alec, and Florian Grisel, "The Evolution of International Arbitration: Delegation, Judicialization, Governance," in Walter Mattli and Thomas Dietz (eds.), *International Arbitration and Global Governance: Contending Theories and Evidence* (Oxford: Oxford University Press, 2014), 22–46

*The Evolution of International Arbitration: Judicialization, Governance, Legitimacy* (Oxford: Oxford University Press, 2017)

Story, Joseph, *Commentaries on Equity Jurisprudence* (London: Stevens and Haynes, 1884)

Stoufflet, Jean, *Le crédit documentaire: Étude juridique d'un instrument financier du commerce international* (Paris: Librairies techniques, 1957)

"Payment and Transfer in Documentary Letters of Credit: Interaction between the French General Law of Obligations and the Uniform Customs and Practice," *Arizona Law Review*, 24 (1982), 267–76

Strindberg, August, *The German Lieutenant and Other Stories*, trans. Claud Field (London: Werner Laurie, 1915)

Stuyt, A. M., "Preface to the 1939 Edition," in A. M. Stuyt, *Survey of International Arbitrations 1794–1970* (Leiden: A. W. Sijthoff, 1972)

"Success of Arbitration," *American Advocate of Peace*, 55 (1893), 151–53 and 162–63

Szramkiewicz, Romuald, and Olivier Descamps, *Histoire du droit des affaires*, 3rd ed. (Paris: LGDJ, 2019)

Tames, Richard, *Economy and Society in Nineteenth-Century Britain* (London: Routledge, 1972)

Tercier, Pierre, "The 1927 Geneva Convention and the ICC Reform Proposals," *Dispute Resolution International*, 2 (2008), 19–26

Terré, François, "L'arbitrage, essence du juridique," in Piero Bernardini, Sébastien Besson, Matthieu de Boisséson, and Jean-Denis Bredin (eds.), *Liber amicorum Claude Reymond: Autour de l'arbitrage* (Paris: LexisNexis, 2004), 309–16

Teschke, Benno, *The Myth of 1648: Class, Geopolitics, and the Making of Modern International Relations* (London: Verso, 2003)

Teubner, Gunther, "Breaking Frames: The Global Interplay of Legal and Social Systems," *American Journal of Comparative Law*, 45 (1997), 149–69

*Law as an Autopoietic System* (Oxford: Blackwell, 1993)

Topik, Steven, and Allen Wells, *Global Markets Transformed: 1870–1945* (Cambridge, MA: Harvard University Press, 2014)

Tourme-Jouannet, Emmanuelle, *Le droit international libéral-providence : Une histoire du droit international* (Brussels: Bruylant/Editions de l'Université de Bruxelles, 2011)

Trachtenberg, Marc, "Clémentel et la diplomatie économique pendant la Première Guerre mondiale," in Marie-Christine Kessler and Guy Rousseau (eds.), *Étienne Clémentel: Politique et action publique sous la Troisième République* (Brussels: Peter Lang, 2018), 375–91

"'A New Economic Order': Étienne Clémentel and French Economic Diplomacy during the First World War," *French Historical Studies*, 10 (1977), 315–41

Tsai, Chen-Wen, "La Chambre de commerce internationale, un groupe de pression international: Son action et son rôle dans l'élaboration, la conclusion et l'application des conventions internationales établies au sein des organisations intergouvernementales à vocation mondiale (1945–1969)" (PhD diss., Katholieke Universiteit te Leuven, 1972)

Tulard, Jean, "Mallarmé (Claude-Joseph)," in Jean Tulard (ed.), *Dictionnaire Napoléon* (Paris: Fayard, 1987), 1122

"Mounier (Claude-Philibert-Édouard)," in Jean Tulard (ed.), *Dictionnaire Napoléon* (Paris: Fayard, 1987), 1203

"Treilhard (Jean-Baptiste)," in Jean Tulard (ed.), *Dictionnaire Napoléon* (Paris: Fayard, 1987), 1653

United Nations, "Foreword," *Reports of International Arbitration Awards*, 15 (2006), http://legal.un.org/docs/?path=./riaa/cases/vol_XV/foreword.pdf&lang=O

Vabulas, Felicity, "Consultative and Observer Status of NGOs in Intergovernmental Organizations," in Bob Reinalda (ed.), *Routledge Handbook of International Organization*. (New York: Routledge, 2013)

Van den Berg, Albert Jan, "Annulment of Awards in International Arbitration," in Richard Lillich and Charles Brower (eds.), *International Arbitration in the 21st Century: Towards "Judicialization" and Uniformity?* (New York: Transnational Publishers, 1994), 133–62

"Enforcement of Annulled Awards?," *ICC International Court of Arbitration Bulletin*, 9, no. 2 (1998), 15–21

"Hypothetical Draft Convention on the International Enforcement of Arbitration Agreements and Awards: Explanatory Note and Annexes," in Albert Jan van den Berg (ed.), *50 Years of the New York Convention*, ICCA Congress Series No. 14 (The Hague: Kluwer Law International, 2009), 649–66

*The New York Convention of 1958: Towards a Uniform Judicial Interpretation* (Deventer: Kluwer Law and Taxation, 1981)

"Should an International Arbitrator Apply the New York Convention of 1958," in Jan Schultsz and Albert Jan van den Berg (eds.), *The Art of Arbitration: Essays on International Arbitration; Liber Amicorum Pieter Sanders, 12 September 1912–1982* (Deventer: Kluwer Law and Taxation, 1982), 39–50

Van den Kerckhove, Sartini, "Une juridiction internationale de droit privé," *Journal du droit international*, 1935, 775–804

Van Hulle, Inge, "Imperial Consolidation through Arbitration: Territorial and Boundary Disputes in Africa (1870–1914)," in Ignacio de la Rasilla and Jorge Viñuales (eds.), *Experiments in International Adjudication: Historical Accounts* (Cambridge: Cambridge University Press, 2019), 55–75

Veeder, V. V., "Chancellor Wirth and the Mologales Concession 1923–1927: The German-Speaking Origins of the 1965 ICSID Convention," in Christina Binder, Ursula Kriebaum, August Reinisch, and Stephan Wittich (eds.), *International Investment Law for the 21st Century: Essays in Honour of Christoph Schreuer* (Oxford: Oxford University Press, 2009), 383–84

"The Historical Keystone to International Arbitration: The Party-Appointed Arbitrator; From Miami to Geneva," in David Caron, Stephan Schill, Abby Smutny, and Epaminontas Triantafilou (eds.), *Practising Virtue: Inside International Arbitration* (Oxford: Oxford University Press, 2015), 127–49

"Investor-State Disputes and the Development of International Law Arbitral Lessons from the Private Correspondence of Queen Victoria and Lenin," *Proceedings of the ASIL Annual Meeting*, 98 (2004), 33–36

"Is There a Need to Revise the New York Convention?," *Journal of International Dispute Settlement*, 1 (2010), 499–506

"The Lena Goldfields Arbitration: The Historical Roots of Three Ideas," *International and Comparative Law Quarterly*, 47 (1998), 747–92

"Lloyd George, Lenin and Cannibals: The Harriman Arbitration; The 1999 Freshfields Lecture," *Arbitration International*, 16 (2000), 115–40

"The Tetiube Mining Concession: 1924–1932: A Swiss-Russian Story (Where the Arbitral Dog Did Not Bark)," in Piero Bernardini, Sébastien Besson, Matthieu de Boisséson, and Jean-Denis Bredin (eds.), *Liber amicorum Claude Reymond: Autour de l'arbitrage* (Paris: LexisNexis, 2004), 325–42

"Two Arbitral Butterflies: Bramwell and David," in Martin Hunter, Arthur Marriott, and V. V. Veeder (eds.), *The Internationalisation of International Arbitration: The LCIA Centenary Conference* (London: Graham & Trotman/Martinus Nijhoff, 1995), 13–23

Veeder, V. V., and Brian Dye, "Lord Bramwell's Arbitration Code 1884–1889," *Arbitration International*, 8 (1992), 329–86

Velissaropoulos-Karakostas, Julie, "L'arbitrage dans la Grèce antique: Époques archaïque et classique," *Revue de l'arbitrage*, 2000, 9–26

Viatte, Albert, "Clause compromissoire: Validité en matière commerciale; Commentaire de la loi du 31 décembre 1925," *Recueil général des lois, décrets et arrêtés – Première partie – Commentaires et revues de jurisprudence*, 56 (1926), 19–24

Viñuales, Jorge, "Experiments in International Adjudication: Past and Present," in Ignacio de la Rasilla and Jorge Viñuales (eds.), *Experiments in International Adjudication: Historical Accounts* (Cambridge: Cambridge University Press, 2019), 11–31

Von Mehren, Arthur Taylor, "International Commercial Arbitration: The Contribution of the French Jurisprudence," *Louisiana Law Review*, 46 (1986), 1045–59

Vulliemin, Robert, *Du recours à l'arbitrage dans les matières commerciales à la fin du XIXe et au début du XXe siècle et de l'organisation de l'arbitrage commercial international* (Paris: Arthur Rousseau, 1931)

Wahl, Philipp, "Enforcement of Foreign Arbitral Awards Set Aside in Their Country of Origin: The *Chromalloy* Case Revisited," *Journal of International Arbitration*, 16 (1999), 131–40

Werner, Jacques, "Editorial: Competition within the Arbitration Industry," *Journal of International Arbitration*, 2 (1985), 1–2

Wetter, J. Gillis, *The International Arbitral Process: Public and Private* (New York: Oceana, 1979)

White, Lyman, *International Non-Governmental Organizations: Their Purposes, Methods, and Accomplishments* (New Brunswick: Rutgers University Press, 1951)

Wilensky, Harold, "The Professionalization of Everyone?," *American Journal of Sociology*, 70 (1964), 137–58

Wilson-Bareau, Juliet, and David Degener, *Manet and the American Civil War: The Battle of U.S.S. Kearsarge and the C.S.S. Alabama* (New Haven: Yale University Press, 2003)

Wood, Allen, "Editor's Introduction," in Georg Wilhelm Friedrich Hegel, *Elements of the Philosophy of Right*, ed. Allen Wood, trans. Hugh Barr Nisbet (Cambridge: Cambridge University Press, 2003 [1821]), vii–xxxii

Xifaras, Mikhaïl, "Après les théories générales de l'Etat: Le droit global?," *Jus Politicum*, 8 (2012), 1–57

"Comment rendre le passé contemporain?," in Nicolas Laurent-Bonne and Xavier Prévost (eds.), *Penser l'ancien droit privé: Regards croisés sur les méthodes des juristes (II)* (Paris: LGDJ, 2018), 33–37

"The Global Turn in Legal Theory," *Canadian Journal of Law and Jurisprudence*, 29 (2016), 215–43

Yackee, Jason, "The First Investor-State Arbitration? The Suez Canal Dispute of 1864 and Some Reflections on the Historiography of International Investment Law," in Stephan Schill, Christian Tams, and Rainer Hofmann (eds.), *International Investment Law and History* (Cheltenham: Edward Elgar, 2018), 70–101

Ziegler, Katja, "Jay Treaty (1794)," *Max Planck Encyclopedia of Public International Law*, 2013

# INDEX

CAMBRIDGE STUDIES IN INTERNATIONAL AND COMPARATIVE LAW

*Books in the Series*

163 *The Three Ages of International Commercial Arbitration*
Mikaël Schinazi

162 *Repetition and International Law*
Wouter Werner

161 *State Responsibility and Rebels: The History and Legacy of Protecting Investment Against Revolution*
Kathryn Greenman

160 *Rewriting Histories of the Use of Force: The Narrative of 'Indifference'*
Agatha Verdebout

159 *The League of Nations and the Protection of the Environment*
Omer Aloni

158 *International Investment Law and Legal Theory: Expropriation and the Fragmentation of Sources*
Jörg Kammerhofer

157 *Legal Barbarians: Identity, Modern Comparative Law and the Global South*
Daniel Bonilla Maldonado

156 *International Human Rights Law Beyond State Territorial Control*
Antal Berkes

155 *The Crime of Aggression under the Rome Statute of the International Criminal Court*
Carrie McDougall

154 *Minorities and the Making of Postcolonial States in International Law*
Mohammad Shahabuddin

153 *Preclassical Conflict of Laws*
Nikitas E. Hatzimihail

152 *International Law and History: Modern Interfaces*
Ignacio de la Rasilla

151 *Marketing Global Justice: The Political Economy of International Criminal Law*
Christine Schwöbel-Patel

150 *International Status in the Shadow of Empire*
Cait Storr

149 *Treaties in Motion: The Evolution of Treaties from Formation to Termination*
Edited by Malgosia Fitzmaurice and Panos Merkouris

148 *Humanitarian Disarmament: An Historical Enquiry*
Treasa Dunworth

147 *Complementarity, Catalysts, Compliance: The International Criminal Court in Uganda, Kenya, and the Democratic Republic of Congo*
Christian M. De Vos

146 *Cyber Operations and International Law*
François Delerue

145 *Comparative Reasoning in International Courts and Tribunals*
Daniel Peat

144 *Maritime Delimitation as a Judicial Process*
Massimo Lando

143 *Prosecuting Sexual and Gender-Based Crimes at the International Criminal Court: Practice, Progress and Potential*
Rosemary Grey

142 *Capitalism as Civilisation: A History of International Law*
Ntina Tzouvala

141 *Sovereignty in China: A Genealogy of a Concept Since 1840*
Adele Carrai

140 *Narratives of Hunger in International Law: Feeding the World in Times of Climate Change*
Anne Saab

139 *Victim Reparation under the Ius Post Bellum: An Historical and Normative Perspective*
Shavana Musa

138 *The Analogy between States and International Organizations*
Fernando Lusa Bordin

137 *The Process of International Legal Reproduction: Inequality, Historiography, Resistance*
Rose Parfitt

136 *State Responsibility for Breaches of Investment Contracts*
Jean Ho

135 *Coalitions of the Willing and International Law: The Interplay between Formality and Informality*
Alejandro Rodiles

134 *Self-Determination in Disputed Colonial Territories*
Jamie Trinidad

133 *International Law as a Belief System*
Jean d'Aspremont

132 *Legal Consequences of Peremptory Norms in International Law*
Daniel Costelloe

131 *Third-Party Countermeasures in International Law*
Martin Dawidowicz

130 *Justification and Excuse in International Law: Concept and Theory of General Defences*
Federica Paddeu

129 *Exclusion from Public Space: A Comparative Constitutional Analysis*
Daniel Moeckli

128 *Provisional Measures before International Courts and Tribunals*
Cameron A. Miles

127 *Humanity at Sea: Maritime Migration and the Foundations of International Law*
Itamar Mann

126 *Beyond Human Rights: The Legal Status of the Individual in International Law*
Anne Peters

125 *The Doctrine of Odious Debt in International Law: A Restatement*
Jeff King

124 *Static and Evolutive Treaty Interpretation: A Functional Reconstruction*
Christian Djeffal

123 *Civil Liability in Europe for Terrorism-Related Risk*
Lucas Bergkamp, Michael Faure, Monika Hinteregger and Niels Philipsen

122 *Proportionality and Deference in Investor-State Arbitration: Balancing Investment Protection and Regulatory Autonomy*
Caroline Henckels

121 *International Law and Governance of Natural Resources in Conflict and Post-Conflict Situations*
Daniëlla Dam-de Jong

120 *Proof of Causation in Tort Law*
Sandy Steel

119 *The Formation and Identification of Rules of Customary International Law in International Investment Law*
Patrick Dumberry

118 *Religious Hatred and International Law: The Prohibition of Incitement to Violence or Discrimination*
Jeroen Temperman

117 *Taking Economic, Social and Cultural Rights Seriously in International Criminal Law*
Evelyne Schmid

116 *Climate Change Litigation: Regulatory Pathways to Cleaner Energy*
Jacqueline Peel and Hari M. Osofsky

115 *Mestizo International Law: A Global Intellectual History 1842–1933*
Arnulf Becker Lorca

114 *Sugar and the Making of International Trade Law*
Michael Fakhri

113 *Strategically Created Treaty Conflicts and the Politics of International Law*
Surabhi Ranganathan

112 *Investment Treaty Arbitration as Public International Law: Procedural Aspects and Implications*
Eric De Brabandere

111 *The New Entrants Problem in International Fisheries Law*
Andrew Serdy

110 *Substantive Protection under Investment Treaties: A Legal and Economic Analysis*
Jonathan Bonnitcha

109 *Popular Governance of Post-Conflict Reconstruction: The Role of International Law*
Matthew Saul

108 *Evolution of International Environmental Regimes: The Case of Climate Change*
Simone Schiele

107 *Judges, Law and War: The Judicial Development of International Humanitarian Law*
Shane Darcy

106 *Religious Offence and Human Rights: The Implications of Defamation of Religions*
Lorenz Langer

105 *Forum Shopping in International Adjudication: The Role of Preliminary Objections*
Luiz Eduardo Salles

104 *Domestic Politics and International Human Rights Tribunals: The Problem of Compliance*
Courtney Hillebrecht

103 *International Law and the Arctic*
Michael Byers

102 *Cooperation in the Law of Transboundary Water Resources*
Christina Leb

101 *Underwater Cultural Heritage and International Law*
Sarah Dromgoole

100 *State Responsibility: The General Part*
James Crawford

99 *The Origins of International Investment Law: Empire, Environment and the Safeguarding of Capital*
Kate Miles

98 *The Crime of Aggression under the Rome Statute of the International Criminal Court*
Carrie McDougall

97 *'Crimes against Peace' and International Law*
Kirsten Sellars

96 *Non-Legality in International Law: Unruly Law*
Fleur Johns

95 *Armed Conflict and Displacement: The Protection of Refugees and Displaced Persons under International Humanitarian Law*
Mélanie Jacques

94 *Foreign Investment and the Environment in International Law*
Jorge E. Viñuales

93 *The Human Rights Treaty Obligations of Peacekeepers*
Kjetil Mujezinović Larsen

92 *Cyber Warfare and the Laws of War*
Heather Harrison Dinniss

91 *The Right to Reparation in International Law for Victims of Armed Conflict*
Christine Evans

90 *Global Public Interest in International Investment Law*
Andreas Kulick

89 *State Immunity in International Law*
Xiaodong Yang

88 *Reparations and Victim Support in the International Criminal Court*
Conor McCarthy

87 *Reducing Genocide to Law: Definition, Meaning, and the Ultimate Crime*
Payam Akhavan

86 *Decolonising International Law: Development, Economic Growth and the Politics of Universality*
Sundhya Pahuja

85 *Complicity and the Law of State Responsibility*
Helmut Philipp Aust

84 *State Control over Private Military and Security Companies in Armed Conflict*
Hannah Tonkin

83 *'Fair and Equitable Treatment' in International Investment Law*
Roland Kläger

82 *The UN and Human Rights: Who Guards the Guardians?*
Guglielmo Verdirame

81 *Sovereign Defaults before International Courts and Tribunals*
Michael Waibel

80 *Making the Law of the Sea: A Study in the Development of International Law*
James Harrison

79 *Science and the Precautionary Principle in International Courts and Tribunals: Expert Evidence, Burden of Proof and Finality*
Caroline E. Foster

78 *Transition from Illegal Regimes under International Law*
Yaël Ronen

77 *Access to Asylum: International Refugee Law and the Globalisation of Migration Control*
Thomas Gammeltoft-Hansen

76 *Trading Fish, Saving Fish: The Interaction between Regimes in International Law*
Margaret A. Young

75 *The Individual in the International Legal System: Continuity and Change in International Law*
Kate Parlett

74 *'Armed Attack' and Article 51 of the UN Charter: Evolutions in Customary Law and Practice*
Tom Ruys

73 *Theatre of the Rule of Law: Transnational Legal Intervention in Theory and Practice*
Stephen Humphreys

72 *Science and Risk Regulation in International Law*
Jacqueline Peel

71 *The Participation of States in International Organisations: The Role of Human Rights and Democracy*
Alison Duxbury

70 *Legal Personality in International Law*
Roland Portmann

69 *Vicarious Liability in Tort: A Comparative Perspective*
Paula Giliker

68 *The Public International Law Theory of Hans Kelsen: Believing in Universal Law*
Jochen von Bernstorff

67 *Legitimacy and Legality in International Law: An Interactional Account*
Jutta Brunnée and Stephen J. Toope

66 *The Concept of Non-International Armed Conflict in International Humanitarian Law*
Anthony Cullen

65 *The Principle of Legality in International and Comparative Criminal Law*
Kenneth S. Gallant

64 *The Challenge of Child Labour in International Law*
Franziska Humbert

63 *Shipping Interdiction and the Law of the Sea*
Douglas Guilfoyle

62 *International Courts and Environmental Protection*
Tim Stephens

61 *Legal Principles in WTO Disputes*
Andrew D. Mitchell

60 *War Crimes in Internal Armed Conflicts*
Eve La Haye

59 *Humanitarian Occupation*
Gregory H. Fox

58 *The International Law of Environmental Impact Assessment: Process, Substance and Integration*
Neil Craik

57 *The Law and Practice of International Territorial Administration: Versailles to Iraq and Beyond*
Carsten Stahn

56 *United Nations Sanctions and the Rule of Law*
Jeremy Matam Farrall

55 *National Law in WTO Law: Effectiveness and Good Governance in the World Trading System*
Sharif Bhuiyan

54 *Cultural Products and the World Trade Organization*
Tania Voon

53 *The Threat of Force in International Law*
Nikolas Stürchler

52 *Indigenous Rights and United Nations Standards: Self-Determination, Culture and Land*
Alexandra Xanthaki

51 *International Refugee Law and Socio-Economic Rights: Refuge from Deprivation*
Michelle Foster

50 *The Protection of Cultural Property in Armed Conflict*
Roger O'Keefe

49 *Interpretation and Revision of International Boundary Decisions*
Kaiyan Homi Kaikobad

48 *Multinationals and Corporate Social Responsibility: Limitations and Opportunities in International Law*
Jennifer A. Zerk

47 *Judiciaries within Europe: A Comparative Review*
John Bell

46 *Law in Times of Crisis: Emergency Powers in Theory and Practice*
Oren Gross and Fionnuala Ní Aoláin

45 *Vessel-Source Marine Pollution: The Law and Politics of International Regulation*
Alan Khee-Jin Tan

44 *Enforcing Obligations* Erga Omnes *in International Law*
Christian J. Tams

43 *Non-Governmental Organisations in International Law*
Anna-Karin Lindblom

42 *Democracy, Minorities and International Law*
Steven Wheatley

41 *Prosecuting International Crimes: Selectivity and the International Criminal Law Regime*
Robert Cryer

40 *Compensation for Personal Injury in English, German and Italian Law: A Comparative Outline*
Basil Markesinis, Michael Coester, Guido Alpa and Augustus Ullstein

39 *Dispute Settlement in the UN Convention on the Law of the Sea*
Natalie Klein

38 *The International Protection of Internally Displaced Persons*
Catherine Phuong

37 *Imperialism, Sovereignty and the Making of International Law*
Antony Anghie

36 *Principles of the Institutional Law of International Organizations*
C. F. Amerasinghe

35 *Necessity, Proportionality and the Use of Force by States*
Judith Gardam

34 *International Legal Argument in the Permanent Court of International Justice: The Rise of the International Judiciary*
Ole Spiermann

33 -

32 *Great Powers and Outlaw States: Unequal Sovereigns in the International Legal Order*
Gerry Simpson

31 *Local Remedies in International Law* (second edition) Chittharanjan Felix Amerasinghe

30 *Reading Humanitarian Intervention: Human Rights and the Use of Force in International Law*
Anne Orford

29 *Conflict of Norms in Public International Law: How WTO Law Relates to Other Rules of International Law*
Joost Pauwelyn

28 -

27 *Transboundary Damage in International Law*
Hanqin Xue

26 -

25 *European Criminal Procedures*
Edited by Mireille Delmas-Marty and J. R. Spencer

24 *Accountability of Armed Opposition Groups in International Law*
Liesbeth Zegveld

23 *Sharing Transboundary Resources: International Law and Optimal Resource Use*
Eyal Benvenisti

22 *International Human Rights and Humanitarian Law*
René Provost

21 *Remedies against International Organisations*
Karel Wellens

20 *Diversity and Self-Determination in International Law*
Karen Knop

19 *The Law of Internal Armed Conflict*
Lindsay Moir

18 *International Commercial Arbitration and African States: Practice, Participation and Institutional Development*
Amazu A. Asouzu

17 *The Enforceability of Promises in European Contract Law*
James Gordley

16 *International Law in Antiquity*
David J. Bederman

15 *Money Laundering: A New International Law Enforcement Model*
Guy Stessens

14 *Good Faith in European Contract Law*
Reinhard Zimmermann and Simon Whittaker

13 *On Civil Procedure*
J. A. Jolowicz

12 *Trusts: A Comparative Study*
Maurizio Lupoi and Simon Dix

11 *The Right to Property in Commonwealth Constitutions*
Tom Allen

10 *International Organizations before National Courts*
August Reinisch

9 *The Changing International Law of High Seas Fisheries*
Francisco Orrego Vicuña

8 *Trade and the Environment: A Comparative Study of EC and US Law*
Damien Geradin

7 *Unjust Enrichment: A Study of Private Law and Public Values*
Hanoch Dagan

6 *Religious Liberty and International Law in Europe*
Malcolm D. Evans

5 *Ethics and Authority in International Law*
Alfred P. Rubin

4 *Sovereignty over Natural Resources: Balancing Rights and Duties*
Nico Schrijver

3 *The Polar Regions and the Development of International Law*
Donald R. Rothwell

2 *Fragmentation and the International Relations of Micro-States: Self-Determination and Statehood*
Jorri C. Duursma

1 *Principles of the Institutional Law of International Organizations*
C. F. Amerasinghe

For EU product safety concerns, contact us at Calle de José Abascal, 56–1°, 28003 Madrid, Spain or eugpsr@cambridge.org.

www.ingramcontent.com/pod-product-compliance
Lightning Source LLC
LaVergne TN
LVHW052029200926
848481LV00005B/1623
*9781108799775*